THE
AMERICAN
WAY
OF
SEX

An Informal Illustrated History

Bradley Smith

BOOKS BY BRADLEY SMITH

The New Photography
Erotic Art Of The Masters: 18th, 19th and 20th Centuries
The USA: A History In Art
China: A History In Art *(with Wan-Go Weng)*
Mexico: A History In Art
Spain: A History In Art
Japan: A History In Art
You Can Save A Life *(with Gus Stevens)*
The Horse In The West
The Horse In The Blue Grass Country
Escape To The West Indies

PRODUCER-EDITOR
Insomnia or The Devil At Large, *by Henry Miller*
My Life And Times, *by Henry Miller*
The Golden Sea, *by Joseph E. Brown*
Art For Children, *by Ernest Raboff* (15 titles)

THE AMERICAN WAY OF SEX

An Informal Illustrated History

Bradley Smith

A Gemini Smith Inc. Book
Distributed by
Two Continents Publishing Company
30 East 42nd Street, New York, N.Y. 10017

Designer:
Bradley Smith

Graphics Directors:
Richard Carter
Curtis Fields

Production Assistants:
Florence Kronfeld
Sharon Weldy

Editorial Assistants:
Elisabeth Girard Smith
Mary Cason

Library of Congress Number 78-61204

International Standard Book Number 0-8467-0567-2

A Gemini Smith Inc. Book
Distributed by
Two Continents Publishing Company
30 East 42nd St., New York, N.Y. 10017

Manufactured in the United States of America

Acknowledgments

A book is never created without the assistance of many people, and **The American Way of Sex** *is no exception. I wish to give my thanks to C. Peter Davis and Lawrence Gichner, Booton Herndon and William R. McHugh for their editorial advice and counsel. I am equally grateful to Paul Gebhard, director, Debbie Richards, researcher and Bill Dellenback, photographer, at the Institute for Sex Research at Indiana University. I am also grateful to Peter Canby, Yvonne Freund, Henry Miller, Jim Moran, David and Evelyn Munro, Marcia Seim, Daniel B. Smith, and Diggory and Doylie Venn. My thanks to the librarians at Harvard, the University of Virginia at Charlottesville, the University of California at San Diego and in particular to Lawrence Dinnean, Curator of Pictorial Collections, Bancroft Library, Dr. Marvin W. Kranz at the Library of Congress and Dr. Mark McKiernan, Director of the historic New Orleans Collection.*

I am grateful to all the publishers, collectors, artists, photographers, libraries and museums that have given permission for me to reproduce or to quote from their works. Their names and affiliations will be found listed under Bibliography or Picture Credits.

Table of Contents

For Elisabeth

Introduction

Sex needs no introduction to Americans, but I would like to take this opportunity to introduce a few of the colorful characters you will be meeting on this sojourn up and down the ways and byways of the American sexual scene.

It may come as a surprise that both male and female homosexuals occupied a specific place and had an important function in the pre-Columbian and the later American Indian social structures. Additional surprises will be found in the prevalence of immoral behavior that occurred with alarming regularity among the explorers of the New World, the Puritans, the pioneers, the Founding Fathers — and fathers generally.

As the history of sex in America is examined over a span of the last 500 years, changes in the seesaw pattern seem to be for the better in terms of less hypocrisy, more sex education, more tolerance and more freedom. With each succeeding generation, the pursuit of happiness (fortunately included in the Declaration of Independence) very slowly came to include sexual happiness — not only for procreation but for pleasure.

The American Indian did not separate the two. Sex was practiced for pleasure, and if progeny resulted, the children were a gift from the gods. Sex was practiced by youths strictly for pleasure long before conception was possible. The expectation that guilt and punishment would follow as a result of sexual enjoyment was imposed entirely by European explorers, settlers, priests and missionaries. But the newcomers were ambivalent; they partook of the sexual freedom offered by the Indians yet, considering it a sin, were critical of the Indians' morality. That they enjoyed looking at the naked Indian women is obvious from their comments, but they could hardly wait to cover their nakedness.

One of Columbus' horny sailors, Michele de Cuneo, wrote that Indian women were plentiful in the New World and easily had. "When they become of the age to procreate," he said, "they procreate." And, "These people eat when they are hungry and have sex openly when they feel like it."

The European explorers had barely landed before the sailors were scurrying off in all directions to get into the bushes with the native girls. The search for gold was slowed down considerably by dalliances with the acquiescent (and sometimes reluctant) Indian women. Ponce de León and Hernán Cortés took mistresses early on, and Pedro de Castañeda was pleased to find that "the virgins had to go around this way [naked] and they covered themselves after they had known man." The Spanish must have supplied an ever-increasing number of garments as they traveled through the West.

While the Spanish were producing the first Spanish-Americans on the West Coast, the East did not lack sexual activity. Pocahontas made a slave of Captain John Smith, married an Indian at the age of twelve or thirteen, then became the captive of the Jamestown settlers and the bride of John Rolfe, granddaddy of the American tobacco industry. As the Indians, hard work and hard winters killed off many New England men, their widows were snapped up as wives to keep the remaining settlers warm soon after their first husbands were cold. That all was not morally correct in Massachusetts is testified to by Reverend Cotton Mather, who, after discovering that a friend and pillar of the church had "been involved in buggery for at least fifty years," exposed him. Actually, this devout fellow had buggered a cow, two heifers, three sheep and two sows. His fellow churchmen hanged them all — including the deacon.

The coming of slavery brought a whole new group of interesting protagonists in the sexual dramas that were played out on the East Coast and in the South. Black girls joined the Indian women and both became bearers of children to white masters. Large numbers of the first slave women to be imported into the United States arrived pregnant by the European sailors who delivered them. Some of the early Virginia planters paid premium prices for these women, getting two slaves for the price of one. Captain Richard Drake logged: "Once off the coast the ship became half bedlam and half brothel. . . . They [captain and mates] stripped themselves and danced with black wenches while our crazy mulatto cook played the fiddle."

In the plantation country you'll meet one of Virginia's most unique characters — lusty William Byrd, who in 1712 wrote in his diary that, in a moment of abandon, he gave his wife a flourish on the billiard table.

"Neither a maidenhead nor a fortress will hold out after they begin to parley," wrote Benjamin Franklin. While both the British and American leaders had mistresses available during the Revolutionary War, the British had the foresight to import a large number of women to sexually service their rank and file. The ordinary American soldier was expected to catch-as-catch-can. By far the biggest sensation on the morals front was the discovery,

after seventeen months of service, that an athletic young soldier, Robert Shurtleff, was actually a woman. She was released from the army and oh! what lectures Deborah Sampson gave after the war.

Not all of the characters you will meet in these pages were famous. Some were infamous, others notorious, and some became regional heroes and heroines. Ah Toy, San Francisco's first Chinese prostitute, became one of the richest women on the West Coast, as well as a high-ranking member of the ruling Hip Sing Tong, San Francisco's Chinese Mafia. You'll also meet famous madams of the West: Julia Bulette from New Orleans, Kitty Leroy from Deadwood City, South Dakota, Calamity Jane from Blackfoot, Montana, and Cattle Kate Watson from Cheyenne, Wyoming. There were others from Valparaiso, Chile, and Paris, France — all well worth meeting.

In contrast, you'll meet Harriet Beecher Stowe, who had a high time writing and discussing her American epic of sex, miscegenation and violence and permanently introduced into the American literary scene Topsy and Eva, Uncle Tom and Simon Legree and his lecherous crew of slave hunters and despoilers; Lillian Russell with her gold-plated bicycle; La Belle Otero and her millionaire lovers; ambitious Evelyn Nesbit, her lover — the lusty Stanford White — and her paranoid husband —Harry K. Thaw — who murdered him.

Moving from east to west, three wicked cities offer in abundance intriguing tales that create a base for the sexual greening of America. There follows an opportunity to meet the radicals of Greenwich Village and of the New Orleans French Quarter. The types of humans that give an insight into the cumulative sexual history of the United States continue to appear. The experimentalists gave a solid base to an ever-expanding freedom in the area of sexual liberation. In its way, the period of sexual liberation between World War I and World War II, with its free-thinking, bob-haired, short-skirted, cigarette-smoking women (meet Edna St. Vincent

Millay and Dorothy Parker), was just as revolutionary as that of the one-piece-bathing-suited, outspoken, sexually liberated daughters and granddaughters of the '40s and '50s.

Because of their proximity to the present, the 1960s are usually considered to be the decade of sexual experimentation and liberation. Yet, as I wrote this book, I found — as the reader will find — that every decade had its own peaks of sexual change. Also noticeable is that, as the effort to achieve sexual freedom slowly gained support, the opposition to sexual liberation slowly dwindled. Periods of progress were followed by moderation in periods of censorship and repression. Slowly, but continuously, there was increasing recognition by the population of the facts of sex.

Within limits, I have tried to use the sexual language prevalent in each given period. When the English first landed at Jamestown, the word "fuck," used as a verb, was still common. But as religious institutions, with their emphasis on the invisibility of all sexual matters, took over, a whole new language — both vague and inaccurate — soon replaced the descriptive taboo words that everyone knew. In the generations that followed, men and women slept together, went to bed together, knew each other or, more scientifically, indulged in coitus or copulated. Occasionally, people had sexual connections, a term that sounds like two railroad cars being coupled. People made love, something that could be interpreted to mean almost anything one wanted it to.

Slowly the old taboo words came back. As early as the 1920s writers of novels were allowed to use two-letter words such as f--k, s--t, c--t and even p---k. Shortly after the end of World War II the missing letters began to reappear. (Although as late as the 1960s comedian Lenny Bruce was brought to trial for publicly uttering the word "cocksucker.") It was not as though every child above the age of eight did not already know the taboo words and occasionally write them on walls or carve them on trees. It was not as though their parents did not know, and often privately use, the taboo words. It was just that until they were used in literature by such accomplished writers as Henry Miller, D. H. Lawrence, Irwin Shaw and Norman Mailer the public disallowed them. Novelists received a lot of help from the playwrights, and by the sixties, on-Broadway, off-Broadway and amateur theaters across the country resounded with "fuck you," "piss off," "tits and ass," "shit" and "cunt." The final acceptance came in the 1970s when famous movie stars, male and female, began to talk dirty. (In passing, the word "asshole" was used by President Nixon to describe colleagues in one or more of the White House tapes.)

If successful, the book does not merely tell the story of the evolving sexual mores in the United States, for the artists, and later the photographers, in each era have observed and recorded in their pictures the sexual life of their times. Not only do fashions in sexual manners and morals change before our eyes, but so do the sizes and shapes of women. The circuitous route from naked Indians, through the various stages of cover-up, to current displays of nudity can be traced in the illustrations. And an ankle exposed in 1840 caused more of a sensation than a naked girl a hundred years later.

The change in sexual manners came very slowly indeed. But as readers will note, there has always been a sexual avant-garde exploring the territory ahead. New England was the first country other than Scotland to pass divorce laws giving women some, though not many, legal rights. Throughout the Republic, prostitution was allowed to exist legally — as a necessary evil. Political leaders, both before and after the Revolution, made little attempt to conceal their indulgence in extramarital sex. Not that Thomas Jefferson was entirely frank about fathering four children by his mulatto mistress.

Radical sexual behavior reached its peak in 1872 when the attractive and persuasive Victoria Woodhull ran for president of the United States on a free love platform. Religious communities such as

Oneida in New York practiced communal marriage that, among other advantages, gave to each woman in the community an opportunity for sex with the male or males of her choice. Among the Mormons women had few sexual rights, but men enjoyed their own type of plural marriage, which freed them to indulge their sexual interests to the extent that their economic status allowed. The idea of controlling fertility was briefly circulated when it was advocated as early as 1831 by Robert Owen's New Harmony socialist commune.

There is some question as to whether the uptight sexual periods in American history were as bad as I have described them. Did everyone lead guilt-ridden lives? Was there as much frustration as the criminal and church records show, or were most of these exceptional cases? Even in their guilt-ridden lives, did not forbidden sex add excitement to the anticipation of that ultimate experience?

It is worth considering that the sight of a bare-breasted native girl in the *National Geographic* or the drawing of a corset-clad woman in the *Sears Roebuck Catalog* may have offered as much visual sexual stimulation as the present gynecological spreads in *Penthouse* or *Hustler* magazines. Only fifty years ago it took flowers, candy, multiple dates and a "line" of conversation to get a girl into bed. Perhaps there was more pleasure in the slow buildup of three or four sequential dates, of a quiet dinner party with champagne in a private dining room and then the ultimate seduction, than the present first date, cocktails and/or a joint, followed by mutually agreed-upon sex.

There must have been great satisfaction in being a censor, an arbiter of sexual conduct, at least until the 1960s. How pleasant it must have been to rest high up on a cloud of moral perfection and look down at the secret sinners. Some men you will meet in these pages — Cotton Mather, Anthony Comstock and Will Hays — found that the theme "keep America pure" kept them in their high offices. Sexual purity was equated with all the other virtues: honesty, intelligence and political respectability. Yet these, and all the other self-appointed censors, doubtless got into the censorship business to satisfy their own perverse tastes. How satisfying to punish, destroy and, most of all, to observe all the diversions and deviations — and to be paid and acclaimed for it as well.

The long line of political leaders who contributed to the sexual mores of America begins with Hamilton, Burr and Jefferson and continues through Harding, Roosevelt and Kennedy. It should be noted that, while none of these men led the respectable life expected of political leaders, the public accepted with equanimity the idea of their temporary sexual liaisons and their mistresses. Even when the facts emerged, the public enjoyed reading the scandals, but these American heroes and lesser political figures were not judged.

To tell the story of a country in terms of its sexual attitudes means dealing with legend and myth, with fact and error. I have tried to base this book on as many primary sources as possible. Yet, inevitably, errors will work their way into the fabric of the fact. Not even the protagonists of some of the lurid tales were always entirely accurate in their reports. At some point legends creep into what purport to be factual narratives.

Billy the Kid and Pat Garrick became David and Goliath; Calamity Jane became a white female John Henry; Silver Heels, a whore with a heart of gold. But, as Vardis Fisher once wrote, "Most of those who read books about the past, or present for that matter, don't want to know what the facts are, if knowing them will disturb their standardized errors."

Yet I have found the facts, so far as I could pin them down, to be more dramatic than the elaborated fictional accounts.

1

The Indians —
Sex before Columbus

A fascinating world of America's sexual prehistory has emerged from the study of myths and legends, cave paintings, pottery, wood and stone sculpture, cliffside etchings and picture writing. From a culture dating back eight centuries before the arrival of Columbus, for instance, a shallow bowl remains. On it is painted a hunter striding home with rabbit in one hand, bow in the other, his penis proudly erect.

What was the sex life of these first Americans like? How did it differ from that of the European explorers, conquistadors and settlers who came and forever disrupted their culture. Fortunately, these first Americans left a vivid, relatively easy-to-read record of their sexual beliefs and practices in their myths and legends, along with much tangible evidence. Revealing tales have been cherished and passed down by shamans through the ages. We know, for instance, that they practiced many

kinds of sexual relationships, life styles were both heterosexual and homosexual. Their sexual mores are part of their verbal and visual history.

These earliest ancestors of the American Indian (Columbus so named them because he believed he had found a new passage to India) were, in the dim past, families and small groups that later developed into tribes and nations. As they fanned out from the now submerged Siberian land bridge, first to the Southwest, then across the great plains and eventually to the Atlantic coastline, their way of life ranged from primitive cultures of simple food-gatherers and wandering tribes of hunters to civilizations of agricultural peoples. By the time the Europeans arrived, Indian life styles included relatively prosperous and sedentary nations as well as scattered nomads existing at the starvation level.

In those groups that settled we have observed visual

records in cave paintings, sculpture and pottery. The depiction of the sexual act in abstract and realistic forms occurs with startling repetition and may be compared in relative proportion to the frequency of the erotic in paintings and photographs of the primitive art of Europe and Asia.

Graphically representing bare breasts, the erect penis and the exposed vagina, Indian artists reveal that nudity was customary and widely accepted. A Carolina Indian chief anticipated twentieth century nudist philosophy by some 300 years when he observed that he could not understand what the white man had to hide by wearing concealing clothing. "We Indians," he said, "have nothing to hide."

Among the earliest traceable cultures were the Hohokam, the Mimbres and the Anasazi in the Southwest. Their mores continued in some form through the 500 years of discovery, exploration and settlement by the white man.

In the Mimbres culture, which existed eight centuries before the voyages of Columbus, artists and artisans attained a high degree of perfection in their realistic drawings and designs. They left hundreds of graphic art-history records, including the hunter with the erection.

Another bowl is more educational; it depicts a man and a woman demonstrating the act of sexual intercourse. The artist has used a cross-section technique to show the penetration of the penis deep into the vagina. Another man and five women look on with interest and concentration; the men, probably shamans, wear elaborate headdresses indicating their importance. This is obviously a serious how-to-do-it demonstration for a select audience.

Pictographs which include cave and rock drawings and paintings in the West and Southwest constitute another vital record of the customs of prehistoric North Americans. More than 200 sites in the state of Texas alone contain these messages from the past. Although this form of art continued after the coming of the European explorers, most of it was produced in the years preceding their arrival.

Such art is often realistic, representing men and women in motion as well as scenes of village and animal life. Phallic symbols such as erect penises, both detached and attached to men and animals, are relatively common. In one painting a man appears with a huge erection. His knees are bent, his hips thrust forward, his arms out. The exaggeration of the penis is too great to have been accidental. It is as though the picture was a satiric statement to show what a burden to the male his sex drive can be.

In rock drawings male figures usually have both penis and testicles. Sometimes the testicles are represented by a small square with the penis as a straight line extending from it; sometimes testicles and penis are in the shape of a cross with the crossbar in the crotch and the base hanging down. In these representations the cross appears commonly as a design and a symbol. This might explain why many missionaries found the symbolic value of the Christian cross so readily accepted by the Indians.

Early artists chose may ways to delineate female genitalia. The most common is a vertical slit with lines representing pubic hair drawn around it, resulting in a delightful sunburst effect. A less glorious vaginal symbol is a simple circle between the legs.

Usually picture writings were placed in inaccessible areas, high on walls and roofs of rock shelters or hidden in shadows under overhanging crags. This custom preserved them not only from the elements but also from sightseers. More than eighty percent of this visual language is pre-Columbian, but the percentage is constantly changing with new archeological findings.

Prehistoric sculptors in the Southwest fashioned stone phalluses about the size of an erect penis, from approximately five to eight inches in length. Occasionally a stone in its natural state, bearing a strong resemblance to male or female genitalia, would be found and kept as a household or tribal totem. Stone phalluses, both natural and man-made, were wrapped in beads or skins by the Northwestern and the Plains Indians, who considered them talismans of sexual potency.

Just as visual records show a healthy and frank recognition of sex organs and sexual activity, so do the Indian myths and legends handed down orally from ancient times. The myths are tales from beyond the world of reality incorporating the spiritual and the supernatural. The legends carry the ring of truth and relate to actual human history.

Written down only after the arrival of the Europeans, these fascinating stories reveal the sexual customs and moral attitudes of pre-Columbian America. Some conjecture is necessary in using folklore to recreate historical events, for modern audiences do not have the native environment that allows their imagination to explore naturalistic magic. Taken out of the psychological framework of the Indians, some of these tales may seem to us fanciful, illogical and unreal. Yet many earlier people believed in them.

Myths dealing with the creation of the world do not necessarily reflect the Indians' real beliefs, although they incorporate some of them. Stories of genesis describe a dim, unremembered past when people ate raw food because they did not know how to make fire or because the ever-burning brands had been stolen away by another tribe. One constant, readily under-

ndable in these myths of the creation, is sex, for it
as believed that copulation with human maidens was
e way the deities (who may have represented ancient
iefs) populated the earth.

At some point in the dim past, all native Ameri-
ns related their tribe or group to a particular animal.
is animal became so strongly identified with the
oup that the tribe believed themselves to be descen-
nts from it, either directly or through some remote
cestor. The exploits of these animals became legends
d a permanent part of the tribe's history. Some
astal groups related their origins and ritual relation-
ip to fish, frogs or lobsters; plains groups to the buf-
lo or the bear, and many other groups to birds both
rge and small. Out of these relationships came great
d wonderful tales, some going back hundreds of
ars, others relating to events in the recent past.

The totem gave the tribe not only an identification
t a hero (and sometimes a villain) in the form of their
ecial fish, animal or bird. A survival of the totem
inciple in modern society can be found in organiza-
ns whose members refer to themselves as elk, moose
lions. Good and evil, acceptable or unacceptable
haviour, were reflected in the duality of totems. One
pe of bird could represent good and another bird evil,
ithin the same tribe. The Indians did not eat their
imal totems — although they could if certain rituals
ere observed — but used them largely for identifica-
n.

Among other things, such identifiable animal
tems helped to keep sexual relationships from becom-
g incestuous. With no written family histories, a
sitive identification was vitally important. Thus, two
embers of the same bear family were not allowed to
pulate with one another, but a member of a bear
mily could mate with a member of a wolf family.

Every Indian tribe had its own version of the crea-
on of earth and man, and each sex played a key role.

In several myths of Pacific Northwest Indians the
ntral character is a spirit called Raven, the represen-
tive of a supreme force. According to these stories,
aven sometimes was a benign power for good, but
ore often his mischievous ways brought trouble to
e tribes. Like the god Zeus in ancient Greece, Raven
as able to change his physical appearance at will.

One fable describes how Raven brought light to
e Northwest, then shrouded in darkness: First he
anged himself into a needle from a spruce tree. When
e daughter of the great chief who owned the Light of
e World went to the river to drink, Raven cleverly ar-
nged for her to accidentally swallow him. As a result,
e girl became pregnant — a sort of primeval imma-
late conception. When the baby was born, it was ac-
ally the spirit Raven — who now had access to the
eat chief's house. One day the baby Raven began to
y. The wise men of the tribe were summoned and

one of them, bewitched by Raven, suggested that the
baby be given the ball of Light of the World to play
with.

When the door was opened, Raven transformed
himself into his true birdlike form, clutched the ball of
Light in his claws and flew away. He winged his way to
the darkest area of the Northwest, then populated with
subhuman forms. He asked them for some of their fish,
threatening to break the magic ball, which would make
blinding light everywhere, if they refused. They did
refuse, and Raven broke the ball of Light. The animal-
men perished, then real humans followed the light to
the Northwest.

Because Raven had provided plenty of daylight for
fishing and also taught the people how to burn oil in
lamps for light at night, they became a great and powerful Indian nation — with their totem the raven.

The Navahos had another version of the story of
creation. It all started after a great flood brought ample
water to the dry earth. The land became fruitful and the
fish and game abundant. Everything seemed perfect,
except for a controversy that arose between men and
women.

"We should have the best treatment," said the
men, "because we build the shelters and we hunt for
the food."

"Not so," said the women. "We are more useful.
We bear the children, plant and harvest the corn, make
the pots and keep the fires burning."

The men insisted that they alone knew the proper
ceremonies and dances which kept the spirits favorable
to the tribe, thus assuring bountiful crops.

Voices of both men and women became angry.
They could not come to an agreement. They split up,
the men going south, the women north. But soon they
found existence apart impossible. Reunited, they
agreed that each sex was as important as the other. This,
say the Navaho, is how their men and women learned
to live together peaceably, as families.

However, by the time the Spanish explorers arrived, the Navaho men had the best of it. As in most Indian nations, the women did the dirty work.

Sexual symbols were also fundamental to the version of creation told by the Pawnee Indians. Their god
Tirawa, wedded to the goddess born from corn, spoke
to the people through the evening star, the mother of
all living things. At his command, the Morning Star
mated with the Evening Star and produced a daughter.
Then Tirawa ordered the alliance of the sun and the
moon, and this resulted in the birth of a boy. Boy met
girl, and their union established the framework of the
earth and sky.

The Luiseño Indians of Southern California had a
dramatic myth of genesis which involved incestuous
sexual relations between brother and sister. In this story
the earth and the sky were originally two great clouds.

They changed forms to become brother and sister; sister earth was below and brother sky above. They mated in the dark void and conceived the children of the earth.

Most Indian tribes, in their mythology, endowed their spiritual ancestors, or totems, with human characteristics as well as magical powers. These spirits were likely to be mischievous and tricky. In one myth, a coyote, representing the creator of the world, arranges his own death so he can come back in a different form to have sexual relations with his daughter. She does not recognize him as her father and gives herself to him. Apparently, when gods or spirits were involved, incest was acceptable.

In most Indian folklore, however, incest was entirely taboo. One myth, which originated in a California tribe, involves a spirit called Bluebird, her daughter, Robin, and her mischievous son, Coyote. Robin had two suitors, Lizard and Swallow. She rejected Lizard, to Coyote's delight, for he wanted her to marry Swallow. But the mother, Bluebird, objected to Swallow. Coyote suggested that the rivals gamble for Robin, but when Lizard won and Robin married him, Coyote was furious. "Tell your husband that we are going to swim in the river," he said. Robin did so, and poor Lizard, not knowing that the river was actually a boiling spring, agreed to go in first. He dived into the hot water and was killed.

"What shall we tell our mother?" Robin asked Coyote.

"Tell her that Lizard has gone deer hunting", he said. So when the mother asked where the husband had gone, Robin replied that he was hunting deer and would be gone several moons. But the moons went by and Lizard did not return. Others came to woo Robin, but she and Coyote gave them the boiling spring treatment.

Eventually, Bluebird found out what had happened to Robin's husband and suitors. Irate, she berated her daughter. "Well," Robin replied haughtily, "do you want me to marry my own brother then?" The distraught mother gave her consent. This was just what Coyote wanted to hear. The brother and sister were married, but they did not live happily ever after. Bluebird, anguished over permitting the incestuous union, killed herself — by leaping into the boiling spring. Not long thereafter, a friend of one of the dead suitors tracked down Robin and Coyote and killed them both.

This tale involving brother-sister incest, murder, suicide and revenge also demonstrates the duality of the totem. For the mother, realizing the evil in her children's incestuous relationship, kills herself; and, as in movies of the 1930s that could not allow evil-doers to escape or be rewarded, a member of a different totem tracked down the sinners.

This story appears in many forms among tribes from different parts of the country, indicating that incest was a major concern among American Indians. Tribal laws banned sexual relations between mothers and sons, fathers and daughters, brothers and sisters, and sometimes extended to aunts and nephews, uncles and nieces.

There were many reasons why incest was unacceptable. The size of the family group and the ease or difficulty of obtaining wives from another group were factors, for incest was a threat to survival when it kept a family or clan from expanding. Incest was not practical; a man's sexual relationship with a daughter or sister would bring him no in-laws to protect him in times of danger nor to share food with him in times of famine. A small group intermarrying within itself would have no protection, no allies, no friends and, most important, no relatives in nearby tribes.

Anthropologists have put forward interesting conjectures and heated arguments as to whether incest is natural instinct or a cultural development. Many mammals have incestuous relationships, yet it seems that with humans, there is an implied cultural decision based on the survival of the individual, the family, and the tribe. At times, the sexual impulse (and bloodline status) has been stronger than the cultural taboo. When no other sexual outlet was possible, or convenient, father-daughter, mother-son and brother-sister relationships have been consummated, though mother-son is by far the least frequent. Apparently, humans generally do not practice incest for either instinctive or cultural reasons, but only when their sex drive has no other outlet.

What the Indians thought of incest comes through in stories like the one the Navaho tell about the Ute clan, whom they considered inferior. In this Navaho legend, a father has sexual relations with his daughter. The bastard child of this incestuous union is abandoned — to become the progenitor of the Ute Indians.

Marriage customs among the Indians ranged from extremely simple (a man moved into a woman's shelter) to complex arrangements based on a bridal price and adoption of the suitor by the bride's family. It was generally accepted that men would have many sexual conquests before marriage, but among young girls chastity was hoped for if not expected. Marriage usually took place within six months of puberty. A virtuous girl, though not necessarily a virginal one, could bring a high bridal price. Some sacred ceremonies could be held only if the girl was actually a virgin, though how this was determined the legends do not tell. Romance was not entirely lacking, and seductions, rapes and elopements were not unknown.

In fact, some of the sexual tribal customs are reflected in modern social behavior. Among the first Americans, when women were scarce, the best way to get a wife was to steal her. The aspiring husband always selected a strong, able friend — a "best man" — to assist him in abducting his bride. It was the best man's job to make the arrangements to snatch the bride, and to fight the rear-guard action to keep her from being recaptured.

The best-man tradition still exists in some primitive societies today, though the action is more dramatic than violent. The family knows the daughter is going to be abducted, as does the daughter; she is prepared to run away. As the couple flee to their secret love nest, family, friends and best man stage a sham battle, taking care that no one is badly hurt. In our modern civilization, the best-man tradition and the stealthy departure for a secret destination are almost exactly the same.

Romantic as these customs may seem, romance itself was of small import in the serious matter of marriage. The syndrome of being in love was recognized, but it was apparently considered to be a temporary form of insanity, a kind of madness that invaded the minds of young people. To be in love was to be possessed by a spirit; it was believed that kind and gentle treatment would cure those so afflicted. When it came to marriage, therefore, among most Indian groups love was less important than the purchase price for the bride.

Trade fairs, sports gatherings, planting and harvest festivals were devised to bring bands together. There men could find women outside their own totem groups. Intermarriage among neighboring tribes with compatible totems strengthened each tribe and reduced the prospect of war. The wider the spread of relations a tribe had with other tribes, the more defenders the family had. In some Indian nations marriages created even stronger bonds. The families of the bride and groom became so closely related that it was almost as though each entire family was marrying the other.

The combined families stuck together. They stood behind any member accused of a crime — be it murder, adultery or stealing. Whether he was guilty or innocent, relatives were expected to come to the accused's defense. If they could not mitigate the punishment, at least they could make entreaties to the authorities and, in the final resort, help the prisoner to escape. In some instances, after punishing or torturing the guilty party and banishing him from the tribe, authorities still turned him over to relatives for nursing or other assistance. This was true not only of husbands and wives, parents and children, but also of extended families — uncles, aunts and cousins.

A girl purchased for a wife by no means became a slave; a rich wife came with slaves of her own. Yet a man could truly become a slave to love, for if he had not accumulated enough skins and dried foods to purchase a bride outright, he could become an indentured servant to his bride's family to pay the bride price.

Most tribes were matrilineal; the man usually moved in with the bride's mother. One reason for the Indians' matriarchal society was that while the identity of the mother of the child was always certain, sometimes grave doubt existed as to the identity of the father. Men may have traveled from one family to another, even from one village to another, but the child always stayed in the mother's village or moved with her. A woman's sisters, daughters and granddaughters formed a permanent matriarchal group; line of descent was traced through the mother.

According to both myths and legends, polygamy was widely practiced. Chiefs could have five to ten wives; the average man had to satisfy himself with one or two. An exception, if legends do reflect the custom, would occur when a man accepted tribal recommendations to marry as many sisters as possible in one family. Again, according to legend, a happy, harmonious group would result.

The second or third wife did not suffer socially or economically, nor did the number one wife have any objections to a new face around the wigwam. There was always more work than any one wife could handle, so two, three or more shared in cultivating and foraging for food as well as in its preparation. Further, as entertaining played an important part in Indian life, a man of wealth and distinction needed many wives to make the extensive arrangements for the feasts he was expected to hold.

Polyandry was not unknown in Indian cultures, but it was much rarer, and controlled by interesting restrictions. Among the Pawnee Indians, for example, a young man was freely allowed to have sexual relations with his maternal uncle's wife. Two brothers were permitted to share the same wife, and, when women were scarce, frequently did so.

As might be expected in a primitive society, the double standard prevailed. Adultery was generally accepted for men but not for women. One witness was enough to declare a woman guilty. The enraged husband, accompanied by some of his relatives, would beat the wife brutally and cut off her long hair, sometimes her nose or one of her lips. Disfigured females were relatively common.

Yet in this harsh masculine society a popular myth among the Cree and adjacent tribes presents a refreshing irony, in which the woman got the last word, in a way. It tells of an adulterous wife whose husband caught her in the act and killed her. This was the approved punishment, but the story did not end there. The wife continued after death to be near him and her children, for, in retaliation, her skull rolled after them wherever they went.

A woman's rights would depend largely on the power and status of her family in the tribe. An unusual example of early women's liberation occurred in the Hopi. Generally, divorce was unknown in Indian society because when a man or woman got tired of the other, one of them simply moved out. But the Hopi wife didn't have to move. All she had to do was put her husband's personal possessions outside her door.

Another pro-female legend recounts the story of a man who left his wife for another woman. To get him back she made a strong medicine. First she cut a long, heavy stalk from a cottonwood tree and stood it in an upright position to represent her missing husband. Then she sat and, weaving baskets all the while, sang songs of love to her husband in effigy, calling him back.

Ten years later he returned. When she heard him coming, she did not even look up. She waited until he came up to her and put his arm around her neck. Then, without saying a word, she ripped up the cottonwood stalk and hit him over the head with it, knocking him senseless. When he recovered, she said, "Why did you come back here? You must go away." He answered that he wanted to come back to live with her. She replied she did not want him back, because he had not treated her well in the first place, and then he had left her.

"Well," he said, "I'll never treat you badly again and I would like to live with you. And I will pay you well for having treated you so badly." So, the story goes, he paid her — and they lived happily ever after.

The rites of passage from one stage of life to another constitute an important theme in Indian myths. Puberty rites, especially those for girls, are often recounted. At the time of her first menstruation, the young girl was confined and restricted. In some groups she was allowed to do no work; in others, she was given very heavy work. In many tribes she would not be permitted to touch any living thing. Her destructive powers were believed to be so great that she could kill large trees, ruin crops, and have an adverse effect on hunting, fishing and planting.

The legend of Pelican deals with such a pubescent girl. As was the custom, Pelican was given a dance at the onset of puberty and presented with gifts of beads for her wrists, ankles and neck. Immediately afterward, she was shut up in a hut especially built for this purpose, away from the village, with enough food for a month. All contacts with the outside world were cut. But one day two of her girl friends came to the isolated hut. She pleaded with them to take her with them into

the forest, and they reluctantly agreed. In the thick woods, she became separated from her friends. A huge beast captured here, bewitched her, stripped off her clothes — *and took away her beads.* She was found by her family but never recovered from her tragic experience. The beads symbolized her virginity; the "huge beast" who raped her was doubtless a man from an unacceptable totem group.

The passage of puberty, of course, meant that the girl was now a woman, capable of giving birth. Indian myths emphasize the magic surrounding the time of birth. The activities of the father, for example, were believed to contribute to the health, happiness, sickness or death of the newborn. Before the birth and for two to four weeks afterward, he had to stay within his house and rest, eat very sparingly, move very little, and not even touch anything. He acted as if he were the one experiencing the pregnancy, childbirth and post-partum recovery.

This curious custom is called couvade, from the French word *couver:* to cover, or sit on, as a female bird would to hatch her eggs. It is not unique among American Indian tribes, and is a well-known custom among many primitive peoples. It is a symbolic statement that the father makes to assert his paternity and his spiritual or magical relationship to the child. Since in matriarchal societies the child takes the mother's name and lives with her, this is sometimes the only chance the primitive man has to call attention to himself as a father.

Among American Indians who practiced couvade, such precautions were not applicable to the mother. She was expected to take care of the house and her lying-in husband, as well as bear the child.

Childbirth was apparently an easy function for pre-Columbian Indian women. When a woman was approaching the time of delivery she would walk into the woods, taking another woman with her if possible. She would not lie prone during delivery, but rather squat or get down on hands and knees. She would hold onto her companion, or a vine or leather thong, during the birth process.

In some tribes a female relative or the tribal midwife would press on the pregnant woman's abdomen with her hands, or tie a bandage around her and tighten it, helping the infant move. In difficult cases, the woman was lifted and moved from side to side while her abdomen was gently manipulated in order to change the child's position.

Immediately after birth, a tight bandage was tied around the woman's abdomen, another around the infant's, to prevent excessive bleeding and to promote faster healing. The mother's bandage also helped in the expulsion of the placenta and thus limited hemorrhage.

Some tribes used herbal teas to facilitate delivery. The Comanche used *helenium microcephalum,* which induced violent sneezing and probably pushed out both baby and placenta. Some shamans advised expectant mothers to eat sparingly during the later stages of pregnancy, so the baby would not grow too large and fat and cause a difficult birth.

Mothers bathed their newborn infants in the nearest creek, river, stream or lake. On the Lewis and Clark expedition, Meriwether Lewis observed in his diary:

"One of the women who had been leading two of our pack horses halted at a rivulet about a mile behind, and sent on the two horses by a female friend. On inquiring of Cameahwait [an Indian translator] the cause of her detention, he answered with great appearance of unconcern, that she had just stopped to lie in, but would soon overtake us. In fact, we were astonished to see her in about an hour's time come on with her newborn infant and pass us on her way to the camp, apparently in perfect health."

Indians undoubtedly practiced some form of birth control for a woman seldom had more than one or two children. A tradition among the Huichol Indians held that by drinking a liquid made with a secret plant, childbearing could be prevented. In the annals of the *New York Academy of Sciences* for May 1952 Clellan Ford argues that Indians were aware of safe periods for intercourse, and that the Hopi knew that the time just before menstruation offered the least likelihood of conception.

In the Southwest it was believed that sterility could be artificially induced. Some Cherokee women, for example, chewed a root of spotted cowbane, but the practice was limited by fear of permanent sterility. In some Nevada tribes the women drank an infusion of roots from stoneweed. (Experiments with mice in recent years have shown that this herb changes the normal estrus cycle and decreases the weights of the sex organs, thymus and pituitary gland. Such tests have not been made on women.)

Even if birth control measures had been completely efficacious, slips were bound to occur. When a woman became pregnant with no spouse, and her family was unable to care for the child, abortion was one solution. She would take herbal medicines to induce miscarriage. If this failed, the Indian mother was capable of going into the woods alone, bearing the child and then killing it. This was also the usual fate of deformed infants.

It may come as a shock to many present-day Americans to learn that some homosexuality was common to most Indian groups. To the European mind, the idea of the uncivilized man, living in a wilderness, leading a "natural life," precludes the possibility of homosexuality. Homosexual practices have always been considered a form of decadence in Europe, as opposed to the time-honored "normal" heterosexual behavior.

Actually, instances of homosexual practices go back to the seventh century B.C., with the Assyrian story of Gilgamesh and Engidu, two legendary heroes who were also lovers. Homosexual activities were frequently described in Greek and Roman literature. Physical anthropologists have noted that animals such as dogs, cows, horses and sheep occasionally indulge in homosexual behavior, while our zoological relatives in the primate order, such as monkeys and apes, do so more frequently. Young male monkeys, for example, have been seen engaging in mutual masturbation and even in oral-genital contact. This is also true of female apes and monkeys but to a lesser extent.

A great deal of research has been done on Indian homosexual attitudes in the last hundred years. Before that, homosexuality was specifically mentioned in the early accounts of artist Jacques Le Moyne (1564), explorer Nicolas le Challeux (1565), colonist-artist John White (1587), and Richard Hakluyt at the beginning of the seventeenth century, among others.

Descriptive words such as hermaphrodite, homosexual, berdache and transvestite were all used by the early chroniclers — Jesuit priests, soldiers and scholars — to refer to men who dressed as women, lived with the women and performed the same or similar duties. Most accounts indicate that when a boy became old enough to hunt, he could go with the men if he wished to; if not, he could stay at home with the women. Homosexuals were not outcasts, and sometimes, as at least one early account describes, they were preferred as wives because they were stronger than women, could do more work and skin more buffalo.

In the Mohave culture, in which the male homosexual was known as an *alyha*, it was more difficult for a husband to separate from an *alyha* wife than from a female wife. Cases are recorded in which irate *alyhas* beat up their mates for infidelity, or chased girls away. This did not mean that they were always faithful, for sometimes an *alyha* would run off with another man. The *alyha* had a definite status in the tribe; if anyone was the subject of ridicule it was more often the man who lived with him than the *alyha* himself.

Among the Navaho, homosexuals were sometimes given greater opportunities in material ways than other members of the tribe. Occasionally a group would make themselves up like clowns and do strange dances to amuse the tribe.

The Zuni word for homosexual was *la'mana*. The *la'mana* was generally considered to be abnormal, but not personally responsible for being that way. In Zuni dances la'manas often appeared in both male and female groups, dancing gaily from one to another. When la'manas died they were buried in the men's cemetery — dressed in women's clothing.

The Yuma, predating Freud by several centuries in psychoanalysis, diagnosed homosexuality as being caused by dreams at puberty. While parents may have been ashamed to have children with homosexual tendencies, they apparently made little effort to repress them. When a homosexual boy reached puberty he began wearing women's clothing, sometimes lived with a man, and often had a peaceful influence on the tribe.

A legend among the Omaha group of Plains Indians tells how, as a young Omaha was fasting for the first time upon reaching puberty, a moon god would appear to him, holding in one hand a bow and arrow and, in the other, a pack strap such as women used for traveling. When the youth would try to grasp the bow and arrow, the moon god would cross his arms quickly and, if the youth was slow or careless, he would catch the pack strap instead of the bow. His sexual course was then set for life. From that time on he would have the characteristics of a woman.

There were female homosexuals too. Sahaykwisa, a Mohave born about 1850, was a famous hwame, or lesbian. Because she was always referred to as a hwame during her childhood, it is believed that at puberty she submitted to the ceremony which officially identified her as a lesbian. In these rites she would have danced the homosexual dance and would have been washed by the women in the river, thereby taking on the status of masculine-oriented lesbian. Rather than the long skirt worn by other women, she wore a short skirt. Like the shaman who told her story, she specialized in caring for the sick, but she also hunted and planted crops like a man, for she supported a wife. Other members of the tribe referred to her as he.

Sahaykwisa's wife was very attractive and much desired by the men in the tribe. They teased her and tried to lure her away from her lesbian mate. "Why do you want such a person, who has no penis, for your husband?" they taunted. They told her that if she stayed with the lesbian, after a while no other man would have her. Though she remained with Sahaykwisa for a time, eventually she ran away. Sahaykwisa began to attend the dances again and flirt with the girls. People laughed at her behind her back and called her hiopan kuoape, meaning split vulva, which was an insult. But no one dared call her that to her face.

Sahaykwisa had no difficulty in getting women to move in with her; the shaman describes at least three wives who lived with her at different times. Apparently in love with them, Sahaykwisa went so far as to prostitute herself to men outside the tribe in order to buy them presents. She was bold in her approach. On one occasion, carrying her bow and arrow, she went to the house of a young woman on the pretext of asking her to grind corn for her. Even though she was married, the young woman could not resist Sahaykwisa. She ground the corn and, after more visits, went away with her. A few months later she returned to her husband, perhaps because of the ridicule she had suffered.

Sahaykwisa kept trying to get the girl back, making regular visits to her house. The husband, who must have been a very tolerant individual, finally had enough. He caught Sahaykwisa from behind, tore off her clothes, and raped her. Sahaykwisa never took another wife. Instead, the tribe believed, she returned to witchcraft and had intercourse with women in her dreams. Telling the story, the shaman philosophized that witches should be killed, and that they themselves actually seek death. At any rate, Sahaykwisa boasted that she had bewitched a man, and two fellows who heard her got fed up and threw her into the Colorado River. That was the end of Sahaykwisa, lesbian and witch.

This type of tale is not considered unusual by the Indians, but is representative of the way of life of both male and female homosexuals among the Indians of the Southwest. Some of them took pride in their assumed sexuality. A male homosexual would be insulted if you mentioned his penis and testicles; he would insist that he had no such thing, only a vagina and a clitoris. A lesbian would be equally insulted if you spoke of her vagina. She would insist that she had only a penis.

Indians also took a comparatively tolerant attitude toward bestiality; many of their legends involve sexual intercourse between humans and animals, and tell of the resulting progeny.

A Blackfoot legend describes a youth who came upon a young buffalo cow caught in the mud. Taking advantage of the situation, he mounted her. She later gave birth to a human child — a wonderful, magical boy. He was reared by his buffalo mother, but when he became a youth he went out among the Indian camps to find his father. After traveling to many camps, he recognized his father among the young unmarried men. Father and son hit it off well, for they went together to the boy's home to see the buffalo mother. The boy warned his father that when they arrived she would dash at him four times and almost hook him with her horns, but if he stood still no harm would come to him. Four times she charged, and four times he stood unflinching. After the fourth time, the buffalo cow turned into a young woman.

The three lived together happily for a number of years. Yet she warned her husband that, no matter what else he might do, he must never threaten her with a stick of wood from the fire. One evening, when he had invited guests, she refused to prepare food for them. Enraged, he picked up a firebrand and struck at her. Immediately she changed back to a buffalo cow, **and the**

16

boy turned into a calf. They ran away together. The Indian father was disconsolate. He wanted them back and sought them out among the buffalo. Covering himself with buffalo dung, he crept close to the buffalo while they were dancing. He recognized one of the calves as his son and spoke to him. The calf-boy told him that if he wished to transform them back to humans, he would have to pass a test which would consist of picking out his son from among all the buffalo calves. The calf-boy promised to help his father by raising his tail as he passed. The young animals began passing in front of the man, and the boy raised his tail as promised, but so did several other calves. Confused, the father selected the wrong one. The herd then turned on him and trampled him to death.

However, the story has a happy ending. From one small piece of bone remaining after the trampling, the father was brought back to life and, by more magic, the calf-boy and his mother became human beings again.

This legend does not, of course, involve actual intercourse between a man and an animal, nor does it imply a human successfully impregnating a buffalo. It is a legend of the past based on relations between a man who was doubtless outside the buffalo totem and had illegal intercourse with a young woman of the buffalo clan. But the tale is more than that, for the totem animal was so closely related in a legendary sense to the actual person, that the woman was, in a magical way, a buffalo cow and her son a buffalo calf.

Labrador Eskimos tell the story of a hunter who returned each day to find his house beautifully cared for, his food prepared, his clothing scraped and cleaned, his fire kept. He came home early one day and discovered a fox in his igloo. The fox stripped off its skin and there stood a beautiful woman. They lived happily together for a short while, until the day he said her odor was too strong. Angered at this, she vanished.

In another story, a man who already had two wives met a young doe in the forest. She was more beautiful than any woman he had ever seen, and he tried to have sex with her. She transformed herself into a woman and permitted him to sleep next to her and embrace her, but she refused to have sex with him until she came into heat. When her season arrived she became a doe again and transformed him into a rutting young buck. He mounted her, but four other young bucks ran up and pushed him off. One after the other, they mounted her. Fortunately he had grown long antlers which enabled him finally to beat off his rivals. Then he took her as his wife, and her sisters and cousins as well. The sons he sired by them became true Indians,

but they and their descendants never forgot that their maternal ancestors were deer. They adopted the deer as their totem, and from that time on they called themselves the Deer People.

Women also often had animals as lovers in Indian tales. One young girl in a North Alaskan tale was in love with her dog. He slept at her feet, and every night he would change into a man and they would have sex together. She became pregnant, and when her parents found out who the father was, they became upset. Her father killed the dog and left the daughter in the cold to starve. She survived, however, and gave birth to five pups — four males and one female — who all miraculously changed to humans.

One of the most elaborate Indian tales deals with sex not only between humans and animals, but between humans and stars. As part of the story takes place in outer space, it's truly universal. The story begins with two girls who made their beds outdoors in order to sleep under the stars. They talked late, as girls are likely to do when camping out.

As they looked up at the sky, one asked the other, "Which star would you like to sleep with, the red one over there or the white one overhead?"

"I would like to sleep with the red star."

"Good," the first girl continued, "I would rather sleep with the white star." They fell asleep, and when they awoke they found that they had been transported to the heavens, where their favorite stars were waiting. The girls were somewhat disappointed to find the white star very old and white-haired, and the red star a redhead. Both were apparently equally unattractive to the Indians. The girls stayed on, living with the two stars for a long time, but they weren't happy about it.

An old woman in the star-world took pity on them and showed them a hole in the sky. Pointing down through it, she said, "That is where you came from." The girls could see the earth and their people down below. They wanted to go home. If they wove enough rope together and made a big basket, the woman told them, they could be lowered down to the world of men. Everything worked out as she'd said, but the basket landed in an eagle's nest high in a tree and they couldn't get down. They saw a bear pass by below and they cried out to him, "Hey, bear, come and get us. You will have to get married some day. This is a good chance." But they did not appeal to the bear and he went right on by.

Next came a lynx. The girls cried out to him, "Come on up and get us. You will need a woman some day." The lynx said he could not climb that high, and bounded away.

Finally, an ugly wolverine appeared. The girls, desperate, called down to him. He was desperate too, for he had not been successful in attracting a mate. He climbed up and brought the girls down one at a time.

He set up housekeeping with his two wives, enjoying sex with both of them. The girls, however, found it less enjoyable and decided to run away. They sent the wolverine up the tree to get a warm robe they said they had left in the nest. While he was up the tree, the girls ran and hid. They asked the trees to help them. When the wolverine came down and whistled to summon them, all the trees whistled back. The wolverine realized he had been tricked and gave up women forever.

The association of sexuality with guilt was completely foreign to the pre-Columbian Indian communities. Sex was considered a necessity, like eating and sleeping. Sexual activity began at puberty, and the children born out of these early intimacies were in no way stigmatized. In almost all clans, fertility was highly valued and the woman who had already procreated was all the more desirable as a permanent partner. To ensure the best chances of survival, some type of birth control was generally practiced. This made it possible for the clan to replace those warriors lost in battle, yet avoided unlimited population growth.

In most pre-Columbian societies within the continental United States, the concept of personal property does not seem to have existed. Essentials for survival — food, crops, canoes, hunting implements — all were owned by the group. This lack of proprietorship extended to women, who were free to leave their men whenever the relationship proved unsatisfactory. A woman could either join another man or remain unattached. Thus a man possessed only what he could use; if he needed three women because he was a great chief or a great hunter, he could have them. But, if he was not using his wife, she would lose no status or prestige (and, indeed, might gain some) by his offering her as sexual hospitality to a distinguished visitor.

Nudity was neither extolled nor proscribed for males or females. Both went openly to the rivers, streams and woods to wash and excrete. Since they did not attach any sexual connotations to these natural functions, they had no idea of shame nor desire for privacy.

The first Americans must have taken great pride in the male and female principles, as attested by their numerous paintings and sculptures of oversized male and female genitalia. Their legends also reveal the existence and importance of the concept of the soul or spirit, which could be male, female or homosexual. Separation between the three sexes in the spiritual world was carried on in the natural world where men, women and homosexuals played out their specific roles. And all nature — the moon, the stars, the wind, the water — not only contributed to the rites of passage such as birth, puberty, pregnancy and death, but pervaded their daily life.

2

Explorers and Conquistadors

While sex and sexuality were free and open, accepted as part of nature by the Indians, it was not so with the first white men who landed on their shores. The European explorers of the New World kept secret as much evidence of their sexual activity as possible. A careful reading of the official documents written by Columbus and his captains, and the Spanish who followed them, gives the impression that sex never entered their minds. Yet, by their letters to friends, their diaries and occasional contradictions in official records, their sexual urges and the means used to appease them are revealed.

Columbus had a wife and a mistress in Spain, one legitimate child, Don Diego, and one bastard, Ferdinand. A postmortem diagnosis of the Admiral's illnesses, made some 500 years after his death by doctors of the San Diego Medical Society, indicates that Columbus probably contracted syphilis during his lifetime and, quite possibly, in

the New World. Yet he and his men, rather than contracting it in the New World, could very well have introduced it. In any case, they did not get it from toilet seats.

On San Salvador in the Bahamas, the first landfall in the New World, the Admiral captured some six or eight Indian women. For the next two months he carried them along from one island to another. This, he insisted, was strictly for research to further his knowledge of "the natives and their language." He gave no hint of any sexual contact, yet it had been more than two months since his expedition had sailed from Spain.

The nudity of the Indian women so interested Columbus that he referred to it in his first letter to Queen Isabel of Spain from the New World. "They go entirely naked as their mothers bore them; and also the women." The repression of the Church in Spain had made nudity so rare that it is not surprising that Columbus and his men never ceased being astonished at it. Over and over, in both official and unofficial documents, references to the beauty and nakedness of the natives are repeated.

When the Admiral's flagship, the Santa Maria, was wrecked on a sandbar off northern Hispaniola, the men were ordered to build a fort and dig a hole in which to store the gold they were expected to find. The natives and the Europeans mingled well together. The crewmen were impressed both by the abundance of the food and the availability of the women. When Columbus asked for volunteers to remain at his first outpost in the New World the entire crew volunteered to stay. Thirty-nine men were selected and the Admiral sailed back to Spain with the rest, promising to return within a year.

Enroute back to the fort at La Navidad, a young sailor, Michele de Cuneo, who had been a boyhood friend of Columbus, wrote a letter to a friend in Italy. It is the first detailed description of rape in the New World. It occurred among the pristine, olive-green islands named The Virgins by Columbus, in remembrance of the martyrdom of Saint Ursula and her entourage of virgins who were raped and killed by the hordes of Attila the Hun in the fifth century. The adventure began when de Cuneo, in a ship's boat, surprised and captured a canoe full of male, female and eunuch Caribs. But let us allow de Cuneo to tell the story himself:

"Since I was in the pursuing boat I took a very beautiful Camballo, whom the Admiral gave me as a present. I took her into my cabin, and since she was naked as they are accustomed to be, I felt the desire to exchange sexual relations with her. When I tried to put into effect my wish she was unwilling and scratched me with her fingernails in a way to make me wish I had never started. But in the end I took a rope and tied her up, she was screaming in an unbelievable way that I had never heard before. Finally we came together and got along so well that I can tell you, in her knowledge she appeared to have been trained in a school for whores."

De Cuneo never mentioned the girl again in his letters, which is a pity for this is the first authenticated account on record of sexual intercourse between a male of the Old World and a female of the New, and it would be nice to know how the affair ended.

The ever-inquisitive de Cuneo in his informal letters continued to comment on the behavior of the crewmen and the Indians. When the ship stopped at the island of Guadeloupe a few days before reaching the Virgin Islands, de Cuneo wrote that eleven men were sent ashore "to rob the Indian villages but they lost their way." A rescue expedition found them and, en passant, captured "twelve very beautiful and fat girls from fifteen to sixteen years old," as well as two boys of the same age. De Cuneo explains the eunuchs at this point. These youths had their genital organs cut off — all the way to the belly. He at first thought the operation had been done to prevent the young men (whom he assumed were captives) from having sex with their captors' women. However, the sailors soon learned — to their horror — that Carib Indians emasculated male slaves and fattened them up to eat.

De Cuneo obviously kept his eyes on the women, for he also wrote to his friend in Genoa that the women's breasts were round, firm and well shaped. He observed that childbearing did not give them folds on their bellies but that their bellies stayed as well shaped as their breasts. He also noted that the women shaved their body hair, using stone knives and sharp canes, and that they pierced their noses. Like Columbus, he mentioned their nakedness but he also related that, after a woman had knowledge of a man, she covered the space between her legs with the leaf of a tree, a cotton patch or a *brachi* (which can be translated from the Italian as "panties"). "When they become of the age to procreate, they procreate," he wrote. According to de Cuneo's letters, the only women with whom the Indian men did not have sex were their sisters; all the rest were available.

"These people eat when they are hungry and have sex openly when they feel like it," he reported. "According to what we have seen in all the islands where we have been (this only included Guadeloupe, the Virgin Islands, San Salvador and Haiti) both the Indians and the Caribs are mostly Sodomites, not knowing (I believe) whether they are acting right or wrong."

He also mentioned that, while they did not worship idols, he did learn about a holy man, so proclaimed, who dressed in a cloak of white satin and never spoke. "In the morning," wrote de Cuneo, "he places himself in the middle of a temple and the first woman who comes into the temple has sexual relations with him — then all the other women go up to kiss her for she becomes worthy if the holy man has had intercourse with her."

The expedition continued past Puerto Rico and back to the little fort at La Navidad. Eleven months had passed and, although the natives came out to the ships to tell them that the Spanish were safe, when the landing boats came ashore they found all thirty-nine Spaniards were dead. Some bodies were still lying unburied in the dust around the fort. Guacanagari, the friendly chief, reported on the fate of the settlement. The Spanish had taken many women, three or more each, and this had finally angered the men. He continued that every Spaniard had eaten enough each day to feed five natives and, although he himself did not join in, the leader from an adjoining village led a war party against them and, either by ambush or direct attack, had killed them all. Thus the first large scale Indian-European sexual-social contact ended disastrously.

There is no doubt that children fathered by some of these Spaniards survived, as they did from later sexual encounters in Hispaniola. Hispano-Indian descendants, almost all of light complexion with an occasional olive-skinned blond among them, still pan gold in Rio Janico in the valley of the Rio Yaque del Norte not far from the original site of the fortress at La Navidad. Every day except Sunday attractive women hitch up their skirts and squat in the stream. With a wooden bowl they catch the earth and rapidly, with a circular motion, sluice the dirt and gravel out. The heavier bright gold dust, and sometimes a valuable nugget, remain. Even now these descendants of the conquistadors and the Arawak Indians take from five to ten dollars a day in gold from the river using only this pre-Columbian method. Back in the days of the conquistadors both men and women over the age of fourteen were forced to pay tribute every three months in the form of either a measure of gold dust or twenty-four pounds of cotton. No one seeing these long isolated people can doubt their relationship to the Spanish.

The explorers who followed the sea trails of Columbus and recorded their impressions of Indian life found much that was incomprehensible to them. Conditioned by the discipline of the Catholic Church and the monolithic European state, they fully expected the manners and customs of the Indians to parallel those of ideal Europeans. The "indecent" new culture of the strange new world was outside their experience and they reacted to it with amazement and horror, and only occasionally with approval. Even though much of what the adventurers saw was beyond their comprehension, many of them filled their journals with detailed notes. Observing the endless forests, abundant with deer, turkey and pheasant, and the coves, streams and rivers swarming with fish, they were also fascinated by the strong, healthy and attractive natives . . . especially the women.

The Spanish explorers of North America included not only military men, but also humble friars, proud priests, adventurers and scholars carrying the moral code of medieval Christianity with them. Like other nations of the world, large and small, they believed themselves to be the chosen people of God. But so did the Indians. They were equally sure that they were "the people" and that the world began with them. The strangers did not belong in their world yet the strangers were there and, after a time, the Indians found that they had the weaknesses of men.

In the early phases of exploration of the New World, major battles were rare. In most encounters the Indians could have easily wiped out the newcomers by sheer force of numbers or by withholding food and letting them starve. Yet a fascination for the clothing, swords, guns and horses of the Europeans brought curiosity and a desire to learn, causing the Indians to overcome their fear enough to welcome the strangers.

The conquistadors considered many of the sexual customs of the Indians immoral and in their journals condemned such behavior as pagan and uncivilized, but this didn't keep them from accepting and enjoying the sexual hospitality offered by the natives of the New World. The explorers, who, after all, had come to seek riches,

brought no women with them. Following the tradition of victorious armies in a defeated country, they soon began treating the native women as sex objects — as well as beasts of burden — to be used, enjoyed, then discarded.

From social custom and tactical necessity, Indian men often did not fight to defend their women. When they did European guile or firearms usually disposed of them. Later, as the foreigners proliferated and began to colonize the country, the Indians tried to fight back. However, by then they had lost their initial superiority and soon men, women and children were reduced to slavery. At the same time, an increasing number of children of mixed parentage were being born. However, it is interesting to note that accounts in some of the newcomers' journals imply that Indian women used a type of rhythm system for birth control, resolutely refusing to have sex at critical times during the menstrual cycle.

As the conquistadors did not bother to note the Indian social structure which separated chiefs, rich people and warriors from wives, concubines, poor people and slaves, they could hardly have been aware of the nuances of the natives' sexual relationships. To the Indian the sex act could be an obligation, a sign of hospitality, or a part-time marriage act in which a man might father a child but not live with the child's mother. Learning what full marriage meant to the Indian, or how difficult it was for a man to earn the price of a wife, was of no interest to the newcomers. With rare exception, they considered rape a normal way to approach a woman sexually. De Cuneo's forcible "coming to terms" on Columbus' ship was standard operating procedure. Sex and rape were synonymous.

In 1513 Juan Ponce de León, another of Columbus' shipmates, began his fruitless search for a virility potion and was the first European to discover the mainland of what is now the United States. This brought him no riches but death at an early age. Successful as the governor of Puerto Rico, Ponce might well have remained in his post there had not Christopher Columbus' son, Don Diego, replaced him. Still much in favor with the King, Ponce was given grants to explore further in the New World.

His initial landing took place in an inlet near the present Daytona Beach, fifty miles south of Saint Augustine. Because it was the Easter season, the day of resurrection, then commonly called Pascua Florida, he named the new territory Florida. Ponce had heard tales of an ever-flowing fabulous spring which could make old men young again and restore their fading virility. Ponce was only thirty-nine, but men aged early in the sixteenth century.

The existence of such a fountain of youth was a persistent myth, as attested by Peter Martyr in 1511, who described its marvelous properties. Some eighty years after the death of Ponce, the historian Herrera also reported in his *Historia General* that native kings went regularly to a "hot spring" and felt renewed. He even noted the case of an old man who was so restored that he could "take a new wife and beget more children." This reference to the fountain of youth strongly indicates that the Indians were talking of hot water spas, common in Florida and Louisiana (and in many of the islands of the West Indies), but Ponce did not find them. After a series of devastating attacks by hundreds of Indians, Ponce de León gave up his quest for the fountain of youth and returned to Puerto Rico.

Eight years later he tried again, but his second endeavor proved just as unsuccessful as the first. While making an attempt to erect dwellings, Ponce's group found itself surrounded and attacked by the natives. During the ensuing fight Ponce was struck in the thigh with an arrow, and most of his men were also wounded. They retreated to the vessels and sailed to Cuba, where Ponce died at the age of forty-seven.

A colleague of his involved in the conquest of Mexico was luckier both in war and love for he fathered the first distinguished bastard to be born in the New World. The child was conceived in the year 1519. His mother was an Indian slave, his father Hernán Cortés. Cortés was descended from a prominent Spanish family. Included in his ancestry were the Pizarros, the Monroys and the Altamiranos. Cortés himself bore the title of Marqués del Valle. A love affair with a married woman had propelled him out of Spain and into the New World. One day when he was climbing a wall up to his mistress' window, the wall collapsed and fell on him. As if the bruises weren't bad enough, word of the accident got back to the lady's husband. Cortés took the first available ship bound for Cuba.

In the New World the young adventurer turned on his charm and wangled an appointment as captain-general of a fleet exploring Mexico. With a tough disciplined army of men and sixteen horses he seized the entire country for Spain by making three symbolic cuts with his sword in a large ceiba tree. Learning that the Indians planned an attack, Cortés ordered horses, the first ever to be seen in North America, brought from the ships and held in reserve. The Indian horde fought well. They were on the verge of victory when Cortés ordered his armored and mounted soldiers to attack them from the rear. Completely terrified by these enormous and grotesque beasts that fought like men, the Indians turned and ran.

Cortés cemented the victory in a meeting with forty chiefs who asked for peace. Before their arrival he had a mare in heat brought out and tethered at a spot immediately in front of the place reserved for the caciques. As soon as her scent was established, Cortés had the earth raked and cleared so that no evidence except her scent remained. He then had his largest cannon heavily loaded and aimed at some nearby trees.

When the chiefs arrived and took their places, Cortés told them that they had made the gods angry, as he would soon show them. Then secretly he ordered the loaded cannon to be fired. It went off with a noise like thunder, and the cannonball sped over the heads of the chiefs and shattered the nearby trees. In the second act of Cortés' drama, a stallion was brought out to the spot where the mare had been tied. Getting her scent, he began to rear, buck, neigh and paw the ground, terrifying the chiefs. Eventually, Cortés had the horse led away and told the chiefs that, because they had come to make peace, he had ordered the beast not to be angry with them.

The terrified and docile chiefs left quickly and returned bearing gifts of gold, cloaks woven from feathers, baskets of fruit and bowls of food. But all this was as nothing compared to the gift of twenty young women slaves — some said to be virgins. One of them was destined to become Cortés' mistress and to bear his son. She would also become the most important weapon the Spaniards had against the Indians. Without her Cortés could not have conquered Mexico.

The coming of these women brought a new spirit to the Spaniards. The priests were alerted and preparations were made for a mass baptism. It was the first mass baptism in the New World. The Spaniards were anxious to get it done quickly for their moral code would not allow them to have sex with non-Christians. Within a few days of the girls' arrival, perhaps even a few hours, they had become Christians and were given Christian names.

Cortés gave one woman to each of his captains. He seems to have been careful in his selection for he presented an intelligent, attractive, graceful young woman, now called Doña Marina, to his favorite among the captains, Alonso Hernández Portocarrero. But Portocarrero enjoyed her for only four months before Cortés sent him back to Spain. Doña Marina moved in with Cortés.

One gets the impression that Cortés and his captain Portocarrero may have exchanged girls easily. For, when a frightened and friendly tribe sent a gift of eight girls (who, like the others, were promptly baptized), Cortés gave the best-looking one, Doña Francisca, to "my brother" Portocarrero — and he had already given him Doña Marina. The other girls were distributed among the soldiers. During and after the conquest, many men and women were branded and sold as slaves at auction by Cortés. Bernal Díaz, the chronicler, writes, however, that the best looking women were liberated by the soldiers and "we kept them as if they were free servants."

After Doña Marina had joined the Spaniards, only a few days passed before it was learned that she spoke not only the language of the Mayans but also the Náhuatl language of the Aztecs. She spoke both languages through an unusual series of adventures. Her name, originally, may have been Malin or Malintzin. She was doubtless named after Malinalxochitl, the sister of Huitzilopochtli, god of the Aztecs. It was this goddess who settled the region called Malinalco. She had the misfortune of being born into a chief's family. Her father died and her mother remarried a young chief. From this union a male child was born and both the mother and stepfather were determined that their son should succeed him as chief. Female children were not of great importance so her parents sold her into slavery to passing traders. She was carried to the south, where in addition to her native tongue, she learned the Mayan language.

Fortunately for Cortés, a Spaniard, Geronomi de Aguilar, had been captured and made a slave by Mayan speaking Indians. Cortés had freed him so Doña Marina and Aguilar could talk to one another. Then Aguilar could translate into the Castilian language of Cortés. In this way, Doña Marina became Cortés' interpreter. In time, in addition to her other two languages, she learned Spanish as well.

But Doña Marina was more than a translator and more than a mistress. She understood the ways of the Indians. She could not only speak for Cortés but could advise him, and he was flexible enough to listen to her counsel. As the small band of soldiers traveled across the valley of Mexico, Doña Marina met every challenge as a translator. When they met a tribe that spoke a language neither Doña Marina nor Aguilar could understand, she had the presence of mind to ask them if there were not among them some Náhuatlatos. And indeed she found that there were two among them who could tell her what the others were saying. This was one of many groups that came to offer their services to the Spaniards to fight against Montezuma. At another point she explained to Cortés that it was the custom for tribes to supply porters to important travelers through their territory. Each slave could carry fifty pounds on his back for five leagues a day. This freed the soldiers to fight; until that time they had been carrying their own heavy knapsacks.

When emissaries from Montezuma arrived wearing richly embroidered robes, with servants surrounding them for safety and fanning them to keep mosquitoes away, Doña Marina explained to Cortés that they were tax collectors from Montezuma. They demanded that Cortés turn over to them twenty men and women to take back to Mexico City to sacrifice to their god. After carefully weighing the words of the messengers Doña Marina told Cortés that Montezuma intended ultimately to capture and make slaves of them all. With this foreknowledge Cortés seized the messengers, sent two back to Montezuma, but kept three as hostages.

It was Doña Marina who explained to Cortés the prophecy and tradition dating back to Montezuma's ancestors of a white god who would be sent to the Indians. Later, when Montezuma spoke to Cortés through Doña Marina, he welcomed him to his nation as the white god and informed him that he had been holding the throne awaiting his coming and governing his kingdom. Now, if Cortés came to rule, he Montezuma, was at his service and the kingdom was his.

It was the knowledge, quickness and intelligence of Doña Marina that kept the Spaniards informed. In addition to her cleverness, she was, according to Díaz, a remarkably brave woman. Even though she heard from bloodthirsty enemies all around the Spaniards that "she would be killed, dismembered and eaten with chili peppers," she showed no sign of weakness. When Cortés became ill with a fever, she nursed him. And, while she may be accused of having betrayed her own people for the Spaniards, she remained a faithful mistress. Whether Cortés valued her more as a mistress or as an interpreter will never be known. That she escaped from the great battle in Mexico City after the death of Montezuma was due to Cortés having her carefully protected by 150 men placed between his forces and his rear guard.

In the year 1523, his conquest of Mexico completed, the captain-general married off Doña Marina to Juan Jaramillo, one of his lesser captains. In four adventurous years, Doña Marina had become a Christian, the mistress of Captain Portocarrero, the mistress of Hernán Cortés and the mother of his son Martin, and had married Captain Juan Jaramillo, with whom she had a daughter, María, — and had been the vital element in the conquest of Mexico by Spain.

The success of Cortés in finding gold in Mexico and shipping it back to Spain encouraged a series of new Spanish expeditions to North America. From one of these came the most intimate observations of Indian life ever made in the South and Southwest. When the Narváez expedition landed in Florida in 1527 with 600 hand-picked men, all except four were soon killed off by the Indians. The survivors were tall, red-haired Cabeza de Vaca, Alonso Maldonado, Andres Dorantes and Esteban, a Moroccan Negro who was Dorantes' slave. They began their epic journey after they found the last of their companions-in-arms had starved on an island in the Gulf of Mexico after turning to cannibalism. "Only the body of the last one was left uneaten," de Vaca wrote in his report, "because there was no one left to eat him."

For the next eight years de Vaca's small band moved ever westward, living with the Indians and observing their ways. Sunbaked in summer and nearly frozen in winter, they traveled the width of the continent from Florida to Arizona, trekking as far north as Colorado. Through a series of captures and successful escapes, de

Vaca and his group became the slaves of many different Indian tribes. For a time they even acted as traders, carrying shells, dried food and fruit from one tribe to another.

Because of the white men's knowledge of things new to the Indians, the latter attributed magical curative forces to them. At first de Vaca and his companions denied having any such miraculous powers. But when the Indians "withheld food from us until we should practice what they required, at last finding ourselves in great want, we were obliged to obey them." Fortunately, their practice of primitive medicine earned them respect and awe in some of the tribes. Playing their shaman roles as they moved westward, they learned more about the customs and character of the Indians in the South and Southwest than any of the earlier explorers in any other part of North America.

Like Columbus, de Vaca wrote of the nakedness of the people, but he noted that the women sometimes used Spanish moss between their legs. (This use of moss and leaves has been common among primitive women throughout the world during their menstrual cycles.) As the explorers traveled west, they found young girls wearing brief deerskin skirts entirely open on both sides.

They also reported that, in some of the tribes, "mothers cast away their daughters at birth for the dogs to eat." The chiefs explained that they chose to kill their surplus females at birth rather than risk having them captured by their enemies. Otherwise, they would mate with their captors, thereby producing more enemies to attack them. When Dorantes suggested that, rather than waste these little girls, they should be allowed to grow up and intermarry within the tribe, one chief became very angry. He said the idea of intermarriage between relatives was thoroughly disgusting to his people, and rather than give the girl children to either their own kin or their enemies, it was better to kill them off.

The de Vaca chronicle described shamans and chiefs who lived with two or three wives, and noted that, when a man had multiple wives, they lived together peacefully. In some of the tribes, men had only one acknowledged wife but kept other women as concubines whenever they could be procured.

Although the ideal way to get a wife was to capture one from an enemy tribe, during times of peace the Indians from East Texas purchased them instead. The price could be as low as a fishnet or a bow with two arrows. Marriages, the explorers wrote, lasted no longer than suited the husband. At the slightest annoyance the wife was dismissed. She carried all the burdens while he carried only his bows, arrows and spears.

Since they were considered neutrals, women were used as intermediaries between tribes. Nevertheless, many taboos kept them isolated. For example, menstruating women were never allowed to prepare or serve food. In most tribes the men could speak words that women were not permitted to utter. Nor were women

supposed to drink or serve a certain type of tea or the spirituous liquor made from cactus. In a few instances, however, women enjoyed a better lot and reportedly wore more elaborate and warmer clothing, such as knee-length shirts of cotton and skirts of scraped deerskin.

Some tribes drank liquor regularly and de Vaca wrote that they "were great drunkards." Smoking (tobacco, marijuana or peyote) was another favorite pastime and, the journal added, "they would give all they possess for a smoke."

De Vaca also makes one of the earliest records of homosexuality among the Indians. Slavery was prevalent everywhere, and some tribes maintained a considerable number of eunuchs by capturing and castrating their enemies.

As soon as the Negro Esteban arrived in a village, de Vaca said, he would ask for women and turquoise. After a while, he began thinking of himself as a chief rather than a slave. His physical size and black skin not only aroused great curiosity among the men but also caused the Indian women to find him sexually desirable.

In 1536, burned almost black by the sun, nearly naked and resembling Indians more than Spaniards, the four adventurers, after extreme hardships, arrived in north-central Mexico just south of the present Arizona border. There they finally met a Spanish contingent — a small, well-armed party hunting for slaves. As soon as they had eaten and had been clothed, they told their compatriots about huge towns with large houses, turquoise ornaments, well-dressed chiefs and beautiful women they had heard about from Indian followers they had attracted in that region. Esteban, especially, had gathered quite a following, including a small harem of Indian girls. Later, as the black and his faithful Indians were guiding a Spanish gold and turquoise expedition, he was captured, stripped of his possessions and murdered. But the stories of riches told by de Vaca and Esteban persisted and were embellished, and a newer and larger expedition, under the command of Francisco Vásquez de Coronado, set out to find and capture the fabled "lost cities of Cibola."

In 1540 this expedition set out from Mexico City in search of the legendary seven cities where, according to rumor, fantastic riches awaited. Pedro de Castañeda, a member of the expedition, kept a journal of its activities. The party consisted of a small army numbering 300 Spanish soldiers and 800 Indian porters.

En route to Cibola, believed to be in what is now southern Arizona, the soldiers moved from one poor Indian village to another, demanding whatever the people had to give. One tribe had nothing to offer except their blankets and robes made of animal skins. The Spaniards took them.

In the rocky region of Acoma, New Mexico, one of the captains left the camp to search for food in a nearby pueblo. There, a shapely young woman, standing with her husband on an upper terrace, caught his attention. Calling up, he asked the man to come down and hold his horse. The Indian came down and the captain climbed up the ladder to the dwelling. He stayed a while, then came down and rode away. When the Indian returned to his wife, he found that she had been raped. He immediately reported it to the chiefs in the village. They formed a delegation to protest to the officer in charge of the Spanish regiment. He agreed to punish the rapist if the husband could identify him, and all the soldiers were brought together. The plaintiff could not pick out the right man — all Spaniards probably looked alike to him — but he had no difficulty recognizing the horse. The general would not accept that identification and refused to punish the horse's owner. That was the end of the matter to the Spaniards, but not to the Indians.

Because the soldiers were too numerous and well armed for them, the natives attacked the horses, killing some and driving off others. In counter-retaliation the Spaniards made a surprise attack on the village and rounded up all its inhabitants. The Indians put down their arms, surrendered and asked for peace. They received a pardon from Coronado; then they were taken to Don Garcia, the lieutenant who had planned the attack. He was surprised and angry to see the Indians alive, because he had ordered the massacre as an example to the other villages. In Coronado's absence Don Garcia ordered the 200 villagers burned alive.

Castañeda writes that no one told the lieutenant a pardon had been granted, "for the soldiers knew as little as he, and those who should have told him about it remained silent, not thinking that it was any of their business." About a hundred Indians died, but the others managed to pull away from their stakes before they were too badly burned, and ran. However, as Castañeda continues, "they had no chance for it was a flat country." The Spaniards pursued them and cut them all down with their swords. Word of the massacre spread quickly, and from then on the conquistadors met with fierce resistance in every village throughout Arizona and New Mexico.

While traveling along the Arizona border, Castañeda continued his journal. Regarding homosexuality, he wrote, "Among them are men dressed like women who marry other men and serve as their wives." He also describes a type of ritual prostitution whereby a selected woman who does not plan to marry is consecrated" . . . with much singing and dancing, at which all the chiefs of the locality gather and dance naked, and after all have danced with her they put her in a hut that has been decorated for this event and the chiefs adorn her with clothes and bracelets of fine turquoises, and then the chiefs go in one by one to lie with her, and all the others who wish, follow them." From the night of this ritual, the woman becomes an official prostitute who cannot refuse sex with anyone who pays her an agreed amount.

Castañeda also observed a ritual similar to the *droit*

de seigneur, whereby a man, after acquiring a woman, took her to a chief-priest who deflowered her to determine whether she was a virgin. If she was not, then her family had to return the purchase price. The man could keep her as wife or not, or allow her to be consecrated as a public prostitute. "At these times they all get drunk," wrote Castañeda. He notes that they produced some kind of wine but, he deplores, "the wine makes them stupid." This account is one of the very specific records of pre-Columbian Indians fermenting beverages and getting drunk on them.

Castañeda wrote that, although some of the men were homosexual sodomites, most of the others had multiple wives and often married groups of sisters. One wonders how Castañeda found out about the high incidence of sodomy. According to his account, heterosexual men and women coupled openly like animals, with the female getting down on all fours and the male entering from the rear. So he may possibly have learned that anal intercourse was practiced as a birth control measure.

The Zuni Indians greatly impressed him, especially with their cloths "made like a sort of table napkin, with fringed edges and a tassel at each corner, which they tie over the hips." He reported that they were ruled by a council of the oldest men, called *papas*, who told the people how to live. "There is no drunkenness among them, no sodomy nor sacrifices, neither do they eat human flesh nor steal, but they are usually at work." The very fact that Castañeda speaks of these Zuni Indians (who still have a reputation for high moral standards, industry and thrift) so glowingly gives credence to the less complimentary descriptions of other Southwest Indian groups with whom he came into contact.

Surprised to see young women going entirely naked in this area where the weather gets very cold, he was told that "the virgins had to go around this way until they took a husband, and that they covered themselves after they had known man." Marriage was a simple matter, he notes. "When any man wishes to marry, it has to be arranged by those who govern. The man has to spin and weave a blanket and place it before the woman, who covers herself with it and becomes his wife. There is a men's house and the individual houses belong to the women. If a man leaves a woman, he goes to the men's house and lives there." Women were forbidden to sleep in the men's house or to enter there for any purpose except to bring food.

Echoing the tone set by the Spanish explorers, a French artist named Jacques Le Moyne reported on encounters between Indians and French explorers in Florida in 1564. He not only left written descriptions, but also made detailed drawings. Among the most interesting are representations of male homosexuals dressed in women's clothing, their hair worn long, carrying the wounded on litters after a battle. Like other early observers, Le Moyne noted that male homosexuals were excused from actual combat. He found these homosexuals to be very strong, and reported that their main duties were to care for the sick and bury the dead. However, they lived among the women and also helped in the women's work of gathering fruit, maize and other food.

It is Le Moyne who has handed down to us one of the few factual accounts of condoned incest among the Indians. He writes of a chief named Athore who married his own mother and had sons and daughters by her. Le Moyne describes Athore as being tall and athletic, grave and modest, and majestic of bearing. Le Moyne remarked that the chief showed off his children to the artist with great pride, and explained that after he (Athore) married his mother, the old Chief Saturiba, his father, moved away. This situation, so tolerantly accepted in this instance, was an unusual exception to the almost universal proscription of incest among the Indians.

However, this may not have been as unique a situation as the French artist makes it seem in his account. The old chief, Saturiba, doubtless had many young wives. There was a custom among the East Coast Indians that allowed a chief to have only one child by a young wife, whom he married as a virgin and then rejected sexually as soon as she became pregnant. This story, then, could mean that the old chief had impregnated and put aside a fourteen-year-old girl. When her son was of mating age, fifteen or sixteen, she would have been no more than thirty and would not have lived with the king for some fifteen years. The son could easily have had children by his mother and they would indeed have lived away from the residence of the old tribal leader. Both the son and the father would have been king or chief in their respective adjacent territories. It is also probable that the young chief Athore had other wives in addition to his mother, according to the prevailing custom.

When the English finally began to settle the East Coast they found similar customs among the Indians there. Like Columbus, John Smith and the Jamestown adventurers and settlers did not make mention of their sexual dalliances with the native women of Virginia. But the English settlers often wrote of native women being naked and unashamed. Shapely Queen Apumatecs was "fatt and lusty with long black hair." She was naked in front, only her back being covered by a deerskin. E. M. Wingfield, a conservative member of the Jamestown settlement, said the Indian women were "using [the men] . . . well during their being with them." And Smith, in a burst of candor, wrote: "Such victuals as they have, they spend freely; and at night where [a man's] lodging is ap-

pointed, they set a woman fresh painted red with *Pocones* and oil, to be his bedfellow."

With the kindness and loving care that was given to white men, as described in their journals, one must conjecture that sex was readily available to the colonists.

How passionate a relationship existed between Captain John Smith and Pocahontas is still debatable. Most historians, analysts and commentators have insisted upon a teenager's "crush" on the part of Pocahontas and a fatherly interest by the captain. They based their opinion upon the John Smith journals which had not only been written for the eyes of the English court and the royal stockholders of the Virginia Company, but had also been carefully edited. Tales of intimate relations between men and women during the reign of James I were not considered publishable. Such a relationship between an Indian princess and an English commoner, even a captain, was unthinkable.

So Smith did not even mention Pocahontas in his first book, published in 1608. It was not until 1624, sixteen years later and eight years after the death of "the little wanton" who saved his life, that Smith set down the "rescue" story in detail. It is from this version (another appeared in 1632) that we have the dramatic and romantic account. It begins as Smith made his way through hostile Indian country toward the head of the Chickahominy River. Against a well-planned ambush by a large force of Powhatan's warriors, he was almost helpless. At first, fear of Smith's pistol shots kept the Indians from getting in too close. Then they encircled him. One of their arrows struck Smith on the right thigh but did not wound him seriously. The Indians triumphed when he backed into a swampy area and began to sink so deeply that he couldn't get out. Only then did the tough captain surrender, throwing his pistol and sword to his captors. For Powhatan's warriors he constituted a prize well worth exhibiting in all Indian camps in the region. They fed him well and he wrote that, after pulling him out of the swamp, the Indians massaged his legs, which were cold and stiff. In every settlement women came running out to see him. To Opechancanough, Powhatan's brother, Smith presented an ivory compass. With a limited knowledge of the Indian dialect but considerable gesticulations, he explained the workings of the compass. What seemed to impress the audience most was the needle which could move but could not be touched because of the glass. The performance probably saved Smith from an immediate execution.

He quickly learned that the Indians were interested in having him join their ranks and attack the Jamestown colony. In exchange, they offered him not only his life but land of his own and all the women he wanted. Smith spurned the offers and even convinced the Indians that there was no way they could prevail against the fort, the handguns and the cannon of the English. Instead, he established himself as a magician by writing a list of things he needed and having the note placed on a rock in sight of the Jamestown fort. Within three days the Indians returned with the supplies he had requested. Now there was no doubt in their minds that Smith had the ability to make paper talk.

Under heavy guard, he was then taken to another village, where a foreign captain had killed the chief and kidnapped some of the people. The head men looked Smith over and admitted he was not the man they were after. The last stop was the village of the great Chief Powhatan. Sitting between two young girls, recent wives who had not yet borne him a child, the chief appeared tall, dour and elderly to Smith. He was flanked by his most trusted men. Behind them were many young women. Water was brought for the captain to wash his hands and feathers were brought to dry them. A great banquet was laid out before him. Powhatan was especially curious about the encroachment of the English up the river. He could not understand why the Englishmen were not satisfied to remain on the coast. Smith's explanation that the English needed more land for planting did not satisfy him. Since it was impossible to reach an agreement, the chief decided the Englishman could be of no more use to him. Two great stones were brought in; strong arms held Smith and pushed his head down onto them. Taking up clubs, the official executioners prepared to beat his brains out. A slim, brown female body interfered. Smith wrote:

"Pocahontas, the King's dearest daughter, when no entreaty could prevail, got his head in her arms, and laid her owne on his to save him from death: whereat the Emperor was contented he should live to make him hatchets and her bells, beads and copper; for they thought him as well of all occupations as themselves. For the King himself will make his own robes, shooes, bowes, arrowes, pots; plant, hunt or doe any thing so well as the rest."

It was the custom throughout the Indian tribes of Florida, Virginia and the Carolinas to offer captured slaves to their women. In some cases, this would provide the women with the rare pleasure of putting the slave to death at a rite where all the women would gleefully torture the victim; sometimes skinning them alive, cutting off their penis and testicles or slicing them up in small pieces. More often, captives were awarded to women, young and old, to help them with their household tasks. These included gathering wood, curing and sewing skins and carrying water.

It is obvious that Smith must have made an excellent slave; for the King he could make hatchets, and for Pocahontas bright trinkets — bells, beads and copper ornaments. So, at least temporarily, the fierce, black-bearded, twenty-eight-year-old Englishman became the slave of a near-naked Indian princess. Pocahontas was thought to be thirteen or fourteen years old, possibly even older, for we have no way of checking the actual date of her birth; we only know that she had passed the age of puberty. She is described as wearing the short leather apron front and back and open on the sides rather than the woven grass G-string worn by pre-adolescents.

Pocahontas' interest in John Smith was real, even intense. For, after Smith was reluctantly released and allowed to go back to Jamestown, she carried food to the colonists at regular intervals and kept Smith notified of the dangerous plans of her powerful father. On at least one occasion her warning saved the little community from being obliterated. And, had it not been for the supplies she brought, the colonists in the fort would have starved on a half-dozen other occasions.

The last meeting in Virginia between the adventurous captain and his young friend was a most romantic one. Captain Newport, with supplies for the colonists and gifts for Powhatan, had arrived from England. Smith's mission was to convince Powhatan to come to Jamestown, where he would be crowned king of the region (which he already was) and presented with coronation gifts from England's king. Instead of finding Powhatan, Smith was intercepted by Pocahontas, who told him that her father was thirty miles away but that she would send for him. During the waiting interval she sprang a surprise on the captain and his men. High-pitched voices, screaming and yelling, suddenly burst from the nearby woods. Smith ordered his men to prepare for a surprise attack. But some thirty naked young women, led by the King's daughter, came running and dancing out of the woods. They were putting on a show for her friend and had painted their bodies in bright colors and tied animal horns to their heads. After chanting and dancing around the camp, they invited the five colonists to a feast. Smith wrote that he was no sooner within the house but that all the nymphs tormented him, crowding, pressing and hanging about him, crying "Love you not me? Love you not me?" How the other four colonists reacted or whether he succumbed to their advances Smith does not record. But he was not the kiss-and-tell type.

Later, when he fell seriously ill and elected to go back to England in October of 1609, Pocahontas' visits to Jamestown stopped abruptly. There is no record of any contact between her and the Jamestown colony for the next three-and-a-half years. She is said to have married an Indian whose name was Kocoum but, historically, he is only a name. No one knows what happened to him; shortly after the marriage he disappeared. Then she was betrayed and kidnapped by the English, who needed a hostage in their dealings with the powerful Powhatan. Who could be better than his favorite daughter? The opportunity came by accident. Indians friendly to the Jamestown settlers informed the English ship captain Samuel Argall that Pocahontas was visiting (and trading with) a chief called Japazaws. According to

John Smith's account, Japazaws was rewarded with a copper kettle for getting Pocahontas aboard the English ship.

Once on board she was made prisoner. Argall told her that, before she could be released, Powhatan must return all the English prisoners he had captured as well as the English guns in his possession. But Argall had overestimated the importance of a girl child to the great chief. Powhatan was in no hurry to ransom his daughter. It was more than three months before he agreed to return seven captured Englishmen and seven muskets which his warriors were unable to operate. The deal was not good enough for Argall; he wanted all the arms back. So Pocahontas remained a captive in Jamestown.

Within a few months a wedding was arranged between John Rolfe — colonist, gentleman, tobacco farmer — and Pocahontas. John Smith's rescuer, the once naked savage, now eighteen or nineteen years old (her true Indian name was Matoaka) was rechristened Rebecca. Serious doubts were expressed within the Jamestown colony about a marriage between an English gentleman and an Indian girl. Rolfe, in a disturbed state and racked with guilt because of his passion for the girl, wrote to Sir Thomas Dale, deputy governor of Virginia, petitioning for his approval. He gave almost every reason but the true one for the marriage. It was "for the good of the plantation, the honor of our country, for the glory of God, for mine own salvation, and for the converting to the true knowledge of God and Jesus Christ an unbelieving creature, namely Pocahontas, to whom my heart and best thoughts are and have been a long time so entangled and enthralled in so intricate a labyrinth, that I was even awearied to unwind myself thereout . . ."

In disclaiming his sexual desire, Rolfe added that if sex was the motive he "might satisfy such desire . . . with Christians more pleasing to the eye." Not only was she a "heathen" but also she happened to be a princess and the council in London considered it treason for the commoner Rolfe to marry a royal princess. Royalty was taken seriously in England. On April 5, 1614, the doubts of some of the citizens notwithstanding, John Smith's heroine was joined in holy matrimony to John Rolfe, colonist. It was the first official marriage, sanctioned by the Church, between an Englishman and an American Indian woman.

Pocahontas, Rebecca now, gave birth to a son the next year — Thomas Rolfe. Even now, hundreds of Virginians, some legitimately, trace their ancestry back to Pocahontas. Approximately two years after their marriage, the ex-Indian princess and the young tobacco grower, with their young son, sailed to England, the guests of the child's godfather and governor of the colony, Sir Thomas Dale. Accompanying them were a dozen Indians, including one special friend and companion of Pocahontas with the unlikely name of Uttamatomakkin. He was one of Powhatan's captains and had

the mission of finding out what happened to John Smith. Evidently, Rebecca was very surprised to see Smith alive for she said that "they did tell us always you were dead, and I knew no other till I came to Plymouth; yet Powhatan did command Uttamatomakkin to seek you, and know the truth, because your countrymen will lie much."

The meeting of Smith and Pocahontas in England was awkward. The captain writes that "after a modest salutation, without any words, she turned about, obscured her face, as not seeming well contented . . . we all left her two or three hours . . . but not long after, she began to talk and remember me well.. . ." Pocahontas had every reason to know how often the English had lied to her father. She also may have been overcome with the shock of being with a man she had once loved and had thought long dead. Smith later wrote that he saw Pocahontas more than once but at no time does he give any indication that they were ever lovers. This does not rule out the possibility of a sexual relationship between the two of them. Indeed, in his voluminous accounts of his adventurous life, he mentioned having been saved from death on three different occasions by women.

During her stay in England Rebecca Rolfe attended balls given by the King and Queen. She met a number of distinguished English writers, including Dr. Samuel Purchase and possibly Ben Jonson. For a very short time she enjoyed great popularity. Soon after a great fête given for the French ambassador in February 1617, Pocahontas became ill, perhaps with pneumonia. She died less than a month later, on March 19, just as she was to return to Virginia with her husband.

The union of the Indian princess with the young English colonist brought hope of long-term peaceful relations between the Virginia Indians and the settlers. Unfortunately, it did not work out that way. Powhatan's brother, Opechancanough, secretly planned an attack. Hundreds of massed Indians fell upon the unwary colonists and killed 350 of them. It was a matter of luck that the entire colony was not wiped out.

As it turned out, intermarriage was not to be the salvation of England's first colony, for its survival was made possible not by the Indian bride but by her husband, John Rolfe. After he returned from England, he was responsible for crossing the homegrown tobacco with West Indian seed brought from the Caribbean. This resulted in a satisfying, smooth smoke. It soon became the New World's most profitable export and put Jamestown on the road to prosperity. Europeans had been smoking West Indian tobacco for a considerable length of time. The earliest users were sailors on Columbus' first voyage; although admonished by the Admiral of the Ocean Sea as to its harmful effects, they replied that they were unable to stop.

Sixty-seven years after Columbus discovered the weed-smoking Indians of Cuba, the French King Francis II sent Jean Nicot to arrange a royal marriage between his sister, six-year-old Marguerite de Valois, and five-year-old King Sebastian of Portugal. The wedding arrangements fell through but Nicot brought back to France tobacco plants to which the Queen, the Court and even the monks became addicted. Nicot's name comes down to us through history as nicotine.

A few years later Captain John Hawkins, adventurer and pirate, brought a parcel back to England which he described as "a kind of herb dried, who with a cane and an earthen cup on the end with fire [a pipe], — do suck through the cane the smoke thereof which smoke satisfieth their hunger."

There was opposition of a most powerful sort against the use of tobacco in England. King James I despised the weed and firmly believed that tobacco was a harmful substance when inhaled. On more than one occasion he warned his subjects against its use and tried to have parliament prohibit its import. But John Rolfe, backed by the Virginia Company and its profit-hungry stockholders, prevailed. And so did all the English, French, Spanish and Dutch men and women who, once hooked, could not or would not give up smoking.

Tobacco prosperity had an important effect on sexual relations in the New World. Using tobacco as money to pay for passage, the settlers over the next fifty years imported "tobacco wives" by the hundreds. At first the going price for wives ran from 120 to 500 pounds of tobacco, which paid the expenses (and offered a neat profit) of the sea captain who brought them over from England. These women, with no prospects of marriage in England, were willing to marry almost any healthy man who could pay the price of their transportation. Why were not more women brought over by the earlier settlers? Robert Beverley, in his *History and Present State of Virginia* (1705), wrote that the men who first came over, if married, did not wish to expose their wives and children to the "fatigue and hazard of so long a voyage, until they saw how it should fare with themselves." As prosperity slowly came to Jamestown, many of these men sent for their wives. But the majority, who were single, either had to work in the tobacco fields to purchase a wife or take the risk of social ostracism, jail sentences and punishment if they fornicated with the pagan Indian women. In a few instances they emulated the Spaniards and christened the Indian maidens to make them respectable. In even more cases men left the community and went into the Indian country to spend their lives with Indian wives and their Anglo-Indian children.

Becoming more and more selective about imported women, some colonists required a certificate attesting to the girl's modesty, good behavior and good health. According to Beverley's account, when a man could buy a young, attractive, healthy woman for one hundred British pounds, he was getting a bargain. Prices fluctuated, depending on the availability of females and especially their health; good health was essential because the death rate was as high as thirty percent and a sickly girl constituted a poor investment.

Despite the presence of English women, important visitors could still enjoy for free the very special Indian hospitality. Beverley described festivities given in honor of such guests, "with overflowing platters of meat, fish and fruit, and abandoned dancers until it was bedtime." Then, says Beverley:

"A Brace of young Beautiful Virgins are chosen, to wait upon him that night, for his particular refreshment. These Damsels are to Undress this happy Gentleman, and as soon as he is in bed, they gently lay themselves down by him, one on one side of him, and the other on the other. They esteem it a breech of Hospitality, not to submit to every thing he desires of them. This kind of Ceremony is used only to Men of great Distinction: And the Young Women are so far from suffering in their Reputation for this Civility, that they are envy'd for it by all the other Girls, as having had the greatest Honor done them in the World."

To conclude his observations, Beverley added some radical comments about intermarriages. Noting that frequent rape of Indian women by white settlers created a dangerous tension between the two groups, he suggested mixed unions as a satisfactory solution. On the one hand, this would bring the colonists more children and give them a good opportunity to convert the Indians to Christianity. On the other hand, it would ensure a continuance of the Indian nations that were broken up by wars and "are now dwindled away to nothing by their frequent removals." These somewhat advanced views were not adopted and the conflicts continued. Against the fire power imported in greater quantity with each incoming ship from Europe the Indians' arrows proved no real match.

Almost one hundred years earlier, in the southwest corner of North America, the Spanish had encountered the same problems. Since fornication with pagans was forbidden, marriage between Spaniards and Indians was at first unthinkable. But we have seen how Cortés got around that obstacle by making baptism for Indians more or less obligatory. And as early as 1514 the Spanish Crown lifted its prohibition against such weddings. Ferdinand and Isabel were both convinced that intermarriage between the new conquerors and the natives would result in more stable settlements. Some unions were consummated but not enough to satisfy the Catholic kings.

In 1556 more laws were passed promoting and legitimatizing intermarriage. Even though it did not ultimately mean that most Spaniards married Indian wives, a great many of them did. The stigma attached to it was always less in the Spanish colonies than in the English settlements. In a total sense, the Spanish policy differed completely from that of the British or the French. The Spanish wanted to Christianize and educate the Indians and proceeded accordingly. As a result, a surprising number of Indians became Christians. Although the soldiers who followed the conquistadors committed numerous rapes, an unexpected number of Spaniards began large families with their Indian wives. True, over a period of several generations a class system made its appearance. Nonetheless, the children born of these mixed marriages always belonged to a given social class, while on the East Coast the Anglo-Indians had nowhere to go except back to their Indian ancestors.

The contrast between the status of the Indians of Mexico and those of the United States is striking. As early as the nineteenth century Mexico elected a pure Indian as president of the country, something that has yet to happen in the United States. This gap can be traced directly to the mentality of the first explorers of these countries. As for the French, they couldn't quite make up their minds one way or the other. Samuel de Champlain offered a *dote* of 150 francs to any Frenchman who would marry an Indian girl. But while they had no objection to having sex with the natives, the idea of marrying them stopped the men short. The rumors of limited fertility among the Indian women (due to their birth control techniques) even caused the French to import girls from France who they thought would be more prolific. These were recruited from cities and farms and shipped off to French colonies. Apparently, they lived up to the high expectations placed on them, for in the fall of 1670 Jean Tallon reported that most of the "King's girls" sent out the preceding summer were pregnant. Still, in some accounts these future mothers of Americans were described as nothing else than whores who had been shipped out of France to other horizons. But perhaps because the French had no John Smith and no Pocahontas, and developed no profitable tobacco trade in the New World, they were unable to found prosperous colonies in the Carolinas or Virginia.

So, in spite of the shock expressed by the European writers at the sexual conduct of the Indians, the natives certainly regulated their sexual behavior far better than the explorers did. The Indians seem to have been closer to the mores of the second half of the twentieth century than they were to those of the sixteenth century. They recognized the rights of homosexuals 300 to 500 years before our civilization reluctantly admitted them as members of our society. They practiced no-fault divorce and a realistic kind of separation of the sexes, in which women and men could come together or stay apart in men's or women's houses, anticipating both communes and informal "living together." Teen-age sexual experimentation, incest, birth control, natural childbirth — all these realities of everyday sex life were met and coped with by the native Americans. Not bad for a bunch of "uncivilized savages."

THREE PIECES OF MIMBRES POTTERY
SHOW SEXUAL ASPECTS OF FIRST AMERICANS.

The ancient pottery of the Southwest, created hundreds of years before Columbus, reveals that prehistoric Americans had a strong interest in sex. In the fascinating Mimbres bowl at right, six female figures watch as a male, possibly a shaman, demonstrates how the penis penetrates the vagina. In the other bowl to the right, a hunter, penis erect, carries a rabbit he has killed with a throwing stick or boomerang.

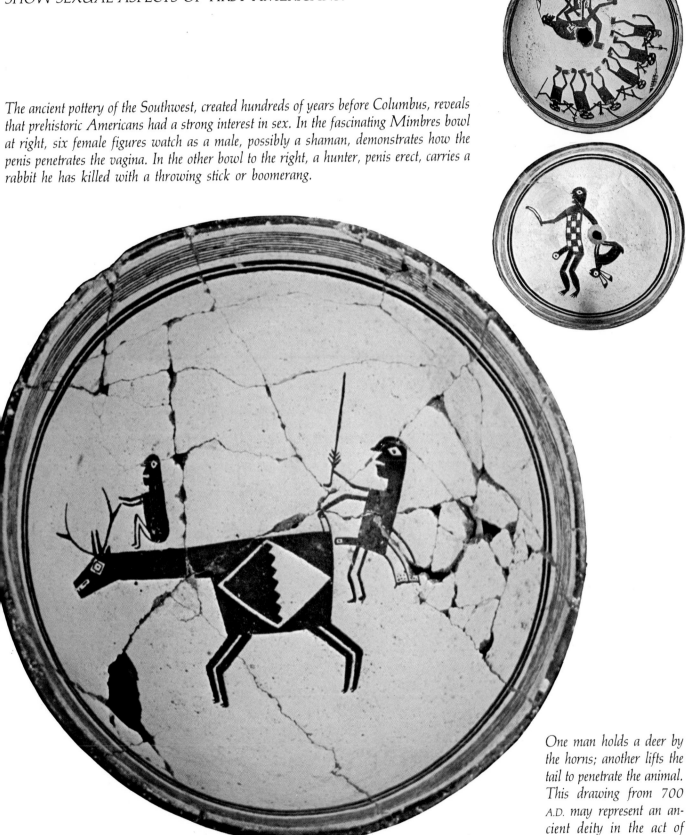

One man holds a deer by the horns; another lifts the tail to penetrate the animal. This drawing from 700 A.D. may represent an ancient deity in the act of fathering the Deer people.

A round stone, possibly of pre-Columbian origin, has been painstakingly chipped and rounded to create a life-size (6-1/8 inch) penis. It was found in Mammoth Cave, Kentucky.

That clothing was worn for decoration rather than for modesty is shown in this portrait of an Indian woman of Florida. It is by John White, 1587, earliest painter of American Indians.

Cast in metal and probably brought over to the Colonies from Europe, this nude figure was used as a bootjack. The heel of the boot was wedged bewteen the spread legs.

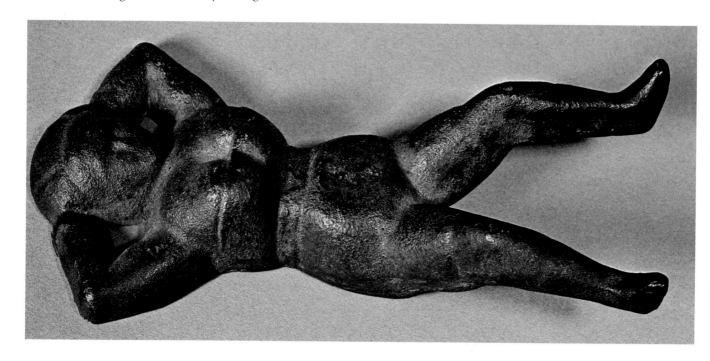

Sexually stimulating paintings such as this Adam and Eve by Bosch, ca. 1500, were seen by America's early settlers in reproductions imported from Europe. In the primitive painting (right) Eve feeds the forbidden fruit to the snake-devil.

Erotic drawings like this one by Thomas Rowlandson were seen by American men ca. 1790-1800 when copies were brought from England into the newly formed United States.

Demure and well-dressed whores in the gaslight shadows solicit beaver-hatted gentlemen as they leave a New York restaurant in the 1850s.

Opposite: American companies decided early that sex sold merchandise. Whiskey advertisers were among the first to use nudity as a sales technique. This advertisement appeared in 1892.

A sensational crime of passion erupted in 1836 when an unidentified pimp murdered Helen Jewett a 23-year-old whore with a hatchet, and set the bed afire.

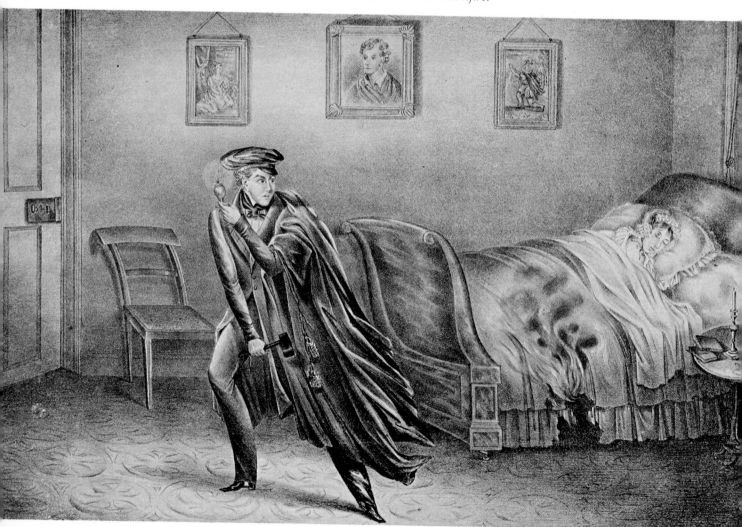

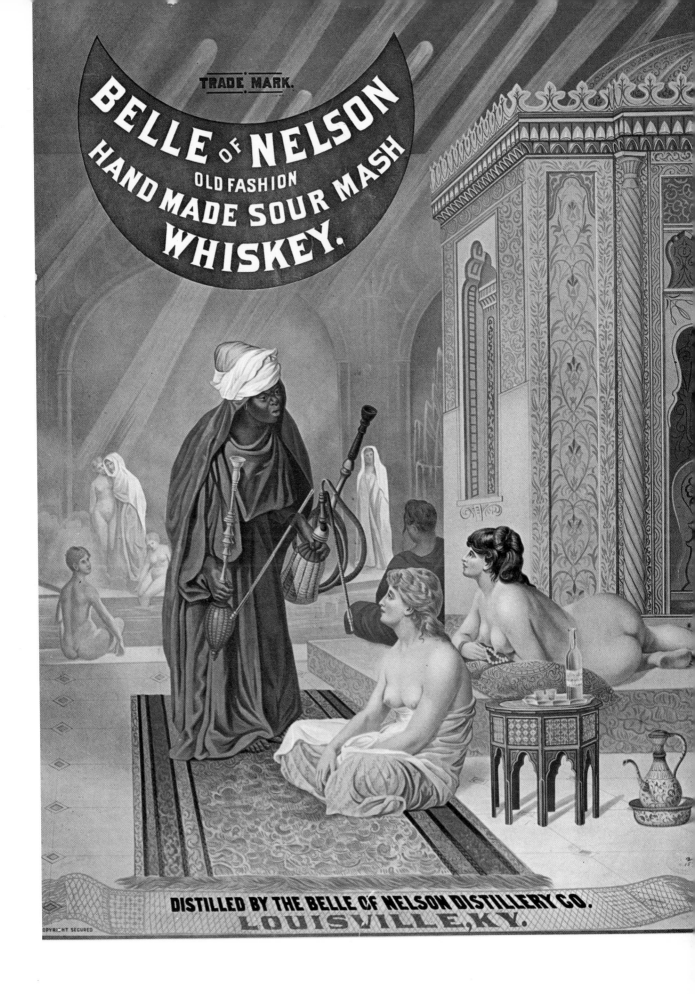

The romantic elements are all combined in this turn-of-the-century postcard: the moon, the sea, a suggestive pose and a "come hither" look in the bathing beauty's eyes.

This was a popular "under the counter" seller in the 1890s. She is an innocent maiden until turned upside down and her face covered.

Cigar cases promised more female exposure than they delivered. Closed, they were cigar size; when extended, the most you could hope for was naked thighs or an advertisement.

Brass counters were exchanged for money by the whorehouse madam. The girl, after satisfying the john, received the coin — later the madam reimbursed her in dollars.

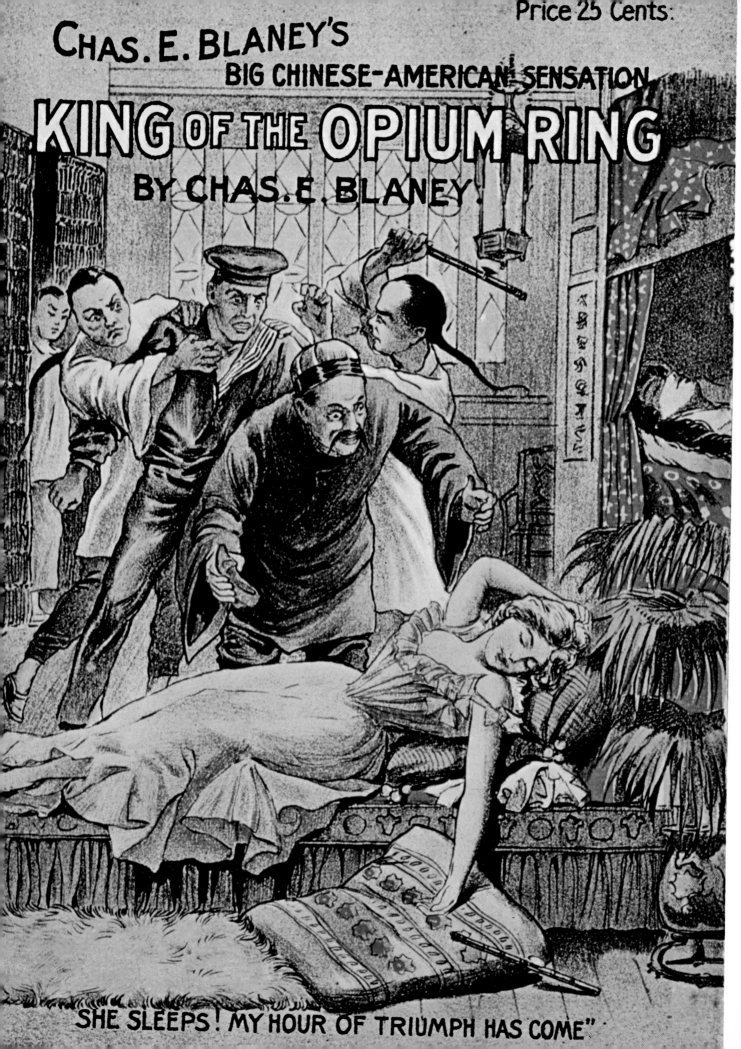

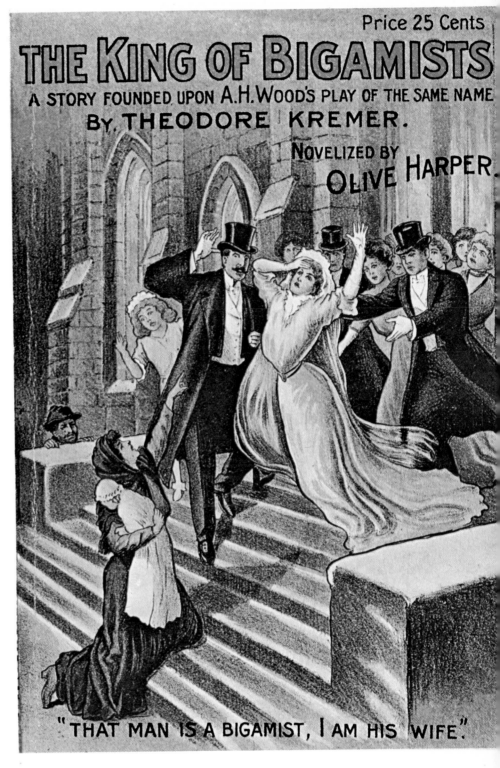

On Broadway in the years between 1890 and 1906, melodramas featured virginity (and the imminent loss of it to dope-driven Chinese rapists) bigamy and daring rescues by the United States Marines.

All artists and their models were suspect in the 1890s. Above a grief-stricken wife discovers a nubile, but well-draped, model with her husband in this typically overstuffed salon.

Tights were worn by dancers as early as 1869 (below) but were not accepted as proper apparel for actresses until the eighties and nineties. Actresses often played male parts.

Knee-length, short-sleeved bathing suits titillated as many people as they shocked. While ministers condemned them, their congregations wore them.

"O what would the congregation say?"

Healthy sexuality is expressed in this lithograph of 1894. Playful cherubs, who could be thought of as the idealized woman's future children, helped to make it respectable.

The public wanted to see more breasts and legs and the artists of the period obliged. This sexy and highly exaggerated circus lithograph was printed in 1892.

Sex was a feature of the covers of paperback novels adapted from popular plays (right). Note that the play "Mlle. Fifi From Paris" was coproduced by Florenz Ziegfeld.

verleaf: Nudity, combined with fantasy and foreshadowing
ter science fiction illustrations, was featured on the cover of
earson's Magazine in 1895.

THE SEPTEMBER

PEARSON'S

READ "THE LOST CONTINENT"
CUTCLIFFE HYNE'S GREAT STORY

10¢ NOW READY 10¢

3

Those Immoral
New Englanders

While the Virginia colony began prospering from the tobacco trade, which paid for the passage of shiploads of marriageable women, Captain John Smith did not remain idle. At the time his friend Pocahontas was being married to John Rolfe, Smith signed on with the Northern Virginia Company to explore the colony's northern coast, which at that time extended to Canada. Smith charted the territory and called it New England. Others had sailed along the North Atlantic coastline before him but it was Smith's favorable description and detailed maps that influenced a group of English dissenters to try for a homeland in New England. Called Puritans, they had broken away from the Church of England because its disciplines, they believed,

were far too permissive, too liberal, too out of touch with the will of God.

For seventeen years, from 1620 to 1637, these religious purists migrated from Europe in ever-increasing numbers to set up their own laws and to establish a Kingdom of God unlike any other in what they considered a degenerate world. The low morality of all of Europe — England, France and Germany — and the opposition of organized Christianity left them no hope of heaven except in a new environment. The foundation of a community of righteous men and women was their hope of salvation.

At the time that the Puritans landed James I of England had a court notable for its immoral revelry and extravagances which, to a degree, condoned homosexuality and adultery — abhorrent to the Puritans. Under Charles I homosexuality, incest and fornication were rarely punished.

True, there had been the execution of the Earl of Castlehaven in 1631. He might have gone free with a light sentence for sodomy and rape — had he performed them on his own wife. But, when it was proved he had also encouraged his servants to have sex with his wife while he watched, the death sentence was inevitable. In addition to forcing her to have sex with him and his servants, the Earl arranged for his stepdaughter of twelve years to be raped by one of his male servants while he observed. His wife and two of his companions testified against him. The stepdaughter and wife told the court their experiences in terrifying detail. It was a major scandal of the day. The Earl and two of his servants were executed. But if everyone had been punished for rape and buggery, the population would have been severely reduced.

For buggery, or anal intercourse, was practiced in high and low places. At least one bishop was executed when found guilty of an affair with another man. Cases of incest, although frequent, rarely resulted in serious penalties.

It was to get away from such immorality and to keep their own young sect from being crushed by the Anglican establishment that the Puritans set out in the *Mayflower* for New England. There they would make their own laws in their own land and live accordingly. Because they insisted upon purity in affairs of both Church and State, and because they were industrious and high-spirited, the disciplinary measures they adopted for themselves served as a base for the conservative society which they formed in the New World.

Like reformer John Calvin, they believed in original sin. Men and women had been damned by God when they learned of sex, symbolized by their enjoying the fruit of the tree of life in the Garden of Eden. Every word of the Bible was interpreted literally. Adam and Eve discovered one another's nakedness, fornicated, understood sexual guilt and were driven out of Paradise by an angry God. They could only be saved by the grace of God. "It sounds," said a young friend of mine recently, "like they were set up to be busted."

In the wilderness of the New World the Puritans created a biblical commonwealth. Between 1620 and 1637 more than 10,000 of them migrated to New England. Communal living was rare, however, for even though the initial settlers needed the full support of one another, they were burdened with England's rigid caste system.

Over the years the religious aristocrats, the Puritans, were hard put to keep their high standards of moral behavior, particularly since many of the second wave of colonists came from the lowest, most vicious elements in England. Prostitutes, pimps, thieves — men and women released from the prisons of London and Liverpool — were shipped off to the New World to work as indentured servants in fields or homes. As many as 13,000 a year, the majority of them women, were arriving in the colonies by 1700. They were sold at an average of ten pounds sterling each and frequently worked harder than slaves: their masters wanted to make sure they got their money's worth during the five- or seven-year's bondage term.

Children were often indentured until they became twenty-one in return for their passage or as payment for a parent who may have died during a voyage.

Two other human elements with divergent moral principles began to mingle in the New England lifestream by the 1650s. These were American Indians and, to a lesser extent, black slaves from Africa. Often unable to adhere to their own moral laws, the Puritan Fathers were less than successful in imposing these upon "inferior" races.

While many Indian tribes remained friendly to the Puritans during the early years of the new settlements, bloody skirmishes were fought with Pequots, Nipmucks and Narragansetts as the century and frontier advanced. Soon the colonists found they had an excess of captives. Indian men quickly proved "ungovernable" as slaves, so they were sold off to West Indies planters. Captured Indian women and children, on the other hand, were usually kept as household servants. It was inevitable that the squaws, deprived of their own men and accustomed to giving sexual favors with no tinge of Calvinist guilt, were often in bed with the colonists.

Detailed church records and court cases give the impression that it was the servants who led their masters into sinfulness and that the new indentured class was unwilling and unable to live up to the rigid sexual code set by the Puritans. Obviously, the newcomers were not the only offenders. Their well-educated masters joined them in the crimes of adultery, miscegenation, bastardy, fornication and sodomy. Murder and theft were relatively uncommon, but sex-related crimes were numerous.

Whether aristocratic landowners or life-indentured servants, men on every social and economic level were on the lookout for white or Indian women. Since marriage was the only sinless way to go, widows rarely slept in cold beds for more than a few months — sometimes only a few weeks.

The first marriage to be solemnized in Plymouth was that of Edward Winslow and Susanna White on May 12, 1621. Winslow had buried his former wife just seven weeks earlier. The bride was also recently widowed, having lost her husband during that first cataclysmic winter at Plymouth. The ceremony was performed by a magistrate because the founders of the colony had decreed that marriage was a civil affair. Having escaped from religious domination, the Puritans were wary of any form of church control.

Their insistence on civil marriage brought the colonists into direct conflict with the Church of England.

When Edward Winslow visited England in 1635 he explained to the Archbishop of Canterbury that "he found nowhere in the word of God that it [marriage] was tied to the ministry." The archbishop was dismayed and disagreed. He abhorred the idea of civil marriage and had Winslow locked up in Fleet Prison in London for seventeen weeks.

In another sharp break with the Church of England, which continued to adhere to the doctrine of insoluble marriage for many years after lusty Henry VIII had defiantly set aside four of his wives, New England elders recognized divorce, the only English-speaking region to do so with the exception of Scotland.

This matter of taking divorce into their own hands was typical of the Puritans — as was their ability to change with the changing times. Among themselves they wiped out much of the hypocrisy that continued to exist in Europe.

The first act that authorized the dissolution of marriage by judicial decree in any dependency of the English Crown was passed by the general court of Massachusetts in 1639. This same year James Luxford was found to have two wives, one in England and one he had married in Massachusetts. All his goods and money were awarded to the Massachusetts wife and her children; Luxford was fined one hundred pounds sterling, was set in the stock for an hour on a market day, then banished and sent back to England on the first available ship. The award to his Massachusetts wife also represented the first instance of alimony in a divorce case in the New World.

The law of 1639 was reenacted in 1658 and read "that there be two courts of assistants yearly kept at Boston, by the Governor, or Deputy Governor, and the rest of the magistrates, on the first Tuesday of the month [March] and on the first Tuesday of the month [September] to hear and determine all and any actions of appeal from inferior courts, all causes of divorce, all capital and criminal causes, extending to life, member, or banishment."

There is considerable doubt that the colony actually had proper authority to establish such a divorce court. The act could have been treated as an usurpation of the authority of the Parliament or the Crown of England and declared invalid. Yet the Founding Fathers of what was to become the United States of America did so act without the permission of the Parliament or the King — and got away with it.

Nine grounds were permitted upon which a marriage could be dissolved: adultery, impotence, bigamy, fornication before marriage with a relative of the husband or wife (a form of incest), malicious desertion, incest, bestiality, sodomy and long absence with the presumption of death.

Special provisions were established for wives or husbands of men or women who sailed from one port to another. The law provided that if a person had not been heard from within three full years, the man or woman who had been left behind would be considered single and unmarried providing this matter were brought before the Governor and his council. A special license could be issued allowing such a person to lawfully marry again. If the missing spouse did reappear after three years, the wife or husband who had remarried could not be prosecuted for bigamy. It was another radical departure from the prevailing Catholic and Anglican dogma for the Puritans to declare that a person legally divorced could have a legal second marriage.

Some idea of the temper of the times is reflected in the case of John and Elizabeth Coggeshall, who came before the court and pleaded that they had parted by "mutual and voluntarie consent." They were granted permission to divorce and for each to remarry.

Civil divorce was also instituted in Plymouth Colony but cases were rare. There are only six divorces on record over a period of seventy-one years. Every one was granted on grounds of adultery.

In an effort to be rid of his wife, one William Tubbs tried an old English expedient. He wrote out a bill of divorcement, had it witnessed by his neighbors and presented to his wife. However, neither she nor the court accepted this simple procedure. The court took over and ultimately granted him a divorce.

The low incidence of divorce does not mean that all went smoothly with husbands and wives in New England. During the years that the six divorces were issued in the Plymouth Colony, more than forty divorces were granted throughout the neighboring Massachusetts Bay Colony.

The court records are sketchy for the years from 1621 to 1650 but there is evidence that in all New England colonies divorces were granted.

One of the most interesting cases in Rhode Island occurred in 1665. Peter Tollman applied for a divorce and, when his wife admitted she had committed adultery, his petition was granted but the wife was sentenced to a fine and a whipping. The fine was ten pounds, the whipping fifteen lashes to be delivered across her bare back at Portsmouth. A week later an additional fifteen stripes were to be laid on at Newport. When petitioned for mercy the court "examined her as to whether she intended to return to her husband." This she refused to do "no matter what the terms or the punishment." She was sent to jail and the whippings carried out.

Details of the divorce cases give considerable insight into the mobile way of life in New England in the last quarter of the seventeenth century, when long distance travel was often necessary for survival. For instance, Mary Sanders obtained a divorce from her husband on evidence that he had committed bigamy in London when he was detained there for three years. Hope Ambrose got a divorce from Daniel Ambrose for desertion, neglecting to maintain her and her children and keeping a mistress in Jamaica. Mary Bishop got a divorce after being deserted for seventeen years and because her husband had another wife in Barbados.

Adultery was also a matter of great concern to the Puritan founding fathers. Evidence of it abounds in long, and occasionally sensational, accounts in the 1640-50 county court records of Massachusetts. The court did not take hearsay or circumstantial evidence but required eyewitness proof. The following account is put into modern language. It is a deposition by Susanna Kennett accusing Mary West of adultery with Richard Jones.

Susanna and another servant, John Tully, were working when they heard odd noises coming from an adjacent room. They both climbed upon a hogshead of tobacco and, looking over the transom, they saw Richard Jones and Mary West on a bed "both arme in arme." Mary reached over and put her hand in Richard's "codpiece and shaked him by the member," and Susanna could not keep from laughing. So they moved away from where they had been watching.

Then, when Mary and Richard moved into a servant's room, Susanna and Tully "slipped a board" in the wall to peep in and "did see the sayde Mary Lye downe upon the bedd with her cloathes upp about her eares and the sayde Richard Jones Laye downe upon her and was betwixt her Leggs.. . ." Then Jones told Mary to "hold up stiff." Mary called to her son George for water to wash Jones. Before he got there with the water, "they had made an end." When the son came back, Susanna testified he cried out "come off my mother." Susanna goes on to say that both she and Tully saw all of this together but that it was no novelty — she had seen it several times before.

Anne Moye confirmed and added to the other servants' testimony. She quoted Susanna and Tully as saying that they had told her "they had seene Richard and Mary West att bedd togeather and they could have taken Richard Jones' cloathes away" and continued that they saw them so near together that "a hott needle might have burnet their bellyes." It was not unusual for servants to testify against other servants but rare for them to testify against their masters and mistresses.

New laws were frequently promulgated to maintain an illusion of high moral standards among the early English settlers. As early as 1676 a Pennsylvania law punished any man who "shall harbor, conceal or detain Contrary to the consent of the husband any married woman, upon penalty of five shillings for every hour that such married woman remains under his roof; after [a] demand [is] made by her husband at the dwelling house where his wife is so harbored, concealed or detained."

Plain, ordinary fornication between consenting but unmarried adults constituted a major crime, punishable by the whipping of both parties. A second conviction for fornication would call for more whipping. But at the next slip, the whipping would take place three times a week for a whole month. Whether the participants in the sex act were both white or white and Indian, the sentence was the same. However, Christian fornicators were forced to ask public forgiveness of the Church congregation.

More serious crimes, like adultery, rape and sodomy, were theoretically punishable by death. As evidenced by the numerous court cases, all three offenses were relatively common. Yet the death penalty was rarely carried out — even when the culprit was convicted. The records show that except for three occasions, the ultimate penalty was reduced to branding, whipping or a fine. Another punishment would consist of leaving the guilty party on a platform with a gallows rope around the neck for one hour or more.

As for sodomy, it was so unspeakable a crime that the Puritans usually referred to it as *the crime against nature*. (This vague description has persisted in the laws of many states.) Since this form of perversion could not possibly result in procreation, it, in theory, broke both the laws of God and the laws of man. Combined with rape or with child molestation, the only appropriate sentence was death.

It took a fair amount of ingenuity for the elders, or judges, to devise punishments for adultery. A conviction for the crime in New England in 1642 required that both parties should kneel before the judges and implore forgiveness. Then, at a later hour each had to submit to a severe flogging. By paying a fine or performing some labor, men often avoided the lash but women, generally stripped to the waist, received anywhere from ten to twenty lashes with the whip across the back. In one instance, while the woman got the lashes, her male partner paid the cost of building a badly needed bridge across a creek in North Hampton County. In another case an adulteress was punished by being dragged through the water behind a boat.

Most women submitted and asked for mercy but others refused to take their punishment quietly. When Edith Tooker of Lower Norfolk was found guilty of sexual relations with a man, she was brought to her parish church during services. Clothed in the usual white sheet of purity, she was led in after the worshipers had taken their seats. But, when the clergymen urged her to repent of the "foul sin" she had committed, she refused and, to the consternation of the congregation, tore and mangled the sheet wherein she was doing her penance. More punishment followed. She was condemned to receive twenty lashes. The whip seems to have had the required effect for, when she appeared in the white sheet in church the following sabbath, there is no record of her misbehaving.

Obviously, the judges, the elders of the church, and the congregation must have enjoyed these spectacles.

Though all claimed to relate the disciplines to biblical admonitions, one sees the human element of sadism creeping into the penalties. Having to admit one's sins before the congregation served to purge the conscience of the sinner who, after becoming the subject of gossip for long periods afterwards, was nonetheless allowed to rejoin the church. After 1650 the rate of adultery increased precipitously as a greater number of indentured workers arrived.

Among the lesser forms of punishment for such crimes as slander and blasphemy, the ducking stool was a favorite. The convicted person was tied to a chair which was mounted on a long board directly over a pond or creek. The slanderer was then lowered into the water until completely covered. Then, just before drowning could occur, the accused was raised, sputtering and choking, presumably remorseful for having committed this offense; if not, the chair was lowered again.

While men must have been as sinful as women, judges and church elders often forgot that it took two to commit adultery. This is not to say that men were not punished. The records show that many were. But more women were tried and convicted. The judges took the position that men were driven to sexual misconduct by their nature, but that women should be able to control not only their passions but also those of the men who seduced them.

In the formative years of the New England colonies the Puritans not only addressed themselves to the problems of human morality, but also to the broader problems of the body politic. In the mother country they had renounced undemocratic legal processes as well as religious conformity. In the New World, while England was troubled by its Civil War, they further asserted their capacity for self-government. One of their earliest documents setting forth rights of citizens was the "Body of Liberties" adopted by the Massachusetts Bay Colony in 1641. This document outlined many principles incorporated into the Bill of Rights in the federal Constitutior 130 years later. Embodied in the new regulations was a prohibition against torture as well as cruel and barbarous punishment. Aliens (that is, foreigners or non-members of the original settlement) were afforded equal protection under these laws. In theory, a decree against cruelty to wives became part of the legal structure. Husbands were forbidden to beat their wives — except in self-defense. In spite of these progressive statutes, the colonists were still bound by orthodox interpretations taken from the Bible.

As political intellectuals, the Puritans were aware of the importance of freedom to think and act but they were heavily saddled with traditional admonitions that they dared not discard. Evidence of this conflict can be seen in Cotton Mather's famous *Magnalis Christi American,* or *The History of New England.* His ecclesiastical history covered the years from 1620 to 1698 and paid homage to the laws of God as interpreted by man.

One instance has to do with marriage between a man and his wife's sister. This was positively prohibited by the law of God. Yet, with the persisting shortage of upper-caste women it seemed natural for a man, upon the death of his wife, to marry her sister. Nonetheless, it was suggested that such people be cut off from communion in the church. The deed was regarded as incest; should it happen, divorce was not only allowable but indicated. Cousins were also dissuaded from coming together in marriage although such unions were not prohibited. Mather's position was that it was easier to abstain from wedlock because "some wise and good men have been so troubled in their minds concerning these marriages."

God was the authority, and self-appointed or congregation-chosen ministers acted as his divine agents administering "justice" to sinners. Intolerance and enslavement of the Indians was excused by the fact that these heathens would not accept the Lord Jesus Christ and that they opposed the armies of the Christians. Because they insisted on the ways of the infidel, they were chastised by the Lord and, more realistically, by the fast-developing military of New England.

Mather was especially concerned with the lack of morality among the Indians. "The Indians are very lying wretches, and they are very lazy wretches, and they are out of measure indulgent unto their children, there is no family government among them." Mather wrote that "now, the judgments of God have employed Indian hatchets to wound us," implying that, because the settlers had adopted some of the Indians' vices, God had used the natives as a weapon to punish them.

The prolific, and sometimes hypocritical, ministers such as Cotton Mather carefully recorded crime and punishment in Puritan New England. Adam's fall was emphasized in Sunday School and church regularly, yet more emphasis was given to Eve. Her fall was far lower than Adam's. Men could, and often did, have their sentences for fornication or adultery commuted or reduced. Not so with the woman. In almost every recorded court case, the judges threw the book at her. There were only two kinds of women, good and bad. Good women disliked, resented, avoided sex. It was unmentionable and unseen. Pregnant women hid their pregnancies because showing them would be an admission that they had indulged in sex at least once. Good women were quiet, industrious, home-loving and hard working. But one slip changed a good woman to a bad one. Bad women were those who knew about sex and accepted it. They were women who had been seduced, raped or were divorced. Even widows were suspect.

Mather wrote of "many secret murders" and of the increasing number of illegitimate children killed at birth because the mother was fearful of punishment for adultery. In his memoirs he tells the story of young Mary

Martin, whose father went back to England and left her in the house of a married man. The latter became so enamored of her, says Mather, "that he attempted her chastity." She yielded to him once and made a vow to herself that she would confess and be made a public example. But, Mather continued, "a chain of Hell was upon her" and she sinned a second and third time after her vows had been uttered.

After obtaining a job as a maid in Boston, Mary found herself pregnant. Bulky clothing hid the fact from her master. And, as Mather puts it, "she concealed her crime till the time of her delivery; and then being delivered alone by herself in a dark room, she murdered the harmless and helpless infant; hiding it in a chest from the eyes of all but the jealous God." Mather doesn't explain how the unlawful birth was discovered. The unfortunate girl denied it, but friends began to search for the dead child. She told them, finally, that the baby was stillborn and that she had burned it, but it was found in her chest. Mary was taken before the judges with the little dead body. Mather continues: "When she touched the face of it before the jury, the blood came fresh into it, so she confessed the whole truth concerning it."

Sentenced to death, the young mother made penitence before her execution and, according to Mather, she acknowledged that she twice tried killing the child before she succeeded. To complete the irony, the unskillful hangman had to make two attempts before Mary died. The story, dramatically told and doubtless embellished, became a favorite Mather sermon.

Infanticide, adultery and incest were not the only moral issues confronting New England settlers. They also had bestiality to contend with. More than once, cows, heifers, sows and pigs were executed for their participation in sexual intercourse with a human.

Mather describes in detail a man of Weymouth, who was a pillar of the church, "devout in worship, gifted in prayer, forward in edifying discourse among the religious, and zealous in reproving the sins of other people; everyone counted him a saint . . . But it was found that he had been involved in buggeries for no less than 50 years." At the gallows they hanged before his eyes a guilty cow, two heifers, three sheep and two sows. His wife and son testified against him. He, too, was hanged.

Bestiality was not confined to New England in the late seventeenth century. In Virginia the shortage of women led to occasional fornication with sheep, goats and calves. One of the most graphic accounts involves Nathaniel Moore, who was seen buggering a calf which was tied to a small tree. Robert Wyard, who testified against him, stated that he had been going home and, upon entering the woods, saw this fellow with the calf. His description, rendered here in modern spelling, follows: "Saw him buggering the said calf four or five times. In his action Nathaniel had the calf by the tail and

his yard thrusting into the calf several times, wiping his fingers on the calf's side and wiped the calf's breech with his hand."

"Peeping Tom" Wyard (who seems to have been behind a tree) beckoned to his wife and pointed out Nathaniel, saying, "Do you see what yonder fellow is doing?" She answered, "Who is it?" And the deponent said, "It is your man [servant], Nathaniel." And she said, "What a villain he is." The curious Wyards stood looking at Nathaniel, who continued buggering the calf; they kept getting closer until, finally, Nat spied them. He turned about the calf, "having not had time to put up his yard."

The deponent said, "Villain, what are you doing here?"

"Nothing, resting the calf. What should I do?" exclaimed Nathaniel.

"You villain, you lie, you're buggering the calf and we stood looking at you," the witness replied, adding, "Villain, you have done enough to be hanged."

Robert Wyard made his mark at the bottom of this statement. His wife, Eleanor, backed him up fully, commenting that she and her husband went up so near to him that they "might have struck Nathaniel with a stick" where the miscreant stood buggering the calf, holding it by the tail.

Nathaniel was found guilty but his punishment is not listed in the county records. He was doubtless hanged.

The task of restraining the amount of gossip, bad language and swearing among the citizenry kept the judges quite busy too.

The English argot used in Virginia in the mid-seventeenth century was highly colorful and graphically descriptive. Some expressions like "a slap in the chops" sound like twentieth-century slang. When Mary Spillman reported that Mr. Wilkins stole a pot of butter and ate it in the park, Mrs. Wilkins became very angry and gave "Mary a slapp in the Chopps and called her whore twice or thrice." This same Mrs. Wilkins is quoted as calling Mary "thou Pissa Bedd Jade." Mrs. Wilkins then hit Mary and "sayed thou pissbedd I'll lay it on. Go home."

Occasionally, an apology in court sufficed to repair calumny. "Whereas I, George Vaux, have disparaged and defamed Alice, the wife of George Travellor, by reporting that Captain Francis Yardley was at bed with the said Alice, and his hands under the clothes of the said Alice, now, know ye that I, the said George Vaux, do ask the said Alice forgiveness in the face of the Open Court and do hereby confess under my hand that I am really and heartily sorry for my said offense."

According to the nature of the profanity used, the sentence could range from "one pottle of Milke per day at the cow pen until the last of September" for calling someone "slut," to a fine of thirty pounds of tobacco or standing in a white sheet in front of the congregation for three or more Sundays. If this was not enough to improve the quality of the language used, a law in 1631 set a fine of one shilling for every swear word uttered. Then, in 1657 a new decree barred from public office any person convicted three times of blasphemy.

In a single term of the Enrico County court in Virginia, as many as ninety cases of "wicked oaths" or swearing were tried. One woman was even charged sixty-five times for profanity. Far from being limited to servants, this inclination for swearing was equally shared by the aristocrats, such as the eminent William Randolph and Stephen Cocke. Once, as a last resort, the exasperated governor and council of Virginia ordered that the laws on bad language be read at least every two months from the pulpit of each church throughout the state.

Language was just as outspoken in the courts of Maryland. Speaking of women who came to Maryland from England, one writer reports that "they have the best luck here as in any place of the world besides; for they are no sooner on shore, but they are courted into a copulative matrimony, which some of them (for aught I know) had they not come to such a market with their virginity, they might have kept it by them until it had been moldy, unless they had let it out by a yearly rent to some of the inhabitants of Lewknors-Lane [a disreputable neighborhood in London]."

Administration of punishment for both men and women was swift and severe whether in Virginia, New England or the Middle Colonies. Women were stripped and whipped, banished or branded; men were whipped and occasionally had one or both ears cut off.

Punishment for most sex crimes was said to be even more severe in the Dutch colony of New Amsterdam than in New England, if that is possible.

A court case of two couples, Laurens and Yutie, Jan and Geeje, is as complex as any modern husband-and-wife swapping arrangement could possibly be, with a few added touches. Laurens sold his wife Yutie to Jan. Jan's wife, Geeje, had committed adultery with Laurens. The four of them were brought before the court and found guilty of living in adultery. The sentences were indeed severe: Laurens, for selling his wife, Yutie, thus forcing her to live in adultery with another man, was condemned to have "a rope tied around his neck, and to be severely flogged; to have his right ear cut off, and to be banished for 50 years." Jan's sentence for living in adultery with Yutie, whom he purchased, was to be "placed at the whipping post, with two rods in his arm, to be banished 20 years and to pay a fine of a hundred guilders and court costs." Geeje, for living in adultery with Laurens, was "to be conducted to the whipping post, and fastened thereto, the upper part of her body being stripped naked, and two rods placed in her hand; to be afterwards conducted in that wise, outside the city gates, and banished the province for the term of 30 years with costs." Yutie was also whipped and banished.

Another interesting, but not unique, case in New Amsterdam was that of Katrina Lane, who asked for a separation and divorce from her husband, Daniel, after he had been arrested for having incestuous relations with their daughter. Daniel broke out of jail and disappeared. The court waited six months, then granted Katrina her divorce.

After the English took over Manhattan from the Dutch in 1664, calling it New York, laws similar to those in New England were established. One such law liberalized divorce when one party was deserted by force of circumstance. This followed the earlier Puritan example of allowing divorce when a husband or wife was absent; but the New York colony law required five years after departing on a voyage assuming that, in such a case, the person would be lost at sea or "imprisoned or enslaved by Turks or heathen." It further intelligently provided that, should the missing person return, they could, by mutual agreement, "enter a release to each other if they should so desire." As in the earlier Plymouth law, if a woman had remarried and her husband had been missing for five years, the court would not consider her marriage bigamous. It would allow the returning party a divorce as well.

Seafaring, of course, was a major business of the New England colonies, and while numbers of sailors were lost on voyages during this colonial period — freeing their wives to remarry — many others returned home with new-found riches, not the least of which was in the form of "black ivory," Negro slaves from the West coast of Africa.

Although the Yankee sea captains generally sold most of their Guinea Coast cargoes to Southern planters, they occasionally saved a few of the choicest to bring home to sell, or to give to their wives. There is evidence that New England tradesmen, as they grew in wealth, welcomed the luxury of having black Africans in their homes as servant/slaves. These were far more tractable than Indians. An English traveler of the period, John Josselyn, kept a diary of his voyages to New England, and his notes regarding slavery are among the most graphic that have come down to us. A passage in his diary of October 1639 records one of the first instances of a white master attempting to use a slave for breeding purposes—a barbarous custom which came to be widely practiced by slave owners over the next two hundred years. Put into modern English, Josselyn's entry reads:

"At nine o'clock in the morning a Negro woman came to my bedroom and in her own language sang very loud and shrill. She showed a great deal of respect toward me and would have expressed her grief in English had she known the language." Informing his host, Master Maverick, of the incident, Josselyn was told that the woman had been a queen "in her own country," which explained the deferential manner in which she was treated by other Negroes. Maverick also revealed the reason for her "grief." He had tried to persuade the black "queen" to go to bed with a Negro man he had in his house. When she refused Maverick ordered the man to take her "will'd she nill'd and to go to bed with her, which was no sooner done than she kickt him out again."

Writing in 1663, almost a generation later, Josselyn noted that although "no person was ever born into legal slavery in Massachusetts, there was a most shocking chronic violation of that law in the Colony and Province for more than a century."

The "law" to which Josselyn refers was probably the Body of Liberties. Article 16 of the document stated with some ambiguity: "There shall never bee any bond slavery, villainage or captivity amongst us unless it bee lawful captives taken in warres, and said strangers as willingly sell themselves or are sold to us. And these shall have all the liberties and Christian usage which the law of God established in Israel concerning such persons do morally require. This exempts none from servitude who shall be judged thereto by authority."

Despite this high-sounding passage, over the next two centuries New Englanders became increasingly involved in African slave trade. After all, Englishmen had been involved in the grisly business since the days of John Hawkins. In 1562 that early adventurer made a voyage to Africa, transporting 300 Negro slaves to the island of Hispaniola. There he bartered them to the Spanish colonists for a highly profitable load of hides, sugar, ginger and some pearls. In 1618 King James I had granted an exclusive charter for trading in Guinea Coast slaves to a group of London merchants.

The first record of black Africans being sold in North America was penned by none other than John Rolfe in 1619. In a report to London he mentioned that a Dutch man-of-war had dropped anchor in Jamestown harbor, adding casually that it "brought not anything but 20 and odd Negroes, which the Governor and Cape Marchant bought for victualle . . . at the best and easiest rate they could."

Only eleven years later we have evidence that blacks and whites quickly learned to mingle sexually. A Virginia court record of 1630 cites one Hugh Davis for "abusing himself to the dishonour of God and the same of Christians by defiling his body in lying with a Negro." The hapless Davis, whose only crime was probably being caught in the act, was sentenced to flogging. The punishment was carried out before an assembly of whites and blacks: the specter of miscegenation was a constant concern to early settlers, although few ever gave slavery a second thought for moral reasons.

For New Englanders black slavery became simply a matter of commerce. A vessel named *Desire*, only seventy-nine feet long, launched in Marblehead in 1636, has the dubious distinction of being the first "slaver" built in the colonies. She took a cargo of dried codfish to the West Indies and returned with a load of Negro slaves. As the century went on, the trading pattern grew more complicated, and more lucrative. New Englanders traded not only codfish but lumber, barrel staves, horses and other necessities to their fellow Englishmen who owned plantations in the West Indies. In return they accepted sugar and molasses. Then the Yankees added a new twist to the trade: kill-devil rum, which they distilled from the molasses. This they shipped to Africa and exchanged for more slaves. And so on. This was the notorious "triangular trade," which made fortunes for many famous New England families.

It was not until years later that the brutalities of the long voyage back to America — known as the "mid-passage" of the triangle — became known to any significant portion of Americans. The voyage was an agonizing time for both crews and their human black cargoes. Men, women and children were chained below decks in separate cramped quarters, reeking of filth and excrement, packed like herrings around the vessel's sides. Their shrieks and groans could often be heard through the night by the crewmen.

Some of the young black women aboard fared slightly better. They became temporary mistresses of the officers and men. If anyone objected to becoming a harlot, she was simply lashed and sent back below, her place taken by a more willing candidate. There were many tragic incidents in this custom, but few brought to light. An officer of an English slave brig later testified that the vessel's captain always selected a woman slave to sleep with him on the outward passage. As he told it:

"There was one young girl he retained for some time as his favorite and kept her in his cabin, until one day, when she was playing with his son, she accidentally tore his shirt. When the Captain learned of it, he whipped her unmercifully with the cat [o'-nine-tails] and beat her up with his fists until she threw herself from him against the pumps and in doing so injured her head so severely that she died three days after. She had been living with him as his mistress for five or six months."

Some of the most lurid and graphic accounts of atrocities and orgies of the mid-passage come from Captain Richard Drake, a notorious slave smuggler, whose memoirs were published two centuries later. He wrote:

"Once off the coast [of Africa] the ship became half bedlam and half brothel. . . . Our captain and his two mates set an example of reckless wickedness. They stripped themselves and danced with black wenches while our crazy mullato cook played the fiddle. There was little attempt at discipline and rum and lewdness reigned supreme. . . . On the eighth day out I made my rounds of the half deck, holding a camphor bag in my teeth for the stench was hideous. The sick and the dying were chained together. I saw pregnant women give birth to babies while chained to corpses which our drunken overseers had not removed."

It was generally common, under such circumstances, for numbers of mulatto babies to be born to black women slaves within the first year after they had landed in the New World. Although degrading, it was expeditious for black women to accept the advances of their callous white masters or overseers if sexual favors would ease their lot.

As the numbers of mixed breeds grew and became more visible, almost every colony passed laws trying to outlaw interracial sexual couplings. These laws also wrestled with the problems of who got a bastard child when it was born, inasmuch as slaves, being non-persons, had no legal rights. Negro children born of Negro slaves, of course, belonged to the master. So did mulatto children born of a white father.

But what about the sticky problem of a white woman having a bastard by a Negro or a mulatto? It was a rare occurrence, but it did happen. In 1663 Maryland lawmakers, noting that "divers freeborn English women, forgetful of their free condition, and to the disgrace of our nation, do intermarry with negro slaves," decreed that children born of such a liaison belonged to the master of the slave. The white woman was also made a slave for the lifetime of her mate. A 1691 Virginia law provided that a white woman having a bastard by either a black or a mulatto would pay a fine of fifteen pounds sterling. If she were unable to pay the fine, she was to be sold for a period of fifteen years. The child was placed under the jurisdiction of a churchwarden until it was thirty. Under the same law any white person marrying a Negro, a mulatto or an Indian was summarily banned from the colony. Massachusetts in 1705 flatly outlawed marriages between blacks and whites, and meted out severe punishment for fornication between the races.

In New England children of liaisons between Indians and indentured servants, "half-breeds" in the language of the day, often grew up to be handsome specimens of humanity and frequently had their own children by a white mate. As generations passed, Indian characteristics disappeared and there seems to have been no stigma attached to mixed-breed children after the third generation. It was not uncommon for an indentured servant, after working out his term, to marry an Indian woman, stake out a land claim far away from his former taskmaster and become a properous freeman farmer.

New Englanders always felt a little queasy about having Indians around — especially after the frontiers wars of the late 1600s when whole villages had been massacred and destroyed. In 1696 a special day of Thanksgiving — to which the Indians were not invited — was set aside in Massachusetts. It was to celebrate the return of "peaceful times" and the council noted happily, "there now scarce remains a name of a family of them [the Indians] but are either slain, captivated or fled." Nonetheless, a hundred years after the founding of Plymouth, there were still Indian slaves in cities like Roxbury, Ipswich, Quincy and Boston.

How did the righteous New Englanders come to condone the condition of servitude, particularly after the strictures in the Body of Liberties? Those who had conscientious objections were swayed by literal interpretations of the Bible. Advocates could find many passages to justify the institution's legal status. "And as for thy bondmen, and thy bondmaids, whom thou mayest have: of the nations that are round about you, of them shall ye buy bondmen and bondmaids" (Leviticus XXV, 44). Or, for those who argued that Negroes were the children of Ham, or Canaan, they could quote Genesis IX, 25: "And he [Noah] said, Cursed be Canaan; a servant of servants shall he be unto his brethren."

It was the Puritans' fundamentalist views which led to another dark chapter in American history — but one which, fortunately, did not last as long as slavery. This was the matter of witchcraft.

Actually, the idea of the prevalence of witches in the New World had traveled from England with the Pilgrims and Puritans. In the mother country between 1610 and 1700 almost everyone believed in witches as well as their demonic and supernatural assistants, called "familiars." Everyday life was lived on a battlefield with God and his angels and Satan and his demons struggling constantly for each soul.

King James I himself contributed to the spreading of belief in demonology. At the time the Pilgrims were consolidating their community in New England, the King issued a tract describing Satan's initiation ceremony of a new follower: "The Witches assembled, commanded a new Disciple (whom they call a Novice) unto him: and if the Divell find that young Witch apt and forward in the Renunciation of Christian Faith, in despising anie of the seven Sacraments, in treading upon Crosses, in spetting at the Time of the Elevation, in breaking their Fast on fasting Daies, and fasting on Sundaies: then the Devill giveth foorth his Hand, and the Novice joining Hand in Hand with him, promiseth to observe and keepe all the Divels Commandments."

Having become a slave of Satan, the witch was endowed with magical powers and could "make Picture of Waxe and Clay, that by the roasting thereof, the Persons that they bear the Name of, may be continually melted or dried away by continuall Sicknesse."

How the King came by all this knowledge has never been explained but he was quite sure there was one absolute test to identify a witch; for the devil, after inducing his disciples to renounce their god and baptism, "gives them his Marke upon some secret Place of their Bodie, which remaines soare unhealed, whilest his next Meeting with them, and thereafter ever insensible, however it be nipped or pricked by any." Consequently, young girls, mature women and grandmothers accused of witchcraft in New England had every inch of their skin examined for such witch's marks.

By the time of the Salem witchcraft outbreak in 1692 there had been forty-four cases tried in New England courts. Punishment had ranged from brutal whipping to torturous standing in the stocks; but only three "witches" had been hanged, which was far fewer than those killed in England during the same period.

In contrast to the dull, goody-goody sermons preached Sunday after Sunday by their dour ministers, the magic of witchcraft, mixed with dark sexual implications, brought a spark of excitement to the drab life of the community. The devil was real — not a spirit that presided over a future Hell — a constant presence who could cause one to be beaten, to fall and break a leg, to sour the milk, to keep the churn (no matter how long it was turned) from making the butter. He could make a man leave his wife, a wife her husband. The struggle with the devil was a daily effort since, in many different forms, he and his assistants constantly tempted the good people of Boston and Salem.

The case of Bridget Bishop is a juicy example of the witchcraft trials. A twice-married woman, proprietor of two taverns, Bridget was accused of wearing scarlet dresses, of having an eye for men and of playing *shovelboard* — enough to cause a great deal of gossip. Also, she was said to have cast a spell over a number of men. As a result, as many men as women named her a witch. Envy, jealousy, pride, distrust and unrequited affection all contributed to these accusations and their sexual implications. As the King had predicted, a group of women "examiners" found what they described as "a witch's tet between her pudendum and anus." Rare was the occasion when the witch-hunter could not find some mole, wen or blemish on the skin of the unfortunate accused. Four of Bridget Bishop's accusers were men and in the night she had appeared to all of them. Samuel Gray felt her disturbing presence at his bedside. While her spirit was in his room his child in its cradle "gave a great screech," and after she vanished, the baby could not be quieted. In time it pined away and died. Samuel Gray accused Bridget of being not only a witch but a murderess.

John Hale reported her to be observing "unseasonable hours in the night to keep drinking and playing at shovelboard." This, he said, caused young people to be corrupted. John Hale attributed the suicide of his friend, Christiana Trask (she cut her throat with a pair of scissors) to a spell put on her by Bridget and proved it with the following argument: "As to the wounds she died of I observed 3 deadly ones; a piece of her wind pipe and Gulle[t] to the vein they call jugular, So that I then judged and still do apprehend it impossible for her with so short a pair of scissors to mangle herself so without some extraordinary work of the devil or witchcraft."

In the mind of Samuel Shattuck, another witness in the infamous trial, there was no doubt that Bridget had bewitched his eldest child, for each time she came to their house "he grew worse and worse: as he would be standing at the door [he] would fall out and bruise his face upon a great step stone as if had been thrust out by an invisible hand oftentimes falling and hitting his face against the sides of the house, bruising his face in a very miserable manner."

John Bly, Sr., and his wife Rebecca claimed that, because they did not pay for a sow purchased from Bridget's husband, the "witch" had caused the sow to have "strange fits Jumping up and knocking her head against the fence."

The apparition of Bridget to Richard Coman was openly sex-oriented. She came "and lay upon my Breast or body." This so oppressed him that he could not speak or stir.

Upon this type of "evidence" Bridget Bishop was convicted of witchcraft. Seven distinguished judges heard the case. The jury promptly found her guilty. In fact, not even the above evidence would have been necessary. Cotton Mather said at the beginning of the trial, on June 2, 1692, "There was little occasion to prove witchcraft, this being evident and notorious to all beholders."

The judges wanted to sentence her to death but could not find a current law on the books of the State of Massachusetts that made witchcraft a capital offense. Quickly adopting emergency measures, they reenacted an old colonial law which rendered the execution possible. Bridget Bishop was immediately hanged on June 10, 1692 on Gallows Hill. Instead of being shocked, the citizens of Salem seemed pleased and their interest in witches redoubled. Within a few days dozens of unfortunate women were accused of relations with the devil.

The shadowy history of witchcraft in Europe and the "wise" words of King James I were only a part of the web of circumstances that created witchhunts in Salem. With games like cards and dice declared illegal, and reading largely limited to religious books, there was little entertainment left other than attending church services and gossiping. Houses were close to one another and every detail, especially anything out of the ordinary, was reported, usually embellished by a "friend" or neighbor.

As early as 1643 an incident of child abuse (not an uncommon occurrence) was turned into a case of witchcraft. One Alice Travellor whipped a child, Elizabeth

Bibby, and then hoisted her up by a tackle normally used to hang deer. After taking Elizabeth down Alice threw her into a creek so far that the child could hardly crawl out. Afterwards, Alice shook the child over the fire, threatening that she would burn her. Further, according to her accuser, Zarah Hart, Alice would run in a fury to the child and molest her. After all this, it is not surprising that the child readily testified that Alice Travellor was a witch.

As in England, women were almost always the victims of witchhunts and the rumor of having looked at a man twice, even in church, was enough to be accused.

From Salem the nasty business spread to Boston. There Reverend Cotton Mather heard of the odd behavior of seventeen-year-old Margaret Rule. During a church meeting he claimed that she had been damned and was harassed by Satan into signing the infamous book of witches. Mather attempted to see the girl privately to exorcise her demons but this proved to be impossible, for other citizens of Boston were equally interested. One observer, who made notes of these semi-public exorcisms, remarked that Margaret insisted on the attentions of men only. When a woman touched her, she cried out. By contrast she seemed to enjoy being stroked across her face, naked breasts and belly by both of the Reverends Mather: Cotton, the son, and Increase, the father. The clergymen piously explained that they were only "laying on hands" to drive away the evil spirits. Later, Margaret insisted that the women leave her room entirely; she said, however, "that the company of men was not offensive to her."

Growing increasingly doubtful of Margaret's possession by Satan, Robert Calef, a witness at these sessions, made copies of his notes and distributed them around Boston. This did not do the reputation of the Mathers any good. The report of his stroking the half-clothed girl "to make people believe a Smutty thing of me" enraged Cotton Mather to the point of having a warrant issued against his detractor. But, when Margaret Rule later identified the spirit that was influencing her as a wizard in the shape of the Reverend Cotton Mather himself, neither Mather nor anyone else appeared in court against Calef. The case was dismissed and, fortunately for Mather, the girl's accusation against him was not widely reported.

After a few private talks, Margaret declared Mather her savior "from the devil and her father in Christ." Not long after, more than a hundred prisoners being held on witchcraft charges were released from jail, and, at the urging of Increase Mather, further trials were halted. Calef did what all investigative reporters like to do: he compiled a book of his observations and of Mather's witch writings called *More Wonders of the Invisible World*.

On the lighter side of colonial New England sexual customs there was the practice of bundling. It seems to have been a common courtship method among some American Indian tribes and perhaps the New England settlers learned it from them. But it is more likely that cold bedrooms, lack of space (one bed), early hours of retirement and a general lack of privacy were the prime causes.

An early French traveler to New England asked his host where to retire after dinner. He was directed to a large bed in the corner of the room in which they were sitting. Embarrassed but exhausted, the guest half undressed himself and got into bed. After a while the lady of the house came to bed next to him, then her husband and finally their daughter. The Frenchman concluded that this kind of familiarity could only proceed from simplicity and innocence.

It was not always so innocent. In Middlesex, Sarah Lepingwell, a maid at the service of the Hawes family, was brought to court on charges of fornication because she had given birth to a child. On this particular evening, she said, she had shared the same bed with her master and his brother, as well as a third man. When all the others were asleep, Thomas, the brother, pulled her next to him. Thoroughly frightened, she kept quiet "but the thing is true that he begete me with child at that time and the Child is Thomas Hawes' and noe man's but his." At the trial Thomas Hawes urged that the testimony of the other man who had been sleeping "on the same side of the bed" be accepted as proof of his innocence. Nonetheless, the jury found him guilty.

While bundling prevailed for a period of 160 years, the custom gradually was confined to villages and the humbler classes of society that could not afford large and well-heated houses. With the increasing laxity of public morals bed sharing was a strong incitement to premarital sex. In fact, the number of bastard children grew so large that in 1668 the general court of Massachusetts passed the first child support law. It made the convicted father of the illegitimate child accept total responsibility for his upbringing.

By 1756 the more sophisticated citizens of Boston, Salem, Newport and New York "forbade their daughters bundling on the bed with any young men whatever, and introduced a sofa to render courtship more palatable and Turkish." On this matter the opinion of the clergy was rather mixed. The Reverend Samuel Peters commented that, although it was rude for a gentleman to speak before a lady of a garter, knee or leg, it was "a piece of civility to ask her to bundle." If both the man and woman had a serious faith in God, it was quite acceptable. But if they were influenced "more by lust . . . they ought never to bundle." Moreover, Reverend Peters claimed that he found ten times more chastity prevailed while bundling than after courting on the sofa was introduced.

As late as 1776 a city clergyman went to a rural church and preached against this "unchristian custom." Far from agreeing, the leading lady of the congregation replied, "Experience has told us that city folks send more children into the country without fathers and mothers than are born among us; therefore, you see, a sofa is more dangerous than a bed." The preacher confessed his error and promised never again to preach against bundling.

The author Henry Reed Stiles tells of a British naval officer who was quartered at a small log hut at Williamstown, Massachusetts, during the Revolution. Seeing only two beds in the house, the officer inquired which he was to sleep in and the lady of the house replied: "Mr. Ensign, Jonathan and I will sleep in this . . . and Jemima and you shall sleep in that." The young man was astonished at the proposal and immediately offered to sit up all night, when the father said: "Oh, la! Mr. Ensign, you won't be the first man our Jemima has bundled with, will it, Jemima?" Then the pretty, dark-eyed girl of sixteen or seventeen years replied: "No, father, not by many, but it will be the first Englishman." This same lieutenant, in his *Travels Through the Interior of America,* published in London in 1781, describes something very similar which he terms *tarrying:*

"When a young man is enamored of a woman, and wishes to marry her, he proposes the affair to her parents (without whose consent no marriage in this colony can take place); if they have no objections he is allowed to *tarry* with her one night in order to make his court. At the usual time the older couple retires to bed, leaving the young ones to settle matters as they can, who, having sat up as long as they think proper, get into bed together also, but without putting off their underwear, to prevent scandal."

After the Revolutionary War the standards of living had improved to the point where bundling was not a necessity any more. Yet, it was the popularity of satirical songs and poems that gave this questionable practice the final blow. Here are a few verses of a widely sung ballad published in 1785:

"Some maidens say, if through the nation,
Bundling should quite go out of fashion,
Courtship would lose its sweets; and they
Could have no fun till wedding day.

"Can this vile practice ne'er be broke?
Is there no way to give a stroke,
To wound it or to strike it dead,
And girls with sparks not go to bed.

"And yet in truth I'm not afraid
For to describe a bundling maid;
She'll sometimes say when she lies down,
She can't be cumber'd with a gown,
And that the weather is so warm,
To take it off can be no harm:
The girl it seems had been at strift;
For widest bosom to her shift,
She gownless, when the bed they're in,
The spark, nought feels but naked skin.

"But you will say that I'm unfair,
That some who bundle take more care,
For some we may with truth suppose,
Bundle in bed with all their clothes.
But bundler's clothes are no defence,
Unruly horses push the fence;

"You're welcome to the lines I've penn'd,
For they were written by a friend,
Who'll think himself quite well rewarded,
If this vile practice is discarded."

And here are some verses from *The Whore on the Snow Crust:*

"Tho' Adam's wife destroyed his life
In manner that is awful;
Yet marriage now we all allow
To be both just and lawful.

"Since in a bed a man and maid
May bundle and be chaste;
It doth no good to burn up wood
It is a needless waste.

"Let coat and shift be turned adrift,
And breeches take their flight,
An honest man and virgin can
Lie quiet all the night.

"But if there be dishonesty
Implanted in the mind,
Breeches nor smocks, nor scarce padlocks
The rage of lust can bind.

"Now unto those that do oppose
The bundling trade, I say
Perhaps there's more got on the floor,
Than any other way."

4

European Women — Native Trade Girls

Sexual behavior, particularly for women, was strongly regulated by law throughout the pre-Revolutionary English colonies. Wives, no matter what the provocation, could not run away from husbands. On the whole, the population indulged in sex as carefully as porcupines, the penalty for fornication being whipping. For repeated offense, the sentence was life imprisonment. And in all the colonies laws against adultery were even harsher.

Once married, thoughtful men carefully spaced sexual relations to avoid continuous pregnancy. William Byrd, the Virginia planter, according to his diary, had sex with his wife only thirty times in the year 1712, about once every two weeks. The year before he had been less active in bed with Mrs. Byrd, reporting only twenty "flourishes" or "rogerings," about once every three weeks.

It made Byrd sad to think how little sexual energy men had compared to that of animals. He observed that rams "jump fifty or sixty sheep" in one night. "This denotes a prodigious natural vigor . . . how short do poor men fall of these Feats."

But there was no form of birth control practiced other than withdrawal, sodomy, or masturbation. These must have been resorted to relatively often although there was a strict religious ban on "unnatural vices." Byrd, owner of far-famed Westover Plantation, wrote that he masturbated occasionally. He called it "manual uncleanliness in bed." And, although he deplored the habit (even praying for himself after the act), he could not control his desire for sexual pleasure. He masturbated not only when he was away on business in Williamsburg but also when he was at home.

It is fortunate for posterity that Byrd kept his secret diary. One learns not only of his sex life and lack of it but much of the morality and immorality of eighteenth-century Virginia. Byrd wrote in his diary every day. He listed his love affairs as a young man in England, the going price of a mistress there (two guineas per visit) and delicately describes how he phased one mistress out — for infidelity. Byrd married twice, the first time for ten years to a wife who died after bearing four children of which two survived; his second wife also had four children.

His diary reflected the belief of many men of his time — that the mistress of the household should be kept barefoot and pregnant. He wrote, "The Agyptians of Old never allowed their Wives any sandals because they had no business to gad abroad, but to stay home and take care of their Family."

Based on other diaries of the Colonial period, the position of the upper-class woman was either that of the sex object or, if she was young, a devil's vehicle for enticement of men. Charles Carroll of Carrollton, Maryland, wrote that he could only be seduced by beautiful women. "I would defy an ugly woman endowed with all the sagacity of a sphinx ever to entrap me." And Landon Carter of Sabine Hall, Virginia, another plantation owner, wrote, "I do believe women have nothing in the general in view, but the breeding contests at home. It began with poor Eve and ever since then has been so much of the devil in woman." He continued that he could not imagine "a more treacherous, interprising, Perverse, and hellish Genius than is to be met with in a Woman. Madame Eve suffered the devil to tempt her; and of such a Tendency has her sex been."

Parties were frequent in Colonial Virginia, with guests traveling long dusty miles to get together. One night Byrd dallied with a friend's wife, staying up and talking with a Mrs. Chiswell. Byrd and Mrs. Chiswell played cards and he "kissed her on the bed till she was angry and my wife also was uneasy about it, and cried as soon as the company was gone." Remorsefully he wrote, "I sought to beg pardon for the lust I had for another man's wife."

Commenting on the sexual activities of his friends, he noted: Jimmy Roscow and a Mr. Lightfoot left for a visit to Mrs. Harrison (Byrd's cousin), "one to make love to the mother and the other the daughter." The next day Byrd went to see the cousin himself "to visit the two gallants and their mistresses."

Never does Byrd admit to having sex with blacks except that he once asked a Negro girl to "kiss" him. On another occasion he wrote that he kissed and "felt up" a wench while he was in Williamsburg. It is possible that he considered sex with a black not important enough to record.

Quarrels with his wife on a number of occasions were settled when he "gave her a flourish." This word and "rogering" were in general use to describe sexual intercourse. Both had become synonymous with intercourse since the early seventeenth century. On one occasion Byrd and his wife were passionately unconventional: "the flourish was performed on the billiard table." One morning he says he lay in bed till nine trying to "bring my wife into temper again and rogered her by way of reconciliation."

Most language before the Revolution (and during it) used elaborate circumlocutions to avoid sexual references. Yet Byrd called a whore a whore and, when he speaks of a nurse on the plantation who got drunk, he explains that she "got laid by the Smith." He also writes of whipping one of his slaves "for being a whore." In this case he did not necessarily mean that they were engaging in sex for money, but in the usage of the time that they were fornicating and unmarried or that they were fornicating outside the marriage covenant. Only virgins and properly married women were respectable. All others were whores.

Two languages, one polite and one vulgar, have always been used for sex matters, and in Colonial America the vulgar words and their meanings had been imported from England. It is our good fortune that a sailor, Captain Francis Grose, set down the impolite language of London between 1770 and 1785, some words, of course, dated earlier. His book, called *A Classical Dictionary of the Vulgar Tongue,* was the earliest dictionary of English "slang." In it was recorded the colloquial "private" language used in seventeenth- and eighteenth-century England and in the American Colonies. It was lusty language for a lusty age. Some expressions are still in use today; others sound archaic. A girl

was said to have "sprained her ankle" if she got pregnant. A sodomite approached his partner by "the back door." A libertine who enjoyed many women was known as a "beard-splitter." A "bread and butter" situation described a man lying on top of a woman. A "convenient" was a mistress. A "bum," a buttock or backside. Loose women were known as "doxies" or "biddies." To give a girl a "flourish" meant to have sex with her clothes on. But one could "roger" her naked. "To hump" was to copulate. A word that had been somewhat respectible before 1700, "fuck," had become completely taboo even in private sex language. A woman could be described as a "good or a bad piece." She could be "knocked" which simply meant to lay her, or she could be "knocked up" which meant getting her pregnant. A "molly" (later to become mollycoddle) was a homosexual. The word "cunt" was used privately — as was "prick." Both of them had been in comparatively common usage before 1600. "Bastard" was accepted and not even considered vulgar but rather described a specific social condition. At the time of the Revolution, it was estimated that in England one out of every six children born was a bastard. The percentage in the Colonies may have been even higher.

Benjamin Franklin, the United States' first social critic and moralist, gives us the most intimate picture of the promiscuity, profligacy and sexual dalliance in the age of the Revolution. Franklin began his long and fascinating career at a very early age. By sixteen he had written a series of short essays in the form of letters which he signed "Mrs. Silence Dogood." Even in these early tracts he showed an interest in women and in satire. The ridiculousness of handling hoopskirts, possible loss of virginity (and worse, not losing it), the importance of education for women and insurance for widows were among the subjects.

While still a very young man, he went to England with a young friend, James Ralph. Ralph was one of those colonists, of which there were a great many, who left a wife and family in America, married another wife and started a new family in England. But before Ralph married for the second time, he had an affair with a young milliner in London. When Ralph walked out leaving his mistress flat broke, Franklin paid her bills. This, he thought, should give him the same sexual privileges enjoyed by his friend. The girl disagreed and threatened to take Franklin to court. Young Ben was frightened off by her threats and nothing came of it.

Franklin did not record his sexual experiences in these early days, but later he wrote in his autobiography:

That hard-to-be-governed Passion of Youth had hurried me frequently into intrigues with low Women that fell in my Way, which were attended with some Expence and great Inconvenience, besides a continual Risque to my Health by a Distemper which of all Things I dreaded, tho' by great good Luck I escaped it." It was this admitted horniness that was doubtless responsible for the illegitimate birth of his first son William. The mother must have been one of those "low women" Franklin mentions. William, the infant son, was taken to live with his father and the new Mrs. Franklin. There is no further reference to his own mother. Ben's marriage to Deborah Reed was strictly a common-law arrangement. They simply moved in with one another and she began calling herself Mrs. Franklin. Common-law marriages such as this one were not at all unusual in the early life of the Colonies. There were occasional, elaborate, formal weddings but these occurred usually when two families of considerable financial and social status were joined. The average marriages of ordinary folk in 1730 went unnoticed. Deborah cared for the illegitimate William and bore Franklin two children, a boy Francis (who died when he was four) and a daughter, Sarah.

Franklin was a happy man all his life and he showed it in his writing and editing. It all began with *Poor Richard's Almanack,* his first big success. In a way it was the forerunner of all our how-to-do-it books. Together with advice to lovers and medical information, one could find cooking recipes, philosophical and psychological counsel, poetry, proverbs and paradoxes, weather predictions, advice to farmers and to city dwellers. The first edition appeared in 1733. Although Franklin credited all the writing to Richard Saunders (and occasionally to his wife) both were imaginary extensions of his own talent and wit. A major reason for the phenomenal success of *Poor Richard's Almanack* was its spicy, sexy and occasionally vulgar material. Advertised were such features as Bachelor's Folly, Game for Kisses, Moon no Cuckold, Conjugal Debate and Catherin's Love. Proverbs and quips were sprinkled throughout the book:

"Neither a maidenhead nor a fortress will hold out after they begin to parley."

"He that lives upon Hope dies farting."

"Keep your eyes wide open before marriage, half shut afterwards."

"Old boys have their playthings as well as young ones, the difference is only in the price."

"She that paints her face thinks of her tail."

"You cannot pluck roses without fear of thorns, nor enjoy a fair wife without danger of horns."

Franklin borrowed freely from humorous (and occasionally serious) writers of the past. His favorites were Rabelais, de La Rochefoucauld, and Montaigne. A brilliant editor, Franklin rephrased the thoughts of these literary giants and cast them in a new setting, that of Colonial Pennsylvania.

Franklin's masquerades and leg-pulling techniques reached their zenith in his *The Speech of Miss Polly Baker.* So carefully written was this tract, purporting to be a statement made to the Connecticut court by an unfortunate and oft-seduced young girl, that its authenticity was not doubted. "Miss Baker" wrote that she had been tried five times for bastardy, having given birth to five illegitimate children. Her speech is a classic plea for justice. "I take the Liberty to say, That I think this Law, by which I am punished, is both unreasonable in itself, and particularly severe with regard to me, who have always lived an inoffensive Life.. . ." She adds that she has never wronged a man, woman or child. "I have brought Five fine Children into the World, at the Risque of my Life; I have maintain'd them well by my own Industry, without burthening the Township, and would have done it better, if it had not been for the heavy Charges and Fines I have paid. Can it be a Crime . . . to add to the Number of the King's Subjects, in a new Country that really wants People?"

"Polly's" letter states that she has not enticed any youth nor debauched another's husband; she never turned down an offer of marriage because she never had one except when she was a virgin and then "I unhappily lost my own Honour, by trusting to his; for he got me with Child, and then forsook me." She further deplores the "great and growing Number of Batchelors in the Country, many of whom from the mean Fear of Expences of a Family, have never sincerely and honourably courted a Woman in their Lives; and by their Manner of Living, leave unproduced (which is little better than Murder) Hundreds of their Posterity to the Thousandth Generation." She suggests that such men should be compelled by law either to marry or pay double the fine of fornication every year. Her final argument is that she only observed "the first and great Command of Nature, and of Nature's God, *Encrease and Multiply.* A Duty, from the steady Performance of which, nothing has been able to deter me; but for its Sake, I have hazarded the Loss of the Public Esteem, and have frequently endured Publick Disgrace and Punishment; and therefore ought, in my humble Opinion, instead of a Whipping, to have a Statue erected to my Memory."

This was perhaps Franklin's greatest hoax. It was picked up by the English newspapers as well as those being printed in the Colonies. It is entirely possible that Franklin, in composing this satiric masterpiece, was not only defending all those innocent seduced women in the colonies but also assuaging his guilt when as a bachelor he had his illegitimate son. The boy was raised by Franklin and given every advantage. Despite his clouded birth (a fact often used by political rivals), William went on to become the royal governor of the colony of New Jersey. He then fathered a bastard of his own and this son, in turn, had an illegitimate child. It has been said that Franklin began a dynasty of three generations of bastards.

During his long, adventurous and successful life, Franklin was romantically or sexually involved with at least five more women of whom there is record. These were met during the seventeen consecutive years he spent away from Deborah Reed in the course of their forty-four years of marriage. Although she knew they would likely be separated for many years, Deborah had refused to go to England with him.

One early romantic encounter was with Catherine Ray, who remained a close friend for thirty-five years. We know he asked her for favors which probably meant more than kisses and which, at least in writing, she refused. Whether or not they had an affair must remain conjecture, although she did write him, "I have said a thousand things that nothing should have tempted me to have said to anybody else, for I knew they would be safe with you." And, "tell me you . . . love me one thousandths part so well as I do you."

When Franklin first went to London in 1757 to represent Pennsylvania, he met Margaret Stevenson. She supplied a comfortable apartment consisting of four rooms on the second floor of her house on Craven Street, not far from British government offices. He lived as part of the household for fifteen years. Margaret was about thirty-eight when they first met. Her eighteen-year-old daughter, named Mary, was called Polly by Franklin. Later, William Temple Franklin, his illegitimate grandson, moved in and was reared by Franklin.

His years at Craven Street were happy ones, and it appears that his affection for the young Polly and her mother was equal. Although his wife in America repeatedly wrote him to come home, he continued to find excuses (quite legitimate ones) for staying on in London. At least one biographer of Franklin has suggested that Margaret served as mother and mistress to the statesman. That Polly was a joy to him there is no doubt. They became intellectual companions. He gave her many books to read and when she spent time away with an aunt their correspondence was personal and intimate. Franklin wrote her poetry and she returned the compliment by making garters for him. When on her twenty-seventh birthday, she told him she felt she was getting old, he wrote to her:

"No hospitable man, possessed of generous wines,
While they are in his vaults, repines
That age impairs the casks; for he well knows
The heavenly juice
More fit for use
Becomes, and still the older better grows.. . ."

Some of Franklin's biographers have seen Polly's relationship as that of a beloved daughter, others as a mistress. When the distinguished American artist, Charles Wilson Peale, visited Franklin unannounced, he found Franklin sitting with a young girl on his knee. The artist made a quick sketch which shows Franklin stroking the girl's breast or unfastening her dress while her hand is in his crotch. It was probably Polly.

The last two women in Franklin's life were charming and intelligent Frenchwomen. Ann Louise Brillon, in her correspondence, did not hide the fact that she deeply loved Franklin but never indicated that theirs was more than a close platonic relationship. Her husband was not only away from Paris a great deal but she found out he had a mistress. She wrote of her grief to Franklin and he consoled her. During his entire stay in Paris when he was in his seventies, Madame Brillon gave him comfort and joy. Was she also his mistress?

Her friend, Ann Catherine Helvétius, was another story. If Franklin, who seemed to have led an active sex life for most of his years, had a mistress in Paris, it would most likely have been the rich, queenly widow to whom he proposed marriage. She turned him down but it may have well been for typical French family-legal reasons. She, too, was no longer a young woman but Franklin found her both physically and intellectually attractive. They enjoyed common interests, especially in conversation and wine. When Franklin left France, Madame Helvétius wrote: "I picture you . . . farther from us at every step, already lost to me and those who loved you so much and regret you so." Franklin returned to America at age seventy-nine and only his beloved Polly, of all the women in his long and full life, was with him when he died. Polly had gone to America and on moving to Pennsylvania in 1786 had become an American citizen. They had been good friends for thirty-three years.

Least printed of all of Franklin's works dealing with sex is an essay in the form of a letter that Franklin called *Old Mistresses Apologue*. A friend, inflamed with sexual desire, has written him for advice. Franklin first recommends marriage as a remedy:

"But if you will not take this Counsel, and persist in thinking a Commerce with the Sex inevitable, then I repeat my former Advice, that in all your Amours you should *prefer old Women to young ones*. You call this a Paradox, and demand my Reasons. They are these:

"1. Because as they have more Knowledge of the World and their Minds are better stor'd with Observations, their Conversation is more improving and more lastingly agreeable.

"2. Because when Women cease to be handsome, they study to be good. To maintain their Influence over Men, they supply the Diminution of Beauty by an Augmentation of Utility. They learn to do a 1000 Services small and great, and are the most tender and useful of all Friends when you are sick. Thus they continue amiable. And hence there is hardly such a thing to be found as an old Woman who is not a good Woman.

"3. Because there is no hazard of Children, which irregularly produc'd may be attended with much inconvenience.

"4. Because thro' more Experience, they are more prudent and discreet in conducting an Intrigue to prevent Suspicion. The Commerce with them is therefore safer with regard to your Reputation. And with regard to theirs, if the Affair should happen to be known, considerate People might be rather inclin'd to excuse an old Woman who would kindly take care of a young Man, form his Manners by her good Counsels, and prevent his ruining his health and Fortune among mercenary Prostitutes.

"5. Because in every Animal that walks upright, the Deficiency of the fluids that fill the Muscles appears first in the highest Part: The Face first grows lank and wrinkled; then the Neck, then the Breast and Arms; the lower Parts continuing to the last as plump as ever; So that covering all above with a Basket, and regarding only what is below the Girdle, it is impossible of two Women to know an old from a young one. And as in the dark all Cats are grey, the Pleasure of corporal Enjoyment with an old Woman is at least equal, and frequently superior, every Knack being by Practice capable of improvement.

"6. Because the Sin is less. The debauching a Virgin may be her Ruin, and make her for Life unhappy.

"7. Because the Compunction is less. The having made a young Girl *miserable* may give you frequent bitter Reflections; none of which can attend the making an old Woman *happy*.

"8[thly and Lastly] They are *so grateful!!* Thus much for my Paradox. But still advise you to marry directly; being sincerely Your affectionate Friend."

Others of the Founding Fathers had their sexual problems. But being a bastard seems to have given Alexander Hamilton few serious political or social difficulties. He weathered a sex scandal, an affair with Mrs. James Reynolds. Her husband chose to ignore Hamilton's sexual dalliance in favor of political blackmail by insisting upon a position in the Treasury Department as the price to keep the affair secret. When refused, he took the story, as threatened, to Thomas Jefferson. The latter had his own difficulties and such sexual promiscuity was common in high places. Hamilton met the scandal head on, admitting his adulterous affair with Mrs. Reynolds to his wife and others. Although Reynolds spread the story around and the incident became well known, Hamilton because of an understanding wife stayed married. Later on it was not scandal that caused his death but political gossip that lead to the fatal duel with Aaron Burr.

Disrepute never touched George Washington. Thomas Jefferson might be more deserving of the title Father of his Country, for Washington was almost certainly sterile (his wife had two children from a previous marriage). Jefferson fathered six children by his wife, Martha, and four illegitimate children by his mulatto housekeeper-concubine, Sally Hemings.

After the death of Martha, Jefferson was appointed minister to France to replace the aging Benjamin Franklin. He was accompanied to Paris by his daughter and her personal servant, fifteen-year-old Sally. According to the reminiscences of Madison Hemings: "During that time my mother became Mr. Jefferson's concubine, and when he was called back home she was *enciente* by him. He desired to bring my mother back to Virginia with him but she demured. She was just beginning to understand the French language well, and in France she was free, while if she returned to Virginia she would be reenslaved."

But Jefferson was uncommonly persuasive. To induce Sally to return "he promised her extraordinary privileges, and made a solemn pledge that her children would be free at the age of twenty-one years." Soon after the return, a child was born but lived for only a short time. However, writes Madison Hemings, "she gave birth to four others and Jefferson was the father of all of them. Their names were Beverly, Harriet, Madison (myself) and Eston — three sons and one daughter."

Thomas Jefferson kept his word. All of these children became free according to his agreement. All married and raised families. The children were light in color and Beverly, the oldest son, went to Washington where he passed as a white man. He later wedded a white woman and their daughter was accepted as white. Jefferson's daughter Harriet also married a white man and according to her brother, her children, too, were never suspected of having black blood. His son Eston married a colored woman in Virginia and left three children.

Jefferson's quadroon son who wrote his reminiscences was named after James Madison, later president. He was born and reared at Monticello, Jefferson's beautiful home near Charlottesville, Virginia. Madison Hemings also speaks fondly and eloquently of his grandmother whom, he wrote, had seven children by white men and seven by colored men. Madison Hemings' memoirs are backed up by those of Israel Jefferson, who for fourteen years made the fire in Jefferson's bedroom and private chamber, cleaned his office, dusted his books and attended him at Monticello. Israel's journal states Jefferson promised his wife on her deathbed that he would not marry again. "I also know that his servant Sally Hemings (mother to my old friend and former companion at Monticello, Madison Hemings) was employed as his chambermaid, and that Mr. Jefferson was on the most intimate terms with her; that, in fact, she was his concubine...this I know from my intimacy with both parties, and when Madison Hemings declares that he is a natural son of Thomas Jefferson, the author of the Declaration of Independence, and that his brothers Beverly and Eston and sister Harriet are of the same parentage, I can as conscientiously confirm his statement.. . ."

Israel later bought his freedom from Thomas Gilmer, who had purchased all of Jefferson's slaves at auction, three years after Jefferson's death. Jefferson provided for the freedom of seven servants only: Sally Hemings, her four children, her brother John and Burrell Colburn, an old and faithful body servant.

Based upon exhaustive research and intelligent conjecture, Fawn Brodie, in her well-documented book *Thomas Jefferson, An Intimate History,* has also made it clear that the reminiscences of Madison Hemings are authentic. Jefferson was not unique in his time. Thousands of mulatto children were fathered by white masters, offspring of white masters and overseers.

Even more interesting are the relationships within the Jefferson family of whites and blacks, for Sally Hemings was the daughter of John Wayles, plantation owner, who was also the father of Martha Eppes Jefferson, Thomas Jefferson's wife. This meant that Sally Hemings was a half sister of Jefferson's wife and the aunt of his daughter Maria as well as her slave and body servant. But none of this seems to have disturbed Jefferson. His affair with his sister-in-law lasted most of his life. She became his mistress sometime between her fourteenth and sixteenth year and she doubtless cared for Jefferson as a father and lover.

Jefferson's affair with Sally began after his traumatic love affair with Maria Cosway. A most attractive young woman, Maria was married to Richard Cosway, one of the most-sought-after miniature artists of Europe. Cosway was a member of the libertine circle close to the Prince of Wales in England. He also secretly painted pornographic pictures on costly snuff boxes. He was a bisexual, for it turned out later (through some of Maria Cosway's letters to her husband) that he had had affairs during the marriage with both men and women. Maria was certainly exposed to the sub-surface sexual world of Paris and London. She studied with the artist Henry Fuseli, painter of some of the most graphic erotica of that period. It was common knowledge that she married Gosway because he promised to take care of her mother and settled upon her 2,800 pounds. Maria also painted and exhibited her work in London. Jefferson seems to have fallen in love with her almost on first sight in Paris. When she left for London, Jefferson poetically wrote in an imaginary dialogue between his head and heart: "All night you tossed us from one side of the bed to the other. No sleep, no rest." Gallantly, Jeferson saw her and her husband off to England.

Months after their parting and much correspondence, Maria returned to Paris alone, and she stayed for three months. Their subsequent meetings do not seem to be as happy as the first ones. Jefferson was still in love, but Maria became more and more worried about being away from her husband which meant loss of her income; she may also have been concerned about her soul as she was a devout Catholic. Her last note to Jefferson before leaving Paris read: "I cannot breakfast with you tomorrow; to bid you adieu once is sufficiently painful, for I leave you with very melancholy ideas." But she was an artist to the end and could not resist commenting, "You have given, my dear sir, all your commissions to Mr. Trumbull [the artist who painted Jefferson's portrait] and

I have the reflection that I cannot be useful to you; who have rendered me so many civilities."

After this Jefferson turned to Sally Hemings. He was quite solicitous and paid the then-large sum of 240 francs to see that the young mulatto had a smallpox inoculation. During almost all of the time that she was in Paris, he had a French tutor for Sally's brother and, in all probability, Sally had lessons as well for she seems to have made great progress in French. And in 1788 Sally began receiving wages for the first time. After about a year in Paris, her clothing became an important item in Jefferson's account books. As Fawn Brodie points out: If a pair of gloves could be had for two francs, an expenditure of 216 francs for Sally's clothing in seven weeks, plus her monthly salary, would seem unusual — especially when there had been no previous expenditures on her behalf in earlier months.

Jefferson's amorous exploits led him beyond his own plantation, however. It is also well known that, when younger, he may have accomplished the seduction of a neighbor's wife, a Mrs. Walker. Other American statesmen are remembered for their romantic affiliations. Aaron Burr, vice president of the United States and almost president, had a series of tempestuous affairs and was notorious for his mistresses. His liaisons around New York as a young man were numerous. He was known to have seduced the wives of a number of his friends and, to add insult to injury, he retained in his files all of the letters written to him by the women with whom he was intimate. Even after his relatively happy marriage to Theodosia Prevost, the attractive widow of a British officer and mother of five children, he continued his amorous escapades. Aaron Burr's relationship with his daughter Theodosia (who had been named after her mother) was so close that more than one writer has conjectured sexual relations between them. They were constant companions and once he wrote telling her that his thoughts followed her "at different hours in the day and night."

After failing in his plan to split the United States and to set himself up as the ruler of the western sector with the help of the British, Burr continued, even in comparative disgrace, his active sexual exploits. Then, at the age of seventy-six he married Elizabeth Jumel, a feisty lady with a checkered past. Two years later she sought a divorce charging that he had been unfaithful. Burr died at eighty, an unrepentent sinner.

While we see that the sexual proclivities of some of the Founding Fathers and their peers were not **above**

reproach, what were the general attitudes and practices at the time of the Revolution? One indicator that applies to all periods in all societies is the state of the world's oldest profession.

Referring to the numbers of prostitutes being transported to the Colonies from England in the years prior to 1776, Benjamin Franklin addressed an open letter in his *Pennsylvania Gazette* to King George III. Franklin wittily suggested that in return for all these loose women, he was shipping the King several rattlesnakes native to the Colonies to stock the royal gardens. Even after the Constitution was ratified in 1789, a ship laden with condemned criminals, men and women, arrived in the new United States of America. It was promptly turned around with cargo intact and sent back to England.

However, it would be a great injustice to brand all of these unfortunate women as prostitutes. Everyone drank a great deal and it was common for both male and female servants to get soused. One visitor from Europe remarked that most "bound" or indentured women were generally immoral and "there is hardly an indentured servant in Philadelphia who can't be had for very little money." The derogatory term "bounder" comes from this period.

Indentured female servants often had to resort to prostitution because there was no other way of purchasing their freedom. Many were taken advantage of by their masters. When attempting to prove a charge of seduction they showed their pregnancy in court or produced a child as evidence. The master usually claimed that no seduction had taken place but the servant had fornicated with him of her own free will. The women rarely won, but if they were able to prove seduction, the men were liable to fines of adultery as well as child support.

It was not the most moral of times. One wag remarked that as the country was being born, so were innumerable bastards.

During the war of the American Revolution, both sides had prostitutes, or camp followers, attached to their armies. Official records are not specific for armies considered them part of baggage trains. But, in reading memoirs such as those of Anne Grant and the works of the British historian Henry Belcher, it is obvious that the number of camp followers was considerable. Belcher spoke of "swarms of prostitutes" following the British forces. Each British regiment had an allotment of wives plus camp followers. Many of these sailed from England with the army but some camp followers were added in America from women sympathizers to the British cause.

Early in the war, among the first regiments sent to put down "the rebellion," were 5,416 men and 480 women, or one woman for each eleven men. Shortly afterwards came the Forty-second Highlanders with 1,168 men and 80 women. Fraser's Corps followed with 2,298 men and 160 women. The British obviously had

learned that men would not fight wars without recourse to sex. They found it easier to bring wives and prostitutes from England than to depend upon the sexual favors of the native population. This was not to remain the case.

After the war had been on for four years, the percentage of one woman for every eleven men rose to one woman to every four-and-a-half men, even though the over-all number of British troops remained the same as England replaced those lost in battle. Obviously, many local women had been picked up by the British soldiers.

Because there was no official nursing corps, and indeed little medical care, women attached to the armies served as nurses as well as sexual partners. The need was so acute that British generals did not turn away women acquired by their men quartered in American villages. There were among the colonists many British sympathizers who believed independence to be a curse. Daughters of such loyalists were dazzled by the uniforms and curious about the virility of the readily available British officers and soldiers.

By contrast there seem to have been few prostitutes active as camp followers in the straggly American Army during the early days of the war. Yet, their numbers increased as the conflict dragged on. One of the important functions of the women camp followers was the smuggling of rum and procurement of provisions for the soldiers. The British Army received regular wages which made the feeding and maintenance of the whole establishment possible. On the other hand, the Americans got little and irregular pay and had to scrounge for all necessities.

There were many juicy scandals during the time of the Revolution, one of the most notorious concerned British General Sir William Howe and Mrs. Joshua Loring. To make it easier to have access to Mrs. Loring, Sir William gave her husband a lucrative post as commissary general of prisoners. A short poem to this effect was written by Francis Hawkinson, one of the signers of the Declaration of Independence:

"Sir William, he, snug as a flea,
Lay all this time a-snoring,
Nor dream'd of harm as he lay warm
in bed with Mrs. Loring."

It was also common knowledge that General Burgoyne always had a good cook, and usually a mistress.

One gets the impression from reading the records that only a few of the women accompanying the British Army were married to soldiers and that the great majority were either ambivalent mistresses or prostitutes. One order which both armies found impossible to carry out was that no children accompany the forces. Nothing is said about how they were going to prevent the women from having babies and, as it turned out, swarms of offspring followed both armies, though there were far more with the British, who could not send them home to grandparents. Few of the English women were allowed to embark upon the ships that returned to England with the defeated soldiers. General Howe ordered that only six women per company embark with each regiment, whereas an average of sixty women per regiment had been allowed on the way over. The consequences proved tragic. When it looked as though the cause was going well for General Burgoyne and the English, many Colonial women attached themselves to the British forces. Then, after the capture of the British Army at Saratoga, they had nowhere to go. Most of these 2000 women had been fed and maintained by the British soldiers themselves. Now, without protection or supplies, they looted and begged from the farmers and small townspeople on their line of march. Hannah Winthrop described some of these women in a letter dated November 11, 1777:

"We thought we should have nothing to do with them, but view them as they passed. To be sure the sight was truly astonishing. I never had the least idea that the creation produced such a sordid set of creatures in human figure — poor, dirty emaciated men, great numbers of women who seemed to be beasts of burden having a bushel basket on their back . . . some very young infants who were born on the road, the women barefeet, clothed in dirty rags, such effluvia filled the air while they were passing, had they not been smoking all the time, I should have been apprehensive of being contaminated by them."

Indentured women sometimes took up with soldiers in either the British or the American Army. When Colonel George Washington took over the command of the Virginia Regiment, he wrote a rebuke to one of his captains who had appropriated an indentured girl without paying her master. In the letter Washington enclosed a bill from the girl's owner. The captain, having had the woman in camp for nine months, was forced to send the ten pounds he owed on her.

The American Army seems to have gotten by with from six to eight women per company. Some of these women were married though most were not. The female contingent was made up of not only prostitutes but loving wives who refused to stay home and followed their husbands to war. Continuous efforts were made to keep prostitutes from following the army, and quotas were continually set, but these proved impossible to police.

In a conference between General Washington and Comte de Rochambeau on a joint plan of operations, they discussed the proportion of women which ought to be allowed to any given number of men and to which of these rations should be allowed. Washington, in August of 1777, forbade any new women taken on as camp followers. He also issued an order to get rid of all of those women who were not absolutely necessary. "Every encumbrance proves greatly prejudicial to the service; the multitude of women in particular, especially those who are pregnant, or have children, are a clog upon every movement."

Two weeks later, when Washington marched victoriously into recaptured Philadelphia at the head of his army, he issued the following order: ". . . Not a woman belonging to the army is to be seen with the troops on their march through the city." According to one observer of this parade, the women were turned off into alleyways and side streets, but not for long. "The army had barely passed through the main thoroughfares before these camp followers poured after their soldiers again, their hair flying . . . their belongings slung over one shoulder, chattering and yelling in sluttish shrills as they went, and spitting in the gutters."

A further order was issued "to prevent an inundation of bad women from Philadelphia," but to little avail.

There was, however, a recorded event which proved that women could make a more emphatic contribution to the war effort. It involved a Robert Shurtleff, a tall, attractive, muscular young man who, after serving seventeen months in the Fourth Massachusetts Regiment, was discovered to be a woman, Deborah Sampson. Deborah was said to be almost as strong as the biblical figure. Bored with her life as a woman and interested in both the cause of freedom and a soldier's pay, she enlisted in the Revolutionary Army. Bathing was a rare event in the American Army and a change of clothing even more rare, so one can understand how the clever Deborah managed to outwit her male colleagues for almost two years.

It was, however, a great shock to the army and citizenry and provoked some wry humor. Deborah and her adventures became the talk of the Colonies. Mustered out of the service on discovery of her gender, she later married, had three children and enjoyed a successful career lecturing on her adventures. Rather than criticize her for the masquerade, most women applauded her spirit and courage.

Some of the most effective accounts of social and sexual conditions during the Revolution were supplied by British women who kept diaries. One such lady was the Baroness Riedesel, whose husband was a general in the British Army. The Baroness was proud of the parties she gave every week "to gain the affection of the inhabitants and provide innocent pleasures for the officers, and thus keep them from visiting public houses and bad company." Prostitution was gaining momentum as the war continued, and venereal diseases were rife.

The Baroness made no apologies in her notes regarding the behavior of her friends. "Madame Foy's old intimacy with the captain of our ship . . . was the reason for not daring to refuse him those liberties of which he had formerly been accustomed." And her chambermaid's adventures ". . . finding among the sailors such licentious friends as she was best pleased with.. . ." One such crony "was an old tippler who often passed the night with her in my forechamber on shipboard."

The Baroness wrote of the wife and daughter of Tory sympathizers who on at least one occasion were stripped naked by American patriots and tarred and feathered. She was no kinder in speaking of her British compatriots. "Long cloaks," the Baroness wrote, "often conceal very bad or dirty clothing." And General Howe, when he should have been organizing his troops, was "singing, drinking and amusing himself with the wife of a commissary — who was his mistress."

Her memoirs also record two girls who were impregnated by their father and another case of a man who, when his son married, found that he preferred the daughter-in-law to his wife. He therefore proposed that they swap mates. The young son agreed to take his mother but only if his father would also give him two cows and two horses as well.

In Warren County, Pennsylvania, Peter Vrashee, a stickler for liberty and freedom, swapped his wife for that of another man — giving him a cow to boot. When the authorities informed him that this was illegal, he became furious at the state for interfering with his personal rights.

The Marquis de Chastellux traveled through the United States during and after the Revolution. He found the American woman modest beyond belief, yet "she showed a desire to please and was direct in showing her emotion." It was no crime, he wrote, "for an unmarried girl to kiss a man — but a heinous one for a married woman to even show a desire of pleasing." However, after moving around from one part of the northeast to another, Chastellux decided that morality in the United States was partly a matter of geography and partly a matter of local option. But he wrote that he hoped that "the barbarous prejudices and punishments of Europe would never come to these shores."

Shortly after the war the distinguished French writer Moreau de St. Méry traveled extensively in the northeastern states, especially New York and Pennsylvania. Although he observed widely, his opinions were highly personal.

He relates an amusing story of a young Frenchman who arrived in New York with a letter of introduction to a prominent family. After officially presenting his letter, he was invited to dine at the home of the businessman and his daughter, a very attractive girl indeed. A day or two afterwards the Frenchman learned that there was a house where a madam supplied young women for a price. He hurriedly arranged a meeting and was stunned to find that his sexual partner was the young girl to whom he had been presented at dinner a few days earlier. St. Méry remarks: "What was he to do? Already the matter had gone too far to retreat, and so the final step was taken — and happiness put a seal upon his lips."

In his view American women were not affectionate. Their hypocritical attitude regarding the use of certain vulgar words and their aversion to the facts of life disturbed him. He mentions that a woman forced her brother to leave the room because she was going to change the diaper of her five-week-old son.

In outlying country districts in Pennsylvania, St. Méry wrote, girls conceded everything "except the final favor for a quarter of a dollar." This doubtless included mutual masturbation. The prostitutes of Portsmouth, Virginia, were both beautiful and available. "They want only to drink liquor," he added. Sailors' wives in Portsmouth prostituted themselves but preferably, he continued, "to Frenchmen."

Streetwalkers of every type — Indian, white and black — abounded in Philadelphia. Not even the virtue of Quaker youths could withstand the attractions of the local whorehouses, according to St. Méry. They were frequented at all hours and by every class. In 1806, with prices going up, a trend was started by a new and more expensive type of streetwalker. These were young and pretty girls, neatly dressed, who promenaded two-by-two late in the evening — at an hour such "that they aren't just out for a stroll. Anyone who accosts them," St. Méry continues, "is taken to their home. They all pretend to be dressmakers yet they fulfill every sexual desire for two dollars, one dollar of which is supposed to pay for the room."

Procuresses were common, according to him. Some were white, some were black, some were widows who would allow their homes to be used for arranged assignations. A young man would be approached and the suggestion made that he could be supplied with an attractive young girl. They would then bring the two together for a meeting. St. Méry reports that on every occasion the lady who has sex with the gentleman is paid three dollars, and she gives the procuress one dollar for making the arrangements and supplying the bed.

Prostitutes, he said, often traveled with him by stagecoach. This, he explained, gave these women an opportunity to meet men. An additional dividend for these female travelers was free wine or liquor during meals. "Politeness," wrote St. Méry, "required this expense to be borne by the men." He seems to have been taken with the bondswomen whom he met and noted their immorality on a number of occasions.

In Philadelphia a rich man's widow is described as being only thirty-two years old and so attractive that a compatriot of the author's moved into her home. He continues to tell how she gave herself freely to this Frenchman and also allowed him to have sex with her eldest daughter, a girl of thirteen. For this special service she charged "a quarter of a dollar." A young girl of eight years who also lived in the house "allowed every sort of indecency for twelve and a half cents."

Girls in Philadelphia, St. Méry said, matured at the age of fourteen and remained fertile until forty-five years old with no dangerous consequences to health as compared to the perils of late childbirth in Europe. He thought the girls unusually large at fourteen and tall and pretty. Until they began to menstruate they wore their hair long and their skirts with closed seams. But at that point they put up their hair with a comb and the back of their skirts had a placket (slit). At this point in their lives, according to St. Méry, they became their own mistresses with freedom to go walking alone and to have gentleman callers.

The young women were addicted to finery and a desire to display themselves, "inflamed," says St. Méry, "by their love of adornment." He cannot resist, however, comparing them to French women and remarks that Philadelphia girls cannot imitate the elegant style of his compatriots.

He was shocked to find that the parents raised no objection to the suitor coming to the house whenever he wished and going on walks with their daughter at will.

For a suitor to enjoy sex without marriage with a young girl and then leave her was not unusual in Philadelphia in 1800 but, should a man seduce a married woman and be caught in adultery, he was not only punished by a jail sentence or whipping but was unable to obtain work thereafter — "not even that of a watchman," says St. Méry. Young married women lived only for their husbands and devoted themselves continuously to the care of the household. In short, St. Méry says, American women were no more than housekeepers after marriage. And to put it more succinctly, he describes the wife as being the one and only servant in the house.

How or where he got his information about female masturbation is not known but he says that young women, although they are rarely without love or passion, give themselves up early to physical self-gratification. He adds that lesbianism was relatively common, that many young women were not strangers at being willing to seek unnatural pleasures with persons of their own sex. He attributes some of this to a custom that he says is prevalent among common people such as shopkeepers and tavern keepers. The daughter of the house, "as soon as she passes infancy, sleeps with the servant," that is to say, from eight to ten years she may have shared the bed with a number of passing servants and these servants may have been possessed of habits that, passed on, could be disastrous to young persons.

American women, he says, do not like to speak of the parts of their body but rather divide it into only two sections: from the shoulders to the waist it is all stomach and from the waist to the foot it is ankles. Although he found young American women attractive, mentioning that they are careful to wash their faces and hands —, he added, "not their mouths, seldom their feet and even more seldom their bodies."

With women still scarce widows quickly remarried. St. Méry observes that a delay of six weeks between the loss of a wife and the choice of another one to replace her is the limit of a man's "outward expression of regret." Divorce in Philadelphia, he writes, was obtained with ease and from this alone he decided that most Philadelphians had loose sexual habits.

He found it hard to understand Americans' love for dancing. Frenchmen, he declared, dance because it's the thing to do while Americans dance for their own amusement.

Bastards seem to have been quite common in Philadelphia. St. Méry observes that there are two principal reasons: "First, the city is full of religious sects with none of them giving their clergymen full authority to enforce obedience." Consequently, he says, there is no way of inspiring shame in women who become mothers for no reason except the pleasure they get out of it. Secondly, when an illegitimate child becomes twelve months old, the mother can get rid of him by farming him out as an apprentice (indentured) for twenty-one years. This makes it possible, concludes St. Méry, for her to commit the same sin again. Also it is so easy to get rid of children, remarks St. Méry, that abortion is not often used.

The female douche, or syringe, was introduced in the early nineteenth century from France. In the beginning there was a great wave of sentiment against their use because it was said they were being used to prevent conception — and indeed they were. Yet they soon became popular and various types were carried in American apothecary shops not only in Pennsylvania but in Massachusetts and New York.

During the Revolution, and no doubt long before, blacks were all but invisible. Their morality went unnoticed; their nudity not even seen — young Negroes and Negresses running about or basking in the courtyards of great houses as naked as they came into the world. Chastellux described young male Negroes "from sixteen to twenty [years] with not an article of clothing but a loose shirt descending halfway down their thighs waiting at table where were ladies, without any apparent embarrassment on one side or the slightest attempt at concealment on the other."

That a well-established commerce in illicit sex existed between white men and Negresses is apparent from the journals of many travelers. Chastellux thoughtfully noted that there was so much mixed sex that at some time in the future, as mulattoes replaced Negroes, and quadroons and octaroons became ever lighter in color and replaced one another, all Negro blood would ultimately be absorbed by the white race.

During the years following the Revolution, and indeed for almost 200 years thereafter, segregation was the rule in New York and Philadelphia. There seems to have been a good deal of crossing over the color line in instances of prostitution. But while it was acceptable for white men to have sex with a black girl, no white person, not even a servant, would consider eating with colored people. Not even in the prisons, among the condemned criminals, did blacks and whites sit down together. St. Méry describes a class of colored women who "seduce young white girls and sell them." The seller collected thirty dollars of which only a small part went to the victim. He wrote that "thus . . . colored people partly avenge themselves for the shocking contempt with which they are treated in Philadelphia."

As the Colonial settlements and towns of the coastal areas developed and expanded, some men eager for economic gain and others who chafed under the restrictions imposed by community law and custom, looked to distant horizons. Farmers and settlers pushed inland for more fertile acres, hunters for more game, trappers for hides and pelts for the growing fur trade. A new type of Colonial began to appear — bold, strong, resourceful. They had been blooded in skirmishes with Indians, in defense of early settlements and in the French and Indian Wars. These wily woodsmen were fearless and fiercely independent. They had to be to survive Indian war parties, wild elements and the unforgiving hazards of the frontier. Like the Canadian *trappeur* to the north, they pressed on over distant ranges, deep valleys and great rivers. In sharp contrast to their more civilized brothers in the towns and cities, we find a new breed of American emerging — the Frontiersman.

As the frontier moved west, contact with the Indians increased and trappers and traders became more adept in using the Indians for their own purposes. But the Indians soon learned they had some interesting objects of their own which the white man coveted. The Indians quickly learned to trade their women for blankets, kettles, knives and even guns.

Blue glass beads became a favorite among both Indian men and women and developed into common currency used in exchange for sexual favors with the traders. As the demand for beaver skins grew (they were made into men's hats much fancied by American and British society), so did the number of trappers and traders trekking in with loads of trade materials. The exchange of goods for women became an accepted side activity and the term "trade girls" was coined. There were plenty of Indian women, but comparatively few white men who could supply the beads, guns, knives, axes and horses that the Indians most desired. Sex did not seem a high price to pay, for earlier adventurers had found the Indian women willing to give it away. One of these,

John Lawson, an explorer, trader, pioneer, made a trip to Carolina as early as 1700. In his narrative he wrote of the uncomplicated life of "Indian girls of twelve or thirteen years of age who as soon as nature prompts them, freely bestow their maidenheads on some youth about the same age, continuing her favors on whom she most affects, changing her mate often." According to Lawson, the number of men an Indian woman mated with did not affect her reputation. Virginity had no value among the Indian men of the Carolinas. He does write of a kind of courtship in which young men and women "converse and travel together for several moons before the marriage is published openly." But he points out, as did others who came in contact with the Carolina tribe, that should a problem arise, the man would exchange his mate for another; should the woman disapprove of her man he set a price upon her services and any other man willing to pay for her could buy her freedom.

Lawson's accounts of Indian marriages tell how the young man would go first to the young woman's parents. Two or more meetings would be held with participants made up of relatives of both parties. The youth would make a payment to the wife's family or, if he did not have money or skins, he would be allowed to move in with the mother and father until his hunting yielded enough to pay the marriage price. During this time, Lawson says, the two lovers would be able to lie together under one covering but would avoid sexual penetration. He ventured the opinion that the Indian men were not so vigorous nor impatient as the Europeans.

An interesting sexual diversion that seems to have been almost universal among Indian tribes before 1700 was night crawling or rambling. The custom was reported by many explorers and is reflected in early Indian legends. Young men move silently through the night from one house to another to find willing women. When they softly awaken sleeping girls and are encouraged, they have sex. Before dawn the man quietly leaves without the parents' knowledge. If, however, the girl is not interested, she turns away from the nocturnal visitor and the man does not persist.

Matriarchal rights seem to have been observed strictly. Although white traders had many children by Indian wives, they were never able to take these children back to their own communities because the latter always became the property of the woman. Even when an Indian man and woman lived together and later separated, all the children would go with the mother. Many white traders became permanent residents in the wilderness, preferring life with their Indian wives and mistresses to the European communities.

As it was in most tribes, incest was forbidden among the North Carolina Indians. Any man who had sexual relations with his sister was burned and his ashes thrown into the river "as unworthy to remain on earth." However, an Indian could marry his brother's wife should he die or marry two sisters at any time. Sodomy seems to have been practiced by some tribes and not by others. Lawson says that it was never heard of among the Indians of North Carolina and there was no word for it.

Among the Carolina Indians wife selling appears to have been common. Lawson writes that he had seen many bargains driven in a day with men selling their wives as men do horses at a fair. "A man being allowed not only to change as often as he pleases, but likewise to have as many wives as he is able to maintain."

Lawson observes that within some tribes they set apart the youngest and prettiest girls as trading girls. They wore a particular type of hairdress to distinguish them from engaged girls or married women. After several years of prostitution, these girls usually married or at least went to live with one man. However, during the years of their prostitution, Lawson remarks that they scarcely ever became pregnant "for they have an Art to destroy the Conception and she that brings a child in this station is accounted a fool and her reputation is lessened thereby."

In nearly every trader's journal, mention is made of the availability of Indian girls for hire, or even purchase. There were some advantages to outright purchase. The trader could use the woman to help him carry his goods and canoe over portages, cook his food as well as satisfy his sexual needs. And many Indian women were willing to enter this kind of life, possibly because they were better treated by the white men. A number of trappers have written that Indian women preferred sex with the Europeans, but this can also be attributed to typical male ego. Some traders married their Indian women according to tribal ceremony.

Some Indian males became very accomplished pimps. Alexander Henry, who was called the younger to distinguish him from his better-known father, wrote extensively about the persistence of Indian men in trading off their women. He was speaking of the men of the Gros Ventre nation, whom he accused of having no shame or modesty. "For a few inches of twist tobacco a Gros Ventre will barter the person of his wife or daughter with as much sang-froid as he would bargain for a horse. . . . The Blackfoot, Blood or Piegan is now nearly as bad." Even when the trader had another woman or a wife with him, these Indians insisted they accept one of their women for the night as well. In some instances, the Indian asked that his wife be used because they wanted to have a white child, yet Henry says, even in this case the Indian expected a gift.

Some strong-willed factors allowed no women inside the forts, but these establishments seem to be rare. In most of the unexplored regions, Indian women were as easily available to trappers, soldiers and settlers as they had been to earlier explorers. Walter O'Meara, who did extensive research with the Hudson's Bay company records, tells the story of a Kwakiutl Indian who sent his wife twice a year as a prostitute to Victoria, a Hudson's Bay Company post. After she had worked there for a while, he returned with her to his tribe with a bale of at least fifty blankets. O'Meara observes that the great feasts, or potlatches, for which the Indians of the Northwest were famous, were sometimes financed with the proceeds of this kind of organized prostitution.

In his *Natural History of North Carolina*, John Brickell does not speak of syphilis or gonorrhea, but he does mention the venereal disease called yaws. He attributes this disease to Christian traders who communicated it to the Indians. However, yaws has been known in the West Indies and in South America for such a long time that it would be difficult to pin down its actual origin.

Another considerable controversy is whether or not liquor was used by the Indians before it was introduced by the Europeans. The records of Cabeza de Vaca and others would indicate the Indians certainly had a fermented type of drink, perhaps nearer to beer than to rum. The use, however, of alcoholic liquors may have been sporadic, some tribes making large quantities of liquor out of cactus or corn, while others made none. There is no question that all Indians took to drinking rum as soon as it was offered by the Europeans. They did not seem to be able to resist rum, being willing to part with any of their possessions (including their women) for it, nor were they able to control the amount they drank. According to Brickell, they got so drunk that they frequently tumbled into the fire, burning their arms and legs, and became cripples. They sometimes fell down breaking bones and yet nothing seemed to deter them from drinking. The Europeans took advantage of this and traded extensively in rum for deer skins and furs. A law was passed as early as 1708 in North Carolina making it a crime to sell rum to Indians but the law was never observed nor even put into force.

So, while the Indians' sexual customs, the taking and the use of slave girls, sexual hospitality to strangers and polygamy in many tribes, was not at first comprehensible to the whites, they soon turned these practices to their own ends. It was the whites who used barter to develop widespread prostitution among the Indians, contributed to the spread of venereal disease and, by introducing liquor, guns and horses to these simpler cultures, brought about their destruction.

Today's geneticists have some interesting theories about this period of American history. Hunger, privation, Indian wars and hard toil had cut down large numbers of the first settlers, leaving a pool of comparatively hardy and strong men. Conditions for survival imposed on the new frontiersmen were even more rigorous. Scientists believe the children produced by these virile, physically superior men with white and Indian women has been a most important factor in the establishment of the gene pool that determined the evolution and the character of the American people.

The exposure of an ankle was as shocking a sight in 1840 as a naked girl was in 1940. She is alighting from a horse car.

Erotic Adam and Eve pipe stamper found near Independence Hall in Philadelphia and dated before 1800. Theme is Garden of Eden.

Colonial America imported erotic art from China. This ceramic snuff bottle includes a crude drawing of a nude couple embracing.

Snuff box covers concealed erotic images. This one reveals a woman, with her breasts and buttocks exposed, and her lover.

This nineteenth-century pocket watch was imported from Europe.
Inside the cover case a Peeping Tom observes a couple having sex.

Obscene orgies were attributed to the Perfectionist members of the Oneida community. Note the man doing housework, upper left.

Two young females were arrested in 1859 for dressing like men and smoking cigars. They got eight years in a reformatory.

General Order
No. 28.

HEADQUARTERS DEPARTMENT OF THE GULF.
New-Orleans, May 15, 1862.

As the officers and soldiers of the United States have been subject to repeated insults from the women [calling themselves ladies] of New Orleans, in return for the most scrupulous non-interference and courtesy on our part, it is ordered that hereafter when any female shall, by word, gesture, or movement, insult or show contempt for any officer or soldier of the United States, she shall be regarded and held liable to be treated as a woman of the town plying her avocation.

By command of   MAJOR-GENERAL BUTLER.

GEO. C. STRONG, A.A.Gen., Chief of Staff.

When General "Beast" Butler occupied New Orleans during the Civil War, southern women, he said, insulted the northern soldiers.

Soldiers found entertainment in New Orleans from the time of its founding. The French Quarter offered whiskey and women to all.

Barbary Coast saloons offered wine, women and sudden death. Above, two customers who were cheated shoot up the brothel.

They were called "pretty waiter girls" but they were usually hardworking whores who took care of customers upstairs and down.

CALIFORNIA POLICE GAZETTE.

A Weekly Chronicle of Crime---Devoted to Local and Foreign Criminal News, Politics, Literature, Theatricals, and Items of General Interest to the Reading Public of the Pacific Coast.

Vol. VIII.   SAN FRANCISCO, CAL.: **FOR THE WEEK ENDING** DECEMBER 28, 1867.   No. 465.

Murder of Celina Bouclet on Waverly Place on the night of July 19th.

EUGENE TUCKER, now in County Jail, charged with Murdering Celina Bouclet.

Suicide of Samuel C. Hopkins, July 20.

Charles Harvey Stabbing Gilmore, Proprietor of the Empire Brewery, in Oakland, July 6th.

Summary Vengeance on a Mongolian Ravisher.

Two suicides, a hanging, murder of a Chinese, a woman shoot-
ing her lover — San Francisco the week of Dec. 28, 1867.

*A backstage romance, upper right, leads to a shocking con-
frontation between a chorus girl, her elderly lover and his wife.*

Daring young girls danced in bloomers in Chicago in the '80s.
But bloomers did not catch on. Soon long dresses were back in.

Stripped to her hoop and engaged in her toilette, Annie Mc-Mahon was shot by one lover while preparing to entertain another.

*New Orleans was headquarters for the recruiting of young women
as whores for Texas brothels. They expected respectable jobs.*

Gay young men cavort on a New Orleans street corner before the turn of the century. Male homosexuals were generally ignored.

Lesbians portrayed on the cover of a newspaper in 1893! The caption read: "Good God! The Crimes of Sodom and Gomorrah Discounted."

To accentuate their sexuality chorus girls in the 1890s often
wore contrasting stockings and garters with their tights.

After English show girls made tights popular, most producers
insisted that stars, such as Jennie Lee, reveal their legs.

5

God and the Devil
in the Communes

Sex for some, sex for none and sex for everyone could have been the rallying cry of any of a number of utopian communes (and more radical leaders) that made their appearance in America in the latter part of the eighteenth and early part of the nineteenth centuries. These were the basic choices that confronted the theologists, philosophers, mystics, spiritualists and economists — men and women — who founded the various communities. All of the communal movements professed to have the secrets of salvation, all were basically religious in nature and all had strong (if often opposing) sexual philosophies.

One such search for utopia led to the formation of the Society of Shakers in 1792. To the Shakers the problem seemed simple: sex was sinful, so they eliminated it. They practiced the celibate life using infinite precautions to keep the sexes apart. Men and women ate apart, worked apart and worshipped apart. Shaker men and women, for instance, did not shake hands — too intimate. They were proud that their discipline resulted in "no scandals." Purification in the Shaker communities went farther than that of most strict monastic disciplines. Meat was not taken. Dress was as plain and simple as possible. No pets were kept except cats to destroy rats and mice. Smoking was prohibited.

With no procreation, perpetuating their order was difficult. The Shakers solved this problem by proselytizing young people whom they reared in special schools — the girls separated from the boys. Each child taken for adoption, whether from a parent or an institution, was legally indentured for a period of time. Should the children prove difficult, they were returned to their parents or the institution from whence they came.

How the community came to be called "Shakers" cannot be specifically traced, but they were called "Shaking-Quakers" before the group left England to travel to the United States. Members of the group splintered off from the Society of Quakers. They were led to America by Ann Lee, later known as Mother Lee. As a young girl, Ann could neither read nor write.

Shortly before the United States declared its independence from England, a revelation instructed Ann to lead members of her society to the Colonies. The revelation continued: "The second Christian Church would be established in America; that the colonies would gain their independence; and that liberty of conscience would be secured to all people, whereby they would be able to worship God without hindrance or molestation." This prediction turned out to be true.

Her revelations, which Ann and her colleagues believed to be of divine origin, of the spiritual world were so remarkable that after her death her sect revered her as the second Christ to appear on earth.

She preached that true Christian communism could only exist through the principle of virgin life which, of course, excluded marriage. Yet Ann herself married in her youth and had four children who died in infancy. One of the key tenets from the Bible that the Shakers lived by was: "For in the resurrection, they neither marry nor are given in marriage; but are as angels of God in heaven" (Matthew 22:30). The four principles of the Shaker religion were: virginal purity, Christian communism, confession and separation from the world.

Filled with religious fervor, carried away by a mutual exhilaration, it was not unusual for religious groups at revival meetings to roll upon the ground or floor, moaning, crying, laughing. In the case of the Shakers, they shook with the passion of purity, hence their name.

It was one of Ann Lee's visions that brought about the practice of celibacy in this originally small, devout group. She claimed to have been transported to the Garden of Eden and to have been a witness to the sex act committed by Adam and Eve that resulted in their expulsion from the Garden and brought about the ultimate depravity of humanity. This shocking manifestation of sin so repulsed her that she preached that no person could follow Christ and involve themselves in the gratification of the lust of the flesh. Celibacy was the only way of life. The true believers around her adopted her beliefs and the battle against human sexual desire was joined.

An interesting poem was published in 1833 by the Shakers in a volume called *Hymns and Poems for the Use of Believers*. In it Adam is innocently hoeing and pruning the Garden when suddenly he feels the beast of lust rising as he views "the beauties of my wife." The poem reads:

"An idle beast of highest rank
　　Came creeping up just at that time,
And show'd to Eve a curious prank,
[Ed.: the first sexual intercourse?]
　　Affirming that it was no crime:—
'Ye shall not die as God hath said—
'Tis all a sham, be not afraid.'

"All this was pleasant to the eye,
　　and Eve affirm'd the fruit was good;
So I gave up to gratify
　　The meanest passion in my blood.
O horrid guilt! I was afraid:
I was condemn'd, yea I was dead.

"Here ends the life of the first man,
　　Your father and his spotless bride;
God will be true, his word must stand—
　　The day I sinn'd that day I died:
This was my sin, this was my fall!
This your condition, one and all."

On Sunday no unnecessary labor was performed. They did not bathe, no food was cooked, no boots or shoes were polished. Not even fruit could be picked on the Sabbath. The only work allowed was milking the cows and feeding the animals. All the members of the community arose upon the ringing of a bell shortly after dawn. They then prayed on their knees, straightened out their beds and blankets and reported to work. Fifteen minutes were allotted. In summer the rising bell rang at four-thirty in the morning; in winter, an hour later. Breakfast was served one-and-a-half hours after rising. Dinner was at noon, supper at six. At seven-thirty in the evening in summer, and at eight in the winter, the bell tolled again. Members retired to their respective dwellings where they had a half hour to themselves before evening worship. At eight o'clock a small hand bell summoned all. They then marched, without speaking, to the church.

All members of the community were forbidden to say anything against their brothers and sisters no matter what their defects. They could, however, take their complaints to the elders. No female was allowed to enter a man's work place unless accompanied by another woman. Male and female workshops were never under the same roof. Whatever leisure time was left to these dawn-to-dusk workers was expected to be used in the performance of some good work.

That sexual contact must have occurred and must have concerned the Shakers a great deal is evidenced by their stringent rules. Male and female members were never allowed to touch one another. And it is significant that another law forbade anyone to play with or handle any beast whatsoever, nor could a calf or cow be given the name of a person. Bestiality may also have been a problem. Should a brother or sister meet an outsider and shake hands with them, especially one of the opposite sex, it was expected that they would report this sin to the elder in charge.

No literary work, no magazines or newspapers, were permitted into the community unless sanctioned by the elders. All trading for the entire community was done by the trustees, who legally held all property. They carried their discipline to incredible extremes: even the simplest actions in life had to be approved by their ministry. When ascending a flight of stairs, one should step first with the right foot. When the hands were folded, the right-hand thumb and fingers must be above those of the left. Kneeling and rising again was done with the right leg first. Even when harnessing a team of horses, the animal on the right had to be harnessed first.

All children under sixteen were completely separated from the community in their working, eating, playing, sleeping and even worship. They saw only their special caretakers. Only on Sunday were they allowed to mingle at meeting with the adults. It was considered proper to cane or use a rod to whip stubborn children. But, generally, such children were returned to their parents or institutions. Recalcitrant animals were handled the same way. They were sold if they did not conform to the rules.

A form of confession was used for both children and adults: the children confessing to their caretakers; the adults confessing to the elders. One estimate made at the time in one of the larger communities was that only about ten percent of the children trained in Shaker ways remained with the cult as adults.

There were eighteen Shaker societies, the largest ones in the northeast. Generally speaking, the rules were the same throughout though some seem to have eaten more meat than others. The largest of the societies in 1823 had about 500 persons including forty-seven children under fifteen. At one time some of the Shaker societies included mulattoes and quadroons among their members. In the Watervliet Society in Philadelphia there were twelve colored women. These women worked outside the community during the day, coming back to the central dwelling place in the evening. Their celibacy prevented miscegenation.

Whether it was their celibacy, their eating habits (eschewing meat generally), their cleanliness (they believed in regular bathing) or their work discipline, it is difficult to say, but the members were known throughout the country for their longevity. Over and over the records show that many members lived to be past ninety and were still hardworking during their eighties. They lived a long time — if you can call their way of life truly living. Their sexual philosophy could probably be summed up in a verse dating back to 1817:

"The adulterous eye shall now be blind —
It shall not feed the carnal mind;
My looks and conduct shall express
    that holy faith that I possess."

Or again, in a dialogue:

"Question: And what is now the greatest foe with which you mean to war?
"Answer: The cursed flesh — 'tis that, you know, all faithful souls abhor."

Having brought with them from Europe a fundamental belief in the sinfulness of sex, one can see how only by giving it up completely could the faithful hope to enter the kingdom of heaven. For the sex act itself had been portrayed from the pulpit as an abomination. It was not only sinful and dirty but it also drained away the vital essences that should be spent in working and worship.

The Shakers believed that theirs was the one society which would lead the individual to perfection. Never in their most impious dreams could they imagine that another group that would call themselves Perfectionists would adopt a completely opposite sexual philosophy.

The Perfectionists began their radical movement about forty years after the Shakers when a young theological student who had attended Dartmouth, Andover and Yale promulgated a new doctrine that would free men and women and make them perfect.

Basically John Humphrey Noyes propounded the theory that all the ills of the world stem from nationalism and can only be cured by absolute integration. He reduced this to the individual, suggesting that every family is a nationalistic unit and that unless the family is broken down there can be no hope of countries or nations coming together peacefully. Furthermore, when a man takes a wife to have and hold exclusively, it sets her up in his view (and he in hers) as being superior to other men and women. When she has children, they build a fence around the house and the nationalistic cycle begins. His children are better than those next door. Personal property creates legal and moral problems. Individual family living, Noyes believed, promotes jealousy, rivalry and hatred. His solution was a community in which *everyone was married to everyone else.* Every child born had as his mother all women and as his father all men.

John Noyes may well have known some of the history of Christian polygamy which had existed at least since the first half of the sixteenth century. In 1534 John of Leyden was the leader of a militant Christian group. Like Luther, he had broken away from the Catholic Church, but unlike Luther, he insisted that his followers adopt polygamy. John Cairncross in his scholarly work *After Polygamy Was Made a Sin* believes that it came about simply because John of Leyden wanted to have sex with two women and he wanted to enjoy them both undisturbed legally — as wives. Only one course was open to him and that was to change the laws of marriage.

John of Leyden had no difficulty in finding precedent in the Old Testament for until the time of Christ there seems to have been no restriction as to the number of wives a man might have. He quoted Solomon and David. His argument was that it was necessary to increase the population of true Christians. Quoting Luther, that the only choice for a woman was marriage or whoredom, he insisted that "better many wives than many whores." John ultimately married four women and proclaimed polygamy legal in the German free city of Münster. So John became king of the first Christian city to fully embrace polygamy. Once started, most of the citizens happily adopted the practice.

Cairncross quotes the case of a husband who refused to send away a younger wife, which so angered his first wife that she picked up a chair and threatened to split his skull with it. She did not live to regret this act, being promptly beheaded for it.

Other women tried to avoid polygamy by marrying only an unmarried man but this was so unpopular politically that they were few.

However, other religious groups in the countryside, Catholic and Lutheran, opposed John's rule. But he was no peaceful polygamist. He had his opponents all put to the sword — excepting old men, children, cripples and pregnant women. These were stripped of all their possessions and driven out of the city gates. Only Anabaptists remained. John seemed happy with his polygamous life but it did not last long. Every free city and principality in Germany, and even beyond, was aware that if polygamy caught on, their government and especially their "morality" would be endangered.

The city was attacked from all sides. John first got all the men behind him by reminding them that the Anabaptist creed insisted upon complete subordination of women to men. The husband was Lord and wives were responsible to their husbands in the same way men were responsible to God. Surprisingly enough, women fell into line quite easily and became strong supporters of polygamy and of John. It may have been the fact that there were at least three women of marriageable age to each man in Münster. The fervor in favor of polygamy was such that there developed a contest to see which men could marry the most wives in the shortest time. One historian wrote that they invaded every house in which there was a woman, girl or maid, each man trying to outbid the other in the number of wives he could attract.

When women became scarce, one of the preachers suggested that it had been ascertained that girls could become pregnant before puberty, therefore permission should be given for them to be married. Girls from eleven to fourteen, eighteen of them in all, were forced into marriage. It should be remembered, however, that the Catholic ruling at that time was that boys were fit for marriage at fourteen and girls at twelve — and if they were capable of copulation earlier, they should be permitted to marry. Finally the city of Leyden's enemies outside sealed it off and kept provisions from coming in. Within months the women were put out of the city and in June of 1535, approximately two years after polygamy had been adopted, the "Kingdom of the Saints" collapsed. Those who stood by their polygamous Anabaptist faith, men and women alike, were executed.

In spite of the repressive spirit prevalent in the early nineteenth century, John Humphrey Noyes succeeded in forming a successful communal society based upon his unconventional ideas. His followers bought forty acres of land at Oneida, New York, and established a commune which became known as the Perfectionist or Oneida Colony. The Bible was "the textbook of the spirit of truth," and they considered their community as a whole to be a church in which the standard of excellence within the community was to lead to a sinless life. But they did not believe that sex was sinful — *bien au contraire.*

Perfectionists did not see any intrinsic difference between property in things and property in people, and they did not think that either should be owned by anyone. In a time when slavery was generally acceptable, they worked toward the complete abolition of human bondage.

Communal, or complex, marriage began a formal experiment in what was termed by some critics free love in the United States. It combined both polygamy and polyandry.

In practice, each member, male or female, who joined the community was a member of an extended family. Every man had the right to have sexual intercourse with any woman in the community — with her permission. She was, after all, his wife. Any woman in the community had the right to have intercourse with any man — he was her husband.

An excerpt from the Oneida rules explains that "complex marriage means . . . that, within the limits of the community membership, any man or woman may and do freely cohabit, having first gained each other's consent, not by private conversation or courtship, but through the intervention of some third person or persons." This strongly discouraged any "exclusive and idolatrous attachments" of any two persons for each other. They taught the pairing of persons of different ages, the young of one sex with the old of the other. But "persons are not obliged under any circumstances to receive the attentions of those they do not like."

Women's rights were rigorously upheld at Oneida. Each woman had her own room, her own bed, her chest which contained her clothes, sewing materials, Bible and other books and, to the horror of the townspeople, instead of skirts Oneida women wore pantaloons. This seemed practical to Mr. Noyes and the elders because women worked just as men did and all of their earnings, as that of the men, went into the communal treasury.

At Oneida an unusual form of birth control was practiced — unusual, that is, for the United States — though it had been practiced in China and India for generations. It is called *coitus reservatus*, the withholding of semen during intercourse. A man was expected to be able to enjoy sex with a woman, give her complete satisfaction and obtain his own without ejaculation. As far back as the writing of the Hindu sex manual, the Kamasutra in India, this has been an ancient discipline.

In addition, certain birth control measures were known by 1840: a type of diaphragm made from a sponge was sometimes used, the vaginal douche and the condom existed, and the so-called rhythm system was recognized. Oneida not only freed women from unwanted children, it set up rules for producing healthy and, it was hoped, superior children. In effect, if any man or woman agreed that they wanted to have a child, they had to obtain the consent of the governing body to do so. If it was decided that these individuals were eugenically unfit to produce offspring permission was withheld. A woman was never forced to become a mother against her will, and venereal diseases were completely unknown in the community.

After a child was born, it stayed with its mother until it was weaned, and the mother could visit her child or play with it, at any time, as could the father. But, as soon as the child could be put into the nursery, it was taken care of by women and men especially suited to the role of substitute mothers and substitute fathers.

As the children grew older, they went to the schools that were organized and operated within the community. A most important belief was that each woman in the community felt that each child was her own and that each man felt his responsibility as well. Every child, therefore, had some 200 fathers and 200 mothers.

Dr. Noyes, as both spiritual and temporal leader of the community, had special privileges, and he took liberal advantage of them, believing that it was important that his genes be passed on (he had eight children after the age of fifty-eight). In his spare time he wrote a small booklet on male continence.

Whether it was the influence of complex marriage, the inspired and passionate leadership of Noyes or the unremitting toil of the men and women who made up the community at Oneida, the result was good. It succeeded on both an economic and a social level. Members of the commune were respected and liked by their neighbors. Yet the radical group was attacked by the Presbyterian Synod of Central New York. Other religious organizations joined in a move to break up the experiment. Pressure became so great on Noyes that in 1879 he proposed to the membership that they give up the practice of complex marriage, "not as renouncing belief in the principles and perspective finality of that institution, but in deference to the public sentiment which is evidently rising against it."

It was a shocking blow to the men and women who had built their lives, and built them successfully, upon the principle of complete communal living. Marriages were performed between individuals who chose to live together. Children were, to a degree, divided up, though many of them continued to be reared in the same traditional ways. All property previously owned in common, with no individual exercising any exclusive right, was turned into a joint stockholding company in which each person's interest in the general holdings was represented by shares of stock in his or her name. The Oneida Community Limited was formed in 1881. The original commune survived intact. Under the new plan the weakest woman fared as well as the strongest man.

John H. Noyes remained president of Oneida Community Limited until his death in 1886, and one of his sons succeeded him. Out of it came the company which became known throughout the world for Community and Oneida silverware. As early as 1906 they had become a multi-million-dollar organization that employed some 2000 workers in addition to members of the society.

A postscript regarding Oneida's experiment in selective breeding: even today the descendants of the members of the commune are tall, vigorous, even athletic, and long-lived individuals.

Another kind of complex marriage in the name of religion was a contributing factor in the reorganization of the Oneida community. As pressure was being put on Oneida, a newspaper article in *The Republican* of Springfield, Massachusetts, editorialized about another sect:

"Let us be fair with these people who are trying a new experiment in sociology. Nothing can be more unfair than to couple them with the Mormons. Mormonism is a gross tyranny of superstition and outrage, the worst example of priestcraft existing in the world; but the Oneida Community is a mutual compact of free men and women. Mormonism, as priestcraft, always cultivates depression and ignorance; the Oneida Community, by the testimony of their most strenuous opponents, cultivates equality and intelligence. Mormonism reduces women, both by theory and practice, to the condition of the harem — the slaves and victims of man; the Oneida Community makes them theoretically, and, so far as we have any evidence, practically co-laborers and companions of man."

What are the facts? Certainly all the evidence of the early stages indicates that the founders of the Mormon religion, Joseph Smith and his brother Hyrum, when they lived in Illinois were interested in having sexual intercourse with as many women as possible. Joseph Smith married Emma Hale when he was twenty-one. A few years later he impregnated a seventeen-year-old orphan that the Smiths had taken in to live with them. When Emma found that the girl was pregnant, she threw her out. Within the next seven years Joseph had eleven affairs with married women (which he called spiritual marriages and did not reveal to his wife). He also physically and spiritually married two unmarried women and managed to keep this hidden as well. During these years it is believed Smith thought of religious polygamy and was, indeed, in a covert manner practicing it. This was made public, though not all at once, when a nineteen-year-old girl turned down his offer.

It should be explained that Joseph and some of his friends, including the youthful Brigham Young, later insisted they were forming their sexual liaisons with the complete approval of God. Their actions followed those of elderly leaders (and some not so elderly) of the Old Testament who had concubines, as well as wives, by the score and seemed partial to young virgins.

One of the early Mormon saints, Dr. John C. Bennett, a "midwife" who was said to have also practiced abortion, wrote an exposé called *The History of the Saints.* He may or may not have exaggerated when he wrote

that the Mormon religion cast women into three categories. At the top were the Cloistered Saints who became secret or spiritual wives. Next, came the Cyprian Saints who were available to all the church leaders. And finally, the Chambered Sisters of Charity, who could only be used for sexual purposes with Joseph's permission. As to the latter, he looked into his peep stone (a corollary of a crystal ball) to see whether it was the will of heaven before giving his permission.

Joseph and his brethren continued their love feasts. But the high rate of pregnancies based on the limited contraceptive knowledge made it hard to keep the saints' secret marriages private. Babies began to be born to widows, to unmarried women and married women as well, to the surprise of some unaware husbands. Unfortunately for Joseph Smith, when the Female Relief Committee was set up, his wife Emma became its chairman. Joseph, rising to the occasion, secretly married almost all the members of the committee. There was one holdout, a Mrs. Whitney, who gave him as a substitute her seventeen-year-old daughter.

Between 1842 and 1844 Joseph married some forty-eight wives in addition to Emma, twenty of them still virgins, between the ages of fifteen and twenty. Six young wives lived at various times in his home. About a year previous to his taking on almost half a hundred women, he had convinced Emma, his wife, that polygamy was here to stay. She reluctantly agreed but only if she could choose the wives. She then selected two of the four girls that were living with them at that time (May 11, 1843). Little did she know that these girls had already been married to Joseph for a while. Not long after this, Joseph got her to consent to two more wives who were sisters. By then a total of five wives seemed to her sufficient. It is probable at this time Joseph offered Emma an extra husband, but only in heaven. This became part of Mormon theology: it was expected that Mormon wives, no matter how plural the family, would remain faithful to one husband on earth and that they would be given another husband in heaven. Emma never did go along with multiple marriage. If she found out about the other forty-six or so wives, it was after Joseph's death. When he and his brother Hyrum were lynched by a mob, she soon found a new husband — a non-Mormon.

It was indeed the polygamy issue that brought Joseph to his death. One faction of the Mormons, opposed to polygamy, set up a press and printed a newspaper exposing Smith and other of the saints. Joseph and his friends instigated a riot in which the printing press was destroyed. He was arrested and was waiting to face trial in Carthage when an irate mob descended upon the jail, removed Joseph, his brother and two other "saints," and hanged them.

In the long run, plural marriage did make for a successful organization. Brigham Young pulled the saints together and they went marching into the wilds of Utah.

Young ended up with twenty-five wives, fifty-six children and the leadership of an economically successful, new religious community.

It is said that Brigham visited each of his wives daily and that they all had separate bedrooms. This could give an entirely erroneous impression, for the spiritual leader slept alone and some of his wives were certainly in name only. But he did have favorites that changed from time to time, and when the family met for dinner he and his favorite occupied the most prominent place at the table. It was Young's decision that plural marriage be taught and practiced within the entire community.

Adultery was not tolerated and at one time was punishable by death. Birth control and abortion were outlawed and intercourse was not to be had during menstruation, pregnancy or while the mother was nursing. Husbands and wives were expected to sleep in separate beds. Mormon boys were supposed to be married by sixteen and girls by fourteen. The aim of their sex, unlike that of the Oneida Community, was never to be pleasure but always procreation.

It may come as a surprise that a much earlier commune existed in the southern part of the United States of America where blacks and whites not only worked together but slept together. This took place thirty years before the American Civil War and the organizer was none other than Fanny Wright, Lafayette's young English mistress, who accompanied the old hero to the States on his triumphant return forty years after the Revolutionary War.

But Fanny turned out to love the United States even more than she loved Lafayette. The romance wound down. He returned to France while Fanny stayed on to author the first play produced by a woman in the United States. It was called *Altorf* and had a brief life. Then Fanny, who was a reformer and an implacable foe of slavery, went on to organize her utopian community. She bought a tract of 2000 acres in Tennessee and she and her sister Camilla established a commune known as Nashoba. There had been many white communes but the idea of a black and white one was new and shocking. Sexual intercourse was by mutual consent.

The community of Nashoba did not recognize legal marriage, and it brought protests not only from the communities in Tennessee but even from far off Washington. A newspaper described it as "one great brothel." Fanny Wright could not understand the furor. She pointed out that white gentlemen had been producing mulatto children for years, that blacks and whites seemed to have no sexual antipathy and that a plantation such as hers, where the "slaves" would be paid for their work and where everyone was free to live as they wished, should be a great asset to the newly formed United States of America.

The plan was for free Negroes (and escaped slaves as well) to move on to the fertile land, where houses would be built and where they would join a nucleus of white socialists. One southern planter sent six of his female slaves. Other escaped slaves were brought to the commune.

Perhaps if Frances Wright had not been so busy bringing the rights of women to the rest of the United States and had applied her organizational and leadership talents to Nashoba, it might have had some small measure of success. But it did not. The community suffered from malaria, floods; the soil was not the best and the fourteen blacks did not get along well at all with the whites. Frances' dream of blacks and whites happily working and mating with one another was breaking down. She insisted that there was no reason why it shouldn't work. She stressed the constant increase in births of mulatto children for many years. "Why not," said Frances, "face this and use it for the nation's good. Perhaps a stronger race, more suited to the southern climate could evolve." She wrote a letter outlining these ideas and it was published in the Memphis newspaper. Then as money ran out her plantation went to ruin.

In 1830, within two years of the beginning of the experiment, Nashoba was a complete failure. The black members of the community found a refuge in Haiti, that small Caribbean country which had recently proclaimed itself a free black republic.

Frances Wright was an influential and major contributor to the liberation of American women. She founded what was called Frances Wright's Hall of Science in Brooklyn, where she lectured regularly on the equality of women.

Then, as so many prominent Americans of her time, she became personally involved with her own ideas of free love. She found herself pregnant by Phiquepal D'Arusmont, whom she had met at the New Harmony commune. They were married shortly before their child was born. When the child died she had another but could never bring herself to be a housewife. She continued her lectures while her husband took care of the house and child. This went on for thirteen years and ended in divorce. Fanny kept on writing and lecturing and became one of the first architects of the American Labor movement.

Whether free love was actually free or not did not matter, a wave of free love communes, most related to the spiritualism religious movement, swept over the United States in the 1830s and '40s. They had been triggered by the widespread religious revivals of the early

'30s. And, along with communal production methods and communal social intercourse, a number of communities adopted communal sex practices. These were not, for the most part, communities of complex marriage, such as Oneida, nor communities based upon plural marriage, as in the case of the Mormons. They were more of an attempt to break away from both the religious marriage vows and the legal marriage contract. The spiritualist philosophy took marriage away from reality and recast it in a more abstract, sometimes called heavenly, form. A Free Lover was a person who held that he or she had the right to make and remake his or her sexual relations without consulting any authority, religious or legal. Not all followers of spiritualism were free lovers, but all free lovers that joined one another in communes were spiritualists.

The passkey to free love, as the spiritualists saw it, was that marriages, literally, were made in heaven, and unless a *spiritual affinity* existed between husband and wife, they were living in a state of sinful adultery. It certainly has been said (and often accurately) that this search for one's affinity was an excuse for getting out of a distasteful marriage. One could move higher on the spiritual level by finding and having sex with one's affinity (whether he or she was married at the time made no difference). It was strictly the spiritual relationship that made it all moral.

Perhaps the most notable and notorious of all the spiritualists were Victoria Clafin Woodhull and her sister, Tennessee. They practiced not only spiritualism but fortune telling and magic healing, and managed to put considerable emphasis on free love to spice up the mixture. Victoria started her long and sensation-filled career at the age of fifteen when, on a Fourth of July picnic, she met a spiritual affinity and lost her virginity. A little later on, although she now had a common-law husband, Mr. Woodhull, she began living with another affinity, Colonel James Blood. It must be said in her favor that she divorced Woodhull for a brief period after taking on Colonel Blood, but soon welcomed him back into the ménage à trois.

Both Victoria and Tennessee were electrifying, rabble-rousing speakers. Both were specialists at outdoor medicine shows where, after describing the glories of their spiritualistic powers and the advantages of free love, Victoria would dramatically cry out as she pointed to handsome bewhiskered Colonel Blood: "There stands my lover — when I cease to love him, I will leave him."

Then they sold the customers a "magnetic life elixir," the prime ingredient of which was alcohol.

It seems beyond belief that such a captain of industry as Commodore Cornelius Vanderbilt could have been taken in by the mixed quartet of Tennessee Clafin, Victoria, Dr. Woodhull and Colonel James Blood. But they were persuasive. And it is just possible that some of the free love the girls were passing out was welcomed by the Commodore. At any rate, he was taken with them and by them. With his financing and advice, Woodhull, Clafin and Company (stockbrokers) was formed and prospered.

It was not long before making money in the market did not provide excitement enough, so the quartet started a weekly newspaper. To the great surprise of everyone, they first published Karl Marx's *Communist Manifesto* in English. As editors they also used the newspaper to promote free love, spiritualism and the advantages of being a spiritual wife. They further urged women who were dissatisfied with their husbands to add other men to their lives instead of getting a divorce, and especially to procreate only with superior men. All these were women's rights — and so, they insisted, was the right to vote.

Other more respectable newspapers were horrified. The churches cried revolution and the state cried treason. The group's headquarters, a large home on Thirty-eighth Street in New York City, became a favorite gathering place for free lovers and freethinkers. There, a century ahead of her time, Victoria Woodhull advocated short skirts, vegetarianism, magnetic healing, an excess-profits tax and world government.

Among her attackers within the religious community was the most powerful minister in the country. He was the tall, handsome, magnetic Henry Ward Beecher, easily the most important minister of the gospel of his time. His Plymouth Church had an influence that reached across the nation. He was a man who could play many parts and did so to the delight of his audiences. His church became known as Beecher's Theater.

After one of his effective sermons, he brought out two young and pretty black slave girls. He dramatically urged the congregation to join him in raising money to buy their freedom. As he described the pathetic life of the slaves, his audience melted into tears. Women stripped themselves of their jewelry while men gave all the money they had — then added their gold watches to the collection plate.

Still, the Reverend Henry Ward Beecher was not beyond reproach. He had been enjoying a guilty love affair with Elizabeth Richards Tilton, an attractive brunette of thirty-five years, married to Theodore Tilton to whom she had borne four children. She had become Beecher's mistress after he had convinced her of their *spiritual affinity* and had arranged their heavenly marriage. But her strict upbringing was too much for her guilty conscience: she had to tell someone, breaking the pledge of secrecy she had given her preacher-lover. She confessed all to her husband. In exchange she got a promise from him that he would not use the information against the minister.

Then Tilton met Victoria Woodhull. He found her extremely attractive and most sympathetic. They spent more and more time with one another. Whether they became lovers was later hotly debated, but the evidence is on the affirmative side. Mrs. Woodhull confessed in an interview that "he was my devoted lover for more than half a year." She continued, "So enamored and infatuated were we with each other that for three months we were hardly out of each other's sight, and he slept every night in my arms."

But Victoria knew how to cover her tracks. After giving out this information to the *Chicago Journalist,* her interview in a New York paper echoed the opposite theme. She denied ever making the previous statement and said, "A woman who is before the world as I am would not make such a flagrant statement even if it were true." This got her even more publicity. At some time in their relationship, Tilton revealed his wife's affair with the minister. Victoria Woodhull waited until she needed Beecher's support and then tried to blackmail him into introducing and sponsoring her at a most important speech she was to give at Steinway Hall.

With no other choice, Beecher agreed to a meeting with Victoria. In privacy, according to her, he said that he was a coward regarding free love. Furthermore, he personally believed that marriage was the grave of free love but if he let his views be known he would be preaching to empty seats. According to Victoria, Beecher wept on his knees pleading for her to reconsider the request that he endorse her. Finally, he refused to come to Steinway Hall that fateful night and it was the wronged husband, Theodore Tilton, who made the introduction. Victoria spoke on The Principle of Social Freedom which "Involves the Question of Free Love, Marriage, Divorce and Prostitution."

It was a big night for Victoria Woodhull and she did not hold back. When someone shouted from the audience, "Are you a free lover?" she shouted back, "Yes, I am a free lover. I have an inalienable constitutional right to love whom I may, to love as long or as short a period as I can, to change that love every day if I please. . . I have a further right to demand a free, unrestricted exercise of that right, and it is your duty not only to accord it but as a community to see that I am protected in it."

Victoria Woodhull was riding high — so high that her followers rented a New York theater, and a unique group of spiritualists, suffragists, Fourierists and members of various communes nominated Victoria Woodhull for president of the United States. Her vice-presidential running mate was Frederick Douglas, the first black ever to be nominated for that high office. But from this point on her career began slipping. Commo-

dore Vanderbilt withdrew his support from the newspaper and brokerage business as well. Hotels refused to accept her. Henry Ward Beecher was polite but said he could not be of any assistance. Unfortunately, she attacked the other women suffrage leaders as being too conservative, and as a result lost the support of her friend Theodore Tilton, who decided to back Horace Greeley, the newspaper editor, for president. Afterward, Victoria attacked Beecher directly in her newspaper. Citing his immense physical potency and his attraction to cultured women around him, she wrote that, because of her position on free love, Beecher had the social, moral and divine right to have had his love affair with Mrs. Tilton. However, she now felt that Henry Ward Beecher was being a hypocrite and that he should admit his love for Mrs. Tilton. She went even farther, saying, "I conceive that Mrs. Tilton's love for Mr. Beecher was her true marriage . . . that her marriage to Mr. Tilton is prostitution. The only fault with which I charge him is not infidelity to the old ideas, but unfaithfulness to the new."

The scandal exploded not only in New York but all over the United States. It was a godsend to righteous young Anthony Comstock of the Young Men's Christian Association, whose ambition was to suppress all vice in the United States. Only ten hours after perusing the newspaper article he got the district attorney of New York County to issue a warrant for the arrest of the sisters. He could not wait even that long: he recollected that Congress had passed a statute making the sending of obscene materials through the mails a misdemeanor. Comstock convinced the federal authorities that what Victoria had written about Mr. Beecher was obscene.

Although an acquaintance offered to put up the bail of $16,000, the two sisters decided it would be better politics and better publicity for them to go to jail. It was there that they spent election day; Ulysses S. Grant won the presidency.

Never numbering more than a few thousand at most, the proponents of sex without marriage, whether they were called spiritualists or free lovers or perfectionists, had an influence on sex in America far greater than their numbers would indicate. The free love movement never became one that the average citizen joined, yet the emphasis these groups placed on sexual freedom for women, on a vigorous intellectual as well as social life and their interest in individual self-development had far reaching effects on future generations.

The women behind the free love movement (and

more women than men were advocates) preached the gospel of making themselves attractive and, even more daring for their times, they insisted that the men with whom they came into contact also make themselves more physically and mentally attractive. The typical, dull routine of marriage, with the woman cooking and bearing the babies, the husband going to work and coming home to smoke his pipe, eat his dinner and go to bed (with occasional, routine missionary-position sex) was an anathema to them. Unwilling to accept the stereotype marriage pattern of their mothers and fathers, they decided one way to avoid this rut was to eliminate marriage.

Dreams of utopia included a large communal kitchen, a gymnasium, an art gallery and, of course, a printing press — a forum from which new ideas could be disseminated to the world. At the Institute of Desarrollo, dreamed up by Thomas and Mary Nichols, there was to be no marriage for, like John Noyes, the Nichols believed that human happiness could not thrive on monogamy. When marriage was born, according to their philosophy, sex died. They were not too far wrong for sex was an unmentionable obscenity in the 1850s. The Nichols wanted it brought out into the open and made respectable. It was a God-given urge, they preached, and should be freely indulged.

Perhaps the Nichols went too far in blaming most of the ills from which their generation suffered not only on poverty, monotony, hypocrisy and intolerance — but also on marriage. Marriage, they declared, was an unnatural restriction on the sexual freedom of both men and women. If women were allowed to freely choose the fathers of their children, such selection would make for a stronger, happier, healthier and wiser new generation.

The two founders of this potential utopia were an unlikely couple. Mary Nichols had previously been married to Hiram Gove, who (according to her later writings) was most unattractive, uninteresting and a male chauvinist. But she came under the influence of Sylvester Graham, a Presbyterian clergyman who, in addition to inventing the graham cracker, preached what was in his day a revolutionary philosophy.

Graham had been the general agent and a lecturer for the Pennsylvania Temperance Society and was one of the first men in America to question the use of additives in food, especially bread. He claimed that bakers, by bleaching the flour, took the strength out of it and further that they adulterated bread with a great variety of chemicals, including alum, sulphate of zinc and even plaster of Paris. As a result he was nearly lynched by the bakers of Boston.

If he had confined himself to his pure-bread program, his influence on Mary Gove would have been minimal. But his other interest was sex education, and here he was treading on the taboos of the religious fundamentalists and the teachings of the church generally. He had the temerity to suggest that young men and

women study human anatomy to learn about their bodies. This mild reformer stimulated Mary Gove to learn what she could about female and male anatomy. As a result she started teaching physiology classes to women, where among other advice she urged that they throw away their corsets. The *Philadelphia Daily Chronicle* severely criticized her for illustrating a lecture by donning a corset (over her clothing) and showing and telling how the various body organs were constricted when she laced it up.

The next step in Mary's sex education came from Henry Wright, a young Englishman who was a proponent of "water" as a cure for everything. Mary became a "hydropathist," prescribing water for everything, especially female problems. She suggested that water be used internally to cleanse the system and recommended the cold douche, the enema (research does not say whether she insisted that the water be cold in this case) and the cold wet sheet for certain ailments. Her water-cure boarding-house on Tenth Street in New York became a favorite meeting place for the radicals of her time; among them were such people as Sarah Josepha Hale, editor of *Godey's Lady's Book,* and the soon-to-be-popular young poet, Edgar Allan Poe.

There is no hard evidence that she and Poe had a love affair but he dedicated at least one poem to her and wrote his famous *The Bells* while visiting her home. She, in return, visited him at his home. The works of George Sand were discussed at her salons. An outstanding intellectual of the time, Albert Brisbane, also came and discussed the ideas of Charles Fourier. Fourier was a French radical reformer who anticipated many changes in the social system. His contribution was part of the socialist movement which began in the United States in the 1830s and continued for some twenty years. It was Fourier's belief that the instinct of the individual had been perverted by society which, in turn, gave rise to his unhappiness and to his inability to cope with daily living. Women, he professed, were the equal in every way of men. Conventional marriage should be abolished.

Society, said Fourier, set up impossible rules which did not take into account the nature of men and women. It should look at people from the point of view of their nature rather than that of religious or political expediency. Property should belong to no one: it is part of the material world and cannot be chopped up into individual parcels without promoting and developing greed, selfishness and, ultimately, violence.

Albert Brisbane introduced Fourierism to America. And, it was a radical philosophy indeed. Women and children, Fourier taught, should never become property. Like men, they too are equal owners in the world they live in.

Fourier also proposed that the secret instinct of the individual is truer than the reasonings of science. For him the monotony of working at the same routine job was both degrading and wasteful. He felt that many women who had to cook meal after meal for their family could easily be freed for more interesting pursuits, "because one vast kitchen with every commodity would replace two or three hundred kitchens."

"Let not the system be excused by saying that the character of woman is particularly adapted to it. It is not so. Her destiny is not to waste her life in the kitchen or in the petty cares of a household. Nature made her the equal of man, and equally capable of shining with him in industry and in the cultivation of the arts and sciences; not to be his inferior, to cook and sew for him, and live dependently at his board. No class could bring so many well founded complaints against the social mechanism as women, for they are truly its slaves."

Fourier envisioned a series of commodities — or phalanxes — which would cooperate with one another. In each phalanx there was a great house consisting of three distinct units. One was for quiet pursuits which included the arts, study, meditation. The productive area was reserved for noisy activity and the children. The third unit contained the banquet halls, kitchens, etc. The plans also included the addition of a building at each end of the commune, one where music, gymnastics and poetry would be practiced, and the other, a place to celebrate men's unity with nature.

Fourier hoped that jobs could be fitted to the personalities of the individuals and their instinctual behavior. Young children, for example, are hyperactive and are especially attracted to dirt and filth. He therefore suggested that the clean-up squads be composed of youngsters. No one should stay on a job too long for monotony was considered a deadly sin. Each person moved from one job to another finding new friends and happiness in his work.

It was the realm of sex that Fourierism ran into its greatest problems in the United States. Since marriage must not exist, if couples were married they had to dissolve their vows. Love was looked on as a universal passion. And Fourier believed that social institutions should see that everyone had a chance at love and sex. Everyone in the community, no matter how unattractive, was to receive his or her share of sex. Certain men and women took upon themselves the pleasant responsibility of providing this minimum amount of sex. Beyond that it was expected that everyone would pursue his or her desires to the extent that their passion took them. There was no criticism of homosexuality, promiscuity or even chastity.

Fourierism envisioned no jails. The only court would be a court of love. Officials were to organize festivals, keep records of the individual's sexual interests and attempt to match their appetites. This court could administer punishment, which most likely would consist of corrective lectures and possible banishment.

Fourier phalanxes reached forty in number in the United States and at least one of them lasted for eighteen years. The influence of Fourier, however, went far beyond the phalanxes. Other communes, such as the intellectual socialist experiment at Brook Farm, Massachusetts, relied heavily on his ideas. Albert Brisbane, with the backing of newspaper publisher-author Horace Greeley, carried the Fourier message throughout the eastern states. Yet, although Brisbane urged adoption of most of Fourier's ideas, he didn't go along with the ultimate sexual freedom that Fourier advocated.

As for Thomas and Mary Nichols, in whose salon Fourierism was incubated, they now launched a program to promote their water-cure theories, opening a medical school with the grandiose name "The American Hydropathic Institute." Within its modest halls Mary held forth on the therapeutic values of water, particularly for the diseases of women and children. And husband Thomas became professor of virtually every other course in the curriculum, including anatomy, physiology, the theory and practice of medicine and surgery, even chemistry. When the institute failed — and that didn't take long — they proposed a School of Life to teach Universal Happiness. They were welcomed to the budding commune called Modern Times, where Josiah Warren, who had been a member of the New Harmony commune, had helped to set up a working organization.

Modern Times was a quiet, tree-shaded colony with some forty-five cottages and was located about twenty-five miles from New York City on Long Island. In the glass-roofed school, children of these spiritualist free lovers learned what a vagina and a penis were, where babies came from and how they got there. It was the first truly avant-garde children's school in the United States.

At Modern Times smoking and drinking were banned. There was no jail. Money was not used, but bank notes, if one had them, were redeemable in food. Marriage couldn't have been simpler. It was observed by tying a red thread around the ring finger and divorce was final when it was untied. No one inquired as to how to identify the father of any of the children born in the group. In this area it was not proper to be curious. As in the Oneida commune, children were taken care of by the community. Outrageous diets were in vogue and at least one young lady died. Her system just couldn't make it on water and unsalted beans. A former minister, when the weather was warm, walked completely naked in the streets. His field of research was "dress reform."

Tom Nichols wrote a how-to-do-it sex handbook called *Esoteric Anthropology,* a best seller in its time with 12,000 copies being distributed. It was a chink in the wall of sexual ignorance and, like Robert Dale Owen's work published in New Harmony in 1831, had an effect far greater than the limited number of copies would indicate. The Robert Dale Owen book, called *Moral Physiology,* not only dealt with women's rights and women's anatomy but also described birth control measures available to women of his time. This included the douche, a primitive kind of diaphragm (the sponge), the condom, *coitus interruptus* and the so-called safe period. Religious groups and moralists tried to ban the volume as obscene but, like Nichol's book, it sold quite well.

As the Modern Times commune began to disintegrate, partly because of the extreme individuality of each member, the Nichols looked for a new location. They moved west to Yellow Springs, Ohio. Except for Antioch College, which had been recently founded, there was not too much going on in Yellow Springs. In a way they found the prime mover of the college, educator Horace Mann, a partial ally. He was a non-drinker, non-smoker and opposed to slavery. He was not, however, a free lover or a spiritualist — rather the opposite.

The Nichols called their commune Memnonia; it was a small one, never numbering more than twenty members, and most of these had come from Modern Times. Having tried absolute freedom, they now tried the opposite, dictatorship on a minor scale. This did not work either. By 1857 the Nichols gave up their good works, joined the Catholic Church and came out publicly for monogamy.

Free love was dead. Of course, other new communes would spring up in coming generations. Free love, spiritualism and all the other "isms" would be popular in the United States at one time or another. But for the moment and for the next forty years sexual experimentation went underground. Anthony Comstock, censorship and sexual ignorance were triumphant.

6

Topsy & Eva, Gold and Girls

The free love movement had been stopped. There was not to be a free love advocate as president of the United States. But as the communes wound down, the issue of black slavery became paramount. The issue was both sexual and economic. Both of these issues, as well as that of human rights, were brought into focus by a brother and sister team. Henry Ward Beecher, whose sexual peccadilloes and spiritual-physical love affairs were touched upon in Chapter 5, and his young sister Harriet Beecher were instruments (of God, they said) that would bring these issues into sharp focus.

Harriet had previously attacked Victoria Woodhull, who was not her type of feminist at all. A petite, demure woman with a modest talent for writing, Harriet Beecher Stowe with newspaper articles, lectures and finally her propaganda bombshell *Uncle Tom's Cabin*, changed the attitudes of millions of Americans toward slavery. Certainly no literary masterpiece, it had a confusing plot, stilted dialogue and dull descriptive passages. But it also had allusions to rape and punishment perpetrated by brutal white slave owners and overseers on delicate, defenseless black females.

Mrs. Stowe's book was a perfect example of what happens with the public when a publication appears at exactly the right time. Writers in the North, and even a few in the South, had touched upon forced miscegenation but, on the whole, they were dry documents. Mrs. Stowe put together a passion play with a saint-like Uncle Tom as her Christ. Sex was never handled overtly but the aura of sadism and sexuality permeated the book.

When a beautiful slave, Rosa, offended her mistress, she was sent to the whipping house for fifteen lashes. The terrified girl says, "I don't mind the whipping so much if Miss Marie or you [her mistress] was to do it. But, to be sent to a man, and such a horrid man, — the shame of it, Miss Feely." The "go-between" that she was addressing, Miss Ophelia, "well knew that it was the universal custom to send women and girls to the whipping houses, to the hands of the lowest men — men vile enough to make this their profession — there to be subjected to brutal exposure and shameful correction." Miss Ophelia intercedes with Marie, Rosa's mistress:

"'But could you not punish her some other way, — some way that would be less shameful?'

"'I mean to shame her. That's just what I want. She has all her life presumed on her delicacy, and her good looks, and her ladylike airs, till she forgets who she is; — and I'll give her one lesson that will bring her down, I fancy.'

"'But, Cousin, consider that, if you destroy delicacy and a sense of shame in a young girl, you deprave her very fast.'

"'Delicacy,' said Marie with a scornful laugh, 'a fine word for such as she. I'll teach her with all her airs that she's no better than the raggediest black wench that walks the street!'"

There is no mistaking what Mrs. Stowe meant in that passage. She wanted her readers to know that the black girls were undressed, examined, whipped and raped. In another passage, when Simon Legree, Mrs. Stowe's incarnation of the devil in human form, goes to a slave auction, she wrote:

"He stopped before Susan and Emmeline. He put out his heavy dirty hand and drew the girl toward him, passed it over her neck and bust, felt her arms, looked at her teeth, and then pushed her back."

Later, when Legree is returning home with his new slave purchases, "Emmeline is terrified; but when he laid his hand on her, and spoke as he now did, she felt as if she would rather he strike her. The expression of his eyes made her soul sick, and her flesh creep . . . 'You didn't ever wear ear-rings,' he said, taking hold of her small ear with his coarse fingers. 'No, mas'r! said Emmeline trembling and looking down. 'Well, I'll give you a pair when we get home, if you're a good girl. You needn't be so frightened. I don't mean to make you work very hard. You'll have fine times with me and live like a lady, — only be a good girl.' Then Legree turned to two brutal slaves who were his overseers. 'Here, you Sambo,' Legree said, 'Take these yere boys down to the quarters; and here's a gal I've got for *you*,' he said, as he separated the mulatto woman [Susan] from Emmeline, and pushed her toward them. 'I promised to bring you one, you know.'"

Descriptions of the violence and the sadistic pleasure taken by slave hunters in catching and torturing escaped blacks, especially women, is standard fare in *Uncle Tom's Cabin.* Tom Loker is described as strong and ruthless, with his brutality revealed in the features of his face. He and his colleagues talk of finding light colored and handsome black women, and they deplore the fact that these black women are difficult to handle especially if they have a child.

"If we could get a breed of girls that didn't care for their younguns," a slave hunter says, "I tell you I think it would be 'bout the greatest mod'rn improvement I knows on."

Slave hunters operated as agents for owners to run down and return escaped slaves. But, as often as not, when they found a good-looking female, they would fail to report her and take her down to New Orleans "to speculate on." In that fast-growing, French-Spanish-American city, there was always a brisk market in prostitutes and potential prostitutes. Girl children from ten years upward brought good prices. Mulatto girls from sixteen to twenty brought the highest prices.

Describing one young mother, Harriet writes, "she was marked out by personal beauty to be the slave of the passions of her possessor and the mother of children who may never know a father."

By the time Mrs. Stowe wrote her book in 1851 when she was forty, slavery was 200 years old in North America. She lived in Cincinnati, Ohio, and just across the river was Kentucky, a slave state. She became an early member of what later became known as the Underground Railroad, a system of passing escaped slaves from one white sympathizer to another until the slave was safely far away from his owner. One night she came in contact with a slave girl that she and her husband sheltered and moved on. Then came a bonanza for a would-be writer. She and her husband employed a mulatto girl as a cook, and she listened avidly as the slave girl told her of the mistreatment of black and mulatto women at the hands of white slave owners and their overseers.

The world of Harriet Beecher Stowe expanded as her conviction that something must be done became ever more pressing. The great debates were beginning. Charles Sumner in the Massachusetts Legislature said: "Slavery is odious as an institution if viewed in the light of morals and Christianity. On this account alone we should refrain from rendering it any voluntary support."

A year before the first weekly installment of *Uncle Tom's Cabin* appeared in a woman's magazine, Henry Clay, John C. Calhoun and Daniel Webster argued the slavery question. Clay declared that he could never vote for slavery and never would. He also said that "there is no right on the part of any one or more of the states to secede from the Union."

John C. Calhoun, representing the South, insisted that the problem could be solved, "The North has only to will it to accomplish it — to do justice by conceding to the South an equal right in the acquired [new] territory, and to do her duty by causing the stipulation relative to fugitive slaves to be faithfully fulfilled — to cease the agitation of the slave question."

Daniel Webster pointed out the impossibility of separating the slave and free states. "We could not separate the states by any such line, if we were to draw it."

The whole country was poised on the brink of war over the status of slaves when *Uncle Tom's Cabin* appeared. It was not so much that its revelations regarding slavery surprised the public as that it satisfied its craving for the drama and excitement as black virtues and white villains were exposed.

In the South the book was not only banned but it

was actually dangerous to own a copy. Although it was hard for Mrs. Stowe to believe, her book had polarized the attitudes of the southern slave holders and the northern abolitionists. From 1853 onward secession and war became an ever greater threat. It is no wonder that, when the war was over and she was received in the White House by President Lincoln, he said, "So you are the little woman who wrote the book that made this great war."

For its time, *Uncle Tom's Cabin* was relatively outspoken. Rape of Negro women and sex with Negro women generally was a taboo subject. Slaves were livestock, for the most part, just as cattle, horses and sheep were and were generally treated in a similar way. That is, except for the young, attractive women who, when ten or twelve, were given house jobs and, by fourteen or fifteen, began bearing children to overseers, masters, managers and, of course, to male household slaves. There are no statistics on how many millions of mulattoes were born in slavery days or how many quadroons and octoroons began passing as white after the Civil War. But the numbers must have been great, and there is no question but that there was an important influx of black genes into the total melting pot that is the United States.

The country's earliest white citizens viewed miscegenation with alarm. But no amount of punishment, exclusion from the church or punitive laws worked. Men and women, Indian, white and black, met and mated. White slave traders — Portuguese, English, Dutch, French and American — impregnated many of the more attractive female slaves before they were even boarded onto ships. Once on the ships, any that they had missed were more than likely to be sexually used by the sailors. So a considerable number of mulattoes were born within the first year that the slaves landed.

White slave owners learned early that mixed marriages between the indentured servants from England and the blacks who worked in the fields with them were a threat to the entire slave system. They well knew that overseers and masters were fathering mulattoes regularly and that this, too, weakened the system of enslaving the blacks. As a result, laws to reduce cohabitation became stricter, punishment swifter.

There have been many conjectures as to the reasons for the phenomenal birthrate among the Africans imported as slaves into the southern and mid-Atlantic states. One explanation might well be that they had no pleasures except the joy of sex and the happiness they took in their children. There were few entertainments. Slave owners were not concerned about the legality of marriage. They were happy to add to the number of workers and to have a stable slave family. There was little or no argument when an overseer or a plantation owner took a female slave as a mistress. She was, in fact, usually pleased at her elevation in status. There was at least some chance that her children by a white man would be freed at some time in their lives. Some attractive black women, no doubt, did all they could to attract the attention of an affluent white man. A considerable number succeeded. There seems to have also been an attitude expressed — when the white man wanted something, he took it. And this applied to sex as well as property.

But what of the dilemma of the black man who found his woman going off to spend her nights in the big house on the hill or at the plantation on the river? For the most part, they too adopted a "what's the use" attitude. They neither approved nor disapproved. It was the only way they could survive. It probably had an ultimate effect on the development of an underlying, continuous resentment against the white man, but this anger was suppressed for the most part or channeled into other areas.

What about the white woman and her sexual relations with the black man? It certainly happened in the earlier days of slavery and continued occasionally into the mid-nineteenth century. But racial prejudice, the enforcement of strict miscegenation laws especially involving women, kept the black male from competing for white women except those women on the lowest economic and social level.

Women immigrating from Europe, Asia and South America, through the menial jobs that they were able to get, frequently came into contact with, and some married, Negro men. On some levels the color line became a mirage. White men occasionally married light mulatto women who could, and often did, pass as whites, and white women sometimes married Negro men who were so light in color they had no idea that they were Negro.

Long ago I heard a story of a white man who asked a mulatto why he thought the white man demanded segregation. He answered, "I don't know. I just can't figure it out — look at my face, it wasn't no black man who hung this face on me."

In plantation households and even in the small farm households where a few slaves were kept, black nursemaids attended the children. There is a saying in the West Indies that it does not matter how many children the white folks have as long as they have black folks to pass them along to.

That the proximity and the intimacy of black girls raising white boys and girls had some psychological effect is likely. There was no great, unfamiliar step to take when a young white man made a black or mulatto girl his mistress. Even as late as 1920 in some portions of Virginia, Louisiana, Mississippi, Alabama, Texas and the Carolinas, black servants, sometimes quite young, had full charge of the rearing of the young, at least up until puberty.

I can vividly remember at the age of five or six having my mulatto nurse undress me, give me a bath and often undress herself to get into the tub with me. The first woman's body that I ever saw or felt was that of my Negro nurse.

Black slavery never became a problem in the Far West. The early settlers — what few there were — had little truck with the institution. California's first newspaper, *Alta California,* reflected this attitude in an early 1848 issue. An editorial proposed that the brand-new state's bill of rights include the phrase: "Neither slavery, nor involuntary servitude, unless for punishment of crimes, shall ever be tolerated." And, indeed, this phrase later became part of California's constitution.

Despite this high-sounding sentiment, slavery of another kind was tolerated and widely accepted from the mouth of the Columbia River south to San Diego: this was the bondage of Indian, Chinese and Mexican women for purposes of sex-for-sale. Long before the Pacific Coast was annexed to the United States, sexual slavery among the Chinook, Flathead and other tribes in the Northwest was well established. Whites were impregnating Indian women before Lewis and Clark reached the mouth of the Columbia River in 1805. Those explorers found evidence of many ships from England, France, Portugal, Russia and the United States putting into harbors along the coast to trade furs with the Indians. Sailors, ships' officers, indeed all of the male personnel, traded for women as well. The asking price, according to Meriwether Lewis, was very little. He wrote:

"Among these people, as indeed among all Indians, the prostitution of unmarried women is so far from being considered criminal or improper, that the females themselves solicit the favours of the other sex, with the entire approbation of their friends and connexions. [Her] person is in fact often the only property of a young female, and is therefore the medium of trade, the return for presents, and the reward for services. In most cases, however, the female is so much at the disposal of her husband or parent, that she is farmed out for hire. The Chinook woman, who brought her six female relations to our camp, had regular prices, proportioned to the beauty of each female; and among all the tribes, a man will lend his wife or daughter for a fish-hook or a strand of beads. To decline an offer of this sort is indeed to disparage the charms of the lady, and therefore gives such offence, that although we had occasionally to treat the Indians with rigour, nothing seemed to irritate both sexes more than our refusal to accept the favours of the females."

Sexual "connections" could last as little as half an hour, a night, a few weeks or months. Occasionally Indian women became permanent common-law wives. But for the most part, these women seem to have been used sexually *en passant.* One young Indian woman, well

decorated by primitive tattoo marks, had the name J. Bowman permanently etched into her flesh. Lewis conjectured that Bowman was a trader or seaman who made regular fishing expeditions to her village. His own sexual relations with Indian women remained unrecorded but Lewis did, in a number of places in his diary, write that his men had such "connections."

These were not, of course, the first Indian women in the Far West to be sexually used by Europeans. That dubious honor goes to the 300 picked soldiers led by Francisco Vásquez de Coronado across what is now parts of Arizona, New Mexico and Oklahoma. As a result of exploratory forays by Europeans between 1540 and 1840, some fifteen generations of hybrid strains had been spawned by the time of the 1849 gold rush. It is not surprising then that these mixed breeds continued to supply women to succeeding generations of Western men. Pioneer trappers, sailors and adventurers had sexual connections not only with pure-blood Indian women but with a myriad of mixed-blood girls. The number of available females was immense. There was no work, almost no way of survival, for girl children of mixed parentage. In addition, West Coast tribes, for the most part, were poor, often hungry, with no resources except hunting and fishing. The coming of white men meant guns with which to procure more food, horses with which to follow game and attack other tribes, blankets to keep warm; knives, axes, candles and other western tools to make living supportable. And rum — that warmed the blood and fired the imagination.

Indeed, the Indians considered the white men quite stupid: they were puzzled why traders would give away such valuable, almost miraculous, products in return for the skins of dead animals or the sexual use of their women.

Personal journals of the early trappers of the Far West, such as that of Alexander Henry, the younger, and his father, the elder, give a fairly clear picture of white-Indian relationships. Both worked for the old Northwest Company, the great fur trading rival of the Hudson's Bay Company. In the son's diary that runs from 1799 to 1814, he admits that he has cleaned up the rough language of the trappers because he did not feel he could use "the blunt speech of the trading post." Yet he spoke freely of the beauty and nakedness of the Indian women, their shamelessness after washing themselves in the river and then drying their bare bodies by the fire. He gives the impression that although his greatest interest was the give and take of trading for furs, he lent a sympathetic ear to the sexual interests of his men. From his diary it is obvious that he indulged himself from time to time in women he believed to be free of disease.

Henry seemed to reject more women who offered themselves than he accepted. One chief, Old Buffalo, brought in his daughter, a virgin who was about nine years old. He wanted Henry to take her as a wife in eturn for a keg of whiskey. Henry said he turned down the offer.

One gets the impression that there was an unwritten but unbreakable law among the Indian tribes — and this appears to have been general throughout the West — that a woman could only be used sexually with the consent of her husband or father. Once, when a comely, slim, eighteen-year-old Indian girl left her husband and moved in with Henry, he reluctantly, but forcefully, returned her to her husband. There she boldly angered her spouse by saying that she loved the white man and was going back to him again. Henry quotes the Indian as saying to her that he would "have the satisfaction of spoiling your pretty face." Whereupon he took a glowing brand from the fire, threw the girl onto her back and held her down while rubbing the fiery stick over her face until the glow was gone. "Now go and see your beloved."

"Her face," reports Henry, "was in a horrid condition. I never had connection with her. She told me that, if I would have her, she would stay always." This is probably just what Henry feared.

Survival was not only difficult for women but for outcast men as well. Some half-breed trappers willingly put themselves into bondage to a trading company for varying periods of time, even life, providing the company would clothe them and supply them with an Indian woman. One of Henry's men offered to go into perpetual bondage in return for warm clothing, a little tobacco and a woman.

A French trapper-guide named Livernois exchanged his expensive mare for a young wife said to be about eight years old. It could be that Henry erred on this point or he usually talks of wives ranging between twelve and seventeen. Henry observed that the mare had cost him sixteen pounds, thirteen shillings and four pence, which Henry remarked was incredibly expensive for any woman, when an overnight connection could be had for as little as a single coat button.

Life was indeed cheap, wild, exciting and dangerous on the frontier. The combination of liquor and women was especially volatile. Trappers beat their wives frequently. One churl, while fighting with his, fell into the campfire and was almost roasted. He crawled out, smoking, with strength enough to bite the woman's nose off.

Extreme cruelty was common among the Indian tribes. Many early Western diarists record how captives were tortured unmercifully and slaughtered. Henry sets forth an incident in which a group of Sioux attacked a small, isolated group of Saultier Indians. The Sioux killed both the men and the women, cut off one man's genitals and stuffed them into his wife's mouth. Bodies were dismembered, scalps were taken, children were enslaved.

The journal sometimes reads like it is describing a scene from a jungle hell. Both men and women indulged in three-day drinking matches. First came the rum, then the fights, more rum and more fights — with guns, knives and axes. But, in contrast, there were peaceful dances in the moonlight where, says Henry, after dancing and singing, Indian couples lay down and openly had sex together.

That wives were virtually slaves in many tribes is indicated by the story of Le Borgne, chief of the Big Bellies. He had many wives and added to them whenever he saw a woman he liked. When one of his wives left him for a younger man while he was away on a hunt, he immediately noticed her absence upon his return. He asked where she was and, when the tent was pointed out, he walked in, dispatched her with an ax, ignoring her lover who was standing nearby.

Homosexuals, who are referred to in Henry's journals as "berdash," were common and he mentions them frequently. These were men who dressed and who were used as women. The word in Indian, as reported by Henry, was *a-go-kwa*. One of them that he describes had many husbands and was a curious mixture of male and female. According to Henry they show the courage of a man but "nevertheless they pretend to be a woman and dress as such. They walk like women, sit like women and flirt with men."

In the Mandan country of the Dakotas Henry verified the reports of Meriwether Lewis by writing that men there offered their wives to the Europeans without solicitation, expecting a mere trifle in return. "They are deeply offended if the sexual favors of their wives are refused — the wives are even more offended." Then Henry adds an interesting custom about Mandan women. He says that those with long vulva lips were considered especially attractive and made exciting bed mates. He describes these exaggerated lips as "a good swinging pair of contrevents." Some of the women, he wrote, had naturally long labia but the others, when they were still young girls, pulled on them (and so did men) and this continued until maturity, when the lips were several inches long on each side of the vaginal opening. Some females suspended weights to make the lips longer.

Not only English, French and American trappers took up with Indian women, but such well-known scouts as Jim Bridger and Kit Carson, two legendary Western heroes, had Indian wives. Actually, the word "wife" as used in books on the West rarely meant a spouse either in the legal sense or even in the common-law sense. A "wife" was a euphemism for having a sexual connection with a woman, sometimes on a temporary, more rarely on a permanent, basis. The early explorers simply did not know how to mention intercourse in their journals. They used words like "connection" and, occasionally, "intercourse" and usually wrote that this chief or that offered his daughter as a "wife." There were actually few wedding ceremonies.

"Prostitute" is another misleading word in these

103

journals. By almost every definition a prostitute is a woman who usually has a limited amount of freedom. Unlike a slave, she is paid for her sexual services, and in most cases has some sexual choices.

The slave, in effect, does not prostitute herself but rather is forced to make herself sexually available. An Indian woman whose body was rented out for a button or a twist of tobacco or a drink of rum, received no recompense herself, nor did she have any part in the sexual arrangements. She — like many of the Mexican, Chilean and especially the Chinese girls later imported into the West — fell into the category of sexual slavery. So before 1800 there were no "prostitutes" in the West.

White women were not just rare in the early West; they were almost nonexistent. Alexander Henry tells a fascinating story of finding a young white lad from the Scottish islands kneeling on the floor of his cabin:

"He stretched out his hands toward me and in piteous tones begged me to be kind to a poor, helpless, abandoned wretch who was not of the sex I had supposed, but an unfortunate Orkney girl, pregnant, and actually in childbirth. In saying this she opened her jacket and displayed a pair of beautiful round white breasts. Her child, born the next day, was the first white child to be born in the Pacific Northwest."

This girl had for three years been masquerading as a man. Only one person, John Scart, who was also from the Orkney Islands, knew that she was a female. It was by him that she had become pregnant. A year after this incident, in 1806, another white woman, Madame Lajimonière, came to the Northwest from Three Rivers, Quebec.

But Alexander Henry's great romantic adventure was yet to come. For the third white woman to arrive on the West Coast was a sexy British blonde, an ex-barmaid from Portsmouth, England, Jane Barnes. She had traveled by sailing vessel, the *Isaac Todd*, for thirteen months sharing the bed of fur-trader Donald McTavish, a rich, adventurous, middle-aged Scotsman who plucked her out of England by making her an interesting proposition. In return for being his traveling companion he promised her a wardrobe of silk and satin dresses, a comfortable trip and a generous settlement when they returned to England. McTavish followed through on most of his promises. The ship was well stocked with wines, beer and tinned beef.

Jane Barnes seems to have had a reasonably pleasant journey to the mouth of the Columbia, arriving on April 17, 1814. None of the men at the trading post of the Northwest Company had seen a white woman for such a long time that Miss Barnes was treated like a queen.

When Alexander Henry went aboard the *Isaac Todd*, he was disappointed by his tasteless breakfast but surprised and delighted to meet a white woman. After walking around the ship and talking to McTavish, he asked for something more to eat before returning to shore. This time, the fare was better: a bit of cheese, brown biscuit and some port wine. A discussion ensued between Donald McTavish, Henry McDougall, one of his clerks, and the flaxen-haired Jane. It was about the easy sexual access that men had to Chinook women and the subject of venereal diseases. Henry, who thought women should be protected from such conversation, objected to continuing it in the presence of Jane.

It is difficult to trace the exact movements of Jane, her lover-benefactor McTavish and Alexander Henry from this point. But Henry met Jane on April 24, one week after her arrival. On the 26th McTavish and Jane came ashore for a couple of hours, and Henry entertained them by opening a cask of bottled porter and a cask of moldy biscuit.

While a room was being made ready for McTavish and Jane, a group of Chinook ladies came to visit. They wanted to look at the white queen and to "trade cranberries and their precious favors." When Henry heard that some of the *Isaac Todd*'s crew had already begun to feel the effects of their "communications" with the Chinook women, he conjectured that these men were certainly infected with a venereal disease.

A few days later, probably after a fight about money, McTavish decided to get rid of the blonde Jane. By mutual consent she was to be turned over to Alexander Henry, who insisted that "affection is out of the question; our acquaintance is too short." On Sunday, May 8, Jane arrived with "bag and baggage," and took up her lodging in Alexander Henry's room. Two days later McTavish and Henry went on a long walk and came to an understanding for future arrangements regarding Jane. By this time Henry seems to have changed his mind about "affection." He said that his course was clear and that in every respect he was determined to support what he conceded were his rights, "even at the displeasure of every person on the Columbia." This indicates that there was probably a good deal of jealousy in the camp and that Henry had decided to keep Jane exclusively for himself.

On the evening this decision was made, three of the staff of the fort each selected a Chinook woman to spend the night with them. Donald McTavish even moved out of his bedroom for the convenience of these other men, and the next morning went back to the ship to fetch his baggage. At the fort he took up lodging in an unfinished room, and shortly afterward he got a Mrs. Clapp into his bed. She was the former Indian wife of B. Clapp, a clerk who left her and later entered the United States Naval Service. McTavish seems to have enjoyed his "*tête plate*," (Flathead woman) for he clothed her in a fine black broadcloth dress which, writes Henry, "cost twenty-three shillings sterling a yard" — a right high price for the time.

The arrangement seemed to be working out pretty well. McTavish had his Indian girl and Henry had Jane

Unfortunately, neither of them enjoyed their women for very long. Just twelve days after Jane moved in and five days after McTavish took up with his squaw, both men were drowned. They had embarked in an open boat to proceed to the opposite side of the Columbia River. Somewhere near the middle a heavy wave struck the boat, which instantly filled and went down.

Comely, statuesque Jane then made another unwitting conquest at the fort. She caught the eye of the son of the chief of the Chinooks, Cassakas, who wore little clothing but kept his body well greased with whale oil. This kept off mosquitoes and other biting insects and may have also helped to keep the Indians warm.) He courted Jane with daily visits and, according to another diarist at Fort George, promised that if she would marry him he would make her mistress over his other four wives, send one hundred sea otters and a huge quantity of dried salmon to her relatives, never ask her to carry wood, draw water or dig for roots and that he would "permit her to sit at ease from morning til night," smoking as many pipes of tobacco as she thought proper. Furthermore, instead of the tree bark apron (which exposed the brown buttocks of the Chinook women), Cassakas declared magnanimously that Jane could wear her western dresses. He ended his plea for her white body by saying that "she would always have an abundance of fat salmon, anchovies and elk."

Jane turned down Cassakas's generous offer. She declared, uncharitably, that she would never cohabit with "a Flathead, a half-naked body and copper-colored skin besmeared with whale oil." Cassakas considered kidnapping her but, after being warned, Jane kept close to the men at the fort and her Indian admirer gave up.

Jane also refused to become the mistress of the fort's surgeon, Dr. Swan, who offered to take her in. But she did stay on for four months at Fort George because there was no place else to go.

The record of Jane's life after this becomes a little blurred, albeit still libidinous. One version indicates that after her dalliance in the Northwest she sailed on to China aboard the *Isaac Todd*. Another account reports that she went to China aboard the U.S. ship *Columbia* (the first U.S. vessel to circumnavigate the globe), which departed the Northwest Territory about a month before the *Isaac Todd*. Jane is said to have become in Canton the temporary mistress of an English businessman. In any event, it is a fact that Captain Robson, of the *Columbia*, gave up command of his vessel in China, and he and Jane sailed back to Europe together on another ship. Once back in England, Jane tried to collect the annuity Donald McTavish had promised her. But she didn't succeed. She may actually have ended up marrying the American captain, for it is believed that she revisited the mouth of the Columbia at a later date as Mrs. Robson.

It was some forty years after Jane Barnes's first visit to the West before women from the East and from Europe began filtering into the Far West. When Richard Henry Dana, Jr., who was gathering material for his literary epic *Two Years Before the Mast*, arrived on the *Pilgrim* in 1834, he commented, as had earlier visitors, on the fact that Indian husbands brought their wives down to the ship to offer them at a price for sexual use.

But conditions in the West were to change radically within the next decades. Three years before the gold rush, on the dockside at Yerba Buena (the village that later grew into San Francisco), a new breed of woman was available for sex to the sailors and trappers visiting northern California. Some girls had been imported or had traveled with their parents or pimps from Mazatlán, Guaymas and San Blas in Mexico. Many came from Peru and represented different mixtures of Spanish Indian, mulatto, Spanish Peruvian, chollas and other mixtures of European, South American and Mexican blood. They were soon to be joined by French women from the Marquesas Islands and a considerable number of women that had made their way from Valparaiso, Chile. There were so many of these that what is now Telegraph Hill in San Francisco was called "Little Chile."

A few North American white women began to trickle westward. Some followed the army that moved into the Southwest at the beginning of the war with Mexico. Others had preceded them into Texas and Oklahoma. But from 1846 they came in ever increasing numbers. In that year General Zachary Taylor attacked and defeated the Mexicans at the battle of Palo Alto. By this time volunteer soldiers were flooding into Texas and New Mexico. With them were a few wives but even more camp followers. These women brought more than sexual satisfaction — with them came the beginnings of a civilization that made the West more livable for explorers, miners and cowboys.

In early western life the barroom was the center of social life. It was frequently the first commercial building completed in a town and its fixtures were crude. Sometimes the bar consisted of a heavy plank set across two boxes. Shortly after the barroom came the whorehouse — usually called (politely) the sporting house, the cat house and the heifer or the cow yard. Even tents were employed for assignations; occasionally, covered wagons became brothels. Sex was available on many levels. There were the camp followers, the local Mexican girls and the occasional women who moved in from the eastern cities to become the first madams of the West.

The woman shortage was so bad that one San Francisco resident wrote, "Dancing is a principal amusement here but it is pretty much of a stag order, as we are short of petticots — except the squaws which indeed wear no petticots — but only a light wrapper. They are an affeckshynut disposition, but all-fired yellar." The miners did indeed dance a great deal and, because of the scant supply of female partners, any man selected to play the woman's role wore a bandana tied around his arm. Occasionally, when drunk enough, a rough, bearded type would tie on a bonnet and a gingham apron — if available — to prance around in.

From 1800 to 1859 the Indian population of California received a great injection of European genes due to this scarcity of white women. Future generations of American Indians could count these white men among their ancestors.

As news of the gold strikes grew in the East, Americans by the thousands went West. At least 45,000 went overland through the central route, 10,000 took the southern route through Arizona and New Mexico, and 15,000 more crowded into clipper ships and traveled around the Horn. During the period from January 1848, when a workman in California's Sacramento Valley discovered gold at Sutter's Mill, until the end of 1852 — five frantic years — about a quarter of a million Americans converged on northern California. Overnight mining villages such as Red Dog and Poker Flat mushroomed.

The population of San Francisco and Sacramento exploded. In June 1847 San Francisco had boasted only 400 people. This had doubled to 812 by March of 1848. Then the migrations began. Within six months the population had jumped to 2000. By 1851 the city had a population of more than 25,000. Inflation was unbelievable. Eggs sold for as much as a dollar each. It cost a pinch of gold, worth perhaps sixteen dollars, to buy a shot of whiskey. The editor of the *Alta California* predicted that San Francisco was "destined to become the first city in industry and importance on the West Coast."

As Eastern men began to journey West to make their fortunes in the gold mines, leaving their wives and children, sweethearts or mistresses, many a song, such as "Joe Bowers," celebrated the hardships involved in making money for the women left behind.

"Says I, 'My dearest Sallie,
    O Sallie! for your sake
I'll go to California
    And try to raise a stake.'
Says she to me, 'Joe Bowers,
    You are the chap to win,
Give me a kiss to seal the bargain,'
    And I throwed a dozen in."

Most of these ballads had a sad ending. When word came to Joe Bowers that his Sallie had switched to another man and had borne a red-haired child, the moral seems to have been that gold was not the answer to happiness.

The discovery of gold had also been a signal heard round the world for prostitutes to gather in California. There were few white women in the earliest western migrations. In the first six months of 1849, 110 vessels brought some 9000 males — but only about 500 females — on the arduous sailing trip around the Horn and up the Pacific Coast. In addition, some 5000 Mexicans made it by land during this brief span and 2000 Chileans arrived by boat. By 1851 at least 2000 whores from New York, New Orleans, France and England were hard at work using their bodies to separate miners and trappers from their gold.

During that first year after the discovery of gold, a noted courtesan, generally known as "the Countess," arrived from New Orleans and established herself in a large house. Judge E. O. Crosby, in one of his many long letters, wrote that the Countess was "one of the pioneers" and that she had as part of her entourage six or eight young ladies, "most of them beautiful girls."

To the Countess must go credit for San Francisco's early cultural evolution. For she gave regular receptions, sending out engraved cards to the prominent men of the city. Few turned down her invitations. There were very few females in the city and the Countess and her girls were always beautifully dressed, always cheerful and charming. Men were delighted by this display of female beauty and they found the appointments — excellent china, soft lights, a piano to accompany the dancers — irresistible. To augment the supply of females for her parties the Countess even invited madams and their girls from the other houses that had sprung up in town. Men who attended wore evening dress and white gloves. The early part of the evening could not have been more respectable. Champagne was served and, after the dancing and whist, an elegant supper was laid out. Afterwards those who wished would withdraw and, as Judge Crosby delicately put it, "a different character of entertainment" made up the balance of the night.

Because few men brought their families to California, the Countess entertained not only judges and members of the legislature, but also business leaders and ministers. An evening with the Countess in the winter of '49-'50 was a rare treat. Six ounces of gold was the price. The judge remarked, "Those girls who took care of their money became very rich."

To understand the role of the western whore in the bringing of civilization to the West, it is necessary to realize the importance of these women to the communities. The demand always exceeded the supply. Respectable women who married were isolated from the all-male community. Prospectors, miners and workmen generally had only one home, usually the parlor houses in the city. The only time they cut their hair, washed or shaved was when they expected to see a woman. In the better whorehouses they not only saw beautiful women but beautiful clothing, luxurious furnishings, books, paintings — and the ever-present music. Some establishments even had string quintets although most settled for a piano. The sporting women brought civilization with hem: not sunbonnets but Paris millinery; not mother hubbards but sequined gowns. They were among the true tamers of the Wild West.

French women were said to be the most talented and most prosperous. Yet every successful parlor house had at least one Jewish girl, red-headed if possible, for it was commonly believed that they were the "hottest" of all women. One madam who made a fortune with a chain of houses had placed a red-headed Jewish girl in every one.

In San Francisco it was said that the respectable women of the town copied the fashions imported by the courtesans. But as travelers went through outlying early towns, stagecoach curtains were often drawn when they would pass the houses in which such women as Contrary Mary, Peg Leg Annie, the blonde pubic-haired Cotton Tail and Velvet Ass Rose guaranteed sexual satisfaction to all patrons.

One physician, Dr. William W. Sanger, was so curious about the "why" of prostitution that he made a survey of two thousand women. Interestingly enough, he found that approximately half of them enjoyed their work and went into prostitution because they preferred it to other endeavors. The other half were mixed. Many answered that they became whores because they had no money. Some were introduced into the profession by their boyfriends; some were deserted by their families.

As San Francisco and other cities in the West grew, so did the other elements of the prostitution trade. Just below the "fancy" houses were the "parlor houses," where a percentage of the girls' earnings went back to their owners. The bottom level, sometimes called the "boat" girls, did their trade in the street "cribs," where, again, they received only a small percentage of their earnings. This bottom class was expendable. Some writers have mentioned that they were not allowed to refuse any customer, which would mean that even the most venereal-disease-ravaged man would have to be accommodated. This seems, to me, doubtful. The Chinese and the French, Spanish and American brothel keepers all knew how valuable their property was. I suspect that at least a cursory examination was made and that there was always a bouncer available to throw out a too-diseased, too-violent or too-drunk customer.

Along with the American and European whores came the Chinese. The Chinese invasion actually started in 1849 when one Chinese man and two Chinese women came to San Francisco. A year later five more Chinese women arrived. By 1852 the number had swollen to several hundred.

The Chinese managed to successfully bring in boatload after boatload of girls for the trade. A typical report of June 9, 1860, stated the "ships *Viking, Renown* and *Early Bird* arrived Tuesday from Hong Kong bringing 1096 Chinese slaves." Within one month, from May 1 to June 9, a total of 3722 Chinese women were landed.

A Chinaman who was convicted in Stockton of keeping a brothel was fined one hundred dollars. He paid the fine with 200 half-dollars — which he received from his customers one at a time. It wasn't long after this before the City Marshall of Stockton declared a war on Chinese prostitution.

Not all Chinese imports were feminine, however. Coolie laborers also began to arrive. As early as the winter of '49, a letter from the mines read, "The Chinese is beginning to come in but the boys don't like their long tails nor the way their eyes is set in their heads." The Chinese were not the only ones the so-called native Americans did not like. Also mentioned were the Irish, the Scotch, the "nigger," the "yellow bellies" and the John Bulls, as well as Australians — even Russian sailors who jumped ship — who were crowding into the mines. Because so many of the native Californians were Mexican, they got a little better break and quite a number of fortunes were mined in early Mexican claims.

If the Chinese were puzzled with American food, American drinks and American customs, they perfectly understood gambling and the sale of sex, more generally known as gash, cunt and pussy. Chinese prostitution trade was better organized probably because the traders took no interest in the sexual charms of their merchandise and graded them more carefully. A well-brought-up young *me-me* would bring a top price as a concubine to a rich merchant, trader or gambler.

One of the earliest Chinese girls to hit it big in San Francisco was a particularly lovely *me-me* called Ah Toy. She had the body of a pocket Venus and the mind of a banker. Soon after starting her career in the crib section of San Francisco, there was supposedly a line of men a block long waiting each day to spend their sperm and their money on her. There were lines in front of other cribs, too, but exotic Ah Toy was most in demand. Within a year she had moved up to the status of madam, with her own house. "Ah Toy," wrote Judge Crosby, was "select in her associations." The judge was right, for her major association was with one of the powerful secret Chinese societies, the Hip Sing Tong (later referred to by Americans as "highbinders"). By 1852 she had become an agent for them and was buying up and placing girls by the hundreds, perhaps thousands. It was a fantastically profitable business, for young Chinese women could be purchased for twenty to one hundred dollars in China and sold in San Francisco for $300 to $3000.

Professing to be benevolent societies, the tongs were in effect a Chinese Mafia. They controlled Chinese prostitution completely. Blackmail was routine and their "soldiers" were "hit men." One of the documents that has survived reads that these men were instructed to "go under orders to all vessels arriving in port with prostitutes on board and . . . be on hand to receive them." If a member should be killed in performance of his duties, the tong paid $500 to his family or friends. Should he be wounded, he would receive ten dollars a month; added to this was $250 if he were maimed for life. Should a member be put in jail, the family would receive ten dollars a month. The memorandum further stated, "Exert yourself to kill, or wound anyone at the direction of this tong." When one considers the amount of vitriol thrown in the faces of prostitutes who tried to escape, and the number of them who disappeared completely, one understands that the tongs expected their instructions to be taken seriously.

The opium trade, relatively uncontrolled, brought great profits to the tongs, even though the opium habit could then be satisfied for as little as ten cents a day. Within an eight-year period at least a half-million pounds of opium was imported into San Francisco. One minister, the Reverend Masters, preached that the love of narcotics was a universal vice: "The Malays had their betel nut; the Persians, Turks and East Indians, hemp; the Chinese opium and everyone tobacco and alcohol." Opium, though bad enough, was not considered as dangerous as alcohol by the clergyman. He reasoned that it was a mild drug and that, while it might kill you, it did not inflame your passions as did alcohol, which could cause you to kill someone else.

The tongs had a tendency to fight among themselves, and Chinese dead from unknown causes were common in early San Francisco. Street wars sometimes started when one tong stole women from another. All of the tongs employed American lawyers, the best that money could buy. If a girl did manage to escape from a house, she was immediately charged with stealing. There was no chance for her to beat the rap; the evidence was carefully manufactured. At the same time she was told that if she returned to the brothel all the charges would be dropped. Rather than go to jail, she usually returned.

It is probable that at least one half of Chinatown paid tribute to the tongs. Yet when the organizations were investigated they seemed to have no official offices nor could the membership be identified. It is not too surprising that the early San Francisco police force couldn't cope with the Chinese gangsters. For one thing, there was not an officer on the force who could speak Chinese.

There were, of course, many Chinese in San Francisco for legitimate reasons. But while many of these wanted law and order, the tongs would only allow them to have it at a price. By 1890 Chinatown was controlled by at least twenty "highbinders," or tong societies.

For an article in *California Illustrated Magazine* of February 1892 Mary Grace Edholm interviewed many prostitutes. She concluded that "Negro slavery does not compare with Chinese slavery in the United States." She recites one case history of a girl who had been kidnapped at the age of eighteen in China and sold for $400 upon arrival. Forced to become a brothel slave, she was

resold for $1700. Another girl had been sold by her parents in China at the age of ten and brought to the United States, where she was purchased right off the ship for $500. Yet another young girl reported that she had been kept under drugs after her arrival, introduced into a brothel and sold for $2970. Most of these unfortunate creatures believed that they were being taken to meet their future husbands. One girl repeated that she had been told: "[She] would have a rich husband and a fine time in California." She had been taught to say, when she arrived, that she was returning to San Francisco and had a husband on Jackson Street. After swearing that she had lived there with him, she was admitted by the authorities — and straightaway was taken to a brothel, where she was starved, beaten and her life threatened. She was finally sold for $1530. One of these girls recalled she was first sold for $185 and then for $600. When she tried to run away, the tong sent a soldier to shoot her. But he missed and she escaped to a Christian mission.

There were two schools of thought among the owners of prostitutes. One group believed it to be better for their workers to have children and add them to the work force as soon as their age would permit. Meanwhile, they were used as child laborers from the age of eight until they were twelve or thirteen. Young children, especially females, brought good prices. At the age of ten, females were sold for as much as $500. But by holding onto them until they reached thirteen or fourteen, their owner could demand, and get, $2000.

The second group believed that children were an added expense; that for at least three months before delivery the girls were useless as prostitutes, and that the support of the children was not worth the amount they ultimately would bring on the market.

Mrs. Edholm describes a slave market on Dupont Street which was called The Queen's Room. There, girls were introduced to potential purchasers, stripped, carefully examined and sold. She wrote that "a device only employed in the case of lower animals" was used on many of the girls. No one knows how many thousands of crude, surgical operations were performed. It consisted of a tubal ligation, the tying of the Fallopian tubes so that pregnancy could not result from intercourse. These operations were performed with no anesthetic other than whiskey or, perhaps in the case of the Chinese girls (upon whom the majority of such procedures were performed) opium may have been used.

While San Francisco was beginning to acquire its sheen of bawdy sophistication, French, Irish and American women who were described as neither maid, wife nor widow — in other words, prostitutes — began to stream into the rugged, upcountry mining regions. Some went by the more delicate handle of "slingers" or "waiter girls" — but all served on the side as bar and dance girls. For twenty-five cents a john could buy a dance with a girl, and that two bits included a drink or, at his option, a cigar as well. The girls got a percentage.

There was little luxury in the lower class whorehouses. Most of the business was done in total darkness — and almost always with some clothing on. Men didn't dare take off their boots or trousers for fear that they would be stolen. The girls usually wore a loose wrapper that could be pulled up above their breasts. Candles and lamps were dangerous. If they got knocked over during a sex bout, the crib or wooden house was likely to go up in flames immediately. It was not unusual, therefore, for the great majority of citizens to have their sexual relations in the dark.

Among the outstanding women of the mining country was Julia Bulette, "the harlot with the heart of gold." She settled in Virginia City when gold was found in the Comstock Lode in 1858. Slowly she developed the most popular parlor house between St. Louis and San Francisco. She was acclaimed for having the best girls and for running a "straight house," which meant that her patrons were protected while on her premises. It was believed that she had come from France, though there were rumors that she was a Creole from New Orleans. Her house became the center of Virginia City. She imported paintings, hand-carved furnishings and brass bedsteads. From her admirers she collected expensive jewels. Unfortunately, one morning she was found dead, strangled on her magnificent bed, her jewels missing. A diligent hunt for her murderer was organized and a general holiday was declared in Virginia City for her funeral. Only the so-called respectable women stayed away. Even their husbands attended.

It took a year for the citizenry to catch her killer. Then John Millain was found with some of her jewelry. The respectable women of the town tried to get him off by advancing the argument that he had done a service to everybody by killing Julia. But the trial was a short one. He was found guilty. The day he was hanged, like the day of Julia's funeral, was a city holiday.

Kitty LeRoy was another of the well-known courtesans. She was a gambler with a fine, professional reputation who built one of the outstanding sporting houses in Deadwood, South Dakota, before going farther West. Kitty, like Julia, was said to be French. That she was a beauty there is no doubt. She was a superb pistol shot. Men found her so interesting that she had married five of them by the age of twenty-eight. She managed to desert, divorce or intimidate (she parted the hair of one of her husbands when she cracked his skull with a pistol) four of them. And, although she was quick on the draw, her fifth husband was quicker. Kitty died at twenty-eight

from heart failure — when a bullet went through it.

Women, with the exception of prostitutes and the occasional school teacher, were never welcome at the mines. Actually, it was generally considered that women were bad luck whenever they came close to a mine. This superstition was laid down in the mines of Europe long before the gold rush but continued as part of Western folklore. It probably can be traced to the fact that women usually came to mines after a disaster to wait to see if their husband or lover was among the dead. Ghost stories are still told of women shrouded in black having been seen around the mines, sometimes in the early dawn, sometimes at night. What has that got to do with sex? Well, in the early days of underground mining, each man carried a candle. And should the candle go out three times, he could be sure that his wife was cheating on him or being raped while he was at work.

The western environment (with the exception of the slave types, Indian and Chinese) produced women who often emerged from the anonymity of the parlor houses and even the cribs. Such a woman was Pearl Hart, shady lady, stagecoach robber and all-round hell raiser. Like a few of her respectable sisters, she was a feminist. She believed in equal rights for women, with a difference. If men could carry guns, so could women. If men could dress in high-heeled cowboy boots and Stetson hats, why not women? She had a lover who was neither a mack nor a loafer but a partner. His name was Joe Boot. Like a considerable number of the women who affected their environment in the West, Pearl was willing to go where men, women, angels and devils feared to tread. After holding up a stagecoach and being identified by the passengers as the robber, she had enough style and enough brains to get herself acquitted by flirting with and confusing a frontier jury. But she was so obviously guilty and the judge was so irate that he insisted that she be tried once more; this time for stealing the stage driver's gun, which was found in her possession. She couldn't wriggle out of this charge and was sentenced to five years. Her lover got thirty.

No one paid much attention to Joe Boot. He escaped easily and was never heard from again. As soon as Pearl got into her cell she began making plans to get out. Her ploy was to insist that she had become pregnant since being put into jail. However, as she well knew, only two keys could open her cell. One was held by the warden, the other by his wife. And the only two people to visit her alone were the governor of the Arizona Territory and the warden. This put her in a strong bargaining position. The governor quickly pardoned her on the condition that she leave Arizona never to return. To the newspapers he reported that her pardon was primarily due to the lack of accommodations for women in the Yuma jail. Pearl had been examined previously by a nurse (whom she may have bribed), who declared her to be pregnant. Whether she actually was pregnant no one ever knew. She got out of town and kept her promise never to come back to Yuma, Arizona.

Another colorful western madam was "Cattle Kate" Watson, who seems to have started her career as a prostitute in Cheyenne, Wyoming. She moved on to Rawlins, Wyoming, where she developed a sideline business by stocking a small homestead with unbranded cattle that she accepted for her favors instead of money. Cash was scarce but cattle rustled from the surrounding ranches was plentiful.

Cattle Kate was about twenty-eight years old when she picked up a friend who had a saloon-grocery store-post office, Jim Averill. Wyoming was a "no woman" country, and even though Cattle Kate was not a great beauty and inclined to be overweight, she was a rare feminine flower to the rough cowhands of the region. Cattle Kate and Jim got along well with each other, Averill running the bar and Kate branching out into a "cow yard" operation.

She and her partner-pimp began to prosper, and Kate's small ranch began to see many mavericks run through it on their way to market. Then the stock growers association, enemies of the small ranchers, decided to keep an eye on Cattle Kate's unbranded stock ranch. Calves belonging to nearby ranchers were found in Kate's corral. Somebody was rustling their cattle and selling them to Kate for money or sex. The ranchers moved in and arrested the pair, saying they had a warrant. In short order the lynchers took Kate and Jim out to some scrub trees and hanged them both. A young boy, Gene Crowder, saw them taken away and ran off to find a friend of theirs, Frank Buchanan, who notified the sheriff. But it was three days before the sheriff's posse finally arrived.

The guilty men were identified but freed on bail. Before their trial Frank Buchanan disappeared, and the chief witness, fourteen-year-old Gene Crowder, died suddenly. With no witnesses, the killers of Cattle Kate went free.

Best known of all the independent women of the West was Calamity Jane. She probably learned her ancient trade in her mother's house — for her mother was the madam of The Bird Cage, a brothel in Blackfoot, Montana. Jane got an early start in the sex-for-pay business. By the time she was seventeen she had been "working on the railroad" taking care of lusty section hands who spent their days laying rails and their nights laying any women available.

Yet Jane was more than a prostitute. She was a deadeye pistol shot, an expert rifleman, and could crack a bullwhip like a man. Her early exploits included shooting up the ground under a cowboy called Darling Bob MacKay after he said something she resented about the odor of her underwear.

By the time she was twenty-four, she was the only woman among 1500 men who left Fort Laramie with a supply train for the United States Army's expedition against the Sioux Indians. Although Indian women had been bathing naked in the streams of the West for hundreds of years, Jane was the first white girl to get caught swimming naked with her male buddies near Sheridan, Wyoming.

She seems to have been egocentric, passionate, promiscuous, energetic and talented. It was said that to get Jane into bed you needed only to buy her a drink. She fought Indians, cowboys and, occasionally, other women. She also boasted that she was the only woman who had been both a whore in, and a patron of, a whorehouse. She once declared that, dressed as a man and using a dildo, she could put on an act that would convince any prostitute that she was a male.

Why was Jane called Calamity? There are three theories. One, because she may have usually been infected with a venereal disease and it was a calamity to have a connection with her. Another, that she was such a first-rate pistol and rifle shot that it was a calamity to be opposed by her. A third may have come from her real name, which was either Mary Jane Conarry or Canary. Perhaps she was known as a child as Canary Jane, which in time became Calamity Jane.

It was a rough life for women in the West, though probably no rougher than it was for men. Western men admitted to only two kinds of women, pure and impure. A pure woman was one who had sex only with marriage, and there were many of these who came west with their husband-soldiers; a great many of them became early widows during the Indian Wars. No one will ever know how many women were actually captured by Indians in the West, then raped and tortured, sometimes killed.

According to Colonel James F. Meline in his first-hand account *Two Thousand Miles on Horseback* published in 1867, long after the gold rush, *all* captive white women were raped by the Indians who captured them. In most cases, according to Meline, the Indians usually "passed her over the prairie," which meant being raped by all the Indians present at her capture. Meline continued, "This is a lot awaiting the female made captive by any Indians west of the Mississippi. It is invariable, and the mere statement of outrage and violation is but a meager indication of such a woman's sad fate." Meline points out that a woman captive would be fortunate to be made the slave of one Indian rather than turned over to the tribe.

Ironically, when white women were rescued, most of them confessed only to privation and hardship. Seldom did one admit sexual contact with her captor. This is understandable when one considers that a woman who admitted sexual relations with her Indian captors would never be able to find a place in respectable society. It was not decorous to be raped. And the stigma of being violated would endure the rest of a woman's life.

The records show that many women refused rescue after they had lived within a tribe for some time. This, too, is understandable. As one woman explained, her face had been tattooed, she was pregnant and she felt that she would be more miserable back with her father than she was in the Indian camp.

As late as 1878 there is a record of a white captive who corroborated Colonel Meline's statements. Josephine Meeker's father, Nathan, was an Indian agent at the White River Agency in Colorado. The Indian Wars were thought to be over. His job, as the Indian agent, was to supply relief food to the Indians and attempt to make farmers of them.

But the Ute Indians of the region were horse breeders and hunters. They protested when Meeker tried to force them into plowing the land to raise crops; they thought this practice would destroy their horse grazing and breeding lands. Nonetheless, Meeker stubbornly insisted that the Utes take up farming. The Indians just as stubbornly refused to give up their horse breeding and horse racing. And so, on September 10, 1879, they killed Meeker and other agency employees and captured Josephine, then twenty, and her mother Arbella.

For three weeks the two women were prisoners of the Utes. After being rescued by the Colorado militia, Josephine was interrogated in Greeley, Colorado, by General Charles Adams. In her testimony she first explained that a young Indian by the name of Persune had seized her. She declared that their treatment had been no better than she expected, since she knew the Utes and their nature quite well. General Adams was careful to point out that the information brought out at this investigation would not be published in the newspapers, but that he did need a complete statement because it would make the difference between life and death for the Indian captives. Josephine at first, like so many women before her, dodged the subject of rape. She said, "We were insulted a good many times." When Adams asked what she meant by insult, she replied, "Of outrageous treatment at night."

Adams then asked, "Am I to understand that they outraged you several times at night?" Josephine answered, "Yes, sir." As to whether any other Indians participated in the "outrage," she said, "No," only her captor.

"Was it done while his own squaws were in the tent?" asked Adams.

"Yes," Josephine answered.

"And they knew about it?" exclaimed Adams.

"Yes, sir." When Adams asked, "Did they [the other Indians] seem to think it was very wrong?" Josephine replied, "No; they thought it was a pretty good thing to have a white squaw. Persune's squaw told me that I must not make a fuss about it; it was pretty good."

Asked if the chief had offered her any insult, Josephine replied, "No, he did not to me, but he did on one occasion to mother. I think that is what made a good deal of the trouble — his squaws were jealous; they did not want her there."

Arbella Meeker went along with her daughter's testimony: "It was made known to me that, if I did not submit, I would be killed or subjected to something of that kind, and after I gave up nothing was said about it. Douglas [as the chief was called] I had connection with once, and no more. I was afraid he had disease."

Perhaps partly because of Josephine's short captivity and her youth, she recovered from her traumatic experience, went to Washington and later became a secretary, but I could find no record of her ever marrying.

The rapes of white women by Indians were reported in as much detail as possible by both the respectable and not so respectable press. At least fourteen women wrote narratives of their kidnapping, including Mary Rowlandson and Fanny Kelly. Such first-person adventures, containing as they did descriptions of both sex and violence, became best sellers. They were, in fact, an important part of the sexual literature of the mid-nineteenth century. There is little question that countless American matrons fantasized sexual experiences with American Indians.

Capture by Indians and violation of white women had little effect on the sexual revolution that followed the Civil War. It seems hardly noticeable more than a hundred years later, yet there were widespread changes in the social-sexual mores of the nation during that disastrous conflict. Conditions during the war resulted in a corner of the curtain separating men from women being lifted ever so slightly.

At the beginning of the war it was not considered respectable for women to nurse wounded soldiers. This was true both on the Union and the Confederate sides. Women were too delicate, too pure, to be exposed to the attendant nudity, blood and excretory functions that were part of daily life in the army and the aftermath of every battle. But death and disease know no sex. As the war progressed, the services of women in hospitals, both makeshift on the battlefields and in their home regions, became essential. It is estimated that during the war more than twice as many soldiers on each side died of disease than were killed. The figures for the North were 93,443 men killed or fatally wounded, while 210,400 died of disease. The Confederate Army lost 80,000 men killed and about 160,000 from disease. Altogether, about a half-million Americans lost their lives, creating a shortage of males that took years to replenish.

There is no record of the number of illegitimate

children born during the Civil War but the figure must have been large. Both northern and southern women went out of their way to look their prettiest and, in many instances, "give their all" to their gallant defenders. Considerable numbers of camp followers moved with the northern troops. This does not seem to be as true in the South,where women stayed home and waited for their men to come back, and where army leaves were more frequent.

The difference between nice girls who would not do *it* at all, not so nice (fast) girls who would do *it* on the sly and whores was well delineated in a letter written by a young Virginia gentleman to his brother shortly after the Civil War.

"I thought that I would try and get hold of some girl or other, so Bruce said he could manage things, so he went round to one of the hotels and made arrangements to tap two Irish girls, we were to tap them that night, but that evening Bruce was introduced by someone to a girl that Bruce thought would go it on a sly as someone told him that she was rather fast, she told B. where she lived and invited him to come round and see her; Bruce found out that there was another girl with her so he came round and told me that he had the triggers all fixed and that we would go round and probably tap them; that night he and I started off in the rain and walked about 1-1/2 miles and after a good deal of trouble found the house which much to our surprise was a hoer house, we thought that it would not pay to go all the way back without getting a tap so we rang the bell and went in. We found the two girls in and we sat down and fooled with them a while and after hugging & kissing them a while took them up to their rooms and slapped it to them like hell, they were beautiful girls and I never had a more glorious time in my life. They were first class hoers they did not curse like those other bitches that I wrote you of. I caught the clap again by it but in a very mild form but have entirely recovered. It is impossible to tell whether they have the clap or not as they keep themselves so clean and nice, they have excellent rooms and well furnished, they perfume themselves and look as nice in every respect as any girl you ever saw. I positively tapped her for about an hour, we pulled off and went to bed and craked it and slapped it to them like hell. We retreated about 12M raining like thunder and as dark as the devil. I went round again and got a nother pull a day or so before I left. I did not knock that damn hoer that I got in to that row with that I wrote you of but merely charged on her and knocked up against her, when she retreated. I had heard so much about the beauty of some of the hoers that I thought that I had as well try some of them as I was going to leave Balto and would not probably have another opportunity for some time. The Bee I got hold of was only 15 or 16 and a beautiful plump girl from West Va or rather the valley, she said that she had only been there two or three weeks, she said that she

came on to Balto on a trip of pleasure and was seduced while going from the Theatre one night by her escort, though they generally tell some such lies, nearly all of them have the clap or pox I am damn glad I got off with the clap only."

An explosive example of male-female confrontation occurred during the last days of the Civil War. General Benjamin Butler occupied the city of New Orleans after it had been effectively isolated from the Confederacy. Butler put on a strong show of strength ,with his officers and men patrolling the downtown streets. Upperclass women at first ignored the Union soldiers and, in one instance, turned their backs flipping up their skirts in a "kiss my ass" gesture. Butler observed,"Those women evidently know which end of them looks best." Other incidents included the pouring of the contents of chamber pots out of a window on the heads of a group of officers. Then a ten-year-old youngster walking down the street with his mother spit upon the uniform of a Union officer, and Butler took dramatic action. He was of an egocentric nature and certain that the order he gave would solve his immediate problem. Because he knew there was no greater insult to a respectable southern woman than to reduce her status to that of a prostitute his order read:

"As the officers and soldiers of the United States have been subject to repeated insults from the women [calling themselves ladies] of New Orleans, in return for the most scrupulous noninterference and courtesy on our part, it is ordered that hereafter when any female shall, by word, gesture, or movement, insult or show contempt for any officer or soldier of the United States, she shall be regarded and held liable to be treated as a woman of the town plying her avocation."

Up to now it had been a gentleman's war, but Butler was no gentleman. This earned him the nickname Beast Butler.

Another Union soldier has come down to us in history. "Fighting Joe" Hooker was a vain, handsome, impetuous general who had a reputation as an avid "quif" hunter. He spent so much time in the red-light districts that the girls there were referred to as "Hooker's Division." And even today the girls who work their tricks on the streets are known as "hookers."

After the war many indigent southern women moved westward. The plantations upon which they had depended were deserted. Thousands of homes were abandoned as desolation and poverty spread throughout the South. Many women faced starvation and many a proud southern belle ended up marrying below her class. Samuel Clemens, one-time soldier later to be famous as Mark Twain, estimated that 300,000 women crossed the plains to the West after the war. Perhaps as many went by sea. Some became teachers, others became prostitutes. And many preferred the sporting life to work in a factory. In most instances there was no other choice. A girl worked harder in a factory — ten or twelve hours a day, six days a week — for very little pay. And she was likely to be forced into a sexual connection with a foreman or boss to keep her job.

The war had a telling effect on women in other ways too. Many middle-class matrons learned to operate their family businesses while their men were at the front. And shortly after the war women's rights groups began to make their opinions felt.

Ironically, one of the first American regions to give recognition to women's rights was the territory of Wyoming. In 1869 Esther McQuigg Morris gave a tea party in Laramie which deserves a footnote in American history. Out of it came the right of women to vote, to serve on juries and to hold public office in the Territory.

Over the next twenty-five years other states began slowly to follow Wyoming's example — particularly in taking some action to permit wives to own and control their own property after marriage. It was the beginning of a long, hard road upward.

By some peculiar twist of the national psyche, the post-Civil War period also saw increased attention given to the matter of solo sexual pleasure. Ever since the 1840s there had been tracts deploring the wasted manhood that theoretically resulted from masturbation. One such work, published in Boston, was widely reviewed in such newspapers as *The Conservative Journal*, the religious paper *Zion's Herald* and *The Phoenix Journal*. The book was called *Manhood* and subtitled: *The Causes of Its Premature Decline with Directions for Perfect Restoration*. As on most advice on sexual matters at this time, only the French were considered authorities. Therefore the book, with a circulation of well over 10,000, was attributed to a member of the Royal Academy of Medicine in Paris, a Léopold Deslandes. It had been translated from the French with many additions by an American physician — who preferred to remain anonymous.

The work was designed to terrify any young man who indulged in what was referred to as "self-abuse." Why and how such a pleasurable preoccupation ever got such a bad name is unexplainable. But, according to the authors of *Manhood*, masturbation was a serious disease. Not only did it usually result in death but it was often entirely overlooked "even by medical men, either from false notions of delicacy, or because their attention has not been drawn by fearful experience to cases which are ascribable merely to onanism."

The pessimistic authors point out that the patient who is masturbating his life away is unconscious of the danger and "perseveres in his vicious habit — the physician treats him symptomatically and death soon closes the scene."

The writers laid it on even heavier when they attributed most of the cases of consumption to the effects of masturbation, continuing, "How many minds have been ruined by self indulgence?" Their opening argument insisted that no one had ever disputed that masturbation or coition may be injurious to the health. Consequently the very act of intercourse may be followed by bad effects. The conclusion reached is, "that venereal excesses, particularly those of masturbation, contribute in a considerable proportion to the ills of already suffering humanity."

Determined to frighten young men out of even touching their genitalia, the authors quoted various authorities. One Reveille-Parise declared: "Neither the plague nor war nor smallpox nor similar diseases have produced results so disastrous to humanity as the pernicious habit of onanism: it is a destroying element of civilized societies, which is constantly in action, and gradually undermines the health of a nation." This, the authors say, is no exaggeration.

They also argue that coition may be less harmful than masturbation but only under certain circumstances. If intercourse is done in the simplest way and considered "only as an excretion of semen," it does much less injury to the individual than if it is combined with other sensations. Thus, intercourse with public women who do not excite strong sensations "is generally attended with less derangement." Passion and love are dangerous. The ejaculation of spermatazoa in intercourse is not too bad as long as the individual feels nothing. It is the pleasure principle which makes sex unhealthy. Masturbation is said to be more pernicious than coition partly because of the state of mind that exists in the masturbator. "Having no material object which is the beginning and the end of its pleasures," he must use his imagination. And this is very bad indeed. For, as the authors point out, this mental labor renders the sensations stronger and the body more disposed to feel them. In addition, the onanist is desirous of prolonging his feeling and he retards his ejaculation. "Thus with fatal skill he gives to this destructive vice all the power it can possess and experiences all the evil which this vice can cause."

Among other authorities the authors quote Jean Jacques Rousseau as saying, "Until the age of twenty the body grows and has need of all its substance: continence is natural and if not observed it is at the expense of the constitution." But this is not all. The enjoyment of sex, with or without a partner, leads to various states of disease. Also, the younger and lighter the individual, the more harm masturbation or intercourse can do. And, unfortunately, the authors point out, it is the younger people from the age of twelve who indulge more than older people. Because the individual does not get his full growth until he is forty years old, up to that age excessive intercourse and any masturbation result in more harm to the body than they do after the age of forty. One of the most noticeable effects is the loss of flesh. As for the loss of semen, it is compared with diarrhea. Therefore, the authors of *Manhood* conclude, it is not uncommon to see such people in "a complete state of marasmay: their frame is reduced to a skeleton and presents in anticipation a picture of the state in which death will soon place them. Many parts as the loins, thighs and lower extremities are often remarkable for their extreme emaciation."

Additional elements that produced the desire to masturbate and that should be avoided were: "lascivious thoughts, voluptuous sights, horseback riding, a warm bed and also everything which produces more general excitement in which these organs participate, as wine, liquors, coffee, spices, etc." It must have been that most young men reading these manuals had difficulty figuring out what was keeping them alive and why they felt so good most of the time. Another result, much to be feared, of masturbation was the shrinking of the genitalia. According to the book *Manhood*, in severe cases of onanism the genitalia became very small.

Not only physical decay but moral depravity is to befall the masturbator. After indulging for some time in "self-pollution," the culprit loses all interest in normal (if there is any such thing) sexual relations. He is unlikely to be able to procreate even if he wishes.

Among the lesser evils attributed to "self abuse" were headaches and dizziness, tics, spasmodic movements of the arms or legs and the loss of hair. But of all the frightening results, blindness and epilepsy were perhaps the most quoted. There is no evidence of how these medical authorities arrived at their findings.

But what to do? Many ways of avoiding masturbation were given not only in this manual but in the thousands of books that followed and were widely sold between 1850 and 1950. Feather beds should be avoided at all costs because "such indulgence induces and encourages lascivious feelings." Hard beds stuffed with horse hair or straw were recommended, and the individual should spend as short a time in bed as possible. Diet was very important, and cold baths should be taken carefully for they could be potentially dangerous. For some subjects the simple sight of their own genitalia was enough to set them off and one young man, whose case was described in detail, on taking a bath, indulged in masturbation by placing his penis into the hole in the bottom of the tub. (The authors did not explain how he ever got into that unique position but, as his penis became erect, he couldn't withdraw it.) Although his frantic screams brought assistance, "it was not easy to remove him from the fetters he had forged for himself."

This book and others were replete with stories of young men who had gotten their penes into many relatively inextricable situations. There was the young man who put his limp penis through the handle of a key and then, of course, couldn't get it out. A locksmith had to be called to file the key off. Another penis entered a copper or iron ring and one even got stuck in the socket of a candle stick. Finally the locksmith delivered the organ, but not without causing considerable pain and some damage.

As every healthy growing boy knows, if he is lucky, a sexy dream, sometimes including visions of intercourse, can induce an ejaculation while asleep. And, as most young men know, it's a very pleasant experience except for messy sheets. But not the way the authors of the sex manuals at the turn of the century saw it: in such a wet dream the loss of semen brought on a state of "fatigue, weakness and malaise." Also, the authors never recounted a pleasant dream but invariably ones where the young man was the victim of hideous and repelling females. "On rising the patient experiences a general and more or less distinct feeling of feebleness and suffering. His loins and limbs seem as if he has taken a long walk, or as if they have been bruised; the countenance is pale, the eyelids are swelled and bluish; the patient is sad and stupid. Finally, he presents physically and morally the consequences of the abuse of venery."

If none of the above recommendations helped, fourteen mechanical devices patented between 1856 and 1919 afforded many kinds of painful restrictions of the penis; most of them completely armored the genitalia so that they could not be touched by human hands. Among the appliances was a metal pouch with an elastic strap and a long adjustable ring with dull points which made an erection so painful as to be impossible. There was another with sharp points which included spring-loaded pressure plates which pushed together as the penis expanded. One of the most ingenious consisted of a tube with an open end into which the penis was placed. Should it enlarge, adjustable contact plates caused a bell to ring. This not only notified the potential masturbator but also alerted everyone else in the house as to what he was up to. It may well have been the first biofeedback device.

Another device to prevent manipulation was described as "a sexual armor, a garment having a metallic crotch portion formed with a central slot, and having a gate normally closing said slot, and provided with a lock for securing said gate in its closed position." Certainly the most complicated one included a leather harness with an electric belt, metal tubes for both penis and testicles and a bell that rang as the penis extended.

Fortunately, there are not too many records of parents forcing their children to wear these fiendish devices but some of them became standard equipment in a few asylums for the mentally disturbed. The sexual armor, patent number 875845, was said to be equally effective on females.

At the same time that human masturbators were being forced to mend their ways, no less than thirty-five anti-masturbatory devices were patented for horses. Off-hand, one would not expect that horse masturbation would be a major problem yet many breeders felt that it was. While the number of horses that learned to masturbate by rubbing their erect penes against the skin of their abdomens has never been recorded, semen was too valuable to be wasted. The technique used for horses was adapted as above to humans. A quotation from the U.S. Department of Agriculture bulletin of 1896 reads:

"Some stallions acquire this vicious habit, stimulating the sexual instinct to the discharge of semen, by rubbing the penis against the belly or between the forelimbs. The only remedy is a mechanical one, the fixing of a net under the penis in such fashion as will prevent the extension of the penis, or so prick the organ as to compel the animal to desist through pain."

Five years after the widely printed book entitled *Manhood* was published, a provocative volume with a frontispiece showing a fairly plump, naked, young woman in a forest setting (which was doubtless designed to be a portrait of Eve, that first sinner) appeared. The book was called *The Secret Habits of the Female Sex*. This too was translated from the French and cast in the form of letters to a mother on "The Evils of Solitude and Its Seductive Temptations to Young Girls, the Premature Victims of a Pernicious Passion with All Its Frightful Consequences: Deformity of Mind and Body, Destruction of Beauty and Entailing Disease and Death; but from which, by Attention to the Timely Warnings Here Given, the Devotee May be Saved, and Become an Ornament to Society, a Virtuous Wife, and a Refulgent Mother." This should probably win some kind of award as the longest subtitle in literary history.

In the preface the author pointed out that the vice of masturbation exists to a large extent among young females. The book was addressed, then, to mothers as a means of preserving the morals of their daughters, and of sparing them the pain and sorrow of seeing them wither and perish at an age when they ought to be the ornament of their domestic circle, when they ought to enjoy health and happiness. Although the horrors that were enumerated were very similar to those admonished to male masturbators, more emphasis was put upon the onset of consumption (or, as it is now called, tuberculosis). "Those individuals who yield themselves up to the enjoyment of solitary pleasure, to secret pernicious habits, soon exhibit, more or less, the symptoms of *tabes dorsalis* (a species of consumption). At first they are not troubled with fever; and, although they may still preserve their appetite, their bodies waste away and they have a sensation as though insects were creeping along their spine."

"Even the most robust girls are soon rendered weak; and sometimes a slow fever, sometimes a rapid consumption, terminates the scene."

In letter number three *"solitary indulgence — the most filthy and most murderous vice — all give rise to*

atrophy." All of this was caused by "unhappy patients and the seduction of solitary pleasures."

The doctors reproduced letters alleged to be from their patients. One wrote: "The following is a description that has been given to me of my fits. I stamp violently on the floor, and then fall with my limbs stiffened, teeth clenched, and the end of my tongue thrust between the incisor teeth. My face and hands have become livid and no doubt, sir, my unfortunate fate is the result of those murderous self-indulgences with which I frequently sought to gratify myself, as before that, I enjoyed an excellent state of health, which was evinced by the freshness of my complexion." This poor girl undoubtedly had an epileptic seizure.

As with men, women were warned not to sleep in soft beds, especially not feather beds.

A diet for women masturbators consisted of: "bread, a little fresh, containing if possible some rye flour; mild, diluent and refreshing vegetables, such as spinage, beet root, sorrel, roots of scoroma, radishes, etc; melons, gourds; fruits perfectly ripe such as cherries, plums, pears, red gooseberries, and oranges." So far as liquids were concerned, gooseberry, orange and lemon juice were recommended. "Buttermilk into which every pint should be put twenty grains of nitre-nitrate (saltpeter) of potash; occasionally some orgeat (barley water flavored with almonds or orange flowers), emulsions prepared without heat from seeds, and sufficiently flavored with acidulate syrups of lemon, gooseberry and pomegranate."

It was recommended that the girls' drink at meals be a cold and light infusion of licorice-root water slightly sweetened, or spring water. They should abstain from eating such vegetables as celery, cabbage, artichokes, asparagus and any other so-called acid vegetables. Certain fruits, such as peaches and strawberries, did not go along with masturbation. And neither did fish, shellfish, crawfish, crabs or other Crustacea. She also had to be careful of roots, garlic, onions, black truffles and skirret (caraway). Boiled white meats were considered preferable for such young ladies for this would not bring on the desire to abuse her genitals. Above all "she must particularly abstain from all the meats called black, from game kept too long for they are acrid, strong and irritating."

Also, girls were advised to take baths in tepid water "whenever the situation permits." Should the skin around the "secret parts" of the girl be inflamed, "leeches might be successfully applied where the inflamation is violent."

Highly recommended in the treatment of girls with a tendency to masturbate were quiet and moderate activities, such as the study of languages, polite literature, history, oratory, poetry, music and painting. Dressmaking and embroidery were equally efficacious. One had to be careful with music, however, for "some music tends to corrupt the mind." Music selected should be of a "noble, sublime, fresh, and lively character." Excursions in the country were recommended but even a limited amount of walking on uneven ground might have a tendency to rub the genital labia together thereby causing excitement — and as for horseback riding, well, it was not only believed that the rocking motion would inflame the genitals, but that a girl might even lose her virginity bouncing against the pommel on a leather saddle. Boarding schools were considered dangerous for both young men and young women, for there young people already addicted to masturbation might teach the neophyte the forbidden pleasures.

The most vicious and non-reversible operation for women was the clitoridectomy introduced in the mid-nineteenth century. Over a period of the next fifty years quite a number of such operations were performed on victims whose only crime was masturbation. For almost a hundred years, at least until the advent of the Kinsey era in the 1940s, masturbation found few defenders. And, in fact, discussions with a number of psychiatrists show that a high percentage of their patients, both male and female, have carried guilt feelings regarding masturbation with them through their lives.

This might be a good time to wipe out the credit, or debit (considering which way you look at it), of the Biblical character Onan, who is usually referred to as the father of masturbation. What Onan actually practiced was *coitus interruptus* — very different from masturbation, indeed. And the reason why the Lord gave him the death penalty was because, by sprinkling his seed upon the ground instead of upon the womb of his brother's widow, he was refusing to obey the Biblical law and raise up children to his deceased brother.

Genesis 38:8: "And Judah said unto Onan: 'Go in unto thy brother's wife, and perform the duty of a husband's brother unto her, and raise up seed to thy brother.'"

But it was much more threatening to use the Lord's wrath against masturbators than punishing sinners who refused to mate with their widowed sisters-in-law. The many volumes published in England and the United States relating to the physical and mental horrors that would be visited upon the male and female masturbator received their impetus from the eighteenth-century Catholic physician Samuel August Tissot, who also became Pope Clement XIII's advisor on public health. In 1758 Tissot's book, from which other treatises stemmed, was printed in Switzerland. According to Tissot, coitus was injurious to the health but masturbation was a thousand times more injurious, it being a sin against the soul as well as the body. Translated into many languages, Tissot's work, *Onanism; A Treatise on The Disorders Produced by Masturbation*, may well have caused more guilt feelings and psychological problems than all the psychiatrists of the world since have been able to solve.

"INITIATING A HIGH ROLLER"

The High Rollers, an all-male coterie of gamblers, held stag parties
to initiate new members. Here a girl is lowered into a vat of beer.

Masked vigilantes often took the law into their own hands. In Indiana in 1887 a man is beaten for his marriage to his aunt.

*Mother and daughter, accused of fornication, are stripped
and beaten by intolerant citizens in an Indiana woodland.*

She is mestiza, the result of a mating of a Spanish man and an Indian woman. Her husband is Indian, the child a cuarteron.

Beautiful women and handsome men resulted from matings of conquistadors and natives. Before, the Spanish women were bare breasted.

For the camera these Indians exposed their breasts. Later, a prankster added a caption: "Dangers of the Indian Country."

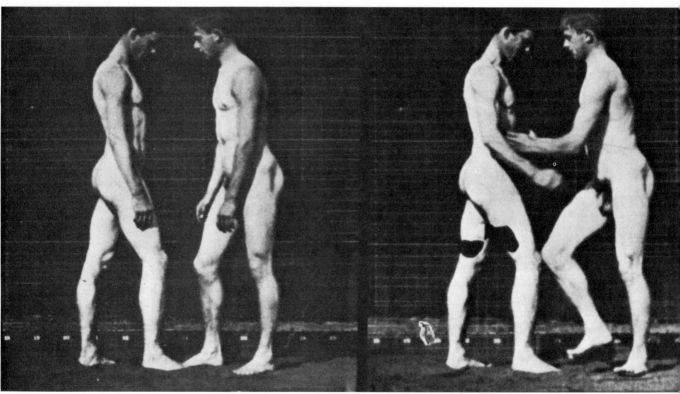

The first nude photographs to be widely published were those
of Eadweard Muybridge, a painstaking and imaginative
photographer who had changed his name from Muggeridge

after killing his wife's lover. Muybridge not only published
the first nudes but showed both men and women in action. His
original purpose was to prove that all four feet of a gallop-

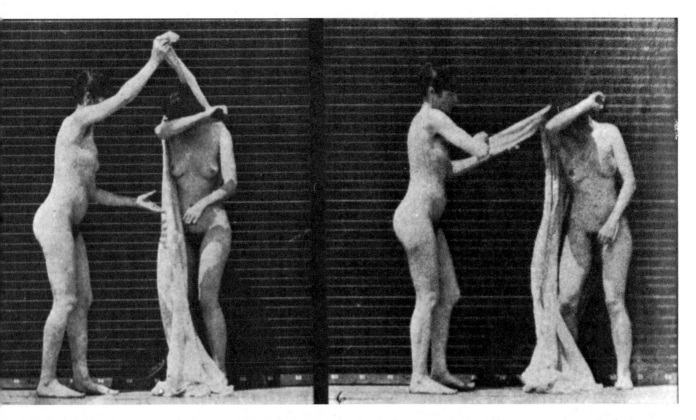

ing horse were off the ground at the same time. Having proved his point, he went on to show other animals and humans in motion. The books were banned in a number of states. In the strip of pictures above, one woman disrobes another. Two naked male wrestlers are shown below. The year was 1878. Later he contributed to the invention of the motion picture.

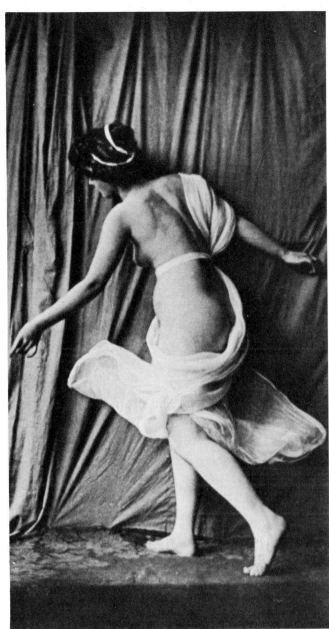

Lacking Muybridge's equipment, photographer Charles Schenk got an in-motion effect by carefully pinning the girl's gauze robe onto his studio drapes. The exposure of her nipples and the cleft of her buttocks was extremely daring in 1890.

125

The radical young woman above is wearing formal bloomers
fitted tightly around the ankle. While bloomers did not last in
the East, western women, perhaps because of outdoor life on
the ranches, often wore cut-down men's trousers or overalls.

Magazines dealing with clothing styles and makeup became popular. Advertisers learned quickly that women wanted to be beautiful.

Kansas City whores Nellie Martin and friend, in lace petti-coats, enjoy a shot of whiskey in a typical parlor house in 1905.

Silver Heels, a whore with a heart of gold, nursed miners during a smallpox epidemic after all the respectable women had fled.

Diamond Lil may not have had a heart of gold but she had a diamond set in a front tooth. Mae West's DIAMOND LIL, was based on her life.

Pearl Starr was the only daughter of the notorious western bandit and sometime prostitute Belle Starr. Pearl became a popular prostitute.

No color line was drawn in mulatto cathouses such as this one, run by Madam Sperber in Kansas City. Taken in 1906, the picture looks as though the photographer asked the girls not to look at the camera. Many young mulatto girls

most of them illegitimate and abandoned, became popular
prostitutes throughout the midwest and western states.

The model's awkward pose was dictated by the time exposure. This, together with her semi-nudity, made her self-conscious.

This parlor house was also known as the House of All Nations. Its madam recruited whores from Europe and Asia.

7

Three Wicked Cities
(Mistresses, Madams and Matrons)

New York

This is a tale of three cities at the turn of the century: New York, San Francisco and New Orleans. From 1880 to 1920 — even before and after for that matter — these have come to be known as the wickedest in the United States. All three have deeper and more pervasive roots in foreign lands than any other cities of the continental United States. They started out as a part of an older culture and they retained those characteristics right up to modern times.

New York had its Dutch, English, Irish, Scotch and Jewish founders; San Francisco its Russians, English, Chinese and Spanish; New Orleans its French and Spanish. By grafting native traditions onto European and Asiatic mores, these cities not only kept their early customs but developed an entirely new, different and sometimes decadent culture. They turned out to be more radical, more romantic, more unmoral (for who knows what immorality is) than the other urban regions. Their roots and seeds were in the Old World but the New World fertilized them well. They grew, they flourished and became, without question, the avant-garde areas of the New World.

There was more of everything: more religion and more vice; more marriage and more divorce; more money and more bribery. Perhaps the only thing there wasn't more of was peace. There was certainly more violence. But in spite of their excesses (or because of them) they became the great cities of character in the United States. For the average citizen living in the interior of the country, visiting one of these metropolises was like going to Paris.

They were places where clerks and farmers, housewives and stenographers, butchers and sailors, could kick up their heels, let off their steam and get drunk on the wine and the freedom.

Because all three cities were major ports, they not only had the advantage of being settled and resettled by a wide variety of peoples, but each day they were infused with new blood, new ideas from the world. Inasmuch as New York is the biggest and the oldest, we will take our first trip through its wild side. Some of the early sexual history of New York has appeared in previous chapters. Now we will pick it up in 1880.

New York's social classes, from 1880 to the First World War, ran a wide gamut. At the top were families with great fortunes — some old, many nouveau riche. Beneath this was a solid layer of pleasure-loving middle class. On the bottom level (with the inevitable involvement of the other two groups) was a city of prostitutes and panderers, a police department on-the-take, and a general attitude of all three levels of live-and-let-live. New York had no law against prostitution as such until 1918, after the entry of the United States into World War I.

This is not to say that fornication was socially acceptable. But it had not been recognized as an offense either by English or American common law. Fornication did become a statutory crime in Massachusetts due to the Pilgrim influence as early as 1692. Later certain states passed adultery and fornication laws. Twelve states, however, have never passed such laws. Yet all states found some way of punishing sex for pay. Open and gross lewdness, for instance, which can be defined in many ways, is illegal in most states. Operating a bawdy house has generally been outlawed on the charge of maintaining a nuisance. Night walking, which is what the modern hooker does in many American cities, has been an offense since 1699 in Massachusetts. There have been many changes in the laws throughout the history of the United States, but to be a prostitute prior to World War I was not in itself a criminal offense. It was in some states regarded as vagrancy. This meant, in a general sense, that a woman had to be a vagrant, a nuisance or a disorderly person to be arrested — when actually everyone knew that what she was really being arrested for was having promiscuous sex for pay.

Most lawmakers had a difficult time deciding whether it should be legal to allow free sex yet punish pay sex. Neither ever met the full approval of the various legislators and all were adamant on one point. They would not allow what is called "licensed vice." Over the years, regardless of the measures taken, no one has been able to solve the problem of prostitution in New York. As early as 1855 the Medical Board of Bellevue Hospital announced in part:

"No rigor of punishment, no violence of public denunciation, neither exile nor the dungeon, nor yet the lingering malady with which Nature punishes the practice, has ever effected [prostitution's] extermination for a single year."

After the Civil War a series of laws were proposed to segregate prostitutes and license them, to give them medical examinations and, one way or another, regulate their trade. But the opposition, mostly from women's groups, was so intense that New York never had such a "red-light" district. The arguments against it were pervasive: men should be held to the same standards of morals as women, therefore making prostitutes unnecessary; besides, the cities could not see any physical or social necessity for men or women to be involved in a life of evil. Finally, the licensing of such a district and of these immoral women would make fornication-for-profit legitimate.

When laws against prostitution were finally passed during World War I, the excuse advanced, of course, was the protection of the young manhood of the country. Whether these men could be equally protected against influenza, yellow fever, bombs or bullets became incidental. Sex was too good for them — or too bad for them — depending upon how you looked at it. The feeling was that prostitution near army camps must be wiped out and that a physically fit army was an army with no sexual contacts. There were, to be sure, some realists. The Surgeon General of the United States once remarked, "We are not trying to eliminate fucking entirely. What we are trying to do is make it more difficult." He was implying that by drastically reducing promiscuous coitus, the incidence of venereal disease would be reduced. This apparently has been the policy of the army medical mentors in both the first and second World Wars.

Although the exploitation of women in New York goes back to the original Indian population, it was the French who seem to have been among the first to organize prostitution on a mass-market basis in the 1890s. Actually, the setup was limited to a comparatively small number of girls who worked for a mack or *maquereau*, French for pimp.

By 1900 young Russian-Jewish immigrants had placed the profession on a businesslike basis, and the Italians and Greeks were moving in fast. Later, as we shall see, the Italian Mafia turned prostitution in New York into big business.

Around the turn of the century, pimps and panderers had at least one well-known organization, called the Independent Benevolent Association. It was scarcely independent or benevolent, but certainly was well organized, with strong connections with the police. The group has been described by Howard B. Woolston in his book of 1921 as "a kind of stock exchange for the trade," where shares in the business were sold and transferred. They collected up to fifty percent of the girls' earnings, managed groups of girls and rotated them into various houses so that they could control them better and offer a greater variety to their customers.

A typical pimp, although he had more hard luck than many of his ilk, was Leo Mersky. He lived in the lower East Side, the Russian-Jewish ghetto area, with relatives, having come from Russia. First he hung around a dance hall, met an Italian pimp and together they opened a small whorehouse. They procured their girls by seducing ignorant young immigrant servant maids. After having sex with the girls, they promised them money and a good time if they would work for them. Then young Mersky was arrested in a gambling raid. To beat that rap, he became a stool pigeon working for the police, informing on the prostitutes and pimps. But being a bright young man, he soon found that he could earn more money from the people that he was exposing by keeping their secrets and being paid off. Unfortunately, when a prostitute complained to the police that Mersky was collecting money from her, he was jailed. The record says that he turned state's evidence, so he probably got out of this jam too. Woolston mentions that Mersky blamed his downfall on the lack of recreation in his neighborhood and vicious companions. He also censured the dance halls, where, he said, "girls were lured into the business of prostitution."

Almost everyone in New York was involved in prostitution. Real estate owners, who represented the most virtuous church-goers, and even acted as agents for church property itself, rented to madams and procurers at high rates. Many of the real estate operators felt that because a certain amount of risk was involved in renting their property for illegal and immoral purposes, they should get a higher return — and they did.

It took all kinds of madams to run the hundreds of

whorehouses in New York. One of the most interesting was Mary Good, who seems to have been not only good in name but also in nature. She started out in New York as a stenographer and, after an illness, took over the running of a rooming house. She soon transformed it into a well-conducted house of prostitution. Upon her insistence, her girls had to attend church every Sunday. Prostitution, she felt, was a necessary evil. But, unlike the police and most of the good women of the community, she thought that it should be controlled by a committee of experienced women who preferred that kind of life, so that girls were not exploited.

Somewhat similar, though less religious, was Harriet Morris, who ran a "respectable" parlor house for thirty years. She took a small percentage from the nine girls in her house and charged them sixteen dollars a week for room and board. Harriet was a strict supervisor; her girls had to stay healthy and the men who visited her house were expected to behave. With her earnings from prostitution she supported her mother and sister and her sister's two children. She also adopted and reared a baby girl who was left on her doorstep.

Without the child ever knowing about her business, she had her educated in a convent and later helped to arrange her marriage. After settling her affairs, Harriet went respectable and moved out West.

The New York taxi driver, and before him the hansom cab driver, was an important factor in getting a customer to the many available prostitutes in New York. During the turn-of-the-century period, horse-drawn cab drivers knew the addresses of all of the "best" establishments and had special girls to recommend who worked out of their own homes or apartments.

Where could one find a girl in New York? There were the parlor houses, roadhouses, hotels, furnished rooms, saloons, cafes, dance halls, in and around theaters, at the railroad stations, the employment agencies and the ambulatory girls on the streets and in the parks.

White slavery. What dark, horrible deeds were reportedly done (and possibly accomplished) under this title? Among many women's groups, it was the number-one topic of conversation between 1880 and 1920. To the morality of the 1900s it was what the Red menace became to the politicians of the 1950s. Based upon the lurid accounts in newspapers and magazines, one would get the impression that a huge, highly organized, international cartel existed, trading exclusively in the bodies of young and innocent females.

But to what extent did white slavery actually exist in New York? The term itself, of course, referred to compulsory prostitution. Women were regularly abducted, drugged, seduced, raped and sold into a life within a controlled brothel. In its strictest sense, white slavery was similar to black slavery. And, in fact, the French call it *traite des blanches,* using the expression to distinguish between the trade in black slaves and white. But each of the investigations of white slavery turned up no evidence of an international conspiracy. The truth of the matter, it would seem, is that a considerable number of individuals and small groups trafficked in female bodies for their own enrichment. These associations were highly informal and no specific international organization was ever prosecuted. But that thousands of women were kept in absolute slavery within houses of prostitution in the United States at the turn of the century is doubtful. What actually happened was that in countries where economic conditions had forced many young people to the edge of starvation, women were recruited by one means or another and were shipped from Ireland, Poland and France to the United States. In many instances, these girls were supplied to existing houses of prostitution. Most of these girls received a percentage of their earnings and a higher percentage of them stayed in "the life" because they preferred it to factory work or starvation, which were usually their only options. In most of the cases, brought to light in the court records of New York in 1900, the girls were seduced, forced to have intercourse with more than one man, then under threats put in a house of prostitution. Very rarely were girls actually bought or sold except among the Chinese and that was prevalent not only in New York but in San Francisco. One French importer, however, reportedly made more than $100,000 by placing prostitutes who came over as either the wives or servants of their seducers.

Among the methods used to keep a girl in line was depriving her of her clothes so that she could not leave the house, keeping most or all of her earnings and regularly beating her. However, it was usually found that the girls worked better if they weren't beaten and they certainly looked better to their customers. Girls who took to the "life" — and there were many of them — often managed to make a reasonable deal with the madam or their pimp and save enough money to get into a higher-class house.

I remember a story about a young reporter who, with an older newspaperman, went over on the "wrong side of the tracks" to visit a bawdy house. As they were walking back late at night, the younger man said, "She was a beautiful young girl. I felt a lot of affection for her and I feel like I ought to do something for her to help her."

The older man said, "Oh, never mind all that sentiment. You're a fifteen-dollar-a-week reporter. What in the world could you do to help that girl?"

"Well," replied the young man, "I think I could get her out of that two-dollar house and into a five-dollar house."

It was estimated, around 1900, that at least 25,000 young girls were procured each year for purposes of prostitution in the United States; that a minimum of 50,000 men and women were engaged full time in finding and living from the earnings of these girls. By the turn of the century prostitution was a big business in the United States.

Besides the Chinese, Latin American girls became sex slaves in New York to some degree. Brought in from Puerto Rico, Cuba or northern Mexico, they spoke no English and once out of their native villages were completely dependent upon their pimp, who usually bought them from a dealer who specialized in importing such girls.

To get the girls out of their villages and into the United States they were invariably promised marriage and the man who lured them always posed as rich and respectable and sometimes even went so far as to participate in a village marriage ceremony. As a citizen of the United States, it was not too difficult for him to get his new wife into the country and sell her to the loosely organized pimps of New York. In the years between 1900 and 1916 many such girls were brought into the country to become virtual white slaves.

Being dependent for their food, their clothing, their lodging, these girls had no choice except to do exactly what they were told. They worked in the cheapest houses or in transient hotels. Most of them were thoroughly beaten up by their pimps if they did not bring in a set minimum amount of money each night. Not too many could escape, for their pimps threatened to slice their faces up with razor blades or knives, burn their bodies with cigars or cigarettes. It was a no-way-out situation and lasted in New York well into the forties, when the reform government cut into the business.

Black prostitutes were often treated the same way by their pimps who, like the Cubans, kept a stable of three to six girls. The girls were known to each other as wives-in-law when they belonged to such a family, and the rare free lance who worked alone without a pimp was called an outlaw.

In Puerto Rico, Mexico, Cuba and the Central American countries, birth certificates were forged to make it seem the girls had been born in the United States, making it comparatively simple for pimps to bring them into the country.

New York also set the standards for illicit sex on the highest levels. European actresses, often of limited talent, were considered the most desirable of sex objects by New York's discriminating rich men. A night spent with one of these courtesans offered more status than membership in the best club or the ownership of a railroad. It was not only a respectable pursuit, this kind of glamorous, romantic affair was looked upon with envy and approval by both men and women.

It is difficult to say which of the turn-of-the-century beauties was the most talented in bed or out. But the most publicized and the greatest money-maker, both from engagements and gifts from admirers, was Señorita Carolina Otero, who, according to the *New York Times* of September 22, 1890, "enjoys a Parisian reputation for unexampled sinuosity." Her arrival in New York was so important that a special craft was chartered. The press, the management of the Eden Musée, and forty other gentlemen boarded it to welcome the beauteous European import. Everyone in the party wore a boutonniere made of a yellow rose and a pink carnation — this in honor of Señorita Otero's national colors.

Boarding the ship that had carried the Spanish dancer, the fifty members of the welcoming party followed her from one deck to another chanting her name in chorus. She moved to the smaller vessel and there, according to the *Times* reporter, she drank her own health a number of times in champagne. She then invited the entire party, including the Royal Hungarian Band, to dine with her and they accepted with cheers and a "tiger" of acceptance.

She was described by the obviously smitten *Times* reporter as being: "highly attractive, above medium height with a lithe and supple and well-rounded figure and a serious, graceful carriage. Her face is of the Spanish type. It is oval in shape with delicate olive complexion, large, dark and lustrous eyes, deep black and perfectly arched eyebrows, full red lips and teeth of dazzling whiteness. These charms are crowned by a wealth of jet black hair which was worn in plain masses on each side of a rather broad forehead. She chatted easily in French and Spanish, but knew not a word of English. She said she was glad to come to America, and expressed her views on other matters of like importance."

The manager of the Eden Musée, Herr Hellman, and its largest stockholder, Count Kessler, were quoted as saying that "she will astonish if not astound New York when she appears at Eden Musée." Her debut was an even greater event, and perhaps it should be mentioned at this time that before her arrival a series of sensational and scandalous stories appeared in the New York press. One article stated that her visit to America was to get away from the unwelcome attention of two members of a royal European family who had threatened to fight a duel to death, with the survivor claiming her. Other stories presented her as the love child of the Empress Eugénie and an unnamed admiral. In another column she was called "one of the most brilliantly beautiful women ever seen in New York." And another journal went so far as to report that once, while performing in Madrid, she was abducted and carried off to the palace of King Alfonso XII by his orders. The story declared that she escaped through a window, climbed down a trellis and left the palace grounds.

This was obviously press agentry, and her press agent concluded his rave review by writing, "Her figure is above the medium in height, stately but full of feminine grace. She possesses an unusual amount of magnetic power." This she certainly did and she used it both on and off the stage. Modestly the *Times* reviewer did not mention the various parts of her anatomy that she shook so well. He observed, "She appears to dance all over, so to speak. Every muscle from her dainty toes to the crown of her shapely head, is brought into play, and the consequent contortions are sometimes startling."

Otero's only rival, a Spanish dancer called Carmencita, had no chance and after Otero's triumphs little was heard from her.

Interest in Otero was wide but comparatively few men could afford her intimate favors. One of the first to suffer was her manager, Ernest André Jurgens. He embezzled large sums of money from the Eden Musée and a year later the law caught up with him. One of Jurgens's impressive gifts to her was a pearl necklace said to be of great value. During the succeeding years, a long list of New York's richest men, including William K. Vanderbilt, contributed jewels. One of Vanderbilt's presents was a diamond bracelet in the shape of a snake, with emerald eyes. It came from Tiffany's and during the ensuing months Otero collected many pieces from that august establishment. According to rumors, Vanderbilt alone gave Otero a quarter of a million dollars worth of jewels.

Because of her beauty and popularity, she was received in a number of respectable homes by socially prominent women.

In the years that followed Otero's success in New York, she had affairs with quite a few distinguished members of European royal families. Arthur Lewis, in his well-researched book *La Belle Otero*, tells the story of a gathering in the private dining room of a famous Paris restaurant eight years after Otero's New York opening night. Five gentlemen were celebrating the thirtieth birthday of Otero — a mistress they had all been sharing for some years. Among those present was King Leopold II of Belgium, Prince Nicholas I of Montenegro, Prince Albert of Monaco, the Grand Duke Nicolai Nikolaevich of Russia and Albert Edward, the Prince of Wales, who became King Edward VII of England.

Among other lovers who came later were Wilhelm II, the Emperor of Germany, and Aristide Briand, premier of France. She described Briand as being a superb lover.

The world came to know her as La Belle Otero and she sang and danced everywhere, making a second triumphal appearance in the United States in 1897. Just before her departure, her first manager and discoverer, Jurgens, after glimpsing his former mistress for a moment, was told to come back later — she was entertaining a gentleman at the time. He went away and committed suicide that afternoon.

Jurgens was not the only man to kill himself over Otero. When one of her admirers threatened suicide if he could not go to bed with her, she is reported to have said, "It would be stupid. You know, if all the men who love me and whom I can't love were to kill themselves, there would have to be a great graveyard especially for them . . . and that wouldn't be too much fun for me."

If you happened to be in Central Park on a Sunday morning in the late 1880s, you might see the rays of the morning sun setting off brilliant flashes as a rider pedaled her gold-plated, diamond, ruby and emerald studded bicycle. The dream that was riding on this two-wheeled treasure, dressed in white, her jaunty Alpine hat bobbing up and down, was Miss Lillian Russell, New York's reigning queen of the theater. If you happened to be at her hotel when she was packing for a tour, you might also get a chance to see the hand-made leather case in which her golden bicycle was shipped from city to city.

The most expensive bicycle ever built was given to Miss Russell by her intimate friend and fellow trencher-man, Diamond Jim Brady. Like Miss Russell, Brady was one of the most publicized figures of what Lucius Beebe once described as New York's "lobster-palace days." Another figure of this set was "Bet-a-million" Gates, who was willing to bet almost any amount at any time on anything — with the exception of women — he knew better than to bet on them. This manufacturer-industrialist once stopped in Kansas City in his special railroad car. A local sport approached to ask whether he would make a bet against him. Gates first ascertained that the local yokel had raised $40,000 cash and was indeed ready to take a chance. Removing a twenty-dollar gold piece from his pocket, Gates said "Heads or tails — you call it," and spun the coin into the air. The unfortunate gentleman picked the wrong side of the coin. Gates calmly accepted the $40,000, put it into his pocket and walked back to his parlor car. The entire event was over in less than five minutes.

Deeply in love with his wife, Gates once decided to surprise her. He bought her a $300,000 dollar townhouse, completely furnished. That would be worth about three million in today's dollars.

But "Bet-a-million" Gates was never the newsmaker that Diamond Jim was. Brady believed that to be rich one should look rich. And his collection of evening dress jewelry sets, a different set for each outfit, included diamonds, emeralds, rubies, pearls and other precious stones. There were thirty sets in all and their value exceeded two million dollars.

In addition to being the most expensively dressed man in New York, Brady was also easily the most incredible gourmand that New York ever produced. He was known to eat a twelve-course dinner (not unusual at the turn of the century) but with it he would consume more than one helping of each dish and, eschewing all alcoholic beverages, have a gallon of chilled orange juice with his dinner and usually a large part of a five-pound box of chocolates. He was reported to have polished off a roasting chicken, two or three ducks, a twelve-egg soufflé, four or five dozen oysters, a saddle of mutton and six venison chops at one sitting — not including appetizers or desserts.

Once, when dining with Lillian Russell and other theatrical friends including Victor Herbert and Sam Schubert, he heard of a new fish course called *filet de sole Marguery*. His informer told the group that the sauce was a deep secret known only to the chef of the Cafe Marguery in Paris. Brady related this information to Charles Rector, the proprietor of the restaurant in which they were dining, and told him that, if he wanted his continued patronage, he'd better start serving his filets with Marguery sauce. Realizing the great publicity value that Brady and Russell had to his restaurant — as well as their personal billings — Rector took his son George out of college and sent him to Paris, where under an assumed name he managed to get a job in the kitchen at Marguery's. Within two months he was in possession of the secret recipe. His father and Brady met him at the dock upon his return and, before the vessel even got to the dock, Brady yelled out: "Have you got the sauce?" As soon as the ship tied up, everyone went to the restaurant and preparations were made for the dinner. Among those present were Marshall Field, Adolphus Busch and the original group. George Rector recalled much later that Brady said: "George, that sole was marvelous. I've had nine helpings and even right now, if you poured some of the sauce over a Turkish towel, I believe I could eat all of it." (The sauce wasn't all that complicated: a white sauce plus egg yolk, white wine, thyme and shallots.)

It was Lillian Russell's association with Diamond Jim that contributed to a unique court case that was the sensation of the 1890s. The beauteous Miss Russell was sued by her manager, J. C. Duff, when she refused to wear tights in a theatrical performance. Duff thought, and justifiably so, that a lot of the audience came to see Miss Russell's legs. There were two points of view expressed vehemently at the trial. Miss Russell contended that the

wearing of tights was endangering her health; they were too drafty, and she was exposed to the changing temperatures on the stage as the seasons changed. Some of her newspaper detractors advanced the argument that she had begun to expand around the hips and thighs — too many of those after-the-theater dinners with Diamond Jim.

The judge disagreed with Miss Russell. He said that she had previously worn tights in both warm and cold weather, and that the time of year had nothing to do with her contract which explicitly stated that she would wear tights. He thought her excuse was, in great measure, "a pretense" and he concluded that "no evidence has been adduced that the costumes of an opera change with the seasons of the year, or that the defendent ever claimed any right to such change."

When Miss Russell began appearing under other management, Duff started another suit to restrain her from working for anyone else because he held a valid contract. A temporary injunction was granted to him and Miss Russell put up a $2,000 bond. The case dragged on for almost two years but was finally decided in favor of Duff. By that time, Miss Russell had made another fortune working for other managers and it meant little to her that she forfeited the $2,000 dollars and court costs. She said she would never appear in tights again — and she never did.

Her decision did not detract one whit from her popularity with her male admirers. One group of six men (among them a Russian and an Austrian prince) had a glittering diamond coronet made for her and had it presented at the end of the second act of her performance of *La Cigale*. As she took a curtain call, a resplendent usher came down the aisle holding high a crimson velvet cushion in front of him. Gleaming upon it was a heavy gold coronet set with 120 small diamonds in the form of a star. Wild applause. The curtain goes down and quickly rises again. Russell is wearing her new crown. Like Otero, she seems to have been able to share herself with a small group of men without them becoming jealous of one another.

Part of the Russell-Brady coterie was Stanford White, architect, connoisseur of champagne, theater and very young women. It was his interest in the latter that abruptly ended his life.

The woman responsible for his death danced and sang well enough to have become a member of the famous Floradora Sextette when she was sixteen. It was reported in the press, and said by many gossipers, that Stanford White was responsible for her theatrical success. Not so. For Evelyn Nesbit made it on her own. She was, as her photographs show, one of the most beautiful women ever to have graced the Broadway stage.

At the age of fifteen she was modeling for such noted artists as Frederick Church and Charles Dana Gibson. The famous sculptor George Grey Barnard produced a sculpture of her which he called "Innocence." It was purchased by the Metropolitan Museum of Art. From the artists' studios this delicately beautiful child went on to become a photographer's model and, after a number of feature stories appeared in the New York press extolling her as "the most beautiful model in America," she received an offer to join one of the most popular singing-dancing acts in the city, the Floradora Sextette.

In the years between sixteen and twenty-one, she had been the mistress of Stanford White and actor John Barrymore, had a miscarriage (she had admittedly been pregnant with John Barrymore's child) and was at the time of White's murder married to the mad multi-millionaire Harry K. Thaw.

While Evelyn Nesbit did not pull the trigger of the gun that sent three bullets crashing through the head of Stanford White, she was the vehicle of fate that put in motion the events that led to his death. For the man she finally married had a streak of insanity that exploded in fits of rage that fed on jealousy. And Evelyn Nesbit, public sex-heroine number-one in New York from 1901 to 1906, told Thaw the most intimate details of her seduction and sex life with White.

It wasn't fair and it wasn't just. True, she was seduced by White while a virgin of sixteen but, according to most of her statements, she truly fell in love. She greatly enjoyed her midnight excursions to his svelte Twenty-fourth Street hideaway, where she would sometimes sit naked on the red velvet cushion of a velvet rope swing in his high-ceilinged studio, while White pushed her high into the air and her bare toes kicked a paper Japanese parasol mounted on the ceiling.

The red velvet swing was only one of White's eccentricities. He was far more than an eccentric. Recognized as New York's greatest architect, White designed the noble arch that still stands in Washington Square. His good taste and skill were responsible for the Century, the Metropolitan, the Lambs and the Players clubs and the Plaza Hotel. Among the many distinctive houses, he designed the magnificent "Marble House" for Mrs. William K. Vanderbilt (wife of man-about-town Vanderbilt, previously mentioned, who lavished jewels on La Belle Otero) in Newport, Rhode Island. He was *the* arbiter of New York taste. White also had the unusual distinction of being killed on the roof of an outstanding building he designed — the roof-garden theater atop Madison Square Garden.

Evelyn Nesbit was the pivotal character, but Harry K. Thaw was the mentally unstable element in the tragic triangle. When it exploded at 11:05 on the evening of June 25, 1906, all three were attending the opening of a gay musical comedy, *Mamzelle Champagne*. The twenty-one-year-old bride of Thaw, Evelyn sat at a table with her husband and two friends, Thomas McCaleb and Truxton Beale. Stanford White, her former lover, occupied a table near the stage.

Fittingly, and by remarkable coincidence, the lead singer had just finished *I Could Love a Million Girls*. Thaw had earlier claimed (and had reported to Anthony Comstock, custodian of the people's morals) that White had debauched no less than 278 virgins.

On the night of his death, according to the book Thaw later wrote, White had come to the theater to see a new seventeen-year-old beauty in the cast. When he went to the stage door, Lionel Lawrence, the show's manager, asked him to "'Please wait until afterwards, we are so troubled this first night.' Worse for him," wrote Thaw. "So White was to die in the very act of trying to debauch another girl hardly past childhood." Thaw continued: "Had he not been waiting for her, he might not have come to his death that night."

But these quotes came later. Thaw was wearing an overcoat, although it was a hot night, to conceal a pistol that he always carried. He rose, put the coat aside and, calmly walking between the tables separating the two, put the pistol close to White's head and pulled the trigger three times. White slid from his chair, dead, turning the table over as he fell, and a glass went clinking down the aisle. The scene froze into a tableau, the dancers motionless, the singers speechless. A policeman appeared and seized the killer's arm. Thaw said to him: "He deserved it, I can prove it." At this point, his wife, according to another witness, ran up to him saying, "Oh, Harry! Why did you do it?"

The trial was front-page news in New York's and the world's newspapers. It became almost impossible for Evelyn Nesbit to go out of her apartment or to make her way to the courtroom. On one occasion, women carrying scissors cornered her to cut locks of her hair as mementos. They tore at her clothing, pleading for her autograph.

As the trial proceeded, the scandal got juicier. Thaw believed that his defense should be "the unwritten law" — perhaps because his dinner companion, Truxton Beale, had gotten off after shooting a man over a woman in California by pleading that he was protecting her virtue. Thaw called his lawyers traitors because they on the advice of his mother (who knew) put in a plea of guilty by reason of insanity. They were right, too, for if ever a man was insane, it was Harry K. Thaw. The trial ended in a hung jury. By the time of his second trial two years later, much more evidence of his insanity was available. He was declared legally insane at the time of the murder and sent to Matteawan State Hospital for the Criminally Insane. Evelyn visited Thaw at the asylum. Then, while in Europe, she bore a son in 1912 and claimed Thaw was the father. Thaw, still in the asylum, denied it. He remained there for five years before escaping to Canada. Canadian authorities wanted no part of Thaw and spirited him back into the United States. After a new trial in New York, he was freed when a jury formally declared him sane again.

Later, Miss Nesbit came out of the retirement she had entered as a wife, and became a popular dancer and singer in vaudeville and musical comedy shows. With her partner, Jack Clifford, she shocked New York and European audiences by doing the new ragtime dances — the one-step, the two-step and the fox trot. In 1916 she finally divorced Thaw and married her dancing partner.

Her fortunes reached one more peak when Hollywood producers paid her $30,000 for giving them permission to tell the story of her life. She acted as "technical consultant" on the motion picture *The Girl in the Red Velvet Swing*, which took her back to the romantic days in Stanford White's studio but left out most of the scandal and all of the nudity.

Meanwhile, Thaw was involved in a number of escapades, including the horsewhipping of a teenage male protégé. (Evelyn wrote that he had once whipped her with a dog whip until she bled.) He was again committed to an asylum where he spent seven years before being again released as sane. His last years were spent in Miami, Florida. He died at seventy-six. But the girl in the red velvet swing lived to be eighty-two and died, in 1967, in a nursing home in Hollywood. Shortly before her death, she was quoted as remarking, "Stanny was lucky, he died. I lived."

On the fringes of the city, in areas that have since become suburbs, passionate religious evangelists pitched their tents and held camp meetings and revivals. Week-long orgies of religious fervor with thousands of conversions and hundreds of pregnancies often resulted. In the late summer the tents could be seen on many a meadow in Queens, Staten Island and the Bronx. Camp meetings operated by religious sects often featured three sermons and an additional songfest every day.

Each day began with a trumpet solo calling the worshipers from their camp beds. Trumpet arrangements included *Love Lifted Me, Shall We Gather at the River* and *Onward Christian Soldiers* was a favorite. The sermons built up an atmosphere of hysteria and spasmodic jumping and even rolling on the ground were not unusual after nightfall. One observer remarked, however, that "more souls were conceived than saved."

Certainly it was a meeting place and there were few enough of them for young men and women. Nor did they need a formal introduction, for both were there under godly auspices. Many a marriage was arranged, many a courtship began. Both revivals and camp meetings had an important effect upon social life, courtship, marriage and propagation, though not necessarily in that order.

But revivals and camp meetings were for those of Christian persuasion who could manage to get out of the city tenements, jam-packed with the Italian, the Irish and Jewish immigrants from Russia, Germany and eastern Europe. In these communities at the turn of the century women had few rights. Men ruled their families and often, when they died or abdicated, the eldest son was liable to take over as the macho leader.

Although legislation had been passed as early as 1860 — due to the efforts of Susan B. Anthony, Elizabeth Cady Stanton and Lucretia Mott — that married women could control their property and, theoretically, control their earnings as well, this was by no means always true in practice. Women and children who worked turned over their wages as household funds. It would have been almost unthinkable among these immigrant groups, for a married woman to dispose of property, regardless of how it was acquired. There were few divorces. Divorce was looked upon as being immoral and unaffordable. Most women in the honeycomb tenements either kept house, sewed, cooked and washed, or worked in a nearby clothing factory, of which there were many.

Sexual independence was almost unknown except perhaps among the prostitutes and certainly not by all of those. Some girls, if they were lucky and played their sexual tricks carefully, could manage to be courted by the man they wanted and pull off a marriage without premarital sex. In other cases they found it necessary to become pregnant and then have the families push the young man into marriage — ready or not.

I can remember a story my mother told me about a young girl she had known who came out of a ghetto environment. She had matured early and, by the time she was thirteen, one young man from a respectable middle-class family had his eye on her. Her mother beat her occasionally because she spent too much time looking out of the window and walking on the street when she should have been in the house. The two families knew one another and one afternoon the young man, with the knowledge of her mother, asked her to come over to visit after school. After entering the house, the girl noticed that he spoke to his younger sister and gave her some coins, telling her to go to the movies. It was then she found that there was no one else at home.

The resulting rape was as painful as it was shameful for her. But she was determined to say nothing of it to her parents. So she was surprised when that same evening the young man, who was then about twenty-one years old, came to call and tell her mother that she was no longer a virgin and that he was ready to marry her, which is what he had planned from the beginning. She had disliked him before she ever went to the house and, of course, now disliked him even more. But she had no choice. She was ruined, she was being offered a respectable marriage by a young man and his family, and they were married.

They had a first child and she determined to leave him as soon as the child was old enough for her to do so. Although he had continuously threatened to slice up her face with a razor blade should she ever try to leave, she did. With her face badly slashed and with scars from which she never recovered, she made her way to New Orleans, where she worked for a time for my family.

How many situations like this may have developed among the rigidly moral, European-influenced citizens of New York no one will ever know. But morality, guarded zealously by the religious leaders and their conservative congregations, was a matter of force not of choice.

Whatever change was felt by the masses of women in New York around the turn of the century was largely the work of Susan Brownell Anthony. She cut her hair short, was one of the early women to appear in bloomers — the first real forerunners of slacks — and she spoke to groups as large as possible as often as possible. Her message: "Free the women now that we have freed the slaves." She spent most of her life campaigning for sexual equality but she died without achieving her ultimate goal: the vote for women. It was fourteen years after her death, on August 18, 1920, that the Nineteenth Amendment, the Susan B. Anthony Amendment, was ratified, and women became full citizens of the United States for the first time in its history.

Sex in advertising began long before the turn of the century, but it was limited to garish outdoor signs, in which women were well-covered, or to overweight harem-type women bursting out of their bras or pantaloons on cigar boxes. In the eighties and nineties whiskey ads began to feature luscious, well-rounded, pink females. Manuals of etiquette and how-to-get-married books carried a few illustrations. However, most of the sexually stimulating material appeared on theatrical and circus posters, on the covers of early dime novels or paperback books containing the texts of Broadway plays.

New Orleans

"Send us some women" went a letter to Louis XV from the man who established New Orleans, Jean Baptiste le Moyne, Sieur de Bienville. This is in striking contrast to the beginnings of the colonies of Massachusetts or Virginia. From its beginning, the French founders of La Nouvelle Orléans realized the basic need of men for women. The king complied with alacrity to Bienville's request. He emptied the women's prison of La Salpétrière. As a result, eighty-eight vagrants, mostly whores and pickpockets, were the first women to arrive to keep the first settlers' beds warm.

Respectable girls followed when the Mississippi Company, charged with developing Louisiana, sent out shiploads of "casket" girls. These were girls from respectable small-town families who were each given a dowry in the form of a petite trunk, or casket. Unlike the first group, who were immediately bedded down, the second shipment was carefully guarded at night lest their purity be sullied. They were paraded out during the day so that men could make their selections. All were soon married. Later Creole families all traced their descent to these respectable girls. One would be led to think that the first group had no progeny at all.

From the very start, due to it being settled by the French, New Orleans enjoyed a spirit of joie de vivre. The weather was warm and the temperament of the people ardent. They believed in taking care of the body during the week and the soul at Mass on Sunday morning.

The early social structure of New Orleans put the Creoles at the top. When the first child was born on one of Bienville's ships, he is said to have written in a letter to the king: "Today the first Creole was born in La Nouvelle France." When New France was sold to Spain, the firstborn children of Spanish parents were called *criollo.* In time, both

French and Spanish sons and daughters of the seminal settlers become known as Creoles. The word took on such social significance that soon there were Creole Negroes, the offspring of blacks from Africa; Creole ponies bred in New Orleans from imported stock, and even Creole cows, pigs and chickens. But the word was never used to describe a person of mixed black and white blood.

In 1803 the United States bought Louisiana from Napoleon, who had taken it back from Spain, for $12 million dollars. This was an even bigger bargain than the Dutch purchase of Manhattan from the Indians, for this piece of land not only included Louisiana and the port of New Orleans, but all French territory north and west of the Mississippi — practically the entire western United States with the exception of California and parts of Arizona and New Mexico, which were Spanish.

The decade after the United States took over Louisiana saw great changes in New Orleans. Fresh new blood poured in from the North and the South. Down the river came riverboatmen by the hundreds. And up the river from the Gulf of Mexico, a continuous chain of ships brought merchants, traders and shopkeepers from the East Coast — Irish, German and Italian immigrants. This was the beginning of New Orleans' uptown, downtown and back-of-town districts. In the oldest section, known as the Vieux Carré (or French Quarter), were the high-class bordellos, gambling houses and cabarets. Further up the river lay a section known as the swamp where sex, whiskey and gambling competed for the patronage of the riverboatmen and the dregs of French and Spanish society. The swamp was a direct ancestor of the licensed red-light district that came into being in New Orleans at the turn of the century.

The spread of prostitution throughout the city was in part caused by the demise of the institution of concubinage which had flourished since 1880. Divorce was unknown in these days and even much later partly because the laws of Louisiana were based upon the French Napoleonic Code. Not even separations could be allowed to break up the family.

There were in New Orleans large numbers of attractive colored girls, the result of liaisons between white men and blacks in previous generations. Many of these mulatto girls had been educated in Paris or in the convents of New Orleans. Some were great beauties, noted for their elegance, their style, their grace. They learned quickly how to dress. These girls with slightly brownish yellow or dusky rose skin were choosy. Because marriage with a white man was impossible, they did not accept any offer lightly, but made the best deal possible in terms of both love and money. The mother checked out the financial and social status of the man and made sure that, should he leave her daughter, there would be property or money for her future support and that of their children.

New Orleans had a special section of the city on upper Rampart Street and the streets intersecting it where small houses were purchased by young men desirous of setting up a mistress and where they kept them, usually with full knowledge of their parents, friends and even wives. Usually, however, these arrangements were made by single men and often the concubine was deserted after his marriage on "the other side of town." Not all these liaisons were on so high a level. Many young men found mulatto girls and kept them as well as they could with or without arrangements with the girl's mother. Sometimes the girl occupied a single room on the edge of the Negro section of town instead of a small house. Many a young man rented a single room in the French Quarter where he could occasionally bring his mulatto quadroon or octoroon mistress.

Great excitement prevailed during the regularly held *Bals Masqués*, generally known as the Quadroon Ball. These were regular occasions designed to introduce "free women of color" to potential rich lovers. Much attention was given to the dress of these light copper colored girls. Their petticoats were ornamented at the bottom with gold lace, their slippers gold embroidered, their stockings decorated with spangles of golden embroidery. Accounts of the balls mentioned tight-fitting velvet jackets, petticoats trimmed with pearl tassels, light-weight cloaks worn as a train which could be removed for dancing. They wore chains of gold and pearls twisted in their hair. It must be remembered that none of these women would be welcome at any white function even though they were not slaves but free. Their balls were well attended by the male socialites and business men of the city, both married and single. By no means were these women prostitutes. If they formed a liaison with a man which was satisfactory to their mother, they lived with him faithfully. It was regarded as an honorable social custom though certainly not approved of by the white women of the city. Women of color had to be careful of their reputation. If they were promiscuous, it became known quickly and they were in trouble with the police. However, should she or her lover part, it was considered entirely reasonable for such a woman to make an arrangement with another man. It was a one-man-at-a-time society.

In addition to meetings at the regularly attended balls, these girls (and sometimes prostitutes as well) strolled at sunset along the New Orleans levee that protected the city from the rising Mississippi River, allowing themselves to be seen. When a young man approached they engaged him in an artful conversation. In many instances, and especially with the youngest and most beautiful girls, chaperones (mothers, grandmothers or aunts) accompanied them to make the bargain. If a young man could not afford a house of his own, arrangements were made with the girl's parents at so much a month (one account says $50 a month) and during that period he would be able to call, have the use of the bedroom from time to time, and "fruit, coffee and refreshments" were served. But he had his meals at his own home, where he also spent most of his nights.

This situation was convenient for the men of the city, unpleasant to the women. The authorities liked it. It kept down prostitution while giving an outlet to young men and an income to the mulatto population. It was in the romantic tradition of the European mistress and can be said to have been a successful sexual experiment that lasted in New Orleans for about fifty years.

There was good reason for young men in many southern cities to be drawn into liaisons with these attractive mulattoes. For one thing, the virginity of girls from well-to-do white families was guarded so carefully that it was rarely possible for a man to be alone with a young woman. Romantic love was not a factor in most Creole marriages. Parents made the arrangements, drew up the papers and often the young people had only a few moments to become acquainted before the ceremony. Discipline was strict, rebellious girls rare. Women of color offered a pleasant and acceptable way out of a young man's sexual dilemma.

By 1900 a major social reorganization occurred in New Orleans. The mulattoes were becoming too important a sexual and economic influence, and the institution of men keeping mistresses too well established, to be tolerated by society. The breakup of this previously condoned system of concubinage helped to spread prostitution over the city.

But before moving on we should mention one great battle that the prostitutes and their supporters won over the city fathers of New Orleans. In the year 1857 the city fathers decided that, because there was so much unconfined, unregulated sex for money — and they couldn't figure out a way to stop it — they would put a tax on it. All prostitutes were to be licensed and taxed. The legal contest began when Emma Pickett, an ambitious madam, applied for a license to operate her bordello. It was granted; she paid for it but made a point that she was doing so under protest. She sued the city to recover her license fee and the courts upheld her claim. It was a great victory and the madams and ladies celebrated for a week. From that time until 1897, prostitutes invaded every part of New Orleans. Some were located on St. Charles Avenue in the center of the expensive American mansions; others settled in the Vieux Carre section, where the Creoles still maintained their status. The situation became so serious (and the sex tax had proved a failure) that, for the legislators, it was either a matter of getting prostitution under control or the city was in danger of becoming one enormous brothel, with sex being sold from the river on the east to Lake Pontchartrain on the west.

There were more than 500 houses and at least 5000 professional whores at work. Yet, when control was suggested, New Orleans' respectable women arose in a body maintaining that to recognize prostitution legally was an affront to southern womanhood. As all over the United States, they did not want it mentioned. They especially wanted to ignore what they considered the animal side of men who patronized women who were both unspeakable and invisible. They intended to keep them that way. And, if a woman was married to a Dr. Jekyll and Mr. Hyde, she would rather not know what Mr. Hyde did when he was away from home and fireside. So the first attempt at a segregated district failed. Taking the side of the respectable women were the landowners and landlords who charged exorbitant rents for their properties throughout the city. Of course, the segregation of the girls would mean a considerable loss of revenue for them.

Then came a far-out idea put forth by Alderman Sidney Story. The measure he proposed, and the law that finally succeeded in confining the prostitutes, read that prostitution could be carried on legally only in a certain defined district. The City Council endorsed Story's motion and the ordinance was passed on January 26, 1897. It was the first time that prostitution had been recognized as a legal business enterprise within the law, and the city of New Orleans was made responsible for its enforcement. Landowners (which included some of the churches) were given time to evict their tenants and, within the year of grace allowed, madams, crib operators and the floating population of sex-for-sale girls packed their finery and moved into "Storyville." It was a perfect name for the district although it was a constant embarrassment to Sidney Story, who had hoped to become known for a more legitimate endeavor.

But the romance of the name Storyville stuck. It became the Storyville where jazz was nursed and weaned, where every kind of sex at every price was available, where the day's work began in the evening and ended at sunup. It was the place where men could gather to drink, gamble, tell jokes and use language that would not be tolerated at home. And they could participate in some of the violence and some of the playfulness of sex. Within this thirty-eight-block square worked more than 2000 registered whores and another 2000 servants, entertainers, bartenders and musicians. Basin Street counted thirty-five elaborate houses offering choice girls, expensive furnishings, good champagne and a gay, congenial atmosphere. Prostitutes ranged from strawberry blondes to exotic Latin types. Many of them were mulattoes, octoroons and quadroons but Negro whores were not allowed to work in the same houses as the white ones.

The madams and some of the girls created their own royalty. Lulu White, an octoroon known as the Diamond Queen, operated a house with beautiful light brown and high yellow girls. It was there that Clarence Williams, the great pianist, wrote his timeless *Mahogany Hall Stomp* as a tribute to the magnificent woodwork in the mansion. The tune later became a Louis Armstrong favorite.

Queen Gertie Livingston once reigned over one of the rougher houses. One of her girls bit off another's finger and she was arrested when an infection set in. Another of her girls testified that Queen Gertie had officiated at the fight and urged them on to more violence. As a result, Queen Gertie threw out the girl who testified, Helen Frank, and seized her belongings, which included four dozen towels. Miss Frank, in an effort to get them back, insisted these were tools of her trade and therefore could not be seized. But Queen Gertie got her comeuppance when her husband cut her up and she was forced to move away. She came back with her royalty status lowered, as Countess Kuneman, and went to work in another madam's parlor house.

To the "Countess" Willie Piazza, another octoroon, goes the accolade for being the first to have a piano player working full time in her spacious living room where her tall café-au-lait octoroons were displayed. The pianist's name has come down by word of mouth in history as John the Baptist.

In the bible of Storyville, known as the *Blue Book*, an annual roster of Storyville's offerings, an entry reads:

"Countess Willie Piazza, 317 North Basin. 'If you have the blues, the Countess and her girls can cure them. She has, without doubt, the most handsome and intelligent octoroons in the United States. You should see them. They are all entertainers.'"

The *Blue Book* began publication as the *Green Book*, or *Gentleman's Guide to New Orleans*, and was published before the segregated red-light district of Storyville existed. There was an edition of 2000 copies in January of 1895. They sold for twenty-five cents each and are collector's items today. At this time there seems to have been a guide called the *Red Book*. But by far the best known, and the one that stayed longest in print, was the *Blue Book*, first published in 1902. It was a small, slim, blue-covered volume with about fifty pages. It was sold by agents at the hotels, railroad stations, steamboat landings, tobacco stands and saloons. It was devoted exclusively to advertising the elaborateness of the houses, the status of the madams and the types and varieties of the girls available.

"The Studio, also known as the House of All Nations, 331-333 North Basin. Kept by Emma Johnson. 'Everything goes here. Pleasure is the watchword. Remember the name, Johnson's.'"

"Diane and Norma, 213-215 North Basin. 'Their names have become known on both continents, because everything goes as it will, and those that cannot be satisfied there must surely be of a queer nature.'"

· Whether queer was being used in a tongue-in-cheek homosexual sense is hard to determine because that word was not in common usage to describe homosexuals between 1902 and 1910.

The coolest, most distinguished madam, Josie Arlington, operated the most ornate, luxurious house in Storyville. It was located at 225 North Basin Street, had four stories with an attractive cupola on the top. Like all the sin palaces, Arlington House was overdecorated but well done. Colorful Persian rugs stretched across the hardwood floors. Damask-covered chairs and sofas adorned the parlor and the rooms upstairs as well. It was recognized as the classiest house in the district. Yet it was not the house but the ten carefully selected, well groomed girls that Josie Arlington featured. She advertised that they were all European and most of her girls were either French, German or Irish. They were a sure complement to her good taste and good business sense. When a fire broke out at the Arlington, Josie and her girls moved to quarters above Tom Anderson's saloon called the Arlington Annex. After they moved back Anderson continued to operate the Arlington Annex.

He became the real king of Storyville because his place was the first stop for a drink in the district. Anderson had great influence over the entire community, having been a member of the legislature for two terms, and the undisputed political leader of the Fourth Ward. In addition to the bar and gambling house, he owned one of the parlor houses on Basin Street and an interest in countless others. Anderson was not much different from other politicians in New Orleans in his time except he was more successful. He was the law in the relatively lawless red-light district.

Jazz existed before Storyville, but was not as nationally known. The distinctive music was actually born out of the French and Spanish marching bands and folk music, the drums and blues of the African blacks, mulattoes and octoroons and the very special vibes of that French-Spanish-American city on the bend of the Mississippi — good old New Orleans.

Many elements contributed to early jazz. Among them were the dancers, chants of the singers and the jungle drums of the blacks in Congo Square. This was an open field located at Orleans and Rampart streets. Voodoo priests, drummers, singers and flute players supplied the music for dancing both before and after the Civil War. The participants were slaves who were allowed to dance in Congo Square on Saturday and Sunday nights. Out of this setting came excellent Negro musicians who worked on Mississippi riverboats as barbers and waiters and at night entertained the passengers. Some of the most talented ones were employed to play at New Orleans dances toward the end of the nineteenth century.

It is important to remember that these were musicians who did not read music but who improvised on tunes that they learned by ear. This required a special skill and, because improvisation was so important, it adapted well to the unconventional style of Dixieland playing. Instead of a group getting together by note, it was crucial for these musicians to get together by sound and empathy, resulting in the polyphonic effect distinctive to New Orleans jazz.

Buddy Bolden was the earliest of the great black jazz musicians to emerge. He played a cornet and it was said that, when he played across the river in Gretna, the sound carried over to New Orleans. He formed a band, worked at many private parties and some of the barrel houses. Bolden is recognized as one of the fathers of jazz. His strongholds were dance halls in the Negro district of New Orleans. Perseverance Hall was one of them. A favorite blues number was *Careless Love* with its story about a girl who becomes pregnant from her careless lover who broke her heart. Its final refrain: "If I was a little bird, I would fly from tree to tree. I'd make my nest up in the sky where the bad boys couldn't bother me."

Some of the song titles and verses were unmentionable and had to be changed so that they could be identified. Such a tune was *Milneburg Joys,* originally called *Pee-hole [pussy] Blues.*

Most of the blues were slow, sad, and some of the bands dragged them out. But there were also blues like *Basin Street* which was upbeat and reflected the fact that both black and white prostitutes lived there. "*Basin Street* — is the street where the light and dark folks meet."

And even in those days you might here a jingle played and sung by a pickup band on a street corner:

> "Mama takes in washing.
> "Daddy's in jail.
> "Baby's on the corner shouting
> "'pussy for sale.'"

While this couplet was not necessarily in the repertoire of the Razzle Dazzle Spasm Band, it could have been. That band was made up of a group of teen-agers who played for whatever pennies, nickels and dimes were thrown to them. They played on street corners, in saloons and ultimately in some of the houses in Storyville. The band included a zither played by Stale Bread, a harmonica played by Cajun, a homemade bass strung with clothesline wire played by Whiskey, a four-string banjo made from a cheesebox played by Warm Gravy and a soapbox made into a four-string guitar played by Slewfoot Pete. Their technique kept improv-

ing and so did their jobs. Much of the personnel changed but Stale Bread stayed with the zither and piano and Harry Gregson (who later became chief of detectives in New Orleans) was the lead singer. Frank Bussy, Cajun's brother, was known as Monk. He played a homemade horn and doubled on a homemade flute. Bussy lived on for many years. During Prohibition he was a bartender in charge of the Press Club. Many an evening, over some illegally imported Johnny Walker, Bussy would recount the high life to which the Razzle Dazzle Spasm Band was exposed.

Hundreds of thousands of words have been written about how the word jazz came into the language. The kind of music that the early New Orleans musicians played was called jass, possibly because the word jazz was a synonym for fuck — you could jazz a girl or you could be jazzed. *Jazz Me Blues* meant fuck me blues. When the word was printed relating to the kind of music that was played in and around the red-light district, it was changed to jass. Ramsey and Smith in their book *Jazz Men* relate that a black band called Tom Brown's Band from Dixieland went to Chicago in June 1915 to work at the Lamb's Cafe. "People were curious to know what jass music really was and they came in droves to find out. Presently the new sign out front read 'Added attraction — Brown's Dixieland Jass Band, directly from New Orleans, best dance music in Chicago.'"

But that was a lot later. Back in Storyville, King Oliver, Freddy Keppard, Kid Ory and Louis Armstrong all played at one time or another in the jazz palaces on Basin Street, the elite section of Storyville. Not much music was heard back on St. Louis and Franklin streets in the cribs. In these small, one-room cubicles with swinging green shutters that could be flipped open enough to let the men look the girls over, the price of pussy ranged from twenty-five cents to a dollar. As the men went by, soft voices in the night would call out, "*Viens ici, chéri.*" By no means did all the girls speak French but I can remember even from my early teens the girls on St. Louis Street calling out to me.

There is a story about a customer who arrived at a parlor house where the madam greeted him in the ornate parlor. He spoke only French and she could not make out just what he was saying. So she called up the stairs, where the girls were, "Does anyone up there speak French?"

And a loud voice came down saying, "Good God — do we have to speak it too?"

"Anything goes" was part of the advertising placed in the *Blue Book* by more than one madam and, within the context of the mores of the time, they meant it.

Some houses specialized in sex entertainment, usually called circuses. Such circuses were held on many different levels. In an expensive house, the customers might be charged from five to twenty-five dollars per person to witness the ritual defloration of a supposed virgin. The girl was always young, pretty and innocent-looking. Her ravisher, who was theoretically paying for the privilege, was often a member of the house's entertainment contingent. Some "virgins" lost their maidenheads three or four times a week.

A few houses had a special room with chinks in the wall so that customers could watch the proceedings at so much per peek. A young girl would enter dressed in white, showing fear of the theoretically innocent customer who expected her to undress and lie down. But she would not allow him to take her clothes off and made him fight every step of the way until she was overcome and reluctantly gave up. While most of these scenes were staged, at other times a legitimate first-time customer would be introduced into such a room situation never knowing that his antics were being observed.

A stage with curtains that could be opened at the beginning and closed at the end of the act was a feature of many houses. Performances often included two lesbians on a couch who were joined by a lusty male, who then proceeded to go through as many sexual positions as a three-way combination could supply. A show might include a white man with an octoroon girl and in the octoroon houses perhaps a black man with a white (or near white) girl.

Uncle Tom's Taillight was a unique act first put on with black performers. A girl would place an unlighted cigarette into the lips of her vagina and another into her mouth. A second girl would light them for her. Then, with buttocks to the audience, she would lean down until her head could be seen between her legs and puff away with her mouth and her pussy keeping the cigarettes glowing. Some girls were said to be especially proficient at this and could also smoke cigars.

Another standard trick was standing a series of half-dollars on edge around a table. Then the performer would pick them off the table, one at a time, by contracting her vaginal lips.

Some shows were accompanied by the house pianist and, in the later days of Storyville, a three- or four-piece band might play the opening number. Even madams enjoyed not only producing but sometimes participating in a circus. Emma Johnson was spectacularly bisexual. She worked as a prostitute, in lesbian acts with other girls and, according to some sources, acquired young men for older homosexuals. Emma specialized in putting on the most graphic and sexually shocking spectacles in Storyville. Yet lesbianism was not acceptable or popular.

On Octobr 21, 1903, the New Orleans weekly newspaper, *The Mascot,* featured on its cover two well-dressed and shapely girls embracing on a couch while a small dog looked on. Their inside story was headlined, "Good God! The Crimes of Sodom and Gomorrah Discounted. A Story Which Only Too True, Recalls a Shocking State of Sin in Our Midst . . . This week the MASCOT is in possession of a story of the love of two women, — licentious, horrible love. One of the girls referred to attracts all eyes as she walks Canal street. She is one of the most beautiful girls in the city. She is virtuous — so far so as repelling the advances of men, but she is viler than the most lost harlot on Basin or Burgundy street. Words would fail to give anything like an adequate description of the horrible orgies she and her chosen friend indulge in. They have been described in the MASCOT office, but modesty must throw over our sheets a veiling which hides from the world the maddening, disgusting practices of the two women alluded to."

The Mascot was all for good healthy heterosexual sex, but it would not tolerate male or female homosexuality, sadism or traffic in virgins. The paper made a great deal of money out of its righteous indignation.

During the twenty or so years that Storyville existed, there were few attacks from the respectable society outside its boundaries. In fact, many church leaders considered it a necessary evil that kept their own daughters pure. No thought was given, nor was it mentioned publicly, that venereal diseases might be spread through visits of husbands and sons to Storyville. Like many other areas, this was a blind spot. Some assignation houses operated quietly outside of Storyville. *The Mascot* in November 1892, attacked "society ladies who have happy homes and loving husbands, yet meet their lovers in assignation houses." The sheet castigated such women for being "impure in mind and body.. . . It is notorious that fallen women have a desire to drag others down to their level, and the social queen, married or single, who indulges in illicit love, is as much a fallen woman as the worst inhabitant of a brothel." *The Mascot* urged that adultery and fornication be made a crime. But the live-and-let-live Louisiana State Legislature would have none of it.

The Mascot wrote not only of the activities in and around Storyville but reported on crime, scandal and political corruption all over the city. While it obviously used sensational material to sell papers, it also defended the rights of working prostitutes both in and out of Storyville. Its sensational cover drawings included one scene in 1890 which shows a group of black musicians with trombone, cornet, drums and clarinet literally knocking down citizens in the street with their blast of

New Orleans music. One man, labeled "property holder," is screaming, as the horses rear and women faint, "For God's sake, stop!"

Another cover showed a sharp-nosed, sharp-eared businessman handing out dollars to a procuress who is buying young girls, hardly more than children. The train in the background waits to speed the girls to Texas whorehouses. When the woman who was buying girls was interrogated by *The Mascot*, she said, "Why? Perhaps you would be surprised if I told you that not a very long time ago a mother brought her three daughters to me and offered them for sale. Two, she said, were bad, and the youngest still unacquainted with vice and the wickedness of the world. She demanded twenty-five dollars for the girls, and expressed her belief that she ought to get more for the guileless maiden."

The Mascot also specialized in exposés and made a decided effort to unmask crooked politicians who, under pressure, would have the very madam seized that they were financing in the white slave traffic.

Some idea of the kind of brawling that went on in Storyville can be gleaned from the account of the fight between Jennie Donahue and John Knipper. Jennie had a boyfriend whose name was Baptiste. He and John Knipper came to blows, "tussled for a short time on the sidewalk, when they rolled into the gutter, and then smashed away at each other for quite a while." Jennie, who was said to be drunk, came out of a saloon and, seeing Knipper on top of her lover, picked up an oyster knife and stabbed Knipper several times. Although the case went to court the next morning and although Knipper was certainly stabbed, Jennie managed to convince the judge that she did not have a knife. The judge "gave the prisoner the benefit of the doubt and discharged her."

That the parlor houses were sumptuous and expensively furnished is proved by both drawings and photographs that have come down from the turn of the century. But at one point five well-known madams found themselves in deep trouble because of their furniture purchases. A gentleman, W. B. Ringrose, who enjoyed the girls in some of these establishments was in the furniture business. He agreed to sell them new house furnishings on the installment plan and promised to make their payments easy. But, regrettably, Mr. Ringrose died suddenly and his family did not feel the same tenderness toward the madams. Much of the furniture was seized and, for a time at least, only the beds were left in these elaborate establishments. However, it was not very long before the debts were paid off and the furniture returned.

The days before Lent, and especially the two weeks before Mardi Gras (fat Tuesday), meant prosperity and overtime hours for the hard-working whores of Storyville. Prices went up for girls and liquor during the gay carnival season. Men arriving by train or boat were often greeted by their friends or guides with the words, "Shall we check into the hotel first, Colonel, or shall we go directly to the whorehouse?" More often than not, the first stop was Storyville. Visitors from all over the world came to marvel at the palaces and the beauty of the girls. No visit to New Orleans was complete without a drink and a stroll through Storyville.

Fortunately, the opulence of the decor and the beauty of many of the girls has come down to us in the photographs of E. J. Bellocq. Bellocq, in addition to other commercial photography, took his glass plate camera down to Storyville to photograph many of the girls, nude and semi-nude, in their unique environment. His pictures included a lovely girl sitting in the window with her small iron bed in the shadows behind her; another showed a frank-faced smiling girl, her high, well-shaped breasts exposed. Interiors, made with time exposure and his large camera on a tripod, revealed the crystal chandeliers, elaborately carved tables, expensive brass bedsteads as well as the now long-forgotten figures and faces who worked their tricks at Storyville.

Bellocq was both a documentarian and a poet with the camera. His girls are never awkwardly posed nor are the backgrounds artificially arranged. They appear as neither glamorous nor degraded but rather as interesting, attractive women who worked at sex in Storyville.

I met Bellocq and bought a series of prints from him shortly before he died. It was thirty-five years later that he was discovered by the Museum of Modern Art which acquired many of the glass plate negatives from which his prints were made. In 1978 he became known to millions of moviegoers as the leading male character in the French director Louis Malle's story of a twelve-year-old prostitute which he called *Pretty Baby*.

Long before Storyville, back in 1870 according to Herbert Asbury, Molly Williams worked as a whore in tandem with her ten-year-old daughter. This combination's price for a night's sexual revelry cost fifty dollars — a very high price in those post-Civil War days. The police ultimately broke up the tandem but the parlor house madam, Josephine Killeen, violently protested. At the court hearing, she insisted that the child was in no way immoral and was only helping her mother to get along in the world.

Storyville did not die. It was shot down by World War I, and more specifically by Secretary of the Navy Josephus Daniels. He issued an order that no prostitution could exist within five miles of a navy base — and New Orleans was a big navy base. Shortly afterwards, Bascom Johnson, War Department representative for the Army and Navy, came to New Orleans, looked over Storyville and informed the city fathers that either they must close the area or the War Department would do it. Because Storyville had been successful in confining prostitution to a limited area; and because New Orleans, using strict supervision, had proved that such segregation was the best method devised for controlling prostitution; and because Storyville had become a worldwide attraction, the city was reluctant to comply. Mayor Martin Berman made a special trip to Washington to tell the War Department that the city government believed that the situation "could be administered more easily and satisfactorily by confining it within a prescribed area." There were rumors that the mayor would win out but he was turned down cold by the Army and Navy. An ordinance was passed condemning Storyville to oblivion at midnight November 12, 1917.

A madam who had been active since 1880, and spent a large part of her life in Storyville, gave up gracefully. In a memoir she wrote that at midnight she stood under the big chandelier in her house on Basin Street and had a last drink of champagne. The whores were crying, she wrote, some were naked, others were dressed with their half-dressed johns coming downstairs. By the time midnight came, the whores were packed and they moved out, some to travel west to Texas, others north to Memphis and Chicago. It was as though a giant hammer had struck a fragile vessel and the fragments were thrown everywhere. The great majority of the whores and madams simply relocated in New Orleans, where many of them lived happily and prosperously ever after. The authorities had made fornication illegal again but, as one of the madams remarked, "They'll never make it unpopular."

Along with sex, music never became unpopular in the crescent city. Only a few blocks from the red-light district on Bourbon Street, the French Opera House had been constructed in 1859. There, for sixty years, the French Opera Company and the most prominent singers from Europe appeared regularly. A number of operas made their American debut in New Orleans. Among them were Saint-Saëns's *Samson et Dalila*, Massenet's *Hérodiade*, *Werther* and *Don Quichotte* and Gounod's *La Reine de Saba* and *Le Tribut de Zamora*. Adelina Patti, one of the great singers of all time, became a special favorite when she made her operatic debut at the French Opera.

From 1859 until 1919, when the Opera House burned down, it continued to be patronized by New Orleans' elite. Because most of its talent was imported from Europe, it had little or no influence on the development of New Orleans' music.

In the area between the French Opera House and the red-light district stood many fine old Creole homes with large Spanish patios and galleries overhanging the narrow streets. By 1915, however, many of the old families were moving uptown, and downtown "studios" were beginning to be used for extracurricular sexual purposes by young unmarried men and older married men as well. These were not really assignation houses but rather a place to bring their girls. These French Quarter studios, to some degree, were related to the earlier institution of white-colored concubinage which was popular between 1800 and 1850. Their popularity continued into the thirties when rent began climbing very high and many buildings were remodeled and repriced by their owners.

After Storyville disappeared in 1917 a new life began to germinate in the New Orleans French Quarter adjacent to it. It became a center for artists, writers and what can only be called experimentalists. Many of the experiments involved a new genre in literature. Sherwood Anderson moved in. He had just written, in *Dark Laughter*:

"Everyone interested in Leopold and Loeb, the young murderers. All people thinking alike. Leopold and Loeb become the nation's pets. The nation horror-struck about what Leopold and Loeb did. What is Harry Thaw doing now, who is divorced, who fled with the bishop's daughter? Dance life! Awake and dance!"

William Faulkner checked in from Oxford, Mississippi. Carl Carmer and Oliver La Farge lighted literary fires that burned as brightly as those of Greenwich Village.

Other artists included Knute Heldner and Leslie Powell, painters, and William Spratling, noted not only for his caricatures of local celebrities in the book with captions by William Faulkner, *Anderson and Other Famous Creoles*, but also for a never-to-be-forgotten prank. One late night he loaded and fired the ancient cannon in Jackson Square. The ball supposedly crossed the Mississippi and landed in Algiers. Spratling was one of the early homosexuals to come out of New Orleans, followed not too many years later by Tennessee Williams. Spratling's career took off in Mexico, where he became a famous silversmith and jewelry designer in Taxco. The Spratling name on a piece of Mexican jewelry soon became a mark of high quality.

John McCrady who, like William Faulkner, came

from Oxford, Mississippi, was an outstanding painter and muralist and colleague of other New Orleans painters, Xavier Gonzales and Paul Ninas.

Among the photographers, Clarence Laughlin documented the great houses and plantations of the region, including their ghosts. In between Bellocq, with his pictures of whores and madams of Storyville, and Laughlin, Arnold Genthe in the late twenties recorded his romantic impressions of the gay and wicked city.

Perhaps the greatest sex radical to stir up the emotions of New Orleanians was a sculptor of Mexican descent residing in the French Quarter. His name was Enrique Alferez. "Rique" had a well-earned reputation for sampling the amateurs on the female sexual scene, with a high percentage of successful beddings. Whenever he saw what seemed to him a beautiful and sexy girl, he wasted no time on courtship but approached her as immediately and directly as possible. His opening, and often closing, gambit was, "Would you like to fuck?" Afterward he reported, "I get slapped a lot of times, but not as often as you would think. The percentage that are willing is well worth the temporary discomfort."

One night, in a New Orleans cabaret, Rique made his proposition to the wrong female. She reached across the table with a champagne bottle and knocked him cold. Fortunately, he had a hard head. It was split open but he lived. This experience did not cool him down. Rique was frequently in trouble with the New Orleans Police, partly because he was drunk and disorderly with dismaying regularity, and partly because he had a tendency to bait them.

An outstanding sculptor (during his apprenticeship he had worked with Paul Manship on the famous gold-leaf sculpture in Rockefeller Center) he had little difficulty getting federal and city commissions. But his realistic sexual attitude showed through in his sculptured figures.

In the late thirties Rique sculpted four figures representing the *Four Winds*. It was a government contract. When the statue was unveiled, it was seen to consist of three nude females and one nude male who was, according to most viewers, well hung. A local official called Rique in and said that it was immoral to "have a man with his privates showing."

After the conference, Rique reported, "He asked me what my mother would do if she knew about it." I told him, "If she didn't know about it, I wouldn't be here." But the flap continued for the officials contended that the figure would be a menace to public morals. It was decided that the penis must go. Alferez took a rifle and stood guard over the statue until the controversy cooled down. It was Eleanor Roosevelt, at the behest of writer Lyle Saxon, who intervened from Washington to save the figure.

Twenty years later, Alferez had another confrontation with the New Orleans censors over a family group designed for the Municipal Court Building. The group showed not only a mother naked but a father and child as well. There were so many complaints from conservative New Orleanians that the sculpture was covered with canvas and auctioned off. At the auction, one municipal court judge, who had complained about the nudity, bid a hundred dollars and said he planned to throw the family into the river. But the warden of one of the prisons considered buying it, saying that he would hang it in the prison courtyard where, he said, "it would entertain the prisoners and take their minds off the food they had to eat." A saloonkeeper with an eye for art bid it in at $2400 — a $600 profit for the city that had only paid Alferez $1800.

The French Quarter was lively in those days. Rique Alferez and his artist and writer friends made it an even livelier place.

San Francisco

California was a golden state from its beginning and San Francisco was the brightest nugget in its glittering lode. Because of the effusion of gold after 1849, it might be said that San Francisco started at the top. It created mansions and palaces alongside cheap frame buildings and one-room cribs where its "soiled doves" sold sex.

It was a man's town in the industrial and economic sense. But it was the civilizing influence of its women — whores and madams, as well as boardinghouse keepers, school teachers and prim matrons — which was the moving force behind the fashionable aura that slowly spread over the once crude village.

Women appeared everywhere and did everything. An early editorial in the *California Police Gazette* chided them: "If forgetting the early principles of virtuous morality instilled in their hearts, during their juvenile days while watched with a parent's care, they will, so soon as they arrive to the years of early maidenhood, throw off the bonds with which they were encumbered and plunge into a vortex of vice, they cannot but expect that they will and must be marked in society and fall from the elevated position they were by nature designed for." The editorial goes on to point out that these women, by going to places of pleasure, appearing at balls, going on moonlight rides on horseback and in buggies, are cultivating the seeds of their destruction.

There was nothing illegal about being a prostitute in early San Francisco, unless trouble broke out. Occasionally a man was arrested for beating up a woman but it was rare for the woman to testify against him in court. One judge, after imposing a fine on a rough-looking type for spanking his wife, said, "It is no great harm to whip some wives, provided the public are not disturbed by the operation." This is reminiscent of a quote attributed to Mrs. Patrick Campbell, the British actress and socialite, who, when told of the sexual peccadilloes of a prominent English couple, said, "I don't care what they do so long as they do not do it in the streets and frighten the horses."

The fine for wife beating was usually ten dollars. Considering San Francisco's affluence in the early days, many men felt that they could afford this luxury.

The city fathers did their best to ignore what went on in the hundreds of brothels, but occasionally such hell broke loose that the whole town felt the shock waves. One evening a whore known as Irish Mary became overly annoyed with Ellen Spizer and, according to the report in the *Police Gazette*, "used brass knuckles on the sconce of Ellen." The damage to Ellen's head being considerable, Irish Mary was fined $200. But this was only the beginning of fiery-tempered Ellen's adventures. A few weeks later she was in bed with another whore, Sarah Ann Drum, when unexpectedly two of their colleagues, Fanny Clark and Margaret Stanley, launched an attack with a hatchet and a pocketknife. Fanny, with her pocketknife, carved up Miss Drum considerably. As Miss Drum in desperation jumped out of the second-story window, Fanny, who was an expert with a knife, threw it with almost fatal accuracy. The blade grazed Sarah Ann and buried itself an inch deep into the wall. Meanwhile, another whore, brandishing a water basin, smashed it over the head of Ellen Spizer. It was a bloody and uproarious evening and occupied an important place in the newspapers for a week. As a postscript, Fanny Clark was convicted of carving up Sarah Ann. She told the court she would be happy with ten years incarceration — because she was very pleased with what she had accomplished. The judge did not oblige her. He fined her $1200 and gave her a short jail sentence.

Violence was common along Kearny Street. Knifings and shootings were almost a daily occurrence. After an argument over a bill for drinks in one brothel, a man refused to pay. When the madam insisted, he drew his gun and shot her and one of her girls. Neither died of their wounds but the newspaper reported: "One ball entered the cheek of the madam knocking out two teeth quicker than a dentist could — and a girl named Nellie was also shot."

During its boisterous heyday the lead stories in San Francisco newspapers were usually devoted to crime, sex or politics. Stories dealing with local prostitution were, however, seldom run. If they appeared at all, it was in small type in the back of the paper. The big sex stories came from New York, Paris and Chicago. One story dealing with prostitution in New York featured a house where twelve- to fourteen-year-old prostitutes were standard bait. A Chicago story dealt with 150 Chicago whores who were arrested and confined to a single cell.

There was seldom mention of either the ornate houses or the mean cribs of San Francisco, Sacramento or Stockton. International murders and killings in the Northeast and New Orleans were always good for a story.

Possibly because of the early shortage of females a considerable number of cases of indecent exposure occurred in early San Francisco. One modest woman took such offense when she saw a flasher outside her window that she picked up her shotgun and blasted away. She was not arrested.

Stories dealing with incest regularly ran in the papers; some involved uncles with nieces, others fathers and daughters. In many cases, when found guilty, the couple was usually allowed to leave town.

Kidnappings also made headlines. One well-documented case involved a seventeen-year-old Mexican girl, Irena Valdez. She and her mother had arrived from Mazatlan and shortly afterward the mother sold the girl's virginity to a local Frenchman for $500. He paid his ante and had possession of the girl for about a month when she escaped. First Irena attempted to get some of the money back from her mother. The mother turned her down and Irena vanished. The case was never solved but it was generally believed that, because the Frenchman disappeared also, he had probably taken off with his possession.

One of the first American chroniclers of the San Francisco scene was Samuel Clemens, who became Mark Twain on his way west — in Virginia City, to be exact. He had traveled west in 1861 and arrived in San Francisco in May of 1864. It was, he said, "the livest, heartiest community on our continent." In that year it had a population of 115,000. There were newspapers and Mark Twain worked for a number of them including the *Golden Era*, the *Californian*, the *San Francisco Call*, the *Daily Dramatic Chronicle*. He also contributed to Virginia City's *Territorial Enterprise*. He patronized its six theaters and its 500 or more saloons. His ascerbic wit and his gift for satire were often demonstrated at the expense of San

Francisco's social set. In his articles on hoop skirts, he wrote: "To get the best effect — one should stand on the corner of Montgomery and look up a steep street like Clay or Washington.. . . . It reminds me of how I used to peep under circus tents when I was a boy and see a lot of mysterious legs about with no visible bodies attached to them. And what handsome vari-colored garters they wear nowadays!" He added, "But for the new spreading hoops, I might have gone on thinking ladies still tied up their stockings with common strings and ribbons as they used to when I was a boy."

Twain earned the enmity of the San Francisco Police on many occasions: "Chief Burke's Star Chamber Board of Police Commissioners is the funniest institution extant, and the way he conducts it is the funniest theatrical exhibition in San Francisco.. . . But it is all humbug, display, fuss and feathers. The Chief brings his policeman out as sinless as an angel, unless the testimony be heavy enough and strong enough, almost, to hang an ordinary culprit, in which case a penalty of four or five days' suspension is awarded."

When Rudyard Kipling traveled from England to the United States in 1889, he also made a number of observations about the women — and the men — that he met. He spoke of San Francisco and "her merry maidens, her strong, swaggering men and her wealth of gold and pride." His descriptions were brief but pertinent.

"I am hopelessly in love with about eight American maidens — each perfectly delightful till the next one comes into the room. O-Toyo was a darling, but she lacked several things; conversation, for one. You cannot live on giggles. She shall remain unmoved at Nagasaki while I roast a battered heart before the shrine of a big Kentucky blonde who had for a nurse, when she was little, a negro 'mammy.' By consequence she was welded on to California beauty, Paris dresses, Eastern culture, Europe trips, and wild Western originality, the queer dreamy superstitions of the negro quarters, and the result is soul-shattering. And she is but one of many stars. Item, a maiden who believes in education and possesses it, with a few hundred thousand dollars to boot, and a taste for slumming. Item, the leader of a sort of informal salon where girls congregate, read papers, and daringly discuss metaphysical problems and Candy — a sloe-eyed, black-browed, imperious maiden. Item, a very small maiden, absolutely without reverence, who can in one swift sentence trample upon and leave gasping half a dozen young men. Item, a millionairess, burdened with her money, lonely, caustic, with a tongue keen as a sword, yearning for a sphere, but chained up to the rock of her vast possessions. Item, a typewriter-maiden earning her own bread in this big city, because she doesn't think a girl ought to be a burden on her parents. She quotes Théophile Gautier, and moves through the world manfully, much respected, for all her twenty inexperienced summers. Item, a woman from Cloudland who had no history in the past, but is discreetly of the present, and strives for the confidences of male humanity on the grounds of 'sympathy.' (This is not altogether a new type.) Item, a girl in a 'dive' blessed with a Greek head and eyes that seem to speak all that is best and sweetest in the world. But woe is me! — she has no ideas in this world or the next, beyond the consumption of beer (a commission on each bottle), and protests that she sings the songs allotted to her nightly with no more than the vaguest notion of their meaning."

Kipling compares the women of London, of Devonshire and of Paris with girls of America and concludes that "girls of America are above and beyond them all. They are clever; they can talk. Yea, it is said that they think."

He was deeply impressed with the fact that women of San Francisco "can take care of themselves; they are superbly independent." He also felt they had a great deal of freedom. "They can go driving with young men and receive visits from young men to an extent that would make an English mother wink with horror."

In spite of this freedom, Kipling wrote, sexual "accidents do not exceed the regular percentage arranged by the devil."

As to the San Francisco men, "The young men rejoice in the days of their youth. They gamble, yacht, race, enjoy prize fights and cock fights — the one openly, the other in secret — they establish luxurious clubs; they break themselves over horseflesh and — other things.. . ."

He observes that the men who made their way across the United States or around the Horn and from all the countries in the world were "as far as regards certain tough virtues, the pick of the earth. The inept and the weakly died *en route* or went under in the days of construction. The result you shall see in large-boned, deep-chested, delicate-handed women, and long, elastic, well-built boys.. . . Him I love because he is devoid of fear, carries himself like a man, and has a heart as big as his boots."

Yet this English writer was wary of the temper of Californians. "It is enough to know that fifty per cent of the men in the public saloons carry pistols about them. The Chinaman waylays his adversary and methodically chops him to pieces with his hatchet. Then the Press roars about the brutal ferocity of the Pagan. The Italian reconstructs his friend with a long knife. The Press complains of the waywardness of the alien." But, he continues, when "the Irishman and the native Californian in their hours of discontent use the revolver, not once, but six times — The Press records the fact, and asks in the next column whether the world can parallel the progress of San Francisco."

But Kipling couldn't stand the fast pulse of San Francisco. "It was with regrets for the pleasant places left behind, for the men who were so clever, and the women who were so witty, for the 'dives,' the beer-halls, the bucket-shops, and the poker-hells where humanity was going to the Devil with shouting and laughter and song and the rattle of dice-boxes. I would fain have stayed, but I feared that an evil end would come to me when my money was all spent and I descended to the street corner."

And Kipling was probably right. For it was easy to run out of money in the honky-tonks, the saloons, the cow yards, cribs and parlor houses. So he traveled north.

By the year 1880 San Francisco's Barbary Coast was well established as the most decadent region in the United States. The center of the district was the block bounded by Broadway, Kearny, Montgomery and Pacific Avenue. This area was known as the Devil's Acre. Within the Devil's Acre, on the eastern side of Kearny Street, was a line of dance halls and brothels. Few of the brothels were equipped with window shades or curtains, so that naked women, and men too, were often visible. Robberies in this section were frequent and the area averaged at least one murder a week.

The Barbary Coast was made up of many kinds of bars, saloons, theaters, parlor houses and dance halls. The proprietors of all except the best and most expensive loaded all the dice against the customer. Even the saloons had some music and dancing, for it gave the girls a chance to find out whether the customer was well-heeled. If he was, she notified the bartender and the first drinks were often on the house. Then, as long as he continued to spend money, he was treated royally. But should he show an inclination to tighten up his purse and leave the joint, his last drinks, again on the house, were likely to contain one drug or another — snuff, sulphate of morphine or a drop of iodine was enough to befuddle him so completely — if it did not knock him out entirely — that he could easily be separated from his money. It did little good for even the toughest type (and some of the seafaring men were very tough indeed) to fight their way out. Because the moment they were outside the bar they were likely to be cracked on the head and robbed.

In addition to the bars that lined the streets of the Barbary Coast, there were concert saloons that featured female singers and dancers. Most of these girls were prostitutes on the side. Almost entirely untalented, ex-

cept perhaps in bed, some of these performers relied upon their outrageous appearance to earn a living. With names like the Dancing Heifer or the Waddling Duck, extremely obese women would perform parodies of classical ballets wearing little clothing. Some entertainers, like the Little Lost Chicken, traded on their small size and innocent appearance. Despite her looks she soon developed a reputation as a pickpocket.

The dance halls and concert saloons supplied small cribs furnished with cots or sometimes only with blankets spread on the floor. After getting her customer plastered, the "pretty waiter girl" would lead him into a cubicle, and during the break between dances they would copulate on the floor without disrobing.

Among the most popular of the combination dance hall theaters were the Louisiana, the Rosebud, the Occidental, Brook's Melodium, the Bull Run, the Billy Goat and the Colliseum. The Bull Run, obviously named for its stench, was perhaps the toughest joint in the late 1870s. It was also known as Hell's Kitchen and Dance Hall. On the corner of Jackson and Kearny streets, also known as "Murderers' Corner," was the Opéra Comique. Herbert Asbury, in his book *The Barbary Coast*, describes the Bull Run as a three-story building with a dance hall and bar in the cellar, a second dance hall and bar on the street floor and a whorehouse upstairs. It was owned by Ned Allen, whose motto for the establishment was "anything goes here." The Bull Run differed from many of the dives along the street in that the drinks served to the girls and the female entertainers were not tea but the real thing. They were expected to drink the liquor purchased for them by their customers. So, instead of hard liquor most of the girls drank beer. This had its problems too. To remedy the fact that they were not allowed to leave the dance floor or the stage except at long intervals, many of the girls wore diapers instead of the usual panties.

Asbury says that if one of the "pretty waiter girls" or performers became unconscious from liquor, she was carried upstairs, laid out on a bed and sexual privileges were sold to all comers while she was sprawled in her drunken stupor. The price ranged from twenty-five cents to a dollar depending upon the age and beauty of the girl. For an additional twenty-five cents a man could watch his predecessor. It was not unusual for a girl to have as many as thirty to forty men in the course of a single night. Theoretically, she was supposed to receive half the revenue from this unconsious prostitution. But, because she had no way of knowing how much she had earned, she was usually cheated.

The best known and lowest of the joints in the Devil's Acre section was originally called the Slaughterhouse and later, in 1885, became the Morgue. It was a hangout for pimps, drunk rollers (who knocked their victims out with a blackjack or a section of lead pipe and then robbed them) and drug addicts, called hoppies, who traded supplies of opium but bought their supply of cocaine or morphine at an all-night drugstore on Grant Avenue.

The corner of Kearny and California streets has the distinction of having been the site of the first topless bar in the United States. This consisted of a dance hall barroom with a few private booths, including a couch — for obvious reasons. The joint opened with its girls wearing only silk stockings and short skirts. When the police ordered the women to be supplied with blouses, the management complied. The apparel was not only thin and transparent, but wide open, the order having failed to state that they should be kept buttoned.

Best known of all these music halls was the Bella Union at Washington and Kearny streets. There, well-known singers and dancers held forth, such as Ned Harrigan, later to be celebrated as half of the minstrel team of Harrigan and Hart, Eddie Foy, who fathered the great theatrical family, Flora Walsh and Lotta Crabtree. Harrigan and Hart, after leaving the Bella Union, went east and became the most popular song and dance team in United States vaudeville around the turn of the century.

The Bella Union became, over a period of years, the most popular theater saloon in San Francisco. Sailors on shore leave, businessmen visiting the city and most of the male residents sooner or later patronized the Bella Union. It had an early start as a gambling house during the gold rush. Later, the decor featured velvet-draped private boxes, and what went on within depended upon the ability and inclination of the performers who visited the booths to sell drinks. It was sometimes a family theater but it was mainly a variety vaudeville house with risqué material. Men never brought their wives. Minstrel shows were especially popular. Short, one-act dramatic plays and knock-about comedy teams were also billed. Although destroyed a number of times, from 1868 until the earthquake of 1906 the Bella Union enjoyed a continuous popularity.

By the turn of the century strong competition came from the Midway Plaisance which featured the popular hootchy-kootchy, a dance that had been made famous at the *Streets of Cairo* show at the Chicago's World Columbian Exposition in 1893. Little Egypt, whom *Variety* described as a hip waver, was one of their entertainers. Like the Bella Union, the Midway Plaisance had a mezzanine made up of small booths heavily curtained. The female performers visited the booths between acts to sell drinks, or whatever else time permitted.

Women who supplied sex for a price were recognized in the West not only as a necessity but as part of the common good, essential to the welfare and development of the country. The attitude seemed to be that the church should be allowed to save sinners but should not be allowed to interfere with carnal needs. And, if the sale of sex brought with it crooked lawyers, greedy landlords and corrupt police and politicians, so did the real estate business.

It was not a question of justifying prostitution. Prostitutes were not only tolerated but encouraged; they performed a needed service in a positive way. It is probable that the kind of limited control over prostitution that existed in San Francisco between 1880 and 1918, which at times included venereal-disease examinations, police supervision and recognized pay-offs, resulted in less bribery, less crime and certainly less syphilis, gonorrhea and crabs — at least until the widespread use of sulpha drugs and penicillin in the forties and fifties.

Prostitution, in a sense, was a legitimate profession, somewhat like bartending or professional dancing. It was not as respectable as being a laundress, a factory worker or a housemaid. But that was largely because to be respectable allowed no sexual pleasure. Generally speaking, sexual pleasure was not even supposed to come to women through marriage. If this could have been managed then prostitution might have become respectable.

The pretty waitresses of San Francisco cafes or the parlor house girls were, like everyone else, looking for opportunities to better themselves. Their greatest hope was that they would catch the attention and interest of a man who might take them out of the "life." Often enough to give some girls hope, this happened.

Back in the gold mining days, a hard-handed miner, Joe Plato, spent a few days in the metropolis of San Francisco and met a young and beautiful (at least to him) whore. He had a claim on the Comstock. Just a claim, and he had no idea of its value. In his frantic effort to spend as much time as possible with the girl, he deeded over half the claim to her. Back on the Comstock, he found he had lucked into a very valuable lode. His claim was worth millions. As soon as he determined its value, he rushed back to San Francisco to buy back what he had bartered away. The price she asked was high — marriage. She got it and turned out to be a very good wife to him. He died quite young and his rich, young widow, who had changed her life completely and had been faithful to him, married a San Francisco businessman and became an ancestor of one of San Francisco's First Families.

Another case was that of Red Stockings, an energetic, independent woman who wanted no pimp and no madam running her business. She started out in a log cabin and built herself up a fortune of at least $100,000 before giving up the life.

Sex was big business in turn-of-the-century San

Francisco. Every possible type of arrangement could be made for sexual purposes. More than one house sold their girls from a catalog, just as though you were shopping for a piece of furniture. A customer walked into a living room or what looked like a business establishment and was shown pictures. He selected a girl and a messenger was sent dashing out to bring her into the adjoining room while the customer was still in the mood.

Perhaps the most secretive operation was one set up in 1907. This was a male whorehouse on Mason Street with twelve young studs. For ten dollars (more or less, depending upon the time and the popularity of the young man) a woman could go through the catalog showing the nude young men and make her selection. She could then go to her bedroom, put on a silk mask if she wished and have her lover knock on the door a few moments later. Heavy bolts were on the inside of the bedroom door. The entrance was off a dark alleyway and absolute privacy was assured. Although business continued for some time, it never caught on. During its short life it was said that a large percentage of its customers were prostitutes out for a holiday.

The first book published in San Francisco was written by a soldier who later became one of the city's first physicians. He was Dr. F. P. Wierzbicki and, in his book, *California as It Is and as It May be: Or, A Guide to the Gold Fields,* he wrote of women in society:

"Women, to society, are like cement to the building of stone; the society here has no such cement; its elements float to and fro on the excited, turbulent, hurried life of California immigrants.... Such is the society of San Francisco. But bring women here, and at once the process of crystallization, if we may be permitted the expression, will set in the society, by the natural affinities of the human heart."

But the good doctor became more specific. He thought that women were needed not only for romantic and sexual purposes but to keep men clean.

"To induce some of the few women that are here to condescend to wash their linen for them, they have to court them besides paying six dollars a dozen."

He even quotes the case of a bachelor who tried to get a woman to wash his clothes and, when she refused, went to the great length of marrying her for "he was determined she should do it at any price, as he was a great lover of cleanliness."

Women who would do what was considered

women's work were so scarce that a group of young men hired a chambermaid to clean up after them at the rate of $240 a month with room and board for her husband and children included.

In these early days when a three-month-old newspaper sold for a dollar or more, prostitutes earned from $200 to $400 a night; that is, with one man spending the night with them. And some writers of the time have mentioned girls getting $500 to $600 for a single sex session. As a result a great many of them were able to retire after only a few months' work. Some went back to France, New Orleans and New York but the majority stayed in San Francisco, some buying land, others putting their money into mining stock.

In the gambling houses, gold in sums of $15 to $20,000 was a common sight at the tables. Women who stood by to drink with the gamblers often got a pinch of dust worth sixteen dollars just to sit by and pass drinks. Even the cigar girls made tips of this magnitude. When one considers that these girls worked the gambling halls in the evening and received customers before and after work, it is easy to imagine how fortunes were rapidly built.

If the girls weren't French, they adopted French names. Famous beauties who used their natural resources in the gambling halls or in bed were known as Marguet, Hélène, Marie, Arthémise, Lucy, Fifi, Emilie, Madame Mauger, Lucienne, Madame Weston, Eléonore, Madame St. Amand, Madame Meyer, Maria, Angéle.

King of the Barbary Coast for at least fifteen years was Jerome Bassity, whose real name was Jere McGlane. During that period, from about 1901 to 1916, Bassity controlled dance halls, saloons, a semi-porno theater and 200 or more prostitutes. His enterprises ranged from a Market Street dive, frequented by such violent criminals that more respectable criminals and even streetwalkers were afraid to enter, to large, ornate, semi-respectable dance halls. Bassity practiced what he preached. According to all accounts, he got his greatest kicks out of patronizing rival whorehouses. His main interests were the new girls and the virgins. A considerable amount of damage was expected because he enjoyed emptying his gun around the feet of some of the girls to increase the tempo of their dance.

Chandeliers and lighting fixtures were also regularly replaced after him, for one of his other pleasures was shooting out the lights of a rival establishment, for which he readily paid. Prominent in the underworld over such a long period of time, he weathered the earthquake and came back with more and better ways to separate men and women from their money.

Around the turn of the century San Francisco also became famous for its excellent "French restaurants," perhaps as much for the intimate private rooms that they afforded as for the excellent food they served. These *chambres séparées,* as they were called in European capitals, had a dining table for two and a divan as well. They made an ideal rendezvous for a quiet seduction with a bird and a bottle and doors that locked from the inside.

One of the most popular restaurants was Delmonico's, located in a building several stories high and with each floor containing private rooms with discreet waiters. To make privacy even more absolute, carriages could drive directly into the building from the street.

Before Delmonico's, there was the Poodle Dog on Bush and Dupont streets. Although not as large as Delmonico's, it also had private rooms, good food and wine and waiters that never appeared until they were summoned by a bell.

The advent of cheek-to-cheek or belly-to-belly dancing contributed to the enormous proliferation of dance halls in San Francisco. Some of them were just that: dance halls. But they were in the minority. For the most part, they were dance halls with bars, tables behind velvet-draped alcoves — and sometimes a couch as well — and nearby rooms, either upstairs or in the house next door. In some of these dance halls men paid admission, women were admitted free. In the great majority, men bought drinks and/or tickets which allowed the customer a three to five minute embrace in motion.

All kinds of girls were available as partners. Some dance halls specialized in Chinese girls, or one could go next door and dance with French girls, or find señoritas from Mexico a few doors down. Other dance halls were like a house of all nations, with mixtures that ranged from black to English to Turkish to Irish.

Among the dances (some of them banned in the more respectable terpsichorean palaces) were the bunny hug, the turkey trot and the Texas tommy. In the dance hall district were many parlor houses but few had as good a reputation as Tessie Wall's place on O'Farrell Street. Tessie believed that men preferred blondes and she backed up her belief by having all-blonde female talent in her establishment. She had also become convinced that men liked their women well-rounded and young. She tolerated no skinny girls.

Tessie's house was respectable as parlor houses go. It had one other distinction. Tessie served good wine to her guests and a lot of it, probably because she herself was a consumer of enormous quantities. Her capacity was Rabelaisian. She often drank half a dozen or more bottles at dinner and, on one occasion, while she was being courted by a gambling man, Frank Daroux, she drank twenty-two bottles of wine with her dinner — without leaving the table! This seems impossible yet it is

testified to by reliable sources who claim that they were there.

It is entirely possible that Tessie consumed even more champagne on her wedding night, for on that memorable evening one hundred guests consumed 960 bottles of imported champagne, an average of more than nine and a half bottles per guest. Those were the days!

It is sad to report that all did not go smoothly with the married life of the sport and the madam. Conventional from the tips of his toes to the dexterous and sensitive fingertips, Frank felt that a woman's place was in the home — not the house. Tessie, however, liked the gay life of her parlor house and San Francisco and refused to move into the country estate he bought for her. They quarreled. Since he could not convince her, he left her. Within a few days she insisted that he come back to her and threatened to shoot him if he failed to return. But he sloughed off the threat and stayed away. On a warm day in the summer of 1916, Tessie followed Frank down the street and carried out her threat. Then as the police arrived, she dramatically cried, "I shot him because I love him."

But Frank was a gentleman and he loved Tessie. Although his wounds gave him a lot of trouble, he refused to prosecute her. He did, however, have sense enough to place 3000 miles between them, moving to New York. Tessie seems to have mourned for a while but went back to the business she loved and spent at least another ten years on O'Farrell Street, wining and dining and exhibiting her girls to the johns for pleasure and profit.

Not many of San Francisco's girls who made their money on their backs lived in the parlor houses. For every one parlor house girl there were probably a thousand or more in the cow yards or the cribs. A cow yard was a big spread, a building that could contain as many as 400 beds. One such brothel, which opened in 1899, made an attempt to use what was then considered modern psychology in the selection of its personnel. It was first called the Hotel Nymphomania and its proprietors had decided to stock its 450 workrooms with women affected with nymphomania. Here was the beginning of an ambitious idea; with this type of female they felt they could give super satisfaction to males and have employees that truly enjoyed their work.

But first they ran into problems with the name; the police would not allow them to use it. This sex supermarket became the Nymphia. As far as the owners were concerned, it was a straight rental deal. Each girl paid five dollars a day for her space and her earnings were her own. Even the name of this business showed imagination. It was called the Twinkling Star Corporation. It had a series of odd rules:

1. Girls must be naked while in their cribs.

2. No man could be turned down on the basis of race, creed or color.

3. Each crib was to allow inspection through a nar-

row window in the door. Each of these windows had an automatic shade which went up for a few moments when a dime was dropped into a slot. This gave the potential customer a chance to check the merchandise and it also provided the passerby an opportunity to see what kind of performance might be going on. It became so popular that metal slugs were manufactured and sold for a penny, which meant that the window shade business became unprofitable. In addition, many of the girls put the shades out of order soon after moving into their cribs.

Uniformed policemen were on hand at all times to keep order. The Nymphia remained in business for about two years but, because of the continuous pressure put on by Father Caraher, a Catholic priest, it was constantly in trouble with the authorities (who were being paid off and who tried to ignore the entire operation). After a major raid, the owners were fined $250 each and the next day the Nymphia opened up again. However, Father Caraher kept at it and in 1903 it was finally closed down.

Another of the large sex-for-sale operations was the Municipal Brothel, which started up a year after the Nymphia closed. A three-story structure with ninety cubicles, it was prospering at the time of the earthquake. After the disaster it was reconstructed and enlarged. The 133 women who worked the Municipal included blacks, Mexicans, French and American girls. Rates were on an ascending scale depending upon the nationality and the attractiveness of the girls. A session cost fifty cents with a first-floor girl, seventy-five cents on the second floor, and the French prostitutes who occupied the third floor got a dollar. The blacks were on the top floor and, because of the long walk, they only received fifty cents. The bargain basement, where rates were only twenty-five cents, was occupied·by the Mexicans.

The Municipal Brothel had only one thing to do with the municipality of San Francisco: it had the protection of the city government, for which the proprietors paid well. In fact, before the brothel opened, protection had been arranged for at least two years. Billy Finnegan, who operated it, was able to assure any whores who rented space that they would have at least two years occupancy. "Brothel" being a rather fancy word, the establishment soon became known as the Municipal Crib. When the Jackson Street trolleys stopped at the corner where the place was located, the conductors often called out, "All out for the whorehouse!" The protection was so carefully set up that other crib houses in the neighborhood were raided or in some way closed down by the police. This left most of the patronage to the Municipal Crib.

It was the last of the huge whorehouses. By 1904 the reform city government was under intense pressure from church groups and citizens' committees. The place closed its doors forever in September of 1907, after a

profitable run of about three years. Two years later the girls almost made it back when two underworld entrepreneurs installed sixty tiny workrooms, which were rented at $35 a week, but they reckoned without the religious element and, especially, Father Caraher. They had the temerity to suggest to the priest that he help them to move all of the brothels and prostitution-infested saloons east of Montgomery Street.

The *San Francisco Globe* lent the prestige of its pages in a campaign to clean up the city and especially to block the opening of this new sex market. As a result, the owners of the building canceled the lease. It was the last try — no other cow yard ever got started.

This did not mean that San Francisco's red-light district was abolished. Many parlor houses, cabarets and saloons continued to sell sex. There was never much effort made to control these places until 1911, when, against a flood of opposition from church groups and respectable citizens, a municipal clinic was set up, empowered to force every prostitute to be examined and treated for venereal diseases. They were charged fifty cents for the clinic visit and were required to report every fourth day for a checkup.

The system was carefully set up, with each prostitute registered and given a booklet which contained her photograph and a record of her regular examinations. So long as she was able to produce this identification, she could work; but should a girl not have such a booklet she could be arrested for vagrancy. If her examination turned up gonorrhea or syphilis, she was required to be treated until cured, and during that interim was expected to give up her occupation. With no unemployment insurance, this made it very hard indeed on the girls.

Although the clinic reduced venereal diseases in the red-light district by sixty-six percent in two years, it was ultimately put out of business by the clergymen — for almost every religious group denounced it. Why? Because the do-gooders believed that the wages of sin should be paid. They reckoned that if the general population thought that a large percentage of the whores were diseased, no man would visit them. This reverse thinking, of course, had little or no effect on the number of men who used prostitutes as a sexual outlet. But the religious forces were triumphant. So, on May 20, 1913, all policing controls were removed. The clergymen were soon rewarded with the knowledge that the venereal disease rate in the city rose precipitously.

When the Barbary Coast was rebuilt after the devastating earthquake of 1906, a new kind of sex entertainment began to take over. These were the "show" places where nudity and sex in varying degrees were portrayed on small stages and even occasionally upon the bar itself. These theatrical dance halls featured semi-nude hootchy-kootchy dancers. The dance of the seven veils was a favorite, although the final veil was rarely, if ever, removed. Along with the usually overweight hip-shaking girl, there were one or two variety acts, sometimes a singer, a juggler or comedian. Such ornate saloon-music halls as the Hippodrome became popular, as did the Thalia, which featured late night, and sometimes all-night, entertainment.

The Barbary Coast degenerated into a slummer's paradise as hundreds of respectable citizens roamed the streets late at night to see how the underworld entertained itself.

Ironically, it was a hypocritical, powerful newspaperman who mounted the ultimate campaign to wipe out the Barbary Coast. This was William Randolph Hearst, who preached staunch, moral conservatism in his newspaper columns and, on the side, lived with and supported a young protégée, Hollywood starlet Marion Davies.

Hearst began his long and famous affair at the time he was beginning to invest in motion pictures. His first major effort in celluloid was with a weekly newsreel, Hearst Metrotone News. A one-man-band type, Hearst determined to make his own feature films, directing them himself. His first and only star was Miss Davies, originally a Miss Douras from Brooklyn, a former chorus girl. She had risen to become a dancer in the Ziegfeld Follies when Hearst was introduced to her. It was not long before she was to become the leading lady at Hearst's Cosmopolitan Corporation and its president as well.

Hearst had a soft spot in his bed for dancers. Millicent Willson, the woman he married, was, like Miss Davies, a dancer. He was a rich, typical stagedoor johnny, who attended the performance of the Willson Sisters in *The Girl from Paris* every night. He married Miss Willson in 1903 and away they went to Europe on their honeymoon. Later, Mrs. Hearst backed up her husband on every necessary occasion. When he was criticized as being depraved (because of his affair with Miss Davies) or charged with neglecting his family, pictures of his wholesome wife and the happy family were immediately and widely circulated in the Hearst papers.

When Anthony Comstock, self-appointed custodian of American morality, managed to suppress the magazine of the Art Students' League because it included paintings of nude women, the Hearst papers defended the censor. At the same time, the Hearst papers were treating their readers to crimes of violence and sex scandals on page one.

Hearst built Miss Davies a small studio bungalow at Culver City and she continued to work with Cosmopoli-

tan Productions for some ten years. Hollywood never questioned her relationship with Hearst. It was generally understood that she was his mistress; but if his wife didn't object, why should anyone else? He traveled openly with Miss Davies to France and frequently to New York. His good friend Father Coughlin, the inflammatory, anti-Semitic Catholic priest, often visited the two of them not only at Hearst's Hotel Warwick in New York, but also at San Simeon.

When Hearst built his $30 million palace in San Simeon he created a very special bedroom for Miss Davies. He and Miss Davies appeared regularly as host and hostess most evenings when in residence there. His wife remained conveniently in the East. Hearst also built a multi-million-dollar residence on the ocean in Santa Monica for his mistress. The estate at San Simeon boasted an art collection that was perhaps the largest, if not the best, ever owned by any one man up to that time. Gala weekend parties were frequently held there for the Hollywood and newspaper elite. Celebrities of the day, from George Bernard Shaw to Winston Churchill, were entertained. The rules were fairly simple — no drinking in the individual suites. A bar was open all day and most of the night but drinking was frowned upon. Hearst was a teetotaler, yet he allowed a cocktail hour where guests were limited to one drink. An informal dinner was staged at nine o'clock. There was a gold dinner service, but guests were expected to dress informally on "the ranch," and paper napkins were used.

Hearst spent at least $7 million trying to develop Marion Davies into the brightest star in Hollywood and she almost made it. When they met she was seventeen (a year younger than his wife when he met her); Hearst was then fifty-four. Davies' biggest film, *When Knighthood Was in Flower,* was produced in 1922. She continued to make films for the next ten years but none ever quite equaled it in popularity.

Hearst acted as a real Svengali to Miss Davies' *Trilby.* He was her coach, her manager, her agent, her director and her lover. It was said that each of his newspapers was ordered to mention her name favorably at least once in every edition.

Miss Davies may well go down in history as the highest-paid mistress. As president of Cosmopolitan Productions, her salary was $104,000 a year. Indeed, she was so rich that, when Hearst had some financial troubles in the years preceding his death, she was able to lend him more than a million dollars.

Throughout his tempestuous life he was a public defender of home and family, violently opposed to divorce and prostitution. His *San Francisco Examiner* had demanded that the Barbary Coast, with its dance halls, harlots and saloons, be wiped out. It got results. The police commissioner forced a resolution barring dancing "in any cafe, restaurant or saloon where liquor is sold within the district bounded on the north and east by the

Bay, on the south by Clay Street, and on the west by Stockton Street." The resolution continued "that no women patrons or women employees shall be permitted in any saloon in the said district." It was further resolved "that no licenses would be renewed on Pacific Street between Kearny and Sansome excepting for a straight saloon."

Hearst's plan was to wipe out commercial sex and "to shut up the market of immoral and vulgar pleasure, and to replace that market with a great market for the sale of wholesome and decent fun" — whatever that was.

For good measure the police banned sidewalk barkers who had previously guided potential customers in by extolling the entertainment inside. Instead of the "fun" that the city had planned to provide, only a dull shell remained.

But even though the bright lights of the Barbary Coast had gone out, red-light districts were still tolerated for another year. A campaign by a combined group of churches, led by the Reverend Paul Smith of the Central Methodist Church, along with Hearst's *Examiner* and the Police Department, caused the enactment of the Red-Light Abatement Act. It took over two years for the California Supreme Court to declare the Abatement Act constitutional. When it did, under its provisions the prominent citizens who owned and rented their property for prostitution were liable to both fines and jail sentences.

More clean-up operations ensued and finally in January of 1917 the mayor promised to close every brothel in San Francisco. A few days later almost every priest and minister in the city delivered a sermon against prostitution. At the same time, citizen committees called a mass meeting for January 25 where they listened to speeches and adopted resolutions demanding that the city government wipe out prostitution.

But the city was in for a big surprise. On that same day the prostitutes themselves held a mass meeting and a parade. All decked out in their finest dresses, girls from streetwalkers to high-class courtesans, escorted by two policemen, marched quietly but gaily to the Central Methodist Church, there to call on their archenemy, the Reverend Smith. They were led by Reggie Gamble, a madam who operated a parlor house on Mason Street.

The women were allowed inside the church, where they sat quietly until the Reverend Smith stepped into the pulpit. Then they all rose and demanded, "What are you going to do with us?" When he urged them to seek refuge in religion, they asked, "Can we eat that?" They also wanted to know whether the congregation would welcome them sitting next to their daughters. A mild argument ensued when Madame Gamble announced that she had been running a house in San Francisco for eight years and that she knew the men and women of the city. She wanted to know how many patrons of the church would accept a woman from the "life" into their homes. The Reverend suggested that they should establish homes but he didn't tell them how. He asked how many had children and three-fourths of them raised their hands. Mrs. Gamble continued, "There isn't a woman here who would be a prostitute if she could make a decent living in any other way. They've all tried it." The women laughed when the Reverend declared that a woman could remain virtuous on an income of ten dollars a week. Several of them shouted that the minimum wage should be not less than twenty dollars a week. And, when the Reverend replied that statistics showed "that families all over the country receive less," Mrs. Gamble retorted: "That's why there's prostitution — come on girls, there's nothing for us here." They left and no one knows what did become of them.

In order to close down the Barbary Coast the entire quarter was surrounded by policemen. Prostitutes were ordered to leave the area and by midnight of February 14, 1917, the district was deserted. A red-light, red-letter day — if ever there was one. Over 1000 women had been driven from their quarters. In addition, one hundred Chinese girls were evicted from the few houses which remained in operation along Grant Avenue. Within the next two weeks forty saloons closed their doors and all the resorts, cafes, cabarets and wine houses were out of business.

But did the Barbary Coast actually ever end? Well, not quite. The spirit of the old San Francisco, now a tawdry, tinsel thoroughfare covering a few blocks on both sides of Broadway, still tries to attract tourists and residents to its girly shows. But it's not the Barbary Coast — that belongs to the San Francisco of the turn of the century.

What with the great hordes of "loose" women and the continuing shortage of women, respectable San Franciscans, as the city grew to middle age, made every effort to build an impenetrable wall around their daughters. Chaperones were an absolute requisite for every occasion when a young woman left the house. As the *San Francisco Chronicle* for January 7, 1900, put it: "There are certain customs and conventions that must be observed and that of chaperonage is one of them.... Here in San Francisco custom requires that a girl be matronized on all important occasions."

Although it was admitted that the duties of chaperones were sometimes disagreeable because of their having to fend off horny young men, "many young men ought to be trusted, some are not." A chaperone was expected to be a combination policewoman, social custom arbiter and, above all, constantly vigilant so that her charge was never out of her sight. They argued that it was a good thing for their charges for it gave them a feeling of security at the theater, when dining out, at parties and balls, or even for a walk along the street. In addition, they should be on hand whenever a young man came to call. they should keep "a watchful eye on young men — so that no wolves in sheep's clothing ever entered the fold."

So in the social sexual life of San Francisco at the turn of the century there was a place for older aunts and cousins. Younger women, even if married, could not be trusted to man the barricades of virtue. Stanford University forbade young women to visit fraternity houses accompanied by a young chaperone — even if she was married. Rules for admission to respectable restaurants and hotels were nonexistent for men but very strict indeed regarding women. When two legitimate actresses made a reservation at Shanley's Restaurant, they were turned away. It was not thought proper for two young women to dine alone. And two actresses were out of the question. They left the restaurant and the next day brought suit in the civil court — and they won.

By the turn of the century San Francisco was an important stop for the theatrical troupes and nationally known actors and actresses who played New York and New Orleans.

Lending their not inconsiderable feminine charms to the theatrical world of San Francisco were three unique women. They were unique not only for their stage presence but also because they exposed more of their bodies in public than had previously been seen in the West — at least by so-called respectable audiences. Adah Isaacs Menken appeared in *Mazeppa*, a melodrama in which her enemies had an opportunity to strip her down until, as Mark Twain described it, "She appeared to me to have but one garment on — a thin, tight white linen one, of unimportant dimensions; I forget the name of the article but it is indispensable to infants of tender age — I suppose any young mother can tell you what it is, if you have the moral courage to ask the question. With the exception of this superfluous rag, the Menken dresses like the Greek Slave; but some of her postures are not so modest as the suggestive attitude of the latter." Twain continues his review of *Mazeppa* by remarking that "she carries on like a lunatic from the beginning of the act to the end of it."

The big scene in *Mazeppa* was after Menken had been stripped down. One of the actors brought in a real horse. Miss Menken was tied onto the back of this "fiery untamed steed" and the horse carried her off the stage. The juxtaposition of the huge, fierce-looking animal and the almost naked Miss Menken brought forth thunderous applause each time. The scene combined enough symbolism (including that of rape, sadism, masochism and bestiality) to give virtually every member of the audience some satisfaction.

Complete nudity was preceded, at least for a few years, by flesh-colored tights. Performers made every effort to obtain perfectly fitting tights, flesh-colored, so that the public, it was said, had to use opera glasses to discern the difference between nudity and clothing. Tights had been a great scandal in the East and Adah Isaacs Menken managed to appear more nude than clothed when she played the male role of the Tartar prince in *Mazeppa*. The tricky thing about it was to keep her fairly large breasts from popping out of her flesh-colored tights. The play was based on the poem by Lord Byron which gave it an aura of respectability. In addition to San Francisco, her performances were sell-outs in New York, Paris, London and Vienna. She and other wearers of tights were roundly denounced before the Women's Suffrage Convention of 1869. "No decent woman," Alice Logan asserted, "can now look to the stage as a career. Clothed in the dress of an honest woman she is worth nothing to a manager. Stripped as naked as she dare, and it seems there is little left when so much is done, she becomes a prize to her manager who knows that crowds will rush to see her." This kind of criticism sold a lot of tickets.

Miss Menken, at thirty-three, had been married more than once which gave her a reputation for being wicked. She wrote poetry and had an affair with Alexander Dumas, the French novelist.

Mistresses were very big in San Francisco before the turn of the century. Lola Montez had been a mistress of Franz Liszt, among others, but was more notorious for her tenure as mistress of King Ludwig I of Bavaria. San Francisco took to Lola Montez as it had to Adah Isaacs Menken. Audiences could not get enough of talented "bad" women. Not that Lola had much theatrical talent. Most of her critics admitted that she couldn't sing, she couldn't dance and she couldn't deliver lines — but they all agreed that it was a great treat to see this fascinating creature on stage.

She was an exotic character — like Menken, a fierce, passionate, independent spirit. Born in Ireland, she successfully passed herself off as Spanish. Her sensuous spider dance, derived from the Italian folk dance, the tarantella, brought her instant acclaim in San Francisco.

But it was a protégée and sometime companion of Montez, the redheaded, charming Lotta Crabtree, who became the permanent darling of San Francisco. She danced in the mining regions north of the city and appeared in Virginia City and Tombstone, Arizona. She started out in San Francisco and, after a number of eastern tours where she developed a national reputation, returned to her home town where she continued her theatrical career.

There was one great difference between Lotta and her mentor Lola. Everyone agreed that she had so much talent that it was not necessary for her to take her clothes off to be a success.

Mesdames Menken, Montez and Crabtree brought a kind of tacky but respectable culture to the sinful city. With the coming of the Philharmonic Society and the opera, things began to look up for San Francisco respectable women's community. By 1886 there was a full-fledged social club for women, the Laurel Hall Club. Meetings did not draw the kind of audiences that the "bad" women's performances had, but at least the topics were high-minded. A Professor Fryer lectured on "The Women of China"; a Miss Lillie Martin described her work in a psychological laboratory; and a Mrs. Purnell, who came from Sacramento to give her talk, compared the women of the 1880s with the women of the time of King Solomon. San Francisco writer Frank Norris was instrumental in forming a ladies' literature society. Unlike other literature societies that had come before, this one was coeducational. By 1887 the Sadik (Truth) Club opened its membership to women. The annual report read: "We saw our error. We corrected our fault. Now we have poetry, music, flowers, grace and beauty."

Talk of women's liberation reached San Francisco by the 1880s. Julia Ward Howe, women's suffrage leader, preached a sermon in the Unitarian Church. Susan B. Anthony touched base in San Francisco and made points with her forceful approach to women's rights.

Women began to make a major impression when the Century Club president, Mrs. George Hearst, set up the Sutter Street clubhouse for discussions involving art, literature and life.

Between 1900 and 1920 sociological questions about the sale of sex were beginning to be posed. Was the mistress or courtesan — as exemplified by Lola Montez, Lillian Russell or Adah Isaacs Menken — a prostitute? Well, not quite. They had rich and famous protectors, or at least bed partners, and were generally accepted socially. What about the female employee (or the male occasionally) who was *nice* to the boss and who would thereby get a better job, less hours or special treatment in one way or another? No, these people were definitely not prostitutes. And, of course, the wife who married for money never fell into that category, although the divorcée, because she had been involved with more than one man, was suspect.

But while women made progress in the West — and elsewhere in America — San Francisco men clung tightly to their famous all-male bastions of respectability.

Two of the most rigid, anti-women clubs were formed as far back as the mid-nineteenth century and still exist today. The Pacific-Union Club, known familiarly as the P.U., is proud of its record of having admitted women only twice in more than 125 years. And the 2000-member Bohemian Club, which has not even the vaguest relation to Bohemians but rather is made up of highly conservative citizens, still excludes women from its membership.

The Bohemian Club is famous for its gargantuan drinking bouts, its annual dinner at which prairie oysters (bulls' testicles) are served, and its outstanding collection of pornography. On occasion women are allowed to join members on picnics in the Bohemian Grove, a beautiful campground which the club owns on the Russian River in the redwood country. In recent years a scandalous exposure almost caught up with some of its membership. During one stag encampment, when hundreds of members gathered to swap stories, drink, talk, and relax in the all-male atmosphere, a relatively large number of high class prostitutes moved into the area. When some of the prostitutes were arrested and brought to trial, one of them turned out to be the kind of witness that would have seriously damaged the reputations of many outstanding members of the club. The court quickly declared a mistrial, not allowing the testimony. Ever since this relatively public exposure, the club has stayed away from any publicity.

This tastefully posed portrait, ca. 1910, is characteristic of photographer E. J. Bellocq, recorder of the whores of Storyville.

Only a few of Bellocq's photographs were of nudes. Some were charming portraits of whores in their fancy stockings and best underwear.

A major influence on sexual freedom was cheek-to-cheek and body-to-body dancing. Vernon and Irene Castle popularized it.

JULIAN ELTINGE
IN
"THE CRINOLINE GIRL"

King (or queen) of female impersonators was singer-dancer Julian
Eltinge. He was a popular star when transvestites were unheard of.

Women were not supposed to have pubic hair before the year 1920. If they did, it was both immoral and illegal to show it.

W.Y.O.D. meant "wear your open drawers." These practical female undergarments kept the legs warm but had an open crotch.

Many a young girl was left pregnant by the soldier she wanted to make happy before he went to war. Here the 69th Infantry says goodbye.

SAFETY FIRST GUARANTEE

THIS CERTIFIES that I, the undersigned, a female about to enjoy sexual intercourse with

....am above the age of consent, am in my right mind and not under the influence of any drug or narcotic. Neither does he have to use any force, threats or promise to influence me. I am in no fear of him whatever; do not expect or want to marry him, don't know whether he is married or not, and don't care. I am not asleep or drunk and am entering into this relation with him because I love it and want it as much as he does, and if I receive the satisfaction I expect, am willing to play an early return engagement.

Furthermore, I agree never to appear as a witness against him, or to prosecute him under the Mann White Slave Act.

Signed, before going to bed, this........day of........................192...

By ....

Address......................................

[SEAL]

Witness..............................

The first views taken with the stereopticon camera were scenics. Later came under-the-counter three-dimensional nudes.

In this sylvan setting two girls seem to be comparing buttocks. Even in these so-called dirty pictures pubic hair is not shown.

Against a studio backdrop three girls, probably prostitutes, put on a
burlesque lesbian act for the camera. Stereopticon humor was rare.

Most stereo pictures were made in the photographer's studio. This
one reveals a young lady dressing. Long hair was still popular.

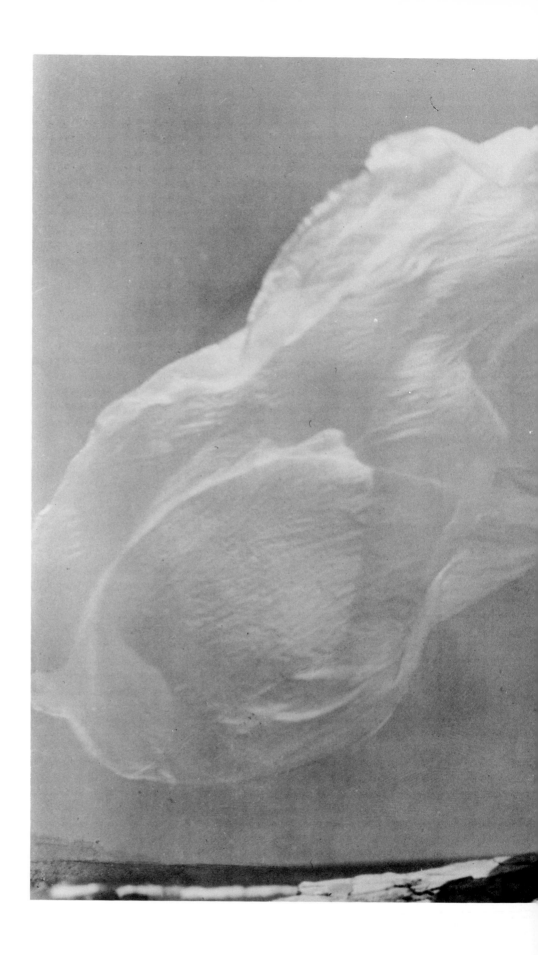

The first widely seen and acclaimed frontal nude called Sea Breeze was made by the late, great photographer William Mortensen of Laguna Beach, California. It caused much comment and was rejected by many of the conservative salons.

When a six-week divorce law went into effect, Reno, Nevada, changed from a western village to a "divorce mill" city.

As the women's liberation movement gathered momentum, hundreds of cartoons appeared lambasting the new uninhibited female.

Women drivers were a new target for cartoonists: here, Lady Godiva, using a modern, underdressed female, and forty Peeping Toms.

Hollywood's sexiest male star of the '30s (off screen) was Charles Spencer Chaplin. Charlie had love affairs with many Hollywood beauties.

Men began stripping in 1918 when Elmo K. Lincoln appeared in TARZAN OF THE APES. *He made up in bulk what he lacked in form.*

Wearing a sexy but not too revealing step-in, the redheaded, shapely "it" girl, Clara Bow, registers outrage and anger.

In India every home has its own household gods; some bring good weather, others health, wealth or good luck. But the most important are the gods of sex or fertility. These are usually erotic figurines. In the United States, dating from the days of the Colonies, a different type of sexual symbol, often having the form of a fertility image, has been ever present. Some members of each succeeding generation have collected erotic cigar cutters, bottle openers, playing cards, corkscrews, erotic plates, plaques and glassware. Some of these symbolic keepsakes are crude, others are exquisitely crafted. All form a small part of the invisible sexual tradition in America.

A pair of sexy scissors that cut both ways, below left. See-through playing card: the sexually engaged figures become visible when the card is held up to the light, lower right. The cherub figure with corkscrew is reminiscent of the much-copied Belgian fountain MANNEKEN PIS.

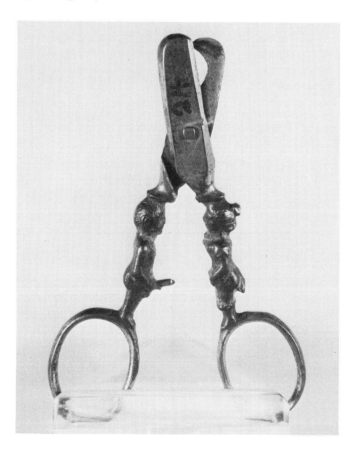

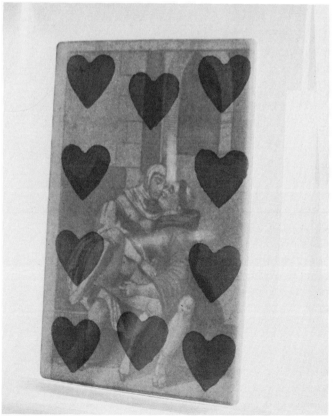

176

8

Toward a Sinless Society

During World War I and the years immediately after the armistice, pundits poured out a spate of profound articles in the "intellectual" magazines, pointing out that America had lost its innocence. What they actually meant was that the United States was emerging from 142 years of sexual hypocrisy into a more open acceptance of the facts of life. But in the years immediately before the war, was there really purity under the celluloid collars, the sack coats, suspendered trousers, union suits and wing tip shoes; or beneath the corsets and open drawers, garters, voluminous skirts and petticoats? It would seem to be only a difference in degree, the difference between exposure and provocative concealment. An ankle revealed in 1870 provoked the same stimulation in men as a knee in 1920. In the "guiltless" days of open prostitution, clandestine meetings of ministers and deacons with their choir singers, was all innocence? Or was it only the appearance of virtue — the great coverup? Sexually, the United States had been repressed, yes; innocent, never!

The United States declared war on Germany on April 6, 1917. Two months later came the draft which was to change the lives and the life style of all Americans. The great uncovering began with World War I. Kisses became longer and skirts became shorter as World War I progressed. Girls who had wanted an excuse to give their *all* now had one. From Maine to California parents were duped, trysts were accomplished, marriages were con-

tracted, sex flourished and the birthrate soared. Many a callow youth off to fight the Hun left his seed to sprout, legitimately and illegitimately. Thousands of "war babies" were born in 1918.

With a depleted male labor source, women began working in defense industries, replacing men as streetcar conductors, taxi drivers, waiters and factory workers. Such jobs inevitably meant different types of clothing. Skirts and petticoats gave way to overalls. Although severely criticized, some women in some jobs wore men's trousers. Most secretarial work that had been done by men went to women. At first, these girls were called "typewriters," after their machines. Stenographers, secretaries and typists came later. Skirts began to rise, lingerie became shorter and more transparent. The one-piece step-in replaced the corset.

A major influence on fashion, and ultimately on more freedom for women, was dancer Irene Castle, who with her husband revolutionized American style. Her gowns revealed her shapely figure but were modestly knee length or longer. Shockingly, she and her mate Vernon danced belly to belly and breast to chest. Fortunately they were married or they might have been lynched. As this graceful team performed the bunny hug, the turkey trot — and especially the tango and the hesitation waltz — excited audiences looked on with feelings of pleasurable uneasiness and envy. The United States Federation of Women's Clubs rose up in wrath and demanded that the tango and the hesitation waltz be banned.

Overseas the boys in khaki were receiving the kind of liberal sex education they would never have found at home. French families deplored billeting American soldiers in their villages and with good reason. Locking up their daughters did little good. Mademoiselle and sometimes madame) met Yank and welcomed him. Somehow the doughboys' promises of marriage and life in the United States did not always work out. Yet some of them did and, after the war, thousands of French girls accompanied their husbands back home.

The *filles de joie* were busy too. No commander who expected cooperation from his men failed to make available as many French prostitutes as possible, although the men often had to stand in line to be served. Such sexual relief provided at least three useful purposes: sexual relaxation, if not fulfillment; some control over the spread of venereal diseases; and fewer seductions and pregnancies among provincial village belles.

The army provided three types of VD control. Condoms were issued liberally. Then there was "short arm" inspection for signs of syphilis and gonorrhea. It was sometimes possible to secure a little cloth bag with a tube of antibacterial salve which, after sexual contact, was spread around the glans of the penis, inserted into the tip, then the penis put into the bag and the drawstring tied. It was intended to be removed after some four hours — although it is doubtful that such a messy inconvenience was so long endured.

This procedure might have given rise to the story about the farm boy who, before intercourse, is asked by the city girl to use a condom which she supplies. When he asks why, she tells him that it would keep her from having a baby. He slips a condom on, has sex with her and goes back to the farm. Three months later, on a hot day in the fields, he says disgustedly, "I'm going to take this thing off — I don't care if she does have a baby."

Sexual relations with American, British and French nurses were inevitable. Girls who probably never would have made it to the altar or even to bed, found love or sex, and sometimes both, as on-the-scene war workers. Ernest Hemingway described such a joyous, though ultimately tragic, affair in his romantic but relatively realistic novel *Farewell to Arms*.

Affairs between servicemen and servicewomen were clandestine, rarely mentioned by the press. Women who went to war were looked upon as innocents, pure angels of mercy. One of the most widely sung war songs extolled the virtues of the Red Cross nurse:

"There's a rose that grows, the soldier knows
It's the touch of the helping hand
'Mid the war's red curse stands the Red Cross nurse
She's the rose of no man's land."

But, as it turned out, all the girls were not so innocent. If the American girls were portrayed as angels, this did not always hold true of the French. Easily the most outspoken of all the war songs that originated in France was *Mademoiselle from Armentières*. One of the many choruses went:

"Mademoiselle from Armentières, parlez vous,
Mademoiselle from Armentières, parlez vous,
Mademoiselle from Armentières, she hadn't been
     fucked in forty years,
Hinky, dinky, parlez vous."

Of course, it depended how and where it was being sung — she hadn't been screwed, she hadn't been laid, she hadn't been humped, she hadn't been . . . in forty or twenty years.

Sex was used to stimulate and titillate in war propaganda. Lurid drawings displayed the hated Hun raping and killing nuns and children. The Kaiser was the beast of Berlin. Unmentionable atrocities were charged against him. On the brighter side, young and beautiful girls on colorful posters urged men to join up to defend democracy. Ziegfeld Follies girls, movie stars and even burlesque queens ("let's show the boys what they are fighting for") were enlisted in the spirit of patriotism to raise blood pressure, money and volunteers.

After the war, the automobile, which had been largely for the rich, brought about a major transformation in the sex habits of the young Americans. Henry Ford was probably responsible for more unwanted pregnancies than any man before or since. His "tin lizzie," or flivver, provided privacy on wheels. It gave young men and women an opportunity to travel out of their neighborhood and to kiss, pet and neck and often go "all the way." This sometimes produced runs in stockings, bruised knees and hip and back dislocations. But it was a great way to get away and get it on.

With the automobile, sex became a kind of game with young unmarrieds. Boys fumbled to get under bras and reach first base. From the nipple, the persuasive and persistent male worked his way down, then up the thigh to the crotch — second base. A finger into the lips of the vagina and third base was touched, with a good deal of panting and a lot of "No — please, not now" and a lot of acquiescence as well. Home base was actually part of going all the way. There were hundreds of Ford jokes. Eddie Cantor sang:

"We went riding
She didn't balk.
Back from Yonkers,
I'm the one who had to walk."

And a joke that went: A couple arrive home early one morning on foot. "What happened?" asked the irate father.

"We were out driving," replies the young man, "the car stopped and we got out to push."

"Yes," adds the girl, "and while we were pushing, somebody stole the car."

The automobile completely changed the courting

habits of American men and women. In the privacy of a car, couples could converse freely, even about sex, without being heard. They could smoke and even have a drink. It's possible that, because of the difficulty of getting into a car with long skirts and voluminous undergarments, the automobile had an influence on fashion. Certainly in the twenties undergarments became scantier and skirts went higher.

For the first time advertising began to mold the appearance of both men and women. Women began to believe that they too could have the perfect complexion of the girls in the ads. The promises offered by advertising were not often realized yet the public continued, and continues, to buy them. Through the last half of the twenties, the ads became bolder. By the thirties women in brassieres and panties could be seen not only in the Sears Roebuck Catalog but on the pages of the daily newspaper. Men wore bathing shorts, discarding the one-piece suits that had concealed their nipples and hairy chests.

An anthology of essays and stories for men was published in 1935 under the title *The Bedroom Companion or A Cold Night's Entertainment.* Amidst the poems, including *Ode to the Impossibility of Rape* by Philip Wylie, appeared a cartoon by Webb of a window washer looking into a bedroom window and saying, "Amateur."

Another feature was a checklist of items for a bachelor's apartment that gives a vivid idea of what advertising had accomplished. Out of the ninety items mentioned, we list a few: "lipstick — six shades; eyebrow pencils — black and brown; Zonite; Lysol; Elizabeth Arden's Orange Skin Food; Murine; bobby pins; perfumes — a wide variety; bath salts; curling iron; Mum; Odorono; electric drier; negligee — one or more (Pajamas shouldn't be worn — a nightie shouldn't be necessary); mules — three sizes; silk stockings — twelve pairs, assorted colors and sizes; garter belt — small, medium, large; K-Y Jelly; Kleenex; [among the books] *Indian Love Lyrics* by Lawrence Hope; *A Few Figs from Thistles* by Edna St. Vincent Millay; any of the works of Dr. Marie C. Stopes; smoked glasses; long black veil; aspirin."

A footnote mentions that "a very natural masculine modesty precludes the mention of various old family standbys [contraceptives] which the gentleman undoubtedly has already. Furthermore the above items will suffice only for a short visit by the average woman."

Another note suggests that certain items should be hidden away, such as pictures of other women, sharp implements and his checkbook.

One of the many limericks quoted in the book:
"There once was a spinster named Gretel
Who wore underclothes made of metal.
When they asked, 'Does it hurt?'
She replied, 'It keeps dirt
From the stalk and the leaves and the petal.'"

Another American phenomenon synonymous with the tin lizzie era was burlesque. It was reaching its peak at the time of the armistice. Burlesque houses played in most American cities to ninety-eight percent male audiences. What a young man hadn't learned about sex in the army or in the back seat of a Ford he could find in the sex-oriented jokes.

It was a world of baggy pants comedians, straight men, talking women and strippers — and a liberal dash of blackouts. Sample: A wife is talking to her husband. "You promised me *big things* before we got married."

He replies, "Fooled you, didn't I?" Blackout.

Or, a short-skirted, low-bodiced French maid enters questioningly. "Is this the place where I'm supposed to be maid?" (Yes, son, that was a joke in those days.)

Or, a baggy pants comedian stretches his belt forward and looks down into his trousers, shakes his head in amazement, looks down again, then at the audience. "Funny," he says, "I didn't have any trouble finding it this morning."

Blackouts dealt with exaggeration, satire, double entendres and seduction in reverse. A beautiful girl invites the comedian into her bed. He jumps in, puts his head under the covers and begins moving around.

"What do you want down there?" she asks.

The comedian surfaces with a harmonica and begins to play. Blackout.

Burlesque bits were specialties of various comedians. The audience expected to hear the same routine, the same joke, week after week, year after year, and their recognition of the gag was part of the fun. A favorite bit was played by a straight man and talking woman on one side of the stage, with a comedian separated from them by a wall. The scene is two hotel rooms, with the audience able to see into both. The straight man and his wife are packing a trunk prior to leaving the hotel. As they try to close the trunk, the comedian, through the thin wall, hears the woman say,

"I think you better get on top." The comedian's interest is aroused as she continues, "Now move around; bounce up and down on it." The man behind the wall perks up his ears.

"This won't work," says the husband, "you try getting on top." In the next room, the man begins to hit himself in the head and pace up and down as he imagines the scene.

"I'm going to get off," the woman says, "you get back on." There is still some clothing protruding from the side of the trunk.

"I can't get it in," he says.

"Try bouncing harder," she replies. Finally she sighs, "I know what we'll do." (By this time the next-door neighbor is leaning against the wall so as not to miss a word.) "We'll both get on top."

The comedian breaks through the wall shouting, "This I've got to see." Blackout.

Another oldie: A young girl meets a straight man on the stage.

He: "I haven't seen you for a long time. What's happened?"

"Well," she says, "I got married."

"Oh," he replies, "so you got married. How old is your husband?"

"Eighty-five," she says, "on his last birthday."

He: "You must have a pretty good time at night — what happens?"

"As I go to sleep," she replies, "I begin to feel old age creeping up on me."

The chief comedian was known as the top banana, an obvious bit of phallic symbolism. Most of the comedians adopted an ethnic accent and clothing to match. Dutch, Jewish and Irish comedians were standard fixtures; so, too, were the dude and straight man and a black, who in those days was called "the nigger," which was never meant as a derogatory phrase. Many of their routines were handed down from one generation to another and all burlesque comedians kept their "bits" in their heads. They were afraid to write them down lest someone steal them.

"Sight gags" were as popular as verbal ones. A good comedian, using a rolled-up newspaper or magazine or a bottle as a phallic symbol, could reduce his audience to hysterical laughter. At the finale of a favorite skit, the talking woman turns her back to the comedian and throws up her skirts, showing her ass — saying, "Take that."

Instead of being insulted, the comedian grins, looks it over carefully, then, with his newspaper held in front of his hips, runs after her shouting, "I do think I'll take that."

But girls and nudity were never treated as a joke. Burlesque took its strippers seriously and sensuously. Strippers had come into vogue just before the war, and the fine art of disrobing in public reached its zenith between 1920 and 1930. When the lights went down, the saxophones moaned and the trumpets groaned. Then came the flash — a deep red or purple spot picked out Ann Corio or Margie Hart, Sherry Britton, Gypsy Rose Lee or Lili St. Cyr posing in a long, body-revealing evening dress. After that came "the parade." With short but smooth steps the stripper took charge of the stage, covering every part of it in time with the drums. As she finished the chorus, she flirted directly with her audience and, as a come-on, removed her hat, her long, white gloves and her necklace. Now she was stripping for action.

During the second chorus, the breakaway dress was unzipped. This was the "tease" section of the routine. After removing her dress, it was traditional for the performer to hold it in front of her until the end of the chorus, doing bumps and grinds behind the dress with just enough hip, leg or breast showing to make it provocative.

Like the comedians, every stripper had her specialty. Ann Corio stripped at a medium pace. Gypsy Rose Lee was a slow stripper. Margie Hart was a fast stripper who sometimes performed a bump (pelvic thrust) with such abandon that you felt that the theater was likely to be demolished.

The third chorus continued the tease but the dancer would slowly strip down to G-string, which just exactly covered the pubes but left the buttocks entirely exposed. "Pasties," small, artificial nipples sometimes set with rhinestones, were applied over the nipple area. These two garments often kept the girls from being picked up by the police vice squads when complaints against burlesque houses were made — usually by citizens who had never seen a show.

An ingenious array of G-strings were invented by designers or by the girls themselves. Gypsy Rose Lee cuddled a mink between her legs with a head that bounced up and down as she gently bumped. In April of 1978, some years after her death, her mink G-string sold at auction for $500 to a British banker.

After her early days in burlesque, Gypsy Rose Lee make it big in legitimate shows in the late thirties and early forties. She never took off very much but managed to keep the audience teased from the beginning to the end of her act. Her last appearance as a stripper on Broadway was in Michael Todd's production of *Star and Garter* in 1942.

Another stripper of less eminence wore a small top hat which kept tilting up as she writhed her bumps and grinds. Still another was adorned with a bell that tinkled in rhythm. By far the most popular accoutrements were rhinestone-encrusted mini-belts. Legend has it that a great stripper could, with struts, bumps and grinds, make a customer feel so good that a man could borrow money from anyone in the audience.

Although not a stripper in the strict show-biz definition, but equally high in the stardom of burlesque, was Sally Rand. During the Chicago World's Fair of 1933, she became renowned for her ability to manipulate two fans in such a way that no one in the audience could be quite sure they had seen Sally's pussy or not.

Performers in the classical school of burlesque (if one will permit such a term) rarely deviated from their routine. Their dances were as traditional as those of the Japanese Kabuki or the temple dancers of Thailand. In "open" towns, such as New Orleans, strippers, when not harassed by the local police, used to offer their customers a quick "flash" at the end of the act, when the G-string was completely taken off. But this flash was so brief that it was almost impossible to tell whether a tiny, flesh-colored supplementary G-string was covering the vaginal lips. Most girls shaved off most of their pubic hair, so the illusion of nudity was heightened. An offshoot of this practice, according to an old Broadway story, is that one producer got rich by manufacturing pubic hair wigs for strippers — frequently known as "merkins."

A number of well-known performers of the late thirties and early forties had begun their careers in burlesque. One of these was Fanny Brice, another was Sophie Tucker, who became famous as the Last of the Red-Hot Mamas. Eddie Cantor was a star in burlesque long before he switched to the movies and more sanitized scripts. Perhaps the most famous of all burlesque songs was written by none other than Irving Berlin. An inevitable part of every nude tableau was *A Pretty Girl Is Like a Melody,* generally sung by an Irish tenor. As the orchestra and tenor joined in harmony, a line of girls wearing white makeup and sometimes white wigs would hold their frozen poses like awkward statues, all nude except for the almost invisible G-strings. In more elaborately staged living-model numbers, a cardboard fountain competed with the cardboard trees and sometimes a paper moon was visible.

By the mid-1920s the Minsky family had twelve burlesque houses going. Slowly the great comedians left, as a result of death or desertion to richer fields, and were not replaced. The acts and the customers kept getting shabbier — and so did the theaters. The burlesque houses became strip or grind houses where one girl after another came out, and removed her clothing while doing an uninspiring series of bumps and grinds. As the patronage dropped off, the stagehand unions became too expensive and live orchestras could no longer be afforded. Burlesque had disappeared from most of the United States when it was outlawed in Manhattan in 1932 by New York's Mayor Fiorello La Guardia. And seven years later it was banished completely from New York City by License Commissioner Paul Moss. Some of the diehards continued to operate in Newark, New Jersey, and some moved to Las Vegas. But it wasn't the burlesque of the twenties.

Historically speaking, burlesque was born some 2200 years ago when the Greek satirist playwright Aristophanes launched his memorable attack on manners and morals in ancient Greece. A master of the exaggeration and the sexual joke, Aristophanes' most famous play, *Lysistrata,* had an overt sexual theme.

The men of Athens have been at war with the men of Sparta for years and their wives have remained unlaid for too long. Claiming not to have been in bed with a man since the war began, Lysistrata, a forceful, passionate female, seeks a way to end the conflict. She organizes the women of Athens, while a female colleague, Lampito, organizes the women of enemy Sparta.

Some of the best lines in the work come when Lysistrata holds a meeting and has all the girls swear: "Lovers of peace, repeat these words after me. I will not open my legs for lover or husband [all repeat this] no matter how stiff he stands." The women pledge they'll drive their men mad with desire and, if taken by force, they will lie "as cold as the ice on the mountain" until the war is over.

The most attractive woman in the play, Myrrhine, a young wife, has to outwit her horny husband, Kinesais, when he comes home on leave. Although she allows him to see her half-naked, she thinks of one excuse after another — taking care of a child, being uncomfortable and needing a blanket, not having had a bath — and finally gets him to the point where he loses complete control. (Aristophanes had his male actors wear erect artificial phalli in some of the scenes.)

When Kinesais, wearing an erect one, can restrain himself no longer, he begins screaming, "Fuck the peace, I want a piece of tail," and agrees to cast his ballot for peace. He tries to catch his wife but she is gone with the ballot. In the final scene, the Spartan herald, wearing an artificial phallus, comes over to announce that a peace treaty has been signed.

This is, of course, a very rough gist of the Aristophanes play. But while burlesque comedy developed from the broad sexual satire of Aristophanes, the nudity of burlesque came from England a lot later. Its beginning can be traced to a performance of the *Black Crook,* a popular melodrama that added an early ballet company wearing tights to brighten up the show. Then, in 1869, came a troupe called *Lydia Thompson and Her British Blondes.* As Miss Thompson said, "It's not the tights you wear, it's the way you wear them," which might have been a slogan for all the strippers who followed: It's not what you take off before an audience, it's the way you do it.

As the world and America changed in the twenties, so did burlesque. Two factors were responsible for the end of the genre. In 1907 Flo Ziegfeld introduced his world-renowned production of the Ziegfeld *Follies* which was, in its opulent way, the rich man's burlesque. Because of the splendor of the costumes and the talent of such comedians as W. C. Fields, Will Rogers, Eddie Cantor and Fanny Brice, Ziegfeld was able to attract women to his audiences as well as men.

Ziegfeld's *Follies* went farther than burlesque had ever been able to go in the magnificence of its nude displays. In one tableau, a long-haired beauty posing as Lady Godiva rode a full-size papier-mâché horse. Semi-nude tableaux showed off the spectacular figures of Faith Bacon, Beryl Haley, and many lesser-known statuesque females. The *Follies* was high-class burlesque and the revues that imitated it, such as Earl Carroll's *Vanities,* George White's *Scandals* and John Murray Anderson's *Little Shows* all paid their debt to the baggy pants comedians and the strutting, posing queens of burlesque.

The tableau with living models was a unique example of life imitating art. The garden at Versailles was reproduced in Ziegfeld's *Follies* with nude girls playing the parts of nude statues. Canova's *The Three Graces* was managed by carefully draping the nipples and crotch. Even men, occasionally, appeared in these tableaux but always with oversize fig leaves.

In 1915, taking a tip directly from burlesque, Gaby Delys peeled off her clothes in the Broadway show *Stop, Look and Listen* to music by the ever-present Irving Berlin in a song:

"Take off a little bit
If that don't make a hit
Take off a little bit more."

Bluenose organizations, including church groups, made attempts to censor these revealing revues. But because most were produced in good taste and so much talent went into them, road show companies of the *Vanities* and the *Scandals* appeared in major cities, where they were sometimes picketed. As the new reviews made it big, burlesque deteriorated, with some shows developing unsavory reputations as traveling whorehouses.

Even though women were shocked and some mothers kept their daughters away from such road show revues as the *Vanities* and the *Scandals*, it was not too difficult for a man to convince his wife or a young man to get a date to go to see such extravaganzas. I remember going to Earl Carroll's *Vanities* at about the age of sixteen with a girlfriend of the same age. Her mother didn't know what the show was about but did read a lurid review in the paper the next day. She called her daughter in and asked, "Claire, how could you sit in the theater next to Bradley and see all those naked girls and listen to those off-color jokes?"

Claire hesitated for a moment and then replied, "But, Mother, I didn't look at Bradley once during the whole show."

A much wider audience of both men and women was being exposed to a broader type of sex education by the movies. Radio had not contributed much, for that medium managed to keep itself spotlessly clean. Eddie Cantor was unable to sing one of his great hits on the air for fear of offending the audience. It was *I'll Say She Does*. The lines especially objected to were:

"When I kiss her, does she shout?
Does she do a lot of things I can't talk about?
Does she?
I'll say she does!"

When the movies came along the censors were taken by surprise. Theda Bara played the femme fatale in many an early flick. She did a somewhat classic version of a strip in her *Dance of the Seven Veils* but actually took off very little. She wore form-fitting, slinky, black dresses, low cut, and moved in what was considered at the time a highly provocative manner. It was okay in the cities but in the rural areas, especially the southern Bible Belt, the nickelodeon was the devil in a new disguise.

Early movies displayed sex in a variety of ways. The first serials were replete with both sex and violence.

One would not have worked without the other. Pearl White began her screen career in 1910 and soon became queen of the Saturday night serial. The most famous of her films was *The Perils of Pauline*. In every thrilling episode, her life and, even worse, her "honor" were at stake. Each installment left her hanging, sometimes literally, on the edge of a cliff or on the brink of violation; but in the next episode her strong and resourceful stepbrother, Harry Marvin, played by Crane Wilbur, came to her rescue.

The durable Miss White was assaulted by Indians, sailors, pirates, gangsters, Chinese and any other bad men that the creators could imagine.

Without being overtly sexy, Pauline managed to have her clothing torn enough to reveal that she was, indeed, a girl. She looked very feminine when wet, which she was fairly often. In the last of *The Perils of Pauline*, the villain is finally drowned; as he vanishes into a watery grave, Pauline and Harry vow that they will marry. It's about time.

The Perils of Pauline was by no means the only serial with a heroine. Among others, *The Million Dollar Mystery*, *The Adventures of Katherine* and *The Exploits of Elaine* were popular. All featured ingenious but vulnerable heroines and machismo heroes. Pearl White, too, came back more than once. Two of her sequels were *The Iron Claw* and *The Black Secret*. In the later years of the serial, Pearl White's greatest rival in popularity was Ruth Roland.

Villains in these early serials were quite often Orientals who were out to drug and rape the heroine. The race, in fact, was portrayed as a veritable "yellow menace" to the American people, and for years preceding the movie serials Asian figures dominated the bad-guy roles in the theater.

The serials also developed techniques to tease the audiences with provocative but harmless sex scenes. One favorite was to show a girl undressing through a window. But just as she was about to step out of her step-in a train would come rattling by — when it had passed, she was well covered by a kimono. A popular story involved a man who came to the movie every night for weeks. Finally, the cashier, who by now knew the customer well, asked, "Don't you ever get tired of seeing this film over and over?"

"No," he said. "I'm a patient fellow — and one night that train is going to be late."

It took a few years to find a combination that would utilize some degree of male and female nudity and get by the newly appointed censors. Then some early Hollywood genius decided to adapt Edgar Rice Burroughs' successful *Tarzan* books to the screen with just the right element of danger from men and animals. These films supplied women with a partly clothed, invincible male whom they could empathize with and, because Tarzan was always non-competitive, men could identify with him also. As for Jane, though not married to Tarzan, she played the perfect shy, but willing, mate.

The first Tarzan of the screen, Elmo Lincoln, wore an animal skin that covered at least seventy-five percent of his weightlifter's body. Gene Pollar and Herman Brix, other bulging-muscle types, were also fairly well covered. But when Johnny Weissmuller, Olympic swimming champion, took over the role, he was stripped down to a pair of leopard-skin trunks. And, as the series progressed, Jane's costume became increasingly brief.

Even before World War I was over, Hollywood actors were beginning to develop a reputation for sexual immorality. William Randolph Hearst, as we have seen, had adopted Broadway's Marion Davies, made her his mistress and produced her films. Miss Davies, along with her lover, backed the war effort with public appearances. But the most important crowd pleasers and money gatherers for the war effort were Douglas Fairbanks, Mary Pickford and Charlie Chaplin, the three most popular people in America and perhaps the world. Sexually, none of them were beyond reproach. During the war, however, the public heard only the vaguest rumors. Douglas Fairbanks (or his press agent) had written in his autobiographical book *Laugh and Live:* "If a man is a manly man, he should marry early and remain faithful to the bride of his youth." Yet, while touring the country with Mary Pickford selling war bonds, he was having a love affair with her. His wife, Beth Sully Fairbanks, stayed home, as did Mary's husband, actor Owen Moore.

Both Mary and Doug — and the movie companies, producers, directors and writers who depended upon them for a livelihood — were desperately afraid that the scandal of a divorce would ruin their respective careers. But the divorces were cleverly managed and, surprisingly enough, they had little or no effect upon the duet's popularity — except, perhaps, to make it greater. Mary and Doug were married secretly on March 28, 1920, and, for the next sixteen years, they became America's symbols of adventure and romance. But not even this true-life fairy tale lasted.

According to Booton Herndon, in his excellent, in-depth biography *Mary Pickford and Douglas Fairbanks,* the movie makers of Hollywood knew that the romance and marriage of the world's favorite lovers was coming apart long before it became visible to the public. During the making of *The Taming of the Shrew* neither of them was happy with the other on the set. It seemed as though Fairbanks was doing a real taming of the shrew with Mary rather than Katrina in the play. At any rate, they were not getting along in the same idyllic manner as before. After that picture, Fairbanks went to England while Mary stayed home and the rumors started. Fairbanks was discreet but the gossip around Hollywood was that he was involved with other women. The couple rocked along together until Fairbanks met Lady Ashley, a former chorus girl named Sylvia Hawkes; it soon became common knowledge in Europe that they were sexually involved. Mary found out about the affair by accident when a bracelet that her husband had ordered for Lady Ashley was delivered to her by mistake. Shortly afterwards, Louella Parsons, the gossip columnist, broadcast the scandal. A few months later, in 1933, Mary filed for a divorce.

By the time they were divorced Hollywood had weathered so many scandals that the new alliances — Mary with Buddy Rogers and Doug with Sylvia Ashley — were already stale news.

During the twenties and thirties, movie fans wanted to believe that Hollywood's movie stars were very special people, glamorous symbols to whom they could relate for a few hours every week as a break in their usually dull lives. They expected a certain amount of intrigue and mild immorality. But outright adultery, especially for women stars, and for men as well, was dangerous. The moviegoers might stop paying to see them. Morality clauses suddenly appeared in Hollywood contracts for both men and women.

Then a series of real shocks spread across movieland. Some of the stars, idols of young girls and boys, and their parents as well, were involved in scandalous behavior beyond acceptance. Wallace Reed, a popular star, died after becoming a heroin addict.

A rotund, gentle-faced, king of movie comedy ($5000 a week), Roscoe "Fatty" Arbuckle, threw a wild party at the St. Francis Hotel in San Francisco. Beginning on the Saturday of a Labor Day weekend, bootleg liquor was flowing freely and by Monday the party had turned into a drunken orgy. An aspiring twenty-five-year-old actress, by no means virginal, Virginia Rappe, engaged in a prolonged sex bout with the 400-pound comedian in one of the bedrooms. It was never exactly clear how it happened but, either with Arbuckle's penis or with a champagne bottle, Miss Rappe's bladder was ruptured. She bled profusely and died as a result. Although it was easily proved that Arbuckle had been sexually involved, money and influence, plus the fact that the death was accidental (no one ever accused Arbuckle of murdering the girl) got him off. He went to trial three times. The first two trials resulted in hung juries. The third time he was acquitted. Though he was technically (according to law) innocent, he was forever guilty in the minds of the movie producers as well as the fans that had previously laughed at his antics. The incident ended his career in films.

William Desmond Taylor, leading director, was mysteriously murdered. The subsequent investigations revealed that at least two pure and innocent screen types, Mary Miles Minter and Mabel Normand, had been sexually involved with him, and both had been at his home the night he was shot. They did not come to trial but their careers in the flicks ended.

Then came the scandal that rocked the entire movie

world. While the Arbuckle and Taylor cases may have been sensational sex scandals of their time, the marriages and divorces of America's favorite comedian, Charles Spencer Chaplin, champion of the noble "little man," were front-page news. Chaplin early became notorious for his predilection for young girls. To avoid being hailed into court on morals charges, he twice preferred to marry sixteen-year-olds — after getting them pregnant. The first of these was Mildred Harris, a barely budding young actress, who became his wife in 1918. After the baby died in infancy, Chaplin quietly managed a divorce.

His next Lolita, believe it or not, was actually named Lillita. At the age of twelve, she worked in Chaplin's movie, *The Kid,* both as a street urchin and then, made up to look older, as the flirting angel in the famous dream sequence. He was so smitten with her that for a time she was given the star's dressing room, which annoyed Chaplin's long-time mistress, Edna Purviance. After *The Kid,* however, Chaplin did not see Lillita again for three years. When he was preparing *The Gold Rush* she visited the studio; he remembered her with great pleasure and was unable to resist her fifteen-year-old charm. He had soon put her under contract to appear in *The Gold Rush.*

According to Lita Grey Chaplin in her book *My Life with Chaplin,* his first attempt was on the beach, then in the back of his curtained Locomobile limousine. But the consummation wasn't accomplished until she went, willingly, to his Beverly Hills home — and ultimately lost her virginity in his steam room. In addition to changing her sexual status, he also changed her name from Lillita McMurray to Lita Grey. They were constant lovers for the next few months until one morning her mother, who had stayed overnight in Chaplin's house, rose early and found them in bed together. Shortly after the confrontation, Lita found herself pregnant. The case became potential publicity dynamite — for Chaplin at first refused to consider marriage. It was not until a court case was threatened, which might have involved a charge of statutory rape of a fifteen-year-old girl, that he reluctantly consented to a secret marriage in Mexico. He successfully protected his public image by living with Lita until two children were born, Charles, Jr. and Sidney. After the birth of the second child, he left his wife almost entirely alone. His nights were then taken up with some of Hollywood's most glamorous stars, including Pola Negri, Claire Windsor, Marion Davies and Peggy Hopkins Joyce.

When Lita decided to divorce him, he couldn't believe it. Not only concerned about his money, he was now seriously worried about his reputation. Perhaps he might have reduced his risk had he made an early settlement, but Chaplin was never a man to take a financial loss if there was a possible way out. Indeed, he took off for New York and Europe hoping that his lawyers could work out a deal whereby Lita would accept twenty-five dollars a week as support for herself and the two chil-

dren — a paltry sum even in those days.

But Lita was now hurt and angry. She agreed to a bill of particulars that her lawyer-uncle drew up and brought a divorce suit against Chaplin. This opened up the scandal to the world. Among the items in the bill of particulars were such tidbits as:

"Plaintiff alleges further that approximately six months before the separation of said parties, defendant was home in the afternoon shortly before dinner, and continued his solicitations and demanded that plaintiff commit the act of sex perversion defined by Section 288a of the Penal Code of California [i.e., oral sex]. That defendant became enraged at plaintiff's refusal and said to her: 'All married people do those kind [sic] of things. You are my wife and you *have* to do what I want you to do. I can get a divorce from you for refusing to do this. That upon plaintiff's continued refusal, defendant abruptly left the house and plaintiff did not see him again until the next day."

Lita's lawyer-uncle was on firm ground, for the California Penal Code did, indeed, forbid oral sex, even between married people. According to Miss Grey, her lawyer said, "If we want to press, he can go to prison for fifteen years." By this time the public was having a picnic keeping up with the daily scandalous headlines. Chaplin was criticized widely as a degenerate Englishman whose favorite pursuit was deflowering virgins. He was denounced from pulpits all over the country for "breaking the laws of God" and, worst of all, some fans began to boycott Charlie's films.

Added to all of this, Charlie had another problem. The Federal Government filed a case against him for non-payment of $1,330,000 in income tax. Chaplin's attorneys renewed their offer of twenty-five dollars a week child support. One women's organization got a group of clubs together in Hollywood to raise money for Lita Grey Chaplin and the children. Anti-Chaplin feeling was rising rapidly. But Chaplin was adamant. He was not going to settle.

At his point, Lita Grey's lawyers prepared to play their trump card: to name in court all the women Chaplin had been intimate with while married to Lita Grey. This was too much for Chaplin to top. He got in touch with his lawyer, asking, "Nate, what shall I do?"

The lawyer said: "Settle."

So the divorce was granted and the press saw to it that all the details were publicized. Custody of the children went to Lita Grey Chaplin, who was made guardian of them and their estates. Each child was awarded $100,000. Lita was awarded $625,000. Chaplin did not appear in court at the settlement. He wanted no more publicity.

While Chaplin's peccadilloes made headlines from the West Coast, another playboy-Lolita affair was about to unfold in New York. A broad-faced, plump and pretty fifteen-year-old, Frances Heenan by name, but nicknamed "Peaches" because of her faultless complexion, fell in love with fifty-one-year-old, rich man-about-town Edward West Browning. They met, she said, at a sorority dance. After a whirlwind courtship, they married on April 10, 1926.

There was nothing illegal about a fifty-one-year-old man marrying a fifteen-year-old girl in New York as long as she had her mother's consent, which she did, but it seemed horribly immoral to New York's so-called respectable citizens and its less-reputable press. The "Peaches-Daddy" romance moved right out of the church into a tabloid newspaper heaven. Everywhere that Peaches and Daddy went reporters were sure to go. He took her to speakeasies and nightclubs and bought her a peacock blue limousine. One of Peaches' great delights was to have her chauffeur drive her back to her old neighborhood in Washington Heights and to visit Fleischers' Delicatessen Restaurant on upper Broadway to treat her neighborhood friends.

The tabloids, especially the *Evening Graphic*, which was competing with the *Daily Mirror* for circulation, invented a new kind of comic strip using composite photodrawings. Peaches and Daddy were shown in the illustrations up to all kinds of antics, with their heads from photographs pasted onto other photographed bodies: Peaches jumping rope, Daddy on crutches. Daddy in a wheelchair, Peaches blowing bubbles.

When Peaches sued for a divorce, the press revived its salacious stories about them. There was no divorce decree but Browning paid temporary alimony of $320 a week until he died in 1934. Peaches was recognized as his legal widow and, in addition to considerable cash, inherited five apartment houses. She continued to be news as she married and divorced three men in relatively quick succession. Prominent in cafe society, she made several attempts in show business, but never quite made it. As the peach faded, the public forgot her as rapidly as it had accepted her.

Two crimes of passion — both saturated with sex — competed with the sex-divorce scandals during the twenties for front-page space. First came the scandal of a minister and the choir singer who, on a pleasant afternoon in September 1922, were found lying next to one another, on their backs, fully clothed, in the shade of a tree on the outskirts of New Brunswick, New Jersey, and quite dead. The woman's head was resting on the man's right arm and her left hand stretched across his knee. At a distance it looked as though they were covered with leaves but, on closer scrutiny, it was found that they were strewn, almost from head to foot, with love letters. The teen-age boy and girl who found the bodies hurried home and breathlessly told their families. When the police arrived and lifted a scarf that covered the woman's throat they found that it had been cut from ear to ear. Both victims had been shot with a thirty-two caliber pistol — the woman's throat was believed to have been slit after she was dead.

Four years later, after a hearing that yielded no evidence of the perpetrator of the crime, the bodies were exhumed and new autopsies performed. At this time, they found that the larynx, tongue and part of the windpipe was missing from the woman who was identified as choir singer Eleanor Mills. This part of the mystery was never solved either. Was her throat removed because she was a singer? Or because someone had observed the couple in illicit and illegal oral sex? Or did she talk too much?

The dead man was the Reverend Edward Hall, an Episcopal minister and pastor of the local church. He had been married to Frances Hall — happily as far as anyone knew — for eleven years. The murdered woman was married to James Mills and had two children.

Now the newspapers had a truly juicy scandal. Investigative newspaper reporters turned up a lot of information — some of it accurate. For one thing Reverend almost certainly had affairs with other members of his choir, in addition to Mrs. Mills. It was believed that his wife knew of his affair with Mrs. Mills. Mrs. Hall, naturally, was the first suspect. But she had an unbreakable alibi for the crucial hours when the murder occurred.

Mrs. Mills' husband, Jim, was never seriously suspected for he, too, had an alibi. Yet soon after the bodies were discovered, Mills sold a package of his wife's love letters to the New York *Daily Mirror* for $500 . The case became even more entangled when a witness who came to be known nationally in the tabloids as "The Pig Woman" (because someone had been stealing pigs from her farm) testified that, after hearing a shot on the night of the murder, she had seen Eleanor Mills running into some bushes.

The town of New Brunswick took on a holiday aura. Reporters, wire services, curious voyeurs poured into town to be present at the trial and to view the colorful characters, especially "The Pig Woman." Newspaper reporters dug up the information that the teen-age girl who first discovered the bodies might have been involved in an incestuous relationship with her father the night of the murders and that one of the married vestrymen had been seen parking in the lane where the lovers were murdered with another member of the choir. Mrs. Mills' sister reported that the minister and the choir singer had intended to leave the country for Japan as soon as Mrs. Mills' daughter graduated from high school.

It took a long time for the news stories to die down. Many suggestions were made as to the perpetrators of the crime. But it was never solved.

Equally sensational, but easily solved, was the crime of passion so clumsily executed that it was referred to by writer Damon Runyon as "a dumbbell murder." That it was a premeditated murder there was never any doubt.

Many observers could not imagine why it took the jury an hour and thirty-seven minutes to reach the decision that brought Judd Gray and Ruth Brown Snyder to the electric chair. She was the seventh woman to be executed in New York State and the second to be electrocuted — the others were hanged.

Ruth Snyder had an unenviable track record as a potential murderess. She had attempted to kill her husband, Albert, seven times before. Her husband was simple-minded enough to sign three life insurance policies, making his death worth over $90,000.

Each of her solo attempts were exercises in futility. First she tried to get him drunk in the garage. Then, after she thought he was asleep, the garage door mysteriously closed. Fortunately, he had not quite passed out and crawled to the door and opened it. She tried turning on the gas when he was sleeping in the living room. But he woke up too soon. She tried it again with the same result. Poison didn't work either; she didn't put enough bichloride of mercury in his whiskey to kill him.

Why did she want to dispose of her husband? Well, it was that old devil, romance. Blonde, thirty-two-year-old Ruth had fallen in love with a handsome corset salesman she had met on a blind date. They soon consummated their passion in an office of Bien Jolie Corsets, where he worked. His name was Judd Gray and, in his own special way, he was probably stupider than she. The affair between Judd and Ruth proceeded in and out of hotel rooms, offices and occasionally at her home in Queens Village outside of Manhattan, for nearly two years. But Ruth was impatient. Her husband was definitely in the way, worthless to her alive but with a value of $90,000 dead. When she suggested that Judd buy a revolver and take up target practice, he turned her down. Finally her womanly wiles prevailed. He agreed to help her.

On March 20, 1927, Judd slipped into the house and waited. Then came the suspenseful moments while the lovers waited for Albert to go to sleep in the next room. Judd, the reluctant killer, had brought along, in his corset case, rubber gloves, a bottle of chloroform, some cotton, a length of picture wire, a bandanna handkerchief and an Italian newspaper. Ruth had located and supplied him with a heavy, lead sash weight. Together they entered the master bedroom. Judd lifted the sash weight and struck down at Snyder's head but he missed and broke the headboard of the bed. Albert woke up; Judd lost the lead weight in the bedclothes. When Albert began choking Judd, Ruth found the weapon and caved in Albert's skull. He seemed dead enough but, to be sure, she saturated the cotton batting with chloroform and shoved it into his nose and mouth. Then they tied his hands and feet. An hour later, for safety insurance, Judd returned and fastened a wire noose tightly around Albert's neck.

Then the clumsy conspirators went to work arranging the evidence to mislead the police. They put Ruth's nightgown and Judd's bloody shirt in the furnace but unfortunately, they didn't burn completely. The bloody sash weight went into Albert's toolbox down in the basement. The Italian newspaper and the bandanna, which were supposed to make the police think that Italian bandits had murdered Albert, were left on the floor. Then to make it look like robbery, they opened and emptied many drawers and, for the hell of it, turned over a few chairs. The final touch was when Ruth had Judd tie her up and gag her.

The police listened carefully to Ruth's story about being attacked by two men with black mustaches. She called attention to the Italian newspaper and bandanna they left behind. The police of New York had never been considered intellectual prodigies but it took them only a few minutes to find the sash weight, the remains of her nightgown and a bloodstained pillowcase that she had put in a laundry bag. To make it all easier for the law, Judd Gray had dropped his tie pin (with his initials J. G.) on the floor of the bedroom — and in the desk was a canceled check for $200 signed by Ruth Snyder — made out to her lover.

Their last words upon being condemned to death were widely publicized. In a metaphor as jumbled as his murder, Judd said, "I hope that my example will be a warning to others and that some who are going wrong will change the rudder and keep off the rocks."

She said, "I am better prepared for death now than if I had continued the life I was leading."

But it was the *New York Daily News* that had the last word or, actually, the last photograph. An ingenious editor had a photographer strap a small camera to his ankle. As the electric current surged into the bound body of Ruth Snyder, he crossed his legs and took a picture of the morbid scene. It ran as a full page next day and became one of the world's most widely published photographs.

Next to the murders the movies occupied the greatest amount of newspaper and magazine space. Bankers and producers catered to the interest of the millions of movie fans by carefully promoting their properties to star status. Smart press agents publicized the fads and follies (respectable ones) of the stars in exposés of their so-called private lives.

Popular sexual specialization followed. Women wanted their male screen heroes to be tall, dark and handsome. As for male preferences, there were tit men, ass men and leg men. For a tit man a forty inch-bust was a feast. Long-legged girls dominated the dance scenes. Choices of mates throughout the country were beginning to be made on a body-type basis.

By the mid-thirties the public had been superficially exposed to some of the ideas advanced by a brilliant, gentle, personally conservative Austrian Jew. His name was Sigmund Freud and he invented the id.

The idea of Freud's id became the popular "it." A Hollywood publicist picked up the idea and christened Clara Bow the "it" girl. Miss Bow managed to combine the healthy sexy look (short skirts and the new bathing suits helped) with a petite, decadent seductiveness that made her a sex queen. She may not have been the most beautiful girl in Hollywood nor the best actress but she had "it." Clara was no dumb bunny and neither were her promoters. Her movies showed as much of her as they dared and almost overnight millions of young housewives and office girls were imitating her makeup, bobbed hair and wardrobe. They all wanted to have "it" too. No one seemed to know or care what "it" was, for most laymen had only vaguely heard of Freud.

In the body of his work Freud distilled his revolutionary psychological concept: that the driving force of the individual was his total unrealized mass of instinctual energy (the "id"). Freud postulated that the individual's ego translates and channels the id into reality. In his theory, the sex impulse is directly related to the id. It can even be said — as many popular writers have — that the id represents the individual's sexual energy flowing into all the areas of human activity. It is almost impossible to emphasize how great Freud's influence was (and still is) on sexual mores.

In a series of epoch-making books he explored the human subconscious mind and the pattern of dreams. Through "psychoanalysis," he developed a technique of allowing the troubled patient to recall repressed memories and used "free association" where one thought progresses to another. Freud, and many analysts since, have been able to induce patients to remember incidents that were at the root of their illnesses and maladjustments. Indeed, he believed that nothing is forever forgotten, but rather buried in the subconscious mind. He inspired all the various modern schools of psychosomatic medicine. Freud, in turn, was indebted for his idea of the id to Georg Walther Groddeck, a German psychologist and philosopher who had used the word "it" to describe the total life force.

Popularizers, writers in magazines and newspapers, only picked up the surface of Freudian thought. Young men, in an effort to get their female acquaintances into bed, lectured them on being repressed or neurotic unless they could happily and joyfully lose their inhibitions. A favorite "line" among them was that female sexual repression would cause obesity, pimples and worse . . . One should not, they had heard, repress one's sexuality lest one become neurotic or perverted. Few people took the trouble to read Freud completely, with ultimate comprehension, for his turgid, technical prose was hard going.

But his doctrine, especially the idea of finding a way for the individual to rechannel his sexual energy to conform to the norms of society, was an important contribution to mankind's knowledge of itself. Incidentally, Freud described three stages of sexual morality which correspond to the development of the pleasure-seeking principle, the libido. According to him every human being requires a certain amount of sexual gratification. The first stage, then, is the free exercise of all sexual impulses. In the second stage, all sexual impulses are suppressed except those leading to procreation. Finally, all sex impulses except those leading to legitimate offspring are stifled in the third stage. Freud pointed out that the restrictions of the second stage, which limit sexual activity between the sexes, have been found historically too difficult for most people. In trying to suppress the sex urge, some become inverts, or homosexuals, unable to love outside their own sex. But the third stage of civilized morality — the one prevalent from 1900 to the 1940s — theoretically required that men and women have no sexual relations until they were legally married. Men and women who did not marry were expected to remain virgins for life. Such abstinence being impossible for most, society's rules — or, in a more fundamentalist religious context, part of the Ten Commandments — had to be broken. Freud believed that those unable to comply with the restrictions imposed by society became neurotic. By neurotic he meant that the natural tendencies of the individual are suppressed yet they inevitably break out in harmful ways, making it difficult for the individual to adjust in society.

Freud's ideas were slow to surface but some of his basic concepts spilled over into the public consciousness. Thanks to them sexual taboos slowly began to vanish.

Writing on a more popular level was Havelock Ellis, an Englishman who, at the age of sixteen, became fascinated with the problem of sex and society. He started off with the traditional years in medical school. But after graduating and going into general practice, he found that to widely disseminate his ideas he would have to write. From then on his life was dedicated to exploring and defining the problems of sex.

It was Ellis who set the stage for all future serious endeavors in the field of sex research. His first great work, *Man and Woman,* was published at the end of the nineteenth century. In studying the differences between men and women, he used the scientific method, by which he concerned himself with not only biological aspects but environmental as well as hereditary factors.

Havelock Ellis was an early, perhaps the first, sex researcher, to speak out against the inferior status of women, maintaining that females are neither inferior nor superior to man. Yet he also insisted that the sexes were not equal. Each has its own place and each balances the other "in their unlikeness."

Ellis's next work, which took him thirty years to complete, was called *Studies in the Psychology of Sex.* He planned seven volumes but for a time it looked like he would never get past the first. For when *Sexual Inversion* appeared at the turn of the century, the bookseller was arrested, charged with selling obscene literature. At that time, no organization existed to defend him against censorship. Ellis never forgave the British censors for banning the book, which was withdrawn from circulation in England. At his insistence, the next edition of *Sexual Inversion* and all of his subsequent books were published outside of England, appearing first in Germany and America.

He was a man of great mental gifts who believed his reason for living was to research, report and comment on the facts of sex as he saw them. Unlike Freud, he used little scientific jargon in his works. He tried to understand the sexual drives of men and women and see how these drives could best be fit into society; or, when that was not possible, how society could fit itself into the sex drives of the people who make it up. He wrote that there was no arbitrary boundary line between normal and abnormal sexual behavior. Some aberrations in sexual matters occur at times in most normal people. And even in the abnormal person, the basic sex impulse is usually normal.

Intelligently organized and lucidly related, his works were widely read. Ellis exploded many long-held, unscientific views about the nature of sex; for one, that the male semen is expelled from the body (as urine might be) because the pressure of the semen builds up until it must be released. He pointed out that semen is not a waste excretion and that this traditional idea was erroneous. He postulated that sexual desire is not constant in either the male or the female but rather periodic, seasonal or, possibly, rhythmic.

The popularization of Ellis' works made his public more conscious of the sense of touch as a most important part of love-making and sexual relationships. He also recognized that the voice of a man or a woman, as well as their smell, are sexual stimuli. However, in his opinion, vision is the most significant of the senses that affects sexual selection; love for beauty, he held, includes and embraces physical nudity and eroticism.

Ellis was not a follower of Freud, though they agreed on the possible benefits of psychoanalysis. He disagreed, however, regarding the Oedipus complex and infantile homosexuality. Ellis wrote that homosexuality developed from the child's concept of sexuality within his environment. Masturbation he regarded as a natural outlet for sexual energy and understood its necessity in a civilization that did not allow sexual outlets to juveniles. A strong proponent of sex education, it was in this area that he was attacked most often. Believing such education essential, he spent much of his time speaking and writing on it, emphasizing that all sex education should begin with the young child.

Ellis often reiterated the idea that there was no single pattern for the sex life. Two consenting adults should be free to adopt whatever sexual practices work best for them — and it should be legal. "Whatever gives satisfaction and relief to both parties is good and right." Ellis' work created a base upon which most current psychologists and psychiatrists have built.

He discussed sexual foreplay, courtship, sex on the honeymoon and foresaw most of the how-to-do-it sex books. As for the many possible positions during intercourse, he advised individual experimentation as the only way for partners to find out what gives them the most satisfaction.

There is a direct line in the field of sexual enlightenment that moves from Freud to Ellis to Sanger to Kinsey to Masters and Johnson . . . and Comfort.

Ellis was doubtless greatly encouraged in his studies by the intimate relationship he formed with Margaret Sanger, a tireless public speaker who popularized his views on sex education. In 1914 she introduced the phrase "birth control" into the English language and subsequently founded the Birth Control League of America. Frequently arrested for making such devices available to women, it was not until October, 1916, that she was able to open her first legal birth control clinic in New York.

It was an uphill fight most of the way. In most states the sale of condoms, diaphragms, vaginal foams and contraceptive jellies was illegal. Many a doctor went to jail for prescribing the use of diaphragms even though this method had been known in the United States since the 1860s. It was not until twenty-three years after the Birth Control League was organized that a federal court ruled that birth control information could be sent through the mail.

Among the aims of the Birth Control League were to allow a husband and wife a period of adjustment before pregnancy occurred, to safeguard the mother's health by allowing at least two years between children and to limit the family to those children for whom a decent standard of living could be provided. Through the twenties and thirties, the Roman Catholic Church, some Orthodox Jewish congregations and many Protestant congregations violently opposed Sanger's ideas, their most frequent objection being that birth control information would increase immorality both among the married and unmarried by freeing the sexual partners from risk of pregnancy.

Actually, the benefits of birth control were felt by the early thirties. Within those groups that had access to sex information there were fewer unwanted pregnancies and more stable families. Another benefit never widely discussed was the great decline in prostitution. Wives on every level, who had sometimes welcomed the idea of their husbands going to a prostitute — rather than being continuously pregnant — learned that with birth control they could keep their husbands happy in their own beds and, in increasingly large numbers, they did just that.

The works of Marie Stopes, who further popularized Ellis's views on sex, also had a profound influence on the American woman.

A doctor of philosophy, Marie Stopes began her first marriage with such a lack of sexual knowledge she couldn't figure out what was going wrong. After some years of connubial non-bliss, she obtained an annulment on the grounds that she was still a virgin. Things changed rapidly after she remarried. Full of new insight and a new awakening, she published her book *Married Love.* It had sensational sales throughout the English-speaking world and became a pillow-side companion for the "liberated" women of the thirties. Inevitably, the book came under fire from diehards both in and out of church circles.

As women like Margaret Sanger and Marie Stopes began to speak out, so did women in the arts, who attacked the so-called superiority of men. One of the most effective was a petite, attractive, young writer and rhymer with a vitriolic pen. Her name was Dorothy Parker.

"There are the Cave Men —
The Specimens of Red-Blooded Manhood.
They eat everything very rare,
They are scarcely ever out of their cold baths,
And they want everybody to feel their muscles.
They talk in loud voices,
Using short Anglo-Saxon words.
They go around raising windows,
And they slap people on the back,
And tell them what they need is exercise.
They are always just on the point of walking
	to San Francisco,
Or crossing the ocean in a sailboat,
Or going through Russia on a sled—
I wish to God they would!"

The incubator of new thoughts, new sexual directions, new freedoms was the twelve-square-block section of New York called Greenwich Village. It is fitting that the limit of the Village is marked with the classic arch built by Stanford White, the radical of an earlier day, who pursued sex and fame to as great an extent as most Villagers did years later. Though a small area physically, by the end of World War I the Village had become a seething center for young people in search of new freedoms — sexual, artistic and political. In the heart of a big city it had a friendly environment. Mistresses and wives got together to discuss politics and sex. An atmosphere of live and let live prevailed.

An important war of ideas and ideals began between America's traditional conservatives and this informal gathering of artists and writers. From this unlikely center the attack spread out. The ammunition included the idea of moral and economic equality for women, self-realization for the individual expressed in a "live-for-today" attitude, freedom of sexual preferences inside or outside of marriage, a mobile society where decaying roots could be left behind and, with all this, the hope of a new society aesthetically oriented.

The magazines and newspapers that represented the more conservative millions fought back. The Villagers were described as long-haired, unwashed radical thinkers mixed up with equally radical, short-haired, immoral women who smoked, drank and practiced sex outside of marriage. It was the conflict of the industrial society against the artistic society — the Bohemian versus the bourgeois.

By the beginning of the twenties, the Village had a well-earned reputation as a Utopian oasis where both men and women had freedom to act as they pleased. Its radicalism rested on a solid base. Avant-garde political and social thinkers had cultivated and planted the seeds of freedom. There were more girls with bobbed hair and short skirts, more girls smoking and drinking and fewer virgins over sixteen than in any other area in Manhattan.

To set history straight, it didn't all start in 1920. Radical days in the Village began as early as 1912. It became the closest approximation to Bohemian Paris that the United States could offer — with the possible exception of the New Orleans French Quarter.

Most important of the early residents was Emma Goldman, a woman with a passion for political justice and absolute freedom for the individual. She called herself an anarchist and she lectured not only in the Village but across the United States. (Young Henry Miller, then set on a career as a cowboy, went to hear her speak in San Diego. He said later that hearing her ideas was a turning point in his future literary career.) Goldman was an advocate of equal rights for everyone — including women. She had no strong objection to marriage but, for herself, preferred to live openly with a lover, Alexander Berkman. At the time he started sharing Emma's quarters, he had been recently released from prison, where he had been tucked away after he shot Henry Clay Frick, the millionaire industrialist and art patron. Actually, Miss Goldman's household was a chic ménage à trois, for when Berkman arrived she was already living with Ben Reitman. (A few years later, they could have been models for Noel Coward's play *Design for Living.*)

Another leading feminist in the Village was Henrietta Rodman, outspoken writer, poet, birth control advocate and pioneer of bobbed hair, whose usual garb was a loose type of garment later known as a muu-muu.

Mable Dodge, a rich divorcee, had moved from Paris, where she had been a friend of Gertrude Stein and Alice B. Toklas. At her "Mabel Dodge evenings," modern art, modern writing, sex — normal and abnormal — were the subjects of intimate discussions. Although this may have become ordinary table talk in the late seventies, in 1913 such matters were never talked over in "polite society." At one of these meetings, it is said, psychoanalysis was openly discussed for the first time. How daring it was then to scrutinize and evaluate the innermost thoughts and actions of each other!

Only a few blocks north of the Village, at 291 Fifth Avenue, was the atelier of Alfred Stieglitz, known as the 291 Gallery. It was here that artists, writers and photographers gathered to plan the post-impressionist show where, for the first time in New York, in 1911, European moderns, neo-impressionists, fauvists, and cubists displayed their works along with avant-garde Americans such as Arthur Dove and Georgia O'Keefe. Marcel Duchamp's strange and wonderful cubist variations of light planes titled *Nude Descending a Staircase* caused an uproar among New York's art critics. When a group of reporters asked dean of art critics Walter Pach to locate the nude figure for them, Pach replied, "Where is the moon in the *Moonlight Sonata?*" Here, for the first time, were the one-dimensional, brilliantly colored nudes of Henri Matisse. Here, too, were the first Picassos to be shown in the United States. But even the shock-proof Villagers were startled by the rumor that photographer Steichen had taken portraits of a woman at the moment of sexual orgasm.

It was a time when three of the great novelties to be seen — and which everyone stopped to view — were: an airplane, a man without a hat and a woman smoking a cigarette. The latter two could be seen every day in Greenwich Village. Plaques with two names began to appear over doorbells, whether the people occupying the apartment were married or not. Usually, they were not but, in the event that they were, the women considered it important to maintain their identify.

Before the war, the monthly newspaper the *Masses* reflected the unconventional views of many Villagers. This did not, of course, include the large numbers of Italian workers and shopkeepers who had no social contact with the avant-garde Villagers. The *Masses* sold for ten cents an issue, or a dollar a year. In it appeared the work of people who went on to become the most important artists in the United States: George Bellows, Stuart Davis, John Sloan, Boardman Robinson, Georgia O'Keefe, Art Young and Jo Davidson. Contributors included Sherwood Anderson, Upton Sinclair, Wilbur Daniel Steele, Max Eastman, William Rose Benet, Carl Sandburg and John Reed.

The *Masses* became famous for its satiric cartoon comments on American life. One cartoon showed a couple in a rumpled bed. The woman is saying to the unshaven man, "Get up, you bum, don't you know this is our wedding day?"

When World War I broke out, Villagers strongly opposed United States intervention. The older Emma Goldman and the young, newly arrived Villager John Reed made impassioned speeches. Reed, who was later to become famous for his inflammatory book *Ten Days that Shook the World,* as well as for his anti-war and pro-Russian position after the war, moved in with Mabel Dodge. With his energy and her intelligence and money, they made events happen.

The most important of the literary magazines was called *Little Review.* One day, in 1918, poet Ezra Pound sent a manuscript from Italy. It was part of James Joyce's literary-history-making book, *Ulysses.* The editor of the *Little Review,* Margaret Anderson, immediately arranged to print it and the novel ran in monthly installments for the next three years. She was hailed into court and charged with publishing obscene material; four times issues of her *Little Review* were burned for obscenity. She and the other editors of the review were found guilty of publishing a lewd manuscript but were fined only one hundred dollars. They were happy in their victory but some of their backers seemed to be disappointed that they didn't become martyrs by going to jail.

In the 1920s, ambitious career girls began to move into the Village. Many enjoyed being sexually promiscuous because, instead of being criticized and shunned, they were respectable — they were also noticed and feted. Nor did it keep many of them from making happy marriages.

A sensitive, young and beautiful woman with advanced ideas in the realm of sex and politics moved into Greenwhich Village just before World War I and proceeded, with her acting, lovemaking and especially her poetry, to make shock waves felt throughout the country. Edna St. Vincent Millay was certainly the most interesting and talented young woman in Greenwich Village between the years 1917 and 1925. She did not merely write extraordinarily well (if unconventionally for her time) but she also lived uncommonly well. She experienced it all, the all-night parties, a series of interesting lovers that possibly included Floyd Dell, Arthur Davison Ficke, Witter Bynner, John Reed and Edmund Wilson — as well as Eugen Boissevain, whom she finally married.

The year was 1923. Miss Millay, called Vinnie by her friends, published a poignant and, for its time, shocking sonnet that began "What lips my lips have kissed . . . ." The poem expressed the intimate feelings of a woman for past lovers. It spoke of kisses given and taken and of forgotten arms in which she once had slept. It was a poetic reminiscence of the pain and pleasure of love clearly evoked in fourteen effective lines.

Her poetry was quoted by hopeful young women (and young men to young women) from the Village to the New Orleans French Quarter to Diversey Street in Chicago and on to the hills of San Francisco. She spoke to all the uptight young women who were tired of virginity, afraid of marriage, caught in a trap between no sex at all or possible pregnancy. She was an early champion of birth control and a radical — but not a rebel. She was not against convention but, rather, advocated radical new directions in which society could and should experiment. She and her comrades in the Village were not so much interested in ending society's double standard, whereby women were to be chaste until married and locked in afterwards, but rather in extending to women the rights that men had taken for themselves. It was not a matter of curbing or limiting male sexual activity but extending those traditional rights to women.

Millay and the Villagers did more than shock. She and her friends carried the cause of feminism forward like a banner. The effects of the Village voices, and the echoes of Victoria Woodhull, Lucretia Mott and Susan B. Anthony were finally heard. In 1920 Tennessee ratified the Eighteenth Amendment. At last women had the vote.

But slim, red-haired Miss Millay and her experimentalist friends wanted much more. They embraced the new in art and began to explore the recesses of the mind through the then-new discipline of psychoanalysis. Even Henry Miller, who was showing his watercolors in the Village, become involved in this new adventure.

Another prime mover of the 1920s Village scene was Eugene O'Neill, whose first plays were written there and produced at the Provincetown Playhouse on MacDougal Street. Through O'Neill's plays, the Village exerted a major influence on dramatic arts throughout the United States. In his play *All God's Chillun Got Wings*, he dealt with the marriage of a Negro man to a white girl for the first time in American playwriting. The year was 1924. Because in one scene the girl, played by Mary Blair, kissed the hand of her Negro friend, played by Paul Robeson, the play was almost closed. O'Neill received threats that his children would be harmed, one of whom, Oona, later married Charlie Chaplin. The theater was threatened with bombs. But the play continued. The censors, however, did decide that child actors could not be exposed to such a spectacle and they were forbidden to appear. Throughout the run of the play, the stage manager read the children's lines while a police cordon guarded the entrance.

Most of O'Neill's early plays had similar problems. *Desire Under the Elms* — dealing with adultery and ending with infanticide — had censorship problems. But these and other O'Neill plays mounted in the Village helped to pave the way for a more tolerant, more mature outlook throughout the country.

Toward the end of the twenties, political attitudes seemed to become less important, sexual attitudes more

important. And the sex life of the Village became the talk of America. Its unofficial mayor, Aimée Cortez, a girl with a beautiful body who liked to show it, would strip down all the way at parties, sometimes leaping into the arms of a man who attracted her, to be carried off to the bedroom. It was the beginning of many combination encounters: boy meets girl, boy meets boy, girl meets girl — and quite often they lived happily ever after.

Unpopular with the longtime Italian merchants in the Village, the avant-garde Villagers were distrusted and disliked. The conventional old-time residents thought, justifiably, that the lives of their children would be affected by all the new ideas in dress, in manners, and the changing moral climate. But the Villagers went their way — citizens, not of the small area they occupied, but of the world. Like the description of human civilization written by Havelock Ellis, they were the avant-garde scouting out the terrain to be traveled in the future. Behind them, but slowly catching up, was the great army of civilization and straggling in the rear, were the decadent.

In the end it was the Villagers who won the war against the bourgeois, but in so doing the stronghold, Greenwich Village itself, was lost — not to conservatism but to sameness — for by 1945, in Terre Haute, Indiana, Santa Monica, California, or Mobile, Alabama, women were smoking, their hair was bobbed, unmarried sex was becoming acceptable, and most of the country had become a widespread Greenwich Village.

The Village left its mark on American culture in other ways. The experimental plays and reviews created by talented Villagers were soon picked up by Broadway producers and moved to the higher-priced uptown theaters. John Murray Anderson, who originated the *Greenwich Village Follies*, went on to produce such Broadway hits as *One for the Money, Two for the Show, Three to Get Ready*. Later he completely modernized the Ringling Brothers', Barnum & Bailey Circus — even teaching elephants to dance — with the help of two close friends, Billy Livingston and Raul Pène du Bois. He was also largely responsible for the success of Billy Rose's lavish Diamond Horseshoe Nightclub.

In the 1930s New York's flashy midtown nightclubs were crowded, with jazz reaching new heights and most clubs featuring torch singers as well as scantily clad singers. Stanley Walker, editor of the *Herald-Tribune*, reported with some shock that dancers at singer Harry Richmond's Club Richmond were nearly naked. The city's most expensive nightclub was operated by a lusty woman, Texas Guinan, who boasted she never had to serve whiskey, so she never had to fear raids by the Feds; after all, her customers could afford to bring their own liquor.

Although the Greenwich Village attitude toward free sex permeated the rest of Manhattan during the thirties, sex-for-pay was by no means wiped out. One of the

191

leaders of this lucrative business was a Sicilian named Salvatore Luciano, who had arrived in New York at the age of eight, and by the age of eighteen was already jailed for selling narcotics. His first rap didn't hold him for long, however, and he soon became an important figure in the New York Mafia.

Because he survived a 1929 "ride" during which he was stabbed and tortured, he was forever after called "Lucky." Lucky Luciano emerged in the early thirties as a racket king with considerable control over the narcotics pushers, the numbers racket and the prostitutes. His success at organizing the business of sex-for-pay was phenomenal. Every time a girl turned a trick in New York, except for a few independents who managed to evade his network, Lucky got a cut.

New York's District Attorney Tom Dewey called him the most dangerous racketeer in New York, if not in the United States. Time after time Lucky was arrested but invariably some underling took the rap or his lawyers managed to spring him — until one of the girls he had been exploiting tripped him up permanently. A twenty-five-year-old, attractive, experienced prostitute, Renee Gallo was lured to the witness stand by Special Prosecutor Dewey. She testified that she earned an average of $260 a week through prostitution but her take-home pay was only thirteen dollars.

"It went this way," she testified. "First the boss [Lucky Luciano] took half. Then Jo-Jo or Pete [her pimp handlers] got half. And then there was board and the doctor — and it went that way."

Renee did not testify alone. After hearing from other hard-working girls who were kept in a kind of white slavery, Luciano was found guilty of compulsory prostitution. He got a thirty-to-fifty-year sentence. Ten years later Dewey commuted Luciano's sentence with the provision that he be immediately and permanently deported to Italy. From the day he was sentenced, the Mafia's hold on prostitution in New York was broken. It was said that Luciano continued to control some of his rackets from prison but things were never the same. At least pimps didn't have to pay off the boss and the girls' incomes increased.

Eagerly reporting every tidbit of gossip during the thirties and forties was a former tap dancer and chorus boy who worked his way up to a preeminent position in the newspaper and radio world. More than any other reporter or writer, Walter Winchell became the king of small talk and trivia, the revealer of who-was-sleeping-with-whom in cafe snobocracy and the teller of inside stories (not always accurate). In his heyday as columnist for the New York *Mirror*, Winchell was drawing $1000 a week from that paper, another $3000 or $4000 a week from syndication of his column, plus a weekly radio stint worth an added $2000. During the thirties he also did a motion-picture short once a month for which he was paid $3500. This short, fast-talking scandalmonger stalked the town by night, learning of budding affairs, imminent separations, divorces and early pregnancies — usually reporting the latter as "Mr. and Mrs. Blank are getting storked."

Winchell had a brisk, machine-gun-like delivery and used his short takes both in the column and on the radio. The entire country became familiar with his: "Good evening, Mr. and Mrs. North and South America and all the ships at sea — let's go to press."

He had almost as many enemies as friends and was as unforgiving to his enemies as Louella Parsons was in Hollywood. Winchell was occasionally witty — "people who live in tin houses should not throw can openers" — but it wasn't his wit, it was his brass, that made his fortune.

Late at night, Winchell often patrolled the streets in his Ford equipped with a police radio, a red light and a siren, outfitted with the permission of the New York City Police Department.

One night he dramatically announced that "Lucille Ball and Desi Arnaz are expecting a bundle from heaven!"

Lucille and her husband happened to be listening and the news came to them as a great surprise. According to Lucille, upon hearing the broadcast, she exclaimed, "It's true! It's true! If Winchell says so, it must be true." She had been trying to have a child for the past nine years, had gone to the doctor for tests the previous Friday. They were positive but the lab called Winchell before they called the doctor. It is probable that Lucille was not the only woman to learn about her pregnancy from Walter. Toward the end of World War II, in one of his broadcasts, he defended Franklin Delano Roosevelt when he was attacked by a congressional committee investigating Pearl Harbor. That night Winchell reported:

"There are some very cheap politicians with their eyes on the next elections who are attempting to blacken F.D.R.'s name — who were not fit to blacken his shoes when he was alive.

"The truth is, ladies and gentlemen, that Mr. Roosevelt was not to blame for Pearl Harbor, but he was responsible for the grand over-all strategy which gave us victory. And that will be repeated again and again, so long as the mighty Hudson he loved flows to the sea, and so long as electrical current runs to this microphone."

By 1945 saloonkeepers had discovered that topless dancers sold drinks. Hip-swinging, breast-bouncing girls did not take it all off.

Bourbon Street in the late '40s featured hot New Orleans jazz and steaming strippers such as Stormy, who danced on the bar.

The old Howard Theater in Boston was known as a great burlesque house but was forced to close down in the '50s.

Exotic lingerie, breast pasties and revealing gowns are sold in all major cities. See-through and open-crotch panties, leather

garter belts and G-strings are usually available. Open-nipple, push-up and push-apart bras that lift the breasts and leave the nipples bare come in small, medium and large sizes. This boutique window is located on New Orleans' Bourbon Street.

Dardy Orlando, one of the great burlesque strippers of the '50s,
poses in the bayou country after finishing her act in New Orleans.

In a revival of the Ziegfeld Follies, Christine Ayres continued the tradition set by Ziegfeld of tall, shapely and beautiful women.

Complete with whip and harness, sexual symbols of dominance and restraint, this is a Christmas card of the 1960s.

Gay entertainers became popular in clubs in the early '50s.
This young gay star poses as a male, left, as a female, right.

Most popular pin-up of World War II was reprinted both during and after the war. Chili Williams was photographed by Ewing Krainin.

An angry young woman ignores the grappling couple behind her in a rocky beach area. Striking photograph by Burk Uzzle.

On a sunny Sunday afternoon in New York's Central Park
lovers, both heterosexual and homosexual, attest to their affection.

At Mardi Gras some viewers try to catch favors thrown from the carnival floats. Others keep eyes on a young woman!

Decorated and signed by a body painter, this young sun worshipper was photographed on an isolated "swimsuit optional" beach.

TAKE YOUR GIRLIE TO THE MOVIES
(IF YOU CAN'T MAKE LOVE AT HOME)

WORDS BY
EDGAR LESLIE
& BERT KALMAR

WATERSON
BERLIN
&
SNYDER CO.
Music Publishers
Strand Theatre Bldg
Broadway at 47 St
NEW YORK

MUSIC BY
PETE WENDLING

Preceding page: The darkened movie houses, in addition to piano or organ music and romantic silent films, offered a haven to lovers for handholding and discreet petting.

Printed cards (below) covering a wide range of sexual interests were passed around by businessmen and sold in tobacco shops and saloons.

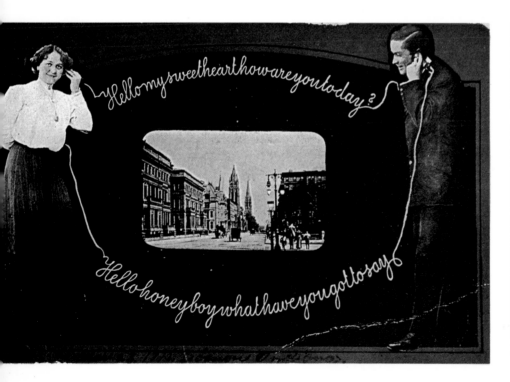

Hello my sweetheart how are you today?

Hello honey boy what have you got to say

Hand-colored stereopticon pictures were widely printed and distributed in the years between 1910 and 1920. Stockings, hat and scarf and amulet all accentuate the nudity of the model.

Here's to Love_
May it's wing never
lose a feather, till your little shoes,
and my little shoes, sit under the
bed together !

Voluptuous nudes dominated the inside covers of cigar boxes. These, and the postcard-size nude picture cards below, never showed pubic hair or nipples — but came as close as they could.

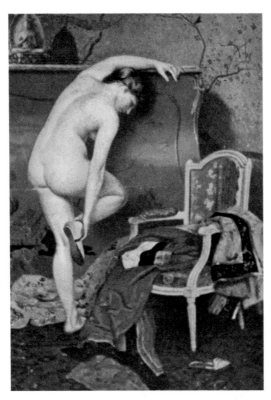

The first published erotic art by an American woman, Clara Tice, appeared in 1927 in a privately printed limited edition in english of MADEMOISELLE DE MAUPIN by Theophile Gautier.

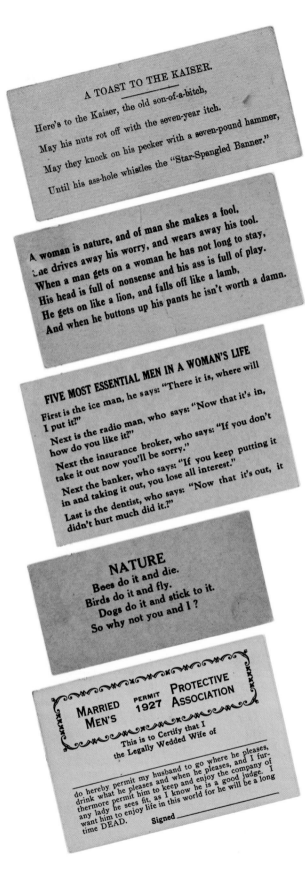

A TOAST TO THE KAISER.

Here's to the Kaiser, the old son-of-a-bitch,
May his nuts rot off with the seven-year itch.
May they knock on his pecker with a seven-pound hammer,
Until his ass-hole whistles the "Star-Spangled Banner."

A woman is nature, and of man she makes a fool,
She drives away his worry, and wears away his tool.
When a man gets on a woman he has not long to stay,
His head is full of nonsense and his ass is full of play.
He gets on like a lion, and falls off like a lamb,
And when he buttons up his pants he isn't worth a damn.

FIVE MOST ESSENTIAL MEN IN A WOMAN'S LIFE

First is the ice man, he says: "There it is, where will
I put it?"
Next is the radio man, who says: "Now that it's in,
how do you like it?"
Next the insurance broker, who says: "If you don't
take it out now you'll be sorry."
Next the banker, who says: "If you keep putting it
in and taking it out, you lose all interest."
Last is the dentist, who says: "Now that it's out, it
didn't hurt much did it.?"

NATURE
Bees do it and die.
Birds do it and fly.
Dogs do it and stick to it.
So why not you and I?

MARRIED
MEN'S — PERMIT 1927 — PROTECTIVE ASSOCIATION

This is to Certify that I
the Legally Wedded Wife of
_____
do hereby permit my husband to go where he pleases,
drink what he pleases and when he pleases, and I furthermore permit him to keep and enjoy the company of
any lady he sees fit, as I know he is a good judge. I
want him to enjoy life in this world for he will be a long
time DEAD.   Signed _____

Beware of Chance Acquaintances

"Pick-up" acquaintances often take girls autoriding,
to cafès, and to theatres with the intention of leading them into sex relations.   Disease or child-birth
may follow

Avoid the man who tries to take liberties with you
He is selfishly thoughtless and inconsiderate of you

Believe no one who says it is necessary to indulge
sex desire

Know the men you associate with

*World War I brought a new awareness of venereal disease. The
American Social Hygiene Society distributed the warning poster above.
By 1916 autoriding had become a cause of pregnancy.*

*Beginning with World War I and continuing to the present, sex-
oriented cards such as these at left were printed and sold throughout the
country. These obviously predate the use of the refrigerator and man's
zipper.*

*Popular cartoon characters appeared in pornographic comic sex books in
the twenties and thirties (right). Fellatio, cunnilingus, sodomy, masturbation, bestiality and straight fucking were crudely depicted.*

Sex and sadism were splashed over the covers of dozens of "detective story" magazines during the days of Roosevelt's New Deal. Note the NRA blue eagle and the slogan "We do our part."

Madams and freelance whores gave out cards in all the big cities, hoping for repeat business. These small hotels and private houses welcomed sex-for-pay customers in San Francisco.

COZY HOTEL
1238 Stockton Street
Near Broadway   14   San Francisco

COME UP SOMETIME
THE CHICO HOTEL
45 SIXTH STREET
NEAR MARKET
SAN FRANCISCO

MIAMI HOTEL
TRANSIENT ROOMS
Attractive Rates

857 Montgomery St.
Near Pacific   San Francisco

Come Up Sometimes
Lolito
CLAUDIA HOTEL
TRANSIENT

248 COLUMBUS AVE.
SAN FRANCISCO

Pros 5308

May
926 LARKIN STREET
SAN FRANCISCO

MISS LENA

924 Geary St.
Sally
San Francisco   Between Larkin & Polk

TRANSIENT
Bernhardt Hotel
ALL COMFORTS
523 Kearny Street
Bet. California & Sacramento
SAN FRANCISCO

DAY   NIGHT

PHONE GARFIELD 9069   *Jean*

HOTEL BRETAGNE

NICELY FURNISHED ROOMS
WITH HOT AND COLD WATER

TWO ENTRANCES
705 BROADWAY, Cor. Stockton
4 CORDELIA ST., at Broadway
5   G   SAN FRANCISCO

WALDORF HOTEL
128
JONES STREET
Bet. Golden Gate & Turk

OAKDALE HOTEL
TRANSIENT
UNDER NEW MANAGEMENT

220 6TH STREET   SAN FRANCISCO

ROOMS
680 GOLDEN GATE AVE.
Corner Franklin Street
SHERRY

1563 ELLIS STREET
Between Fillmore and Webster
HOTEL MADELEINE
San Francisco

ask for Elizabeth

426 Pacific Avenue

SAN FRANCISCO

1224 STOCKTON STREET

THE REGGY ROOMS

ROOMS BY DAY OR WEEK - TRANSIENT

BETWEEN PACIFIC & BROADWAY

EVA, MANAGER
Model Hotel
37
Sixth Street
HIGH CLASS ROOMS
SIDE ENTRANCE ON
STEVENSON ST.   SAN FRANCISCO

ELEANOR HUGHES, OWNER

WELCOME ROOMS
(Always Welcome)

691 FOLSOM STREET
CORNER OF THIRD ST.   SAN FRANCISCO
173

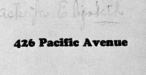

ROOMS
716 BROADWAY
NEAR STOCKTON ST.   SAN FRANCISCO

Nightclubs, big and small, expensive and cheap, were always crowded in the mid-forties. At right are a group of over-age strippers in a small Philadelphia club. Below opposite: Special lighting (including ultraviolet effects) were used effectively in two New Orleans Bourbon Street night spots.

Beginning in the mid-forties, Frank Sinatra proved Havelock Ellis' theory that the voice had a powerful sexual effect. Thousands of young girls fell in love and hundreds fainted under the spell of the Sinatra voice and personality.

216

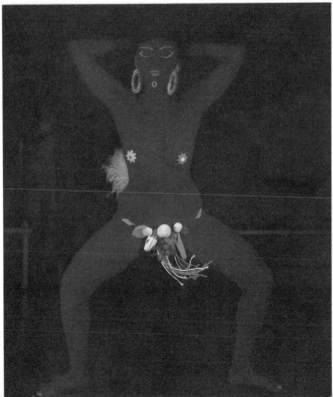

Vertès

ex Announcement of Show with Society of Illustrators NYC 5-6-49.

In advertising, the artist Vertès, with his sketchy, sexy style, was in great demand. This poster was for a Society of Illustrators announcement in 1949.

Messages on buttons, some cheery, others satiric or sexy, gained in popularity in the fifties and sixties. Each year brings a new, up-to-date crop.

In the sixties, gift shop items included nude playing cards (opposite), a call girl service buzzer and the bathing suit of the future — two Band-Aids and a cork!

Playboy Magazine was a huge success from its beginning in 1953 with America's sex symbol, Marilyn Monroe, on its first cover. Most American males (and a great many females) welcomed its special blend of naked girls, wit and high quality short stories and essays.

Left: By the mid-1970s, swim-suits had become optional in many private pools and on a few isolated beaches.

Right: Love, sex, rape, war, music and dance are all graphically represented in the gigantic bas-relief frieze facing the Kennedy Center for the Performing Arts in Washington, D.C. This is a fantastic step forward from the days when depicting humans naked was a mortal sin.

Overleaf: A sexual fantasy-land is reflected in this intimate scene at Plato's Retreat, New York's luxurious sex club. The imaginative color photograph was taken by R. Scott Hopper for PLAYBOY magazine.

This suggestive fountain is a modern copy of a Roman original — it is part of the outdoor decoration at the MGM Grand Hotel in Las Vegas.

221

9

The Age of Information

The elements that would act as catalysts in the new formula of sex in the United States were in place. By the end of World War II, censors of books and films in cities and towns found their bans overruled either by state law or by order of the Supreme Court. Birth control information became widely available, even though it was still illegal to distribute information or to sell devices in some states. Thinner and more sensitive rubber condoms were manufactured at lower prices. And women by the millions were being fitted by their doctors with diaphragms and IUDs. Although from time to time teachers and principals went to jail for allowing sex education in the schools, most school boards had scrapped the birds-and-bees approach. Children got the answers to their final question. For hundreds of years they had been asking how the new baby got inside the mother. Now they found out it took a male and a female to make a baby. The cabbage patch and the stork moved into folklore.

The occupation of Japan by the Americans gave many a GI a new awareness of sex. Japanese girls were more direct than American girls, taking the attitude that sex was an important part of everyday life and that it was in no way sinful. Their American lovers became used to hot baths followed by gentle, soothing massages and being led to bed. GIs by the thousands left mistresses in Japan (and many illegitimate offspring), but others brought their girlfriends home, defying the policy of the Pentagon. Thousands of GIs stationed temporarily in Germany brought back German brides. Sex began to take on an increasingly international flavor in the United States.

World War II also had a major effect on blacks. For the first time they were genuinely accepted in the Army as soldiers and officers. This inevitably led to a greater intermixture of blacks and whites. Blacks married British, French, German and Japanese girls and brought them back to the States after the war. There was resentment, however, because it was illegal for whites and blacks to marry in more than half the states in the United States. Later, the Civil Rights Amendment forced integration in schools and colleges. It was 1967 before the Supreme Court voided all state miscegenation laws.

Three hundred thirty-five thousand young men killed meant a man shortage by the end of World War II. Women kept the jobs that they had taken during the war — they did not have to relinquish them because the men did not come home — and through the loss of husbands and lovers independence was forced on a great number of young married women. Forced to become economically and socially independent, a great many couples were led into the state of living together without marriage.

Sexual language had undergone a number of changes during the war. Phrases like "pissed off," "fucked up," "screwed up" and "knocked up" (with only the latter one having any relationship to sex) were common expressions. There is a story about a young soldier who takes a bus from camp on furlough and finds himself sitting next to a talkative, gray-haired old lady. He tries to read his comic book but she continuously interrupts him with questions about what he is going to do on his leave. Exasperated, he finally tells her:

"When I get off this fuckin' bus, I'm gonna take the first fuckin' taxi I can fuckin' find. I'm gonna drive up to a fuckin' whorehouse, knock on the fuckin' door and, when the fuckin' madam opens the door, I'm gonna go in, look over the fuckin' girls, take one up the fuckin' stairs to the fuckin' bed, get out of this fuckin' uniform — and then, madam, we're gonna have intercourse."

In literature the long-taboo four-letter words became acceptable in postwar novels. Some readers were shocked at seeing such words in print written by an obviously sensitive and creative author. Even though they already knew the words. The taboo words had been handed down by one generation of children to another for hundreds of years. It would seem obvious that their parents must have used them privately, for "shit", "piss," "cunt," "prick" and "fuck" were so clearly descriptive that they were literally the only non-scientific words available to adequately and succinctly describe the excretory functions, the male and female genitalia and the act of sexual penetration.

Parents found substitute words, many with no apparent meaning at all, such as "poo-poo," "ka-ka," "doo-doo," "tinkle," "wee-wee" and "pee-pee." When it came to non-scientific descriptions of the sexual organs, it became more difficult. Most parents avoided any mention at all of the female genitals, acting as though they simply did not exist. Mothers were known to say to a daughter taking a bath, "Wash down as far as possible, then wash up as far as possible — then wash possible."

It was impossible to ignore the sex organs of little boys for there they were — obviously protruding. So there was a "tee-wee," a "peter," a "peenie," a "weenie" and a "pecker."

The word "fuck" had many substitutes. People "made love," which did not describe the sex act at all; they copulated, if they were of a scientific bent; and they had intercourse, which again has a somewhat scientific or literary connotation. There is a story of a man who goes to a psychiatrist because his mind is confused about sex. The psychiatrist gives him a set of questions to answer.

"What is it that men do standing up, women do sitting down and dogs do on three legs?"

He answers, "Shake hands."

"What do dogs do in the yard that people try not to step into?"

"Dig holes."

"What is it that sticks out of your pajamas that you can hang your hat on?"

"Your head."

"What is a four-letter word meaning intercourse?"

"Talk."

Perhaps a favorite synonym for fuck was "to sleep together," which, of course, need have no relation to sex. Wayland Young, in his excellent book *Eros Denied*, points out that in a London trial a lawyer who was defending a prostitute against some serious charges learned that her defense would rest on her exact relationship with a certain man. He asked her, "Did you sleep with this man?"

She answered "No."

Because of his background, which was entirely different from hers, he did not understand that she meant just what she said — she had not passed the night with him nor had she fallen asleep in his company. But they had fucked, as he later found out, and this information helped to acquit her in the case.

Lots of women have slept with men and had no other sexual relationship with them. It would seem, then, that there is really no word in the English language that exactly and precisely defines the sexual act except fuck.

So, by the mid-forties the stage was at least set for meanings to become more precise in sexual literature and in life. A longtime holdout in the liberalization of language was New England, the fountainhead of literature in America. The fame of many of its authors — including Daniel Webster, Nathaniel Hawthorne, Henry James, Oliver Wendell Holmes, Henry David Thoreau, Herman Melville and Harriet Beecher Stowe — and many of its poets — John Greenleaf Whittier, Henry Wadsworth Longfellow and Emily Dickinson — had reached all parts of the growing country. The cultural center of this early intellectual and creative ferment was Boston, Massachusetts.

As the twentieth century unfolded Boston's literary core became increasingly jealous of the works that reached it from outside New England. Many of the new books were considered alien to the conservative American tradition. And indeed they were. The censors of Boston began to consider themselves the keepers of American literary morality. Boston, like the Vatican, developed a long list of books, poems and plays that were banned.

The sexual patterns of New England that had remained concealed added to the repression of books that viewed sexuality openly. In the twenties and thirties being banned in Boston may have had some adverse influence on the sale of a book, but by 1945 such a ban was not taken seriously by the rest of the country. In fact, to be banned in Boston was to mean increased book sales. A book was likely to be considered spicy by the very fact of its being forbidden.

In 1946 Edmund Wilson, one of America's most distinguished critics and a celebrated author, wrote a book that was not only banned in New York but managed to get itself banned in San Francisco as well. It was *Memoirs of Hecate County*, a book of six long short stories. At least one of them, *The Princess with the Golden Hair*, could be called a novelette. It was in this story that a description of the female vagina occurred, poetic but graphic, romantic but all too real for the censors. The paragraph that got Mr. Wilson into trouble read:

But what struck and astonished me most was that not only were her thighs perfect columns but that all that lay between them was impressively beautiful, too, with an ideal aesthetic value that I had never found there before. The mount was of a classical femininity; round and smooth and plump; the fleece, if not quite golden, was blond and curly and soft; and the portals were a deep

tender rose, like the petals of some fleshly flower. And they were doing their feminine work of making things easy for the entrant with a honeysweet sleek profusion that showed I had quite misjudged her in suspecting as I had sometimes done that she was really unresponsive to caresses. She became, in fact, so smooth and open that after a moment I could hardly feel her. Her little bud was so deeply embedded that it was hardly involved in the play, and she made me arrest my movement while she did something special and gentle that did not, however, press on this point, rubbing herself somehow against me — and then consummated, with a self-excited tremor that appeared to me curiously mild for a woman of her positive energy. I went on and had a certain disappointment, for, with the brimming of female fluid, I felt even less sensation; but — gently enough — I came too.

American GIs who had been stationed in France became familiar with the works of an expatriate writer, Henry Miller, who had been published by the small but experimental Obelisk Press, presided over by Jack Kahane, and later by Maurice Girodias at Olympia Press. These presses distributed Miller's books, and other books unpublishable in the United States and England, and they were sold throughout France. While a few of the copies being smuggled in by the GIs were confiscated, thousands reached the United States. *Tropic of Cancer* was a book that many wanted in their libraries.

For the first time an American author writing in English had used contemporary language, including all the taboo words, in a natural way. Miller's men and women did not "sleep with one another" — they "fucked." His characters, all drawn from Miller's eventful life, were happy with their sexuality and proud of their sexual organs. One of his characters says, "I washed my prick out of politeness" before fucking an attractive whore.

D. H. Lawrence's *Lady Chatterley's Lover* also used taboo language. Constance Chatterley is lying naked with Mellors, the gatekeeper, in his cottage. They are deeply in love.

All the while he spoke he exquisitely stroked the rounded tail, till it seemed as if a slippery sort of fire came from it into his hands. And his finger-tips touched the two secret openings to her body, time after time, with a soft little brush of fire.

"An if tha shits an' if tha pisses, I'm glad. I don't want a woman as couldna shit nor piss."

Connie could not help a sudden snort of astonished laughter, but he went on unmoved.

"Tha'rt real, tha art! Tha'rt real, even a bit of a bitch. Here tha shits an' here tha pisses: an' I lay my hand on 'em both an' like thee for it. I like thee for it. Tha's got a proper, woman's arse, proud of itself. It's none ashamed of itself, this isna."

Like Henry Miller's *Tropic* books, *Lady Chatterley's*

Lover was first published in France, but it reached the United States public through the efforts of a young American publisher, Barney Rosset of Grove Press. After being banned in the United States for twenty-nine years, in 1957 *Lady Chatterley's Lover* was held by the United States Supreme Court to be not only a work of serious purpose but also a work of high achievement. It was not considered obscene.

It took almost as long for Henry Miller's milestone books that dealt with sex in a realistic and imaginative way to be published in the United States. In 1961 Grove Press published Miller in the United States. His autobiographical "novels" had a sexually liberating effect upon a whole generation of Americans. He wrote about sex with wit and joy, seriously, realistically and imaginatively. His people lived and breathed, sometimes smelled badly, farted, pissed, shit — just like everyone else. Yet his books were not pornographic. "Obscene, yes. People are often obscene and so are some incidents in my books. But pornographic, never," said Miller to me once. Miller did not isolate sex but rather wrote of sex as a part of the human condition. He wrote of friends, of loyalty, of betrayal and he wrote poetically and romantically of love. Sex was a vital element in most of his characters, not as a theme of the book, but as part of the life force that makes men and women human.

Miller looked at the act of sex dispassionately at times. At heart he was a romantic and the affairs of the heart that he had he did not record. The affairs of the body he was able to detach and view through his rich and creative imagination. In *Tropic of Cancer*:

Llona now, she had a cunt. I know it because she sent us some hairs from down below. Llona — a wild ass snuffing pleasure out of the wind. On every high hill she played the harlot, and sometimes in telephone booths and toilets. She bought a bed for King Fredl and a shaving mug. She lay in Tottenham Court Road with her dress pulled up and fingered herself. She used candles, Roman candles, and door knobs. Not a prick in the land big enough for her, not one. Men went inside her and curled up. She wanted extension pricks, self-exploding rockets, hot boiling oil made of wax and creasote. She would cut off your prick and keep it inside her forever, if you let her. One cunt out of a million Llona.

Miller once said to me, "I think I wrote about sex because it was such a big part of my life. Sex was always a dominant thing. To be honest, I haven't written much about my real loves."

Taboo words were not used by Miller to shock or to call attention to his writing. He is far too good a writer for that. But Miller saw sex in the context of life. Sex was not confused by illusion.

I snuggled up to her and buried my head in her bosom. I slid my head down and licked her navel. Then farther down, kissing the thick clump of hair. She drew my head up slowly and, pulling me on top of her, buried her tongue in my mouth. My cock stiffened instantly; it slid into her just as naturally as an engine going into a switch. I had one of those long, lingering hard-ons which drive a woman mad. I jibbed her about at will, now over, now under her, then sidewise, then drawing it out slowly, tantalizingly, massaging the lips of the vulva with the bristling tip of my cock. Finally I pulled it out altogether and twirled it around her breasts. She looked at it in astonishment. "Did you come?" she asked. "No," I said. "We're going to try something else now."

Miller describes the attitude of many of the men of his time (the twenties) in *Tropic of Capricorn*:

What he disliked especially was the way Curley talked about his aunt. It was bad enough, in Hymie's opinion, that he should be screwing the sister of his own mother, but to make her out to be nothing but a piece of stale cheese, that was too much for Hymie. One ought to have a bit of respect for a woman, provided she's not a whore. If she's a whore that's different. Whores are not women. Whores are whores. That was how Hymie looked at things.

Miller could not help exposing an almost constant inner laughter in his attacks on taking sex too seriously.

Veronica, as I say, had a talking cunt, which was bad because its sole function seemed to be to talk one out of a fuck. Evelyn, on the other hand, had a laughing cunt. She lived upstairs too, only in another house. She was always trotting in at mealtimes to tell us a new joke. A comedienne of the first water, the only really funny woman I ever met in my life. Everything was a joke, fuck included. She could even make a stiff prick laugh, which is saying a good deal. They say a stiff prick has no conscience, but a stiff prick that laughs too is phenomenal. The only way I can describe it is to say that when she got hot and bothered, Evelyn, she put on a ventriloqual act with her cunt. You'd be ready to slip it in when suddenly the dummy between her legs would let out a guffaw. At the same time it would reach out for you and give you a playful little tug and squeeze. It could sing too, this dummy of a cunt. In fact it behaved just like a trained seal.

Evelyn was always lying in the cabbage patch with legs spread open offering a bright green leaf to the first comer. But if you made a move to nibble it the whole cabbage patch would explode with laughter, a bright, dewy, vaginal laughter such as Jesus H. Christ and Immanuel Pussyfoot Kant never dreamed of.

Three years after the war the nation was in for a major sexual shock — the *Kinsey Report*. It was sparked and devised by Dr. Alfred C. Kinsey, who was a biologist and an early professor of sex education and marriage at the University of Indiana. Realizing that he knew little of the actual sex habits of the American people, whose children he was teaching, he decided on a major interview survey to find out what Americans actually knew about and did about sex. His first book covered 5,300 white males and dealt with such subjects as their marital histories, their sex education, their nocturnal sex dreams, masturbation, their heterosexual and homosexual history and animal contacts.

I shall never forget the day the book appeared. I had a number of gay friends, and one lived in the building where I had an office and photographic studio. On the day the book appeared he called me and asked me to come up to his apartment for a drink. I found him in a state of happy excitement. He greeted me by saying, "Bradley, I'm just like everybody else. Dr. Kinsey says one-third of all the men in the United States have had homosexual contacts."

This wasn't exactly the case, but Dr. Kinsey's figures did indicate that 37 percent of all males experience at least one homosexual experience to the point of orgasm at some time. He also wrote, based on his interviews, that 50 percent of the male population have either some homosexual contact or arousal with or without orgasm in their lifetime.

Kinsey also relieved a lot of people's worries about masturbation. It turned out that practically all males had some masturbatory experience. His survey indicated that masturbation among boys is most popular between the ages of eleven and fifteen; that although it drops off after that, perhaps as many as half of the single males are still masturbating at the age of fifty. Surprisingly enough, the survey showed that married males masturbated too — as much as 42.1 percent aged twenty-one to twenty-five years.

In his book that followed shortly after *Sexual Behavior in the Human Male, Sexual Behavior in the Human Female,* Kinsey's team gave aid and comfort to the worried female as well. At least two-thirds of the females practiced masturbation at some time. His research indicated that it was the technique (even more than intercourse) that was more likely to lead to orgasm. No less than 95 percent of the women surveyed who masturbated reported achieving orgasm.

In the area of premarital intercourse, young men were divided into three classifications, and among those who never went beyond grade school almost all had sexual intercourse before marriage. The high school group showed that 84 percent had sex before marriage but the percentage dropped considerably among the males who went to college. Only 67 percent of them made it with the girls.

Among the unmarried women at the time of the *Kinsey Report,* which was 1945, 17 percent experienced sexual orgasm prior to marriage through intercourse. But two-thirds of the total number of married women had experienced some type of sexual orgasm either through masturbation, necking or petting.

About half of the men in Kinsey's survey had affairs outside their marriage.

Kinsey came to the conclusion that "the human male would be promiscuous in his choice of sexual partners throughout the course of his life if there were no social restrictions." He suggested that it didn't matter whether a happy or unhappy marriage was involved — men still strayed.

The *Kinsey Report* relieved many other different types of anxiety by revealing that most so-called sexual aberrations were nearer to the norm than anyone had believed. Farm boys felt pretty good when they found that among rural males on the college level 25 percent had had some experience with animals to the point of orgasm. He reported that sex with animals — sheep, calves, goats, chickens — varied from once or twice in a lifetime to several times a week. The statistics did not, however, find this true of women. Either the ladies didn't report it or such relationships do not occur with females, or occurred so rarely as to be insignificant in a large survey.

Kinsey did not go into another area that should be mentioned in any survey of American sexuality. Farm boys, according to musician, writer, publicist James Sterling Moran, have such a strong sex drive from an early age that, in addition to animals, they also make it with vegetables and fruits from time to time. In his book *How I Became an Authority on Sex,* he reports that at about the age of seven he happened upon a young friend of about the same age in a field of watermelons. Jim was unduly surprised to find that Ralph was actually fucking one of his grandfather's prize watermelons. After carving a hole in the sun-warmed melon, he "was pumping away like crazy. When he finally rolled off, drenched with sweat and covered with dust, he got his breath back and snuggled up to the deflowered melon, patted the hole with proprietary affection and invited me to have a go at it. I politely declined. If it had been flesh-colored, I might have been tempted, but a green watermelon at my age? Never!"

Moran afterwards remembered the conversation and Ralph's advice: "Never fuck a watermelon in the morning — too cold — wait until the sun warms it up. Watermelons are better than cantaloupes because you got more to hold on to."

Jim describes his first sexual experience at about this time (age seven). His seven-year-old friend Susan was willing to go along with a mutual examination. After he had "a good closeup look at the mystery of all mysteries" under Susan's skirt, she examined him. "By fondling my penis and scrotum, she brought on an erection about the size of a cigarette (regular, not king-size) which she said was bigger than her brother's."

Moran's experiences struck a responsive chord in me because I remembered vividly my own first sexual experiences, at the age of six. I have already described the baths given me by my naked mulatto nursemaid, but I was much more interested in an eight-year-old convent girl who decided it was her mission to teach me the facts of life. We not only went through the examination-of-each-other stage but, having watched her mother and father through a keyhole, she knew what to do next. Every afternoon for a few weeks she led me into her parents' bedroom, laid down on her back on the bed, fondled me into an erection and showed me where to put it. I don't remember it being any more exciting than riding my three-wheel bike or having an ice cream cone but it was a pleasant sensation.

By the time I was eight I was able to take charge of the doctor games played in the haystacked barn in Lafayette, Louisiana, where we had moved from New Orleans. My companions there were two boys, six and seven, and their sister about eight. With my superior knowledge I was always the doctor, the two boys were my assistants, and the operations were always performed on the girl. We didn't hurt her. We examined her carefully and sometimes, if she was willing, we fucked her. But it was the examinations that satisfied our visual and tactile curiosity about sex.

Shortly after this I met a boy of ten who had a very attractive eight-year-old sister. These two were very popular among the seven-to-ten-year-old set because they gave demonstrations on how sex worked. There were secret meetings in an abandoned barn where the two demonstrated various positions and seemed to enjoy their performance, which was highly applauded by their schoolmates. These demonstrations were going on between 1916 and 1918, and I can testify from personal experience that most of the children I knew in New Orleans and in Lafayette, Louisiana, were taking care of their sex education themselves. I don't remember any sex education at all at home or at school . . . but who needed it.

My young friends could have modeled for a book called *Show Me* published in 1972. The first portion of the book pictured two nude six-year-olds showing their genitals to one another. The book progressed to naked adolescent boy and girl exploring each other's body. The boy was shown with an erection and the book ended with the two adolescents fucking. The book was banned in a number of states but, being honestly and tastefully done, was sold openly and without problems in most. Having already accepted female nudity in magazines like *Playboy* and *Penthouse* and male nudity in nudist magazines, *Cosmopolitan* and *Playgirl* few book buyers were shocked by the nude kids. But this was in 1972.

Playboy Magazine had become by far the most popular men's magazine in the United States by the 1960s. Started in December 1953 by Hugh M. Hefner, who had previously worked at *Esquire Magazine*, it offered excellent literature in the short story field by recognized

and sometimes undiscovered young writers. Its interviews with the great of the nation ranged from sports, rock and movie stars to sex queens, literary figures and even the president of the United States.

But *Playboy's* greatest attraction for men was its naked girls. Many types of beauties were displayed, but the great majority had the girl-next-door look — that is, if you could get to see the girl next door naked. Nudity was approached directly, although body makeup and careful retouching was, and is, a part of each provocative color photograph. In addition to showing the girl next door nude, *Playboy* also showed her at her job, sports, sometimes knitting or swimming. The big feature was the centerfold that offered a luscious, unclothed beauty more than one-third the size of an average woman.

An important part of *Playboy's* appeal is in two well-edited sections of the magazine. Letters from readers make "The Playboy Advisor" provocative and stimulating reading. It was in one of these letters that a young woman asked whether swallowing male semen during oral intercourse would make her gain weight. *Playboy* played it straight, got its answer from a physician and a chemist and was able to assure the reader that there were not enough calories in semen to cause a weight gain. Over the years questions and answers continue to be surprising, amusing and often witty.

The other section, called "The Playboy Forum," tackles contemporary issues in the general field of sexual behavior. In this section the editors have defended the rights of homosexuals and have kept an eye on court cases involving oral sex and sodomy. A *Playboy* legal defense team, subsidized by the magazine, is available to assist sex offenders who that publication feels are guiltless. The *Playboy* Foundation has also made grants to the Institute for Sex Research at Indiana University and made other research grants.

There have been many imitators, but none have come up with the combination of good taste and an *au courant* approach to the continuing sexual revolution — and those luscious girl-next-door nudes.

Three women's magazines appeared on the sex scene in the sixties and seventies. *Cosmopolitan* was a born-again magazine and its mother was Helen Gurley Brown, author of the best seller *Sex and the Single Girl*. Ms. Brown changed *Cosmopolitan* to the most popular sex, fashion, diet and self-help publication. Provocative articles include "New Styles of Coupling, Including Marriage" and "Some Bizarre, Maybe Helpful Thoughts on Love and Love-making." Its appeal is aimed at young unmarried — and married — women. In addition to its strong how-to-do-it emphasis, *Cosmopolitan* excerpts important books dealing with the modern woman and usually prints a romantic novelette. Although *Cosmopolitan* did not continue the feature, it was the first magazine to publish a male nude fold-out. The subject was Hollywood's Burt Reynolds.

Playgirl, subheaded *Entertainment for Women,* has used the *Playboy* formula, switching to athletic-type naked males. Feature articles deal with women's sexual, marital and financial problems. There is a *Playgirl* interview. Men are photographed as sex objects. Each issue features a center spread of a naked man, semi-hard penis exposed. There is usually a second feature and sometimes a third, so that women get to see male genitalia in a variety of sizes, shapes and colors. In fashion stories women are featured, with men often appearing as incidental decoration in the background.

The women's liberation movement is represented by *MS,* a magazine edited and researched by women for women. Articles press for the Equal Rights Amendment and women in the migratory labor camps, and deal with whatever happened to the most popular girl in your class and similar subjects. It defends both lesbian and gay sex from the intellectual viewpoint.

In 1955 Olympia Press, in France, was responsible for the first publication in English of two sex-oriented novels that were banned in Boston, as well as in other cities of the United States. In neither case were the bans effective. Both books soon became best sellers.

The first one, *Lolita* by Vladimir Nabokov, had a world-wide influence after it was published in the United States by G. P. Putnam's Sons. The story is of a twelve-year-old, sex-ridden nymphet (a word coined to describe her by Nabokov). His satire on life in America, using Lolita, her mother and a mad trip across the country to tell his story, was so real and became so popular that Humbert Humbert and Lolita became part of American folklore. Lolita did not lose her virginity to Humbert, however. When she was away at camp, she and her girlfriend Barbara took turns fucking the thirteen-year-old son of the camp's manager in the woods. Humbert Humbert had, indeed, been seduced by Lolita's mother before the daughter began her flirtation with him.

Reviews of *Lolita* were uniformly excellent, for this was major satire by an important writer on American life in the fifties. And fortunately it was banned in enough cities to help the bookstores sell more than seventeen hardcover editions and millions of paperbacks.

The same publisher picked up a wild satiric romp written by Terry Southern and Mason Hoffenberg in Paris in 1957. The Olympia Press edition was credited to a nonexistent author, Maxwell Kenton. The book was a satire based loosely on Voltaire's *Candide;* and the nubile, empty-headed heroine Candy continues to "feel needed" as she moves to "an understanding" of why it is necessary for her to be ravished by various minority groups, including freaks, gays and a psychiatrist. Always searching for her father, she finally lands in bed with him. As with *Lolita,* both self-appointed and official censors in various states attacked the book and it, like *Lolita,* sold in the millions.

One of the many hilarious scenes in *Candy* occurs when she meets a Dr. Johns in a bar. Johns immediately suggests that he give her a gynecological examination in the men's toilet. After taking off her skirt,

"Now, the little panties," he said, pulling them down. "Lovely things you wear," he added and lifted her up on to the stool.

"Now you just stand with one foot on each side of the stool, limbs spread, that's right and . . . oh yes, you can brace yourself with your hands against the walls . . . yes, just so . . . Fine!"

He bent quickly to his kit and took out a small clamp and inserted it between the girl's darling little labia, so that they were held apart.

"Good!" he said. "Now I just want to test these clitorial reflexes," he said, "often enough, that's where trouble strikes first." And he began to gently massage her sweet pink clit. "Can you feel that?"

"Good grief yes!" said Candy, squirming about, "are you sure that is . . ."

"Hmm," said Dr. Johns. "Normal response there all right. Now I just want to test these clitorial reflexes to tactile surfaces." And he began sucking it wildly, clutching the precious girl to him with such sudden force and abandon that her feet slipped off the stool and into the well of it. During the tumult the flushing mechanism was set in motion and water now surged out over the two of them, flooding the tiny cabinet and sweeping beyond the door and into the bar.

There was a violent pounding at the door.

"What in God's name is going on there?" demanded the manager, who had just arrived. He and the bartender were throwing their weight against the door of the cabinet which by now was two feet deep in water as the doctor and Candy thrashed about inside.

"Good grief!" she kept saying. They had both fallen to the floor. The doctor was snorting and spouting water, trying desperately to keep sucking and yet not to drown.

Finally with a great lunge the two men outside broke open the door. They were appalled by the scene.

"Good God! Good God!" they shouted. "What in the name of God is going on here!"

A police officer arrived at that moment and was beside himself with rage at the spectacle.

The doctor had lost consciousness by the time he was pulled to his feet. Both he and Candy were sopping wet and completely disheveled. She was naked from the waist down.

"He's a doctor!" she cried to the policeman, who was dragging him about like a sack and pulling her by the arm.

"Uh-huh," said the cynical cop, "Dr. Caligari, I suppose."

Candy didn't like this kind of flippant reference to an art film. "This happens to be an examination," she said with marked disdain.

"You can say *that* again, sister," said the officer, taking a good look himself.

"Good grief!" said Candy, snatching the clamp out from between her labes.

The manager and the bartender were speechless with fury.

"You . . . you . . ." stammered the manager, shaking his finger at Candy.

"This so *happens* to be a private examination by my doctor," said Candy with great haughtiness.

"You are barred from the Riviera!" he shouted with the finality of doom itself.

The doctor had regained consciousness now, but was still lost in his insane desire for the girl and flung himself against her in such ardor that they tumbled back into the cabinet with a splash, Candy shrieking, "Good heavens!"

Along with the new freedom in novels came a new freedom in poetry. Allen Ginsberg was a young poet deeply disturbed by the United States environment during the years between the two wars and after World War II. His poems became a part of the hip, or hippie, culture that was to develop in the fifties. He dedicated his book to Jack Kerouac, the radical American prose writer who helped to bring the hippie movement into focus. He called his poem *Howl*. It began: "I saw the best minds of my generation destroyed by madness, starving hysterical naked," and read in part:

> who let themselves be fucked in the ass by saintly motorcyclists, and screamed with joy,
> who blew and were blown by those human seraphim, the sailors, caresses of Atlantic and Caribbean love,
> who balled in the morning in the evenings in rosegardens and the grass of public parks and cemeteries scattering their semen freely to whomever come who may,
> who sweetened the snatches of a million girls trembling in the sunset, and were red eyed in the morning but prepared to sweeten the snatch of the sunrise, flashing buttocks under barns and naked in the lake. . . .

Ginsberg went on to become *the* prophet of the hippie revolution. When *Howl* was published in the fall of 1956, it was seized by the United States Customs and the San Francisco police. After a long court trial the book was considered not to be obscene. It has sold over a half million copies.

Allen Ginsberg and Jack Kerouac inspired the flower children, with their long skirts and blue jeans, long-haired boys and girls who were the relatively peaceful sex revolutionists of the fifties and early sixties. The roots of their movement lay in Greenwich Village, the New Orleans French Quarter and Chicago's Diversey Avenue, but, unlike the creative, rebellious spirits in those communities, the hippies were literally rebels without a cause. Unable to cope with the demands of a society they had not been educated for, in many instances not being able to find jobs, feeling their sex drive

without a means to appease it within conventional society, thousands of young men and women left their homes and set out to find a new way of living.

Yet another type of new culture was developing during the ten years between 1955 and 1965. In the early sixties Timothy Leary, a Harvard professor with a brilliant potential future, began experimenting with the drug LSD. He was fascinated with the idea of expanding mental consciousness, using LSD to induce bizarre and unusual hallucinations. Leary suggested that some of his students join him in both marijuana and LSD highs, which unfortunately just as often turned out to be lows.

One bright young man that I met at a wedding in New York spent an hour explaining the benefits and importance of the mind-altering techniques he was undergoing with Professor Leary. A few months later, under the influence of LSD, he killed himself. Nonetheless, Leary went on to become the guru of the new drug culture. He was arrested from time to time yet managed to gather around him a hard-core group of pioneers in LSD and marijuana experimentation. This group peaked in the Haight-Ashbury section of San Francisco, then traveled downhill. By the seventies, Leary and his experiments were on their way to being forgotten, except by a few faithful followers.

A very large number of the hippies ended their journey in the semi-tenement Haight-Ashbury section of San Francisco, which soon became the most visible drug-oriented quarter in the United States. Hippies literally took in each other's washing to eke out a living. Unwilling to work in factories or even in conventional low-level jobs, many sold flowers on the streets. Theirs was a confused philosophy. They attempted to embrace the disciplines of Buddhism without knowing very much about it. But many youngsters with a flare for original craftsmanship slowly began to produce salable commodities. Talented hippie musicians were midwives in the birth of rock music.

Sexually they traced their roots to the free lovers of the late nineteenth century. Living in small, and occasionally large, communes, there was little formal marriage. Yet for the most part, one-to-one sexual alliances, heterosexual and homosexual, became the rule. But casual sex, separated from sex with love, became common. By considering love as one element, it was possible for many of the hippie youngsters to stay on a one-to-one basis with a lover and yet have casual sex with a friend who wanted or needed "pleasuring." The pill helped to keep the pregnancy rate down.

Great segments of the hippie group searching for meaning in their life found it in fundamentalist Christianity. The branch that did not stay with Buddhism and thereby evolve into the Hare Krishna and other pseudo-Buddhist groups, became Jesus Freaks, men and women often setting out, sometimes alone, sometimes with a small group, to found a Biblical commune. In the late sixties some of these communes worked out quite well both economically and socially. Small parcels of land were purchased and worked, crude dwellings were constructed, children were born at home, drugs were banned, and slowly all but the most decadent of the hippies began to come of age one way or another and to fan out from their centers in San Francisco, Chicago and New York to the countryside.

While hippies were going back to Christ and organizing experiments in communal living, two sexologists were ready to publish their findings. William H. Masters, M.D., and Virginia E. Johnson wrote *Human Sexual Response*, based upon intensive sex research between 1953 and 1965. Unlike Kinsey, Masters and Johnson were most interested in the physiological responses of individuals to sexual stimulation. In their scientifically equipped laboratory, motion picture cameras with high-resolution macro-lenses that could photograph changes in the vaginal color and secretions were used. An artificial penis, electrically powered, made of plastic and designed so that actual photographs could be made through it was important in their research program. It was also used to time orgasmic responses.

Master and Johnson started out with prostitutes, 118 females and 27 males. In later years they also worked with volunteer individuals and couples. Within the twelve years of experimentation before publication of their first book, 694 individuals, which included 276 married couples, participated in the experiments. All were able to reach orgasm during masturbation and/or coitus while being closely observed by the doctors and/or the camera. A careful screening kept out applicants who could not reach orgasm so that no time would be wasted.

As a result of the Masters and Johnson experiments much information was added to the Kinsey findings. One of the important results of their experiments was finding that women were naturally multi-orgasmic — that a woman who could come once could usually come again almost immediately afterwards. Prostitutes reacted orgasmically in the same way as non-prostitutes. Masters and Johnson's interrogations also indicated that most prostitutes went into their profession for economic reasons first but that sexual pleasure rated a high second.

In their book a number of sexual fallacies were exposed. There were no differences perceived in the sensitivity of a circumcised male and an uncircumcised male. The chief cause of male impotence, they found, is fear — of not being able to perform. Both males and females in good health and with a stimulating partner maintain sexual functions into the eighty-year-old and older group. It had long been thought that the more times a man had sex with his wife during her period of ovulation the more possibility there would be of pregnancy. Not so, said Masters and Johnson. Because it took the average male thirty to forty hours after an ejacula-

tion for his sperm production to come up to normal, frequent intercourse would be less likely to deliver enough healthy sperm to the area of the ovum. The researchers also found that it was more important to know when and how to have intercourse if infertility problems were to be solved. They noted that more often than not the problem has been on the male side — that males were responsible for at least 60 percent of the failures to effect pregnancy.

The book, though strictly a scientific study, created a sensation. As usual, most of the reviews attacked it as immoral, indecent and possibly pornographic. Some criticized the fact that elderly people were used in the experiments, giving the impression that reviewers felt that sex was either too good or too immoral for people over sixty. The result, of course, was to make the book a best seller. And in time the Masters and Johnson findings became acceptable both to the scientific community and the lay public.

Masters and Johnson proved another important sexual fact that George Bernard Shaw had commented on years earlier. "Marriage," he wrote, "is popular because it combines the maximum of temptation with the maximum of opportunity."

When they began their research, both authors were married to someone else. Masters divorced his wife in 1972. Johnson had divorced her husband in 1956, and shortly after Masters' divorce was final Masters and Johnson became Mr. and Mrs.

To bring the sex surveys up to date, three of the most important ones to follow Masters and Johnson were conducted by the Research Guild, Inc., responsible for the publication of *Sexual Behavior in the 1970s* by Morton Hunt. Their surveys, done between 1973 and 1974, covered only half as many people as the *Kinsey Report*. However, 10 percent of the subjects were black. The study was interesting as a comparison and update to the *Kinsey Report*, especially since it appeared twenty-five years later.

Among the findings were that some 75 percent of the unmarried women interviewed had intercourse before they were twenty-five. And half of the women who married before twenty-five had premarital sex. Eighty percent of all the younger married women had lost their virginity before marriage.

Among the men in the non-college group, 75 percent had had an experience in intercourse by the age of seventeen. A new finding was in the field of adultery or extramarital sex: more than 50 percent of the divorced males and females said that their divorces were caused by adultery on the part of one or the other. Divorced women, and men as well, had become respectable. Ninety-one percent of the divorced women were sexually active, having an average of three and a half partners per year. The average number of sex partners in the course of a year for men came to an average of eight.

Prostitution had dwindled to half what it was in the forties. There didn't seem to be much change in the extramarital activity of husbands, but among young wives 24 percent, as compared to 17, admitted to extramarital affairs.

Oral sex was found to be far more common — or more often reported. Hunt reported that more than 80 percent of single persons between twenty-five and thirty-four participated in oral sex. And about 90 percent of married persons under the age of twenty-five had experienced both cunnilingus and fellatio.

As was to be expected, sex acts with animals were less common twenty-five years later. This could be partly attributed to the fact that there were fewer boys on the farms, fewer animals — and girls were becoming available at an earlier age. Heterosexual anal intercourse seemed to be on the increase, with about 25 percent of the females and more than 25 percent of the males being involved in anal intercourse at least once. About 25 percent of the couples studied under the age of thirty-five had indulged in anal intercourse at least once during the year 1973, according to Hunt.

This study did indicate that the average number of times of sexual intercourse for married people twenty-five years or younger was about three times a week. For thirty-five to forty-four-year-old married people — twice a week. And for married people beyond the mid-fifties — about once a week. All of these figures would indicate that all groups are fucking from 10 to 15 percent more often than they were at the time of the Kinsey survey.

At least three times as many women were found to reach orgasm as in the *Kinsey Report*. And, although homosexuality was indicated as being more noticeable, its frequency does not seem to have increased.

The book in its conclusions stated that "Americans are much more tolerant of the sexual ideas and acts of other persons than formerly and feel far freer to envision various previously forbidden acts as possible for themselves — and, hence to include such acts in their own sexual repertoires."

The event that was to have the greatest effect upon sexuality in the United States and, ultimately, in the world was the release of the birth control pill. The first such pills were called Enovid and marketed throughout the country in 1960. For the first time in history a 99.9-percent-sure method of preventing pregnancy was available. During the early years the pharmaceutical houses marketed the pill under other names and used slightly differing chemical formulas.

These were not new drugs, nor was the principle on which they worked new; only the demonstration in 1960-64 of the effectiveness and relative safety in human female fertility control was new.

Oral contraceptives are balanced combinations of estrogenic hormone and progestational hormone. The drug suppresses ovulation as long as it is taken; normal ovulation, hence fertility, resumes when the drug is discontinued. The drug prevents the immature ova (eggs) from maturing; it is therefore conjectured that, since the number of ova in each ovary is fixed at birth, the use of oral contraceptives may actually prolong the duration of a woman's reproductive life.

The demand for pills exceeded the supply during the early years. Mothers who had had enough children, women who did not want to have children and especially unmarried women all got "on the pill." Mothers with sexy daughters put out their pill with their morning milk. High school pregnancies dropped considerably. The total birth rate in the United States between 1960 and 1970 was cut in half. Young women who would never before take a chance on sex with their boyfriends for fear of pregnancy, and married women as well, adopted new attitudes toward sex. Sex for procreative purposes exclusively was finished. It was the beginning of sex for pleasure — sex for love. The resulting freedom changed the sex habits of the nation. Arguments raged over whether the knowledge on the part of both the man and the woman involved in sex that fucking could not lead to procreation would be stifling the instinctive urge, would make the act of sex into a less deeply felt emotional experience. But it was generally agreed that, although there were some dangerous side effects, on the whole the pill was safer than abortion and even childbirth. Dr. Alex Comfort, author, biologist, psychiatrist and sexologist, went a step farther in his best-selling book *The Joy of Sex*. He wrote that the pill was safer than aspirin.

The Joy of Sex was subtitled *A Gourmet Guide to Love Making* and sections included "Starters," which could have been called "Appetizers." Among the hors d'oeuvres are such intriguing items as *Foreskin* — Comfort thinks it's better to leave it on than cut it off; *Frequency* — here he agrees with Ellis: as often as both participants enjoy it; *Come Again* — both men and women could. Exercise and practice recommended.

Among the main courses: *Cuissade* — a half rear-entry position; *Kisses* — anywhere on the body and given with lips, tongue, penis, labia or eyelashes . . . *Quickies* — inspired, unpremeditated and mutual.

In the "Sauces and Pickles" department: *Anal Intercourse* — has drawbacks, worth trying at least once; *Feathers* — heron or egret are best; *Indian Style* — includes love cries, love blows and love bites. Positions are reminiscent of the Kamasutra.

Comfort also includes an excellent section on sexual problems. Both his *Joy of Sex* and its sequel, *More Joy of Sex*, are by far the best advice-and-position manuals published in the seventies. They are witty, informative and useful.

While millions of copies of *The Joy of Sex* were sold, even more men and women went to the movies for sexual stimulation and information. The pornographic film had been made ever since the motion picture camera and projector were invented. The first ones were simple, voyeuristic, black-and-white films known as "blue" movies. They were short, most of them running five to twenty minutes. The producers recouped their investment by selling copies for projection at stag and private parties.

Themes were frankly sexual and often funny. Two men in a 1920s Ford pick up two girls wearing voluminous skirts, shirtwaists, high-button shoes and picture hats. They motor a few miles out into the country and get out of the car. In seconds the girls are on their backs, skirts over their heads, their underpants off; the men, pants at half-mast, are on top of them banging away. This scene lasts for perhaps fifteen or twenty seconds. The men roll off and the girls jump up, get into the car and drive away, leaving the men trying to run after them with their trousers around their knees.

One of the most amusing of the very early films shows three naked girls on a beach. A young man is separated from them by a high fence, which he peeps through. The girls see him and make signs that he should put his penis through a knothole in the fence and they will satisfy him. He frantically works up an erection and sticks it through the knothole. Meanwhile, the girls have found a goat on the beach and backed it up to the knothole. On one side of the fence the youth cries out in ecstasy what a gorgeous piece of tail he has; while on the other side the girls holding the goat laugh hilariously. The end.

Over the next thirty years, the "blue" movies became more sophisticated — but not much. Then in the early sixties — perhaps stimulated by topless bars and nude nightclub acts — the porno film, with its "X"-rated status, became popular, if not quite respectable. The first films to be released took the form of sex education lectures with phony European professors, speaking in heavy accents, who introduced a series of male and female models to show how the sex act should be performed . . . in various positions. Such films as *Sex Education in Sweden*, *Sex and Health* and *How to Make Love* soon gave way to more imaginative productions. The "X"-rated movie, however, did not become truly popular until director Gerard Damiano directed *The Devil in Miss Jones*. It had a classic theme: An attractive woman in her late thirties has been completely passed by sexually. In

despair she commits suicide in a carefully orchestrated, sensitively photographed opening sequence. She finds herself in a strange other world where she asks for the chance to fulfill her sexual longings. Her wish is granted and she proceeds to enjoy masturbation, fucking, lesbianism and oral sex. At the end of the film she reaches a sexual high when she is fucked in cunt and ass simultaneously. After this ultimate experience she finds herself alone in a cell, unable to reach an orgasm by masturbation. The realization slowly dawns upon her that she has gone to hell.

The sex was handled more lightly in *Deep Throat*, also made by Gerard Damiano. The amusing premise is that an attractive young woman finds, after experimenting with many men, that she has no sensation in her vagina. By a caprice of nature, her clitoris, instead of being in the usual place, is located deep in her throat. When, after lessons from experts, she finally succeeds in getting a penis far enough down her throat to bring her to orgasm, bells ring, fireworks go off and it's graduation day!

There were a few more well-done "X"-rated films, most of them made by director Henry Paris, a pseudonym for a director of a considerable number of respectable Hollywood films. In the late seventies "R"-rated movies began to take some of the audience away from the "X"-rated films. Nudity became relatively common; fucking was shown, often in detail, as in *The Sailor Who Fell From Grace with the Sea*, with Kris Kristofferson and Sarah Miles in action. An "R"-rated film, *Pretty Baby*, was directed in impeccable taste by Louis Malle and showed life in a New Orleans whorehouse, circa 1915, as witnessed by the twelve-year-old daughter of one of the whores. There were few complaints in the United States but the film was banned in Canada.

On the literary horizon, women writers in the seventies began using four-letter words and describing realistic sexual situations in a field heretofore largely dominated by men. Erica Jong created a sensation with her first-person characterization of Isadora Wing in her best seller, *Fear of Flying*. In it was born the phrase "the zipless fuck," which she fantasized as completely detached sex with a stranger. One-night stands had been written about before but not as realistically as Erica's essays on the zipless fuck. It was, in addition to being a well-written and provocative novel, an attack on the hypocritical attitudes toward sex held by most Americans.

As the gay movement gained impetus, more books — some useful, some frivolous — analyzed the homosexual in American society. One of the most provocative, *The Gay Tapes*, by Dr. David I. Gottlieb and published in 1977, turned out to be an excellent analysis of the homosexual position in American society and the author's view of it. Written by a psychiatrist, the book is largely made up of interviews with homosexuals, whose identities are concealed. Gottlieb covers social and medical problems, sadism and masochism, friendship, jealousy, infidelity and the reality of coupling. It is the kind of book that could not have been published in the sixties.

Conservative school boards throughout the United States have looked askance at teachers who have revealed their homosexuality. In theory, but only in theory, many school board members see no connection between the sexual preference of a teacher and his or her ability to teach. Faced with the growing gay organizations, and in spite of the Equal Opportunity Act and the Human Rights Amendment, some school boards have removed gay teachers.

The churches face an even greater issue. Many homosexuals have been devout members of congregations for many years. They have only admitted to their homosexuality within the past few years, sometimes months. Most churches have expressed compassion for the homosexual condition, but those with a strong biblical base find it difficult to accept homosexuals unless they are willing either to give up sex entirely or to make an attempt to become heterosexual. As Freud would have said, either of these alternatives is likely to make the individual mentally or physically ill.

In the recent 190th General Assembly of the United Presbyterian Church, held in San Diego, California, it was overwhelmingly voted that gays, male or female, could not be ordained as ministers. There is obviously still a strong belief in many quarters that straight heterosexual sex is the only way to heaven.

Heterosexual groups are swinging right along. Perhaps the most prestigious organization that makes an attempt to bring the unmarried upper strata together is Who's Who International. This is a carefully structured, international club with fifty-five chapters and 3000 members. Its members are society-minded, some single socialites, some singles aspiring to be socialites. The club is dedicated to having the rich rub elbows — and possibly other portions of their anatomy — and affords its exclusive unmarried membership every opportunity to get together. Most members like to think of Who's Who as an exclusive singles club especially designed for the mobile life of the unmarried social set. Meetings are held throughout the United States on regular nights in the private rooms of large hotels and restaurants.

Fashionably dressed, carefully coiffured, unmarried women between thirty and fifty — give or take a few years either way — meet with affluent single men in roughly the same age group. To become a member one must attend, with a sponsor, a number of meetings, then pay a $300 initiation fee and $75 a year thereafter. In addition, it costs from twenty to fifty dollars to attend a gathering, which includes drinks and dinner. No couples. Technically, everyone pays their own bill, though there are occasional exceptions. Any members may attend any other chapter's parties should they happen to be alone in the big city, and there is a good chance that they'll meet a congenial opposite.

Though there is no question that the primary purpose of the club is to give the upper crust a chance at romance, Who's Who also taxes every member 10 percent for charity at every party. Members who doubtless know better like to think of the club as primarily philanthropic. But in their hearts they know that it's a big, international, incorporated swinger's club where everybody hopes to find either a temporary or a permanent mate.

It reminds me of the story of a man who is waiting for a commuter train and asks an older man next to him what time it is. The man replies that he doesn't know the time and goes back to reading his paper. A few minutes later the young man notices him looking at his watch and can't help inquiring, "Sir, why, when I asked you what time it was, wouldn't you tell me?"

The older man replied, "Look, if I tell you the time, we'll get to talking, you'll sit next to me on the train, maybe we'll get off at the same station, we'll get friendly and pretty soon I'll invite you over to the house, maybe for dinner. You'll meet my wife and my daughter and my daughter might become interested in you."

"What's wrong with that?" asked the younger man.

"I don't want my daughter to marry anybody who can't afford a watch." In Who's Who International everyone has a watch.

On a more carnal level, we come to Sandstone, the *in* club in California where the elite meet to fuck. Located a few miles northwest of Los Angeles, no clothing is de rigueur. It is more like a luxurious resort where open sexual contacts are encouraged than a crowded city club. The underlying idea at Sandstone is release, or finding oneself through free-association sexual experiences. (Whatever that is.) No one has to have sex with anyone, but sex is the primary reason for belonging. The atmosphere is conducive to not only nudity but possible sexual contacts with people other than your mate. Whether having sex with a group of people does, indeed, have any psychological-release value is, of course, questionable. Probably with some people it does and with others it doesn't. Sandstone is not made up of typical swappers. It is more like a coterie of intelligent, professional men and women attempting to intensify their sexual pleasure — and in a relaxed, unhurried atmosphere. Sandstone is expensive.

At a far lower level are the hundreds of swap clubs that are for some reason especially popular in California and Florida. The greatest number of swap clubs are in Los Angeles County, which is also perhaps the largest county in terms of population in the United States. The San Francisco area probably places second, with New

York, Miami and Chicago following. The most recent information from the Institute for Sex Research at Indiana University indicates that the West Coast of the United States has almost 25 percent of all the swap-swingers in the country. New members are reached through advertisements in confidential columns of newspapers such as the *Los Angeles Free Press* and the *National Enquirer*. Some of the clubs publish their own magazine or newsletter.

Swap clubs have as many as 150 member-couples — 300 people. Groups meet to swap wives or mistresses as often as once a week; some as seldom as twice a year. But the usual swap club meets on at least a monthly basis. Membership changes often and, although there are all kinds of clubs, the rules are fairly simple. Their swinging is usually based on complete honesty with themselves and their marriage partners. It takes at least two — or rather four — to swap.

At least one club schedules sexual relations with each permanent member of the group for any new members. After both the male and female in the couple have been fucked by the permanent members, they are voted on. And a vote of approval makes them permanent members. All clubs, however, require that before initiation a nude photograph be furnished to the membership committee.

One booklet published commandments for the group:

1. Thou shalt love thy neighbor as thyself.
2. Thou shalt love thy neighbor's mate as thy own.
3. Thou shalt be sterile for the protection of thy neighbor's peace of mind.
4. Thou shalt be free of VD.

A new era may be opening up for the swappers. In 1978 in New York City, Plato's Retreat, the ultimate center for sexual freedom, opened on 74th Street. It has become the most popular swinging sex club in the nation. Its advertising reads: "If you haven't been to Plato's Swing Club you might as well be living in Kansas." It's a couples-only pad big enough to hold 300 of each sex. This means many private rooms with mattress, air and water beds available. Admission in 1978 was thirty-nine dollars a couple — and what do you get? Well, there is a clothes-optional discotheque; most visitors opt for dancing with clothes off. There are Jacuzzis big enough for twelve to play in, a large, warm swimming pool (swimmers are rare), a steam room and a free soft drink and buffet bar. No liquor is served, for the state of New York does not allow unclothed people to drink or to serve drinks in public.

Who goes to Plato's? Doctors, lawyers (and doubtless an occasional Indian chief), school teachers, actresses, nurses, career girls of all kinds. King of all this

communal sex is a happy character named Larry Levenson, who says that "everybody comes to this voyeur's heaven to look but most of them stay to be looked at." So popular has Plato's become that smaller clubs, including one for gays only, have opened in Manhattan. And at least one club with separate sections for straights, gays and lesbians has become popular in San Francisco.

Successful political leaders have always kept a low sexual profile.

Neither Calvin Coolidge nor Harry Truman added any spice to the American political-sexual scene. Truman was known to enjoy dirty jokes and told them well. But he never strayed. Nor, based on the evidence at hand, did Richard Nixon. And the most President Carter ever admitted to was lascivious thoughts:

"I've looked on a lot of women with lust. I've committed adultery in my heart many times," he said in a *Playboy* interview.

Neither intimates of the president nor the press revealed during his lifetime the love affair of Warren G. Harding with Nan Britton and the birth of their illegitimate daughter.

A similar secrecy kept the two extramarital romances of Franklin Delano Roosevelt from surfacing. It was widely known that Roosevelt had an early affair with Lucy Mercer. After Eleanor had had her sixth child, she discovered Franklin's love affair with her secretary, Miss Mercer, and never shared his bed again. Although both Eleanor and Franklin pressed for divorce, Franklin's mother, Sara, pointed out that she would withhold the financial support she was giving them and that his political career would be finished. Franklin agreed to break off the affair and he kept his word. Franklin and Eleanor stayed together and were the only presidential couple to occupy separate wings in the White House so far.

Intimates of the president and members of the press also knew of the long love affair between Franklin and his devoted secretary, Missy LeHand. For many years of his life, Missy was not only secretary but also nurse and mistress and on most occasions occupied a room next to the president. Mrs. Roosevelt and the children knew of the intimacy between Franklin and Missy but seemed to take the position that what was best for the president was okay with them.

After the death of Missy, Roosevelt renewed his relationship with Lucy Mercer, who had been married and widowed. She was a gentle, attractive and intelligent woman still in love with Franklin and he with her. She was with him at Warm Springs, Georgia, on the day he died.

No such delicacy on the part of the press prevailed in the 1976 Washington scandals that involved Congressmen Wilbur Mills and Wayne Hays.

Conservative Congressman Wilbur Mills was one of the great fiscal experts in the government, but his knowledge did not extend to women. With a loyal wife back home, Wilbur had an affair with Argentine sex-bomb Annabella Battistella. They kept their affair private but one night, after Wilbur had had a few too many drinks, and ebullient Annabella had joined in, they parked near the Washington Tidal Basin and Annabella indulged in a public striptease.

Mills was chairman of the Ways and Means Committee and, as one of the newsmen put it, "She had the ways, he had the means." Mills lost his chairmanship but did just manage to hang onto his job as congressman from Arkansas. Annabella, who had changed her name to Fanne Foxe, came out ahead. She put together a nightclub act and, because she was talented in and out of bed, made a success of it.

Not long after this a blonde beauty turned up on the payroll of Congressman Wayne Hays. She didn't go to the office and for a time — not too long a time — the investigative reporters could not figure out what she did to earn her salary. Then Elizabeth Ray began to tell all. Miss Ray was a smart girl and before she made her affair with Congressman Hays public, she had begun her book, *The Washington Fringe Benefit*, which as Washington confessions go went pretty far. According to *Playboy*, she says she was giving Hays an Academy Award performance every week — easier than pounding the typewriter. Miss Ray headed for Hollywood after the story broke.

But the confessions of Elizabeth Ray and Fanne Foxe did not compare in popularity with the national shock waves caused by the confessions of Judith Campbell Exner, the attractive brunette who shared John F. Kennedy's bed both before and after he was president. Before becoming a national public figure Kennedy had been involved in affairs with a number of attractive women. And, thanks to their tact and that of Judith Campbell Exner, an attractive woman introduced to him by Frank Sinatra, there was no gossip about their affair until November 1975 (twelve years after his death). Information about the Exner-Kennedy affair was triggered by a report by the Senate Committee on Intelligence Operations. One sentence in the report read:

"Evidence before the Committee indicates that a close friend of President Kennedy had frequent contact with the President from the end of 1960 through mid-1962. FBI reports and testimony indicate that the President's friend was also a close friend of John Roselli and Sam Giancana and saw them often during this same period."

The Washington *Post* broke the story of the intimate relationship between President Kennedy and a woman who was also involved with two Mafia figures who, in turn, were said to be involved with CIA plots to assassinate Castro. As with the Watergate scandal, the information was leaked slowly, but after Ms. Exner had been exposed as an intimate of the president and branded as a possible spy, she decided to write a book telling her version of the affair. Judith Campbell Exner tells how she met Frank Sinatra and, through him, Sam Giancana. John Kennedy was not then president but had entered the primaries. She, Giancana and Sinatra discussed a man named Kennedy but, she wrote, she did not connect the name Kennedy with the potential candidate. She had an affair with Sinatra and even went to Hawaii to share a bed with him.

Back in Las Vegas, on February 7, 1960, she met Jack Kennedy at Sinatra's table at the Sands Hotel. He was with his brother Ted and the group, including Judith and Sinatra, had dinner together. Then she and Jack spent a long afternoon together. While in Las Vegas they made arrangements to meet at the Plaza Hotel in New York on the evening of March 7, the day before the New Hampshire primary. In room 1651 she and the president-to-be went to bed together for the first time.

During the campaign, according to Mrs. Exner's account, she visited Kennedy at his Georgetown home and fell in love. They rendezvoused in Washington and at the Fountainebleau Hotel in Miami, among other spots. After Kennedy became president meetings became more difficult but they were arranged, and the press, if it was aware of the affair, ignored it. In her book she told of her visits to the White House, for intimate moments with the president, in considerable detail. Besides the White House trysts, they also met at the Mayflower Hotel and, according to Judith, it was there that he gave her a large diamond and ruby brooch with nine or ten rubies in the center and about thirty full-cut diamonds set in platinum along the edge.

Throughout the fall of 1961 and the winter and spring of 1962, Jack and Judith continued their affair. In addition to New York and Washington, now there were meetings in Palm Beach. Slowly, according to Judith, they began to fall out of love. Telephone calls from Kennedy dwindled and the affair ended in June of 1962 — it had lasted a little over two years. Judith Campbell Exner kept her secret for the next fifteen years, and when she revealed the love affair it did not cause a great uproar. Sexually, America was growing up. A man's sex life was his own business — even a president's.

The attempt to collect taxes on sex, eliminate the pimp and let the state get the money instead had been tried a number of times in the United States, with varying degrees of success. Usually, as in the case of New Orleans and San Francisco, it was the underworld rather than the state that collected most of the profits. Then Nevada in 1974 officially recognized sex as a respectable industry, just as they had recognized gambling 43 years before. To see that the tax money was spread around and that the business would be controlled licenses for whorehouses were limited to towns with less than 200,000 inhabitants. This technicality eliminated Las Vegas and Reno. Yet it is a technicality — the licensed "sex ranches" can be reached in less than an hour by car or by bus from either of those cities.

There are now four such ranches. The ranches themselves are licensed on the basis of less than seven girls working or more than seven girls working. Each ranch pays $500 per girl per week in state taxes if there are less than seven, and $1000 per girl in state taxes if more than seven are employed. It is easy for the girls to get a work permit. They have to prove that they are over eighteen and have $3 which is what the permit costs. They are photographed and fingerprinted and girls are refused work if they have a criminal record. Each institution has a weekly venereal disease check by a doctor. Records for 1977 indicate that there is less VD (an incidence of about 5 percent) among prostitutes in these licensed houses than in the high schools throughout the country.

Things have been made somewhat more difficult for the pimps. Girls who come to the ranches are not allowed to be accompanied. But the girls get a week off every three or four weeks, depending upon the house they work in, and for the most part go off to join their boyfriends; based on the behavior of prostitutes in the past, they may well turn over a portion of their savings. Some housewives who live not too far away work the whorehouses over the weekend and let their husbands keep house. But by no means are all the whores tied up with a man. Many are college students. Some of them work only during summer vacation.

The standard rate at the time of this writing is about a dollar a minute, with a minimum of fifteen. But that first fifteen minutes can sometimes be spent without getting anywhere at all, and the average expenditure is closer to thirty dollars per fuck than fifteen.

Nevada has had some racial problems, but the biggest of the ranches admits blacks through a separate entrance, and some houses have at least one or two black girls.

The prostitution picture changed dramatically during the seventies. Three major organizations of prostitutes appeared. COYOTE (Call Off Your Old Tired Ethics), headed by Margo St. James, an ex-prostitute, has put together a loose organization of women. New York has its group called PONY (Prostitutes of New York). But California leads it in numbers for it has a second organization called CAT (California Organization of Trollops). These organizations put on an annual convention and a ball as well. Such annual hookers conventions and balls have been held in San Francisco, Los Angeles, San Diego, New York and other large cities. The thrust of all of these organizations of prostitutes is legalization of prostitution without taxes. Churches don't pay taxes, they say — why should prostitutes? They both offer suffering humanity needed services.

The United States finds itself in the same dilemma that all countries have faced. They can't get along with prostitutes and they can't get along without them. France banned them in 1946 and today they have more than ever. (And theirs are beginning to organize too.)

Yet, prostitution occupies a smaller and smaller place in the sex scene of the late seventies. The licensed ranches of Las Vegas are much more a novelty than they are a trend. For the trend is toward a fair exchange between sexual partners. Few young men, except for sailors in a strange port, businessmen away at conventions and men too unattractive or too lazy to find a girl to share sex with them, lack for free sex these days. Pick-up bars, television dating services and computer dating services, along with the organized church functions, make it possible for almost every girl to meet a man and vice versa. There are clubs for singles, clubs for single parents, clubs for juniors and clubs for seniors.

Women's liberation is no longer coming — it has been here for some time. In La Mesa, a suburb of the conservative city of San Diego, California, a club called the Classic Cat cannot accommodate all the women who try to get in every Wednesday evening to see a series of nude male dancers. It's a joyous crowd with women ranging in age from 18 to 60, with the younger women predominating. They surround the two glittering, mirrored stages, where in the glare of bright spotlights muscular, young heterosexuals (as far as I could tell) tease girls by starting their dance in a caftan or tight blue jeans and slowly stripping down. The girls at ringside shriek and squeal as the naked dancers do bumps and grinds. One girl said, "They have such a great advantage over female dancers — with all that stuff they have to throw around."

And throw it around they do. Dances are sometimes slow and provocative, more often frenzied and athletic. A kind of sexual rapport, an intoxication by the rhythm of the dance and the nakedness of the men drives the girls to reach out to the stage trying to touch legs or penises. The men pull away just in time. Occasionally, a girl simply cannot stand the pressure. She hesitantly crawls up onto the stage and joins in the dance. It isn't long before she's stripped off her shirt or blouse, as the dance becomes more frenzied and more sexual. Some of the girls strip off pants and panties and match the male dancer step for step. There's no sexual contact. The lights go down, the loud disco music diminishes, the girl quickly puts her clothes back on and joins her friends to accept their plaudits. Another husky male takes the spotlight.

What, then, is the direction of human sexuality? Having reached equality, or come very close to it, and having made the pleasure of sex available without the worry of procreation, what next? There are two directions that should be considered. Will a conservative swing take sex back into a deep freeze? Or if the current trend continues will future sex warm up for everyone?

The first Americans, the Indians, did not talk about it much and their picture writing was limited. Our own ancestors kept it so quiet that, had it not been for the pregnancies and sex crimes, it would have seemed not to exist. One gets the impression that the more information that is disseminated — the more sex is written and talked about — the less actual intercourse there may be. Have the modern permissiveness, gynecological knowledge, the diaphragms, condoms, foams and finally pills changed the sex drive from a life force to a pleasant kind of mutual masturbation? With the ultimate urge for procreation completely missing, is the instinctive force of sex in individuals being dissipated?

Based upon the dress of men and women, their insistence upon a single sexual standard, we seem to be moving toward the unisex or bisexual individual. Thus far, nature, or evolution, or whatever one calls it, has provided stimulation whenever there seemed to be a danger of human sexuality drying up. After each war skirts have gone up, there have been more nudity, more provocative plays and books. Now, are the almost-nonexistent bikini, nude beaches, nude theater, naked male and female dancers, swap clubs, Plato's Retreat, Sandstone and the naked boys dancing for the naked girls a last desperate attempt at the survival of the human race?

Recently I had a conversation with a history teacher in one of California's largest high schools. He had been conducting a personal survey among the boys in his class. An unusual number of them confessed that their greatest ambition was to get a girl pregnant. It was not that they wanted a child. They had no objections to abortions. But, he said, there seemed to be a desperate need among the boys to prove that the procreative power was still with them. Many of them felt that because of the pill the cards were permanently stacked. It just wasn't possible to impregnate a girl any more. Perhaps this is why the number of pregnancies in high schools has been increasing. And maybe girls want to know whether they still have procreative powers too.

10

Next?

It is the year 2028. Inside a square room in a plastic honeycomb building two students are lounging in form-fitting chairs, while two others stretch out on a soft plastic rug. Three walls of the cell-like room are covered with a material that glows faintly. In the fourth wall a life-size TV screen is recessed. The pupils wear one-piece, lightweight, weatherproof, black jumpsuits. All look very much the same except for two important differences. The females' garments have a vertical zipper that runs from the neckline down between the legs and up to the back waistline. They also have two smaller zippers at the breast-line. The males' costumes are exactly like the females' except for an oversize pouch reminiscent of the codpieces in the ancient Dutch paintings by Breughel, or of the exaggerated jockstraps worn in the classic motion picture, made over fifty years ago, *A Clockwork Orange*.

Both males and females wear makeup and have short hair, which contributes to their look-alikeness. Yet, even without the slightly exaggerated breast and buttock curves of the females and the convex protuberances at the male crotch, their erotic jewelry would help to identify their gender.

A soft chime sounds and the words "SEX HISTORY 1, Discussion Leader John OXY2PhD" appear on the three-dimensional color screen; almost simultaneously a young man in his early forties, dark-haired with a light brown complexion and wearing a one-piece jump suit similar to that of the students, appears and begins the class.

"Today we will be involved in a discussion of the comparative values in sexual relations in earlier cultures, especially those directly leading up to our present sexual freedom. Fifty years ago," he continues, "our problem was sexual freedom. Now that it has been gained, the issue is to find ways for our society to cope with the multiple types of sexual freedom we have achieved.

"No longer is our society concerned with the propriety of two persons of either the opposite or the same sex living together, with or without a contract. Unlike the narrow position held by both Church and State in the 1970s and '80s, all types of relationships are acceptable. We have the open-relationship contract, the swinging relationship, gay relationship, lesbian relationship, brother relationship, sister relationship; and they are, depending upon one's preference, equally socially acceptable. Even the ancient, traditional, religious, monogamous marriage is tolerated."

As the leader, pauses, a voice-activated switch allows a student to speak.

"I don't quite understand," asked Mary 1XYJr., "what you mean by brother relationship or sister relationship. Are you talking about siblings?"

"No, not at all," came the reply from the screen. "Incestuous relations involving brothers and sisters, while not punishable today by law, are generally taboo. With no possibility of progeny, such relations are harmless enough, but the tribal rules against incest were enforced for so many hundreds of years that society generally finds incest distasteful. Does that answer your question?"

"Yes," replied Mary 1XYJr., "but what is a sister relationship?"

"It is," he answered, "ideally, a relationship between two or more females that completely excludes males from their lives sexually, economically and often, though not necessarily, socially. I am surprised that the question should even come up today, for the sisterhood involving two or more females has been growing since the moves toward women's liberation in the late 1940s."

"Does the sister relationship mean that the females involved are all lesbians?"

"Not at all," replied the discussion leader. "I'm sure all of you are familiar with women's bars and cocktail lounges; women's banks, clubs and restaurants, where males are often employed as waiters, cooks and menials; and the nightclubs where erotic male dancers entertain female audiences — not to mention the supermarkets that cater especially to females. The answer to your question is that in female-to-female relationships sex is incidental. The sisterhood must be considered to be in a continuous state of evolution. Females practicing heterocoitus often prefer to have males in their lives for strictly sexual purposes. Yet these same females may resent the domination that sometimes occurs when the relationship becomes totally male-oriented. Even gay females enjoy male company at times, but they don't want to depend upon it."

"What about the brotherhoods?" asked John 1AXB6Jr. "Did they begin and develop in the same way as the sisterhood?"

"No, they did not. And they are almost nonexistent today. For physiological and psychological reasons, males have not adjusted to a brotherhood concept eliminating females as well as females have adjusted to sisterhood. Even though, as you all are aware, total sexual pleasuring is available to everyone in our society, more males are driven — perhaps by animal instinct — toward a dominant, traditional, male-female, heterosexual relationship. Although rare, there are still occasional conflicts over females. Jealousy has made the open-marriage type of contract increasingly difficult to maintain."

"Isn't that an oudated concept now — open marriage?" asked Mary 2AXC1st.

"Not entirely," replied the leader. "The concept of open marriage, meaning that each partner in either the traditional or contractual marriage had the freedom to make any kind of sexual or non-sexual contact outside of marriage, began to lose adherents in the seventies. The lack of sex education and the pressures of economic life at that time contributed to the difficulties. If, indeed, a contractual female housemate went off for a weekend or a week with another male or female the husband's jealousy — and his problems with housekeeping — caused verbal battles and sometimes splits. The same thing happened if the male housemate utilized his sexual and social freedom. Yet this style of cohabiting has survived."

"But why?" asked John 2BX1, a broad-shouldered, athletic type wearing an extra-large codpiece.

"Largely because of the acceptance of bisexuality and partly because of the separation between sex for procreation and sex for pleasuring. Let's take up the history of bisexuality first. In the late sixties the bisexual movement officially began. But it was not until after the year 2000 that, much as gay men and women had been accepted earlier, bisexuality became the rule, rather than the exception, in society. In the beginning, fifty years ago, Don Fass, the founder of the bisexual liberation organization wrote:

"'Being bisexual may not be for every person, but for those who have grown into it or would like to, whether coming from a gay or straight background, we believe bisexuality to be the fullest expression of human liberation. It is a state in which we can love and grow, reaching out with warmth, openness and our fullest potential to any individual we care about — be they genetic females or males.'"

The group leader continued, "As all of you now know, the International Bisexual League is the largest and most respected sex organization in our United Western Hemisphere. To understand its growth, you should know that before males were able to completely eradicate their distrust, disgust and hatred of gay males, before they could understand their own machismo attitudes, which caused them to indulge in violence against both gays and straights, they had to learn something about their own male and female attributes. Bisexuality enabled males to accept males and females on the same sexual level and gave males (even those who did not practice bisexuality) an understanding of, and a way to accept, one another. Jealousy and violence against other males, gay or straight, while not completely eliminated, was greatly reduced by society's mere acceptance of bisexual behavior.

"Now let us discuss the effects of the separation of sex for procreation and sex for pleasure, for it is this area, with all its social and legal implications, that has contributed to our ability in this generation to cope with our sexual — and indeed our total — liberty. The most important step was the limitation of fertility by statute in the 1990s. Every voter and every politician was cognizant that with the continued unlimited production of babies in both the North and South American states revolutions and famines based on lack of living space and lack of food, and all the concomitant problems of unlimited population growth, would have to be faced.

"As far back as 1916, more than a hundred years ago, often-jailed, anarchist-feminist lecturer Emma Goldman told her audiences:

"'If everyone followed the injunction of the Bible and Theodore Roosevelt [twenty-sixth president of the territory formerly referred to as the United States] to be fruitful and multiply, every tenement house would be turned into a lunatic asylum by the excessive number of children . . . A child has a right *not* to be born.' Three years later Miss Goldman was banished from the country.

"Fertility control was a taboo subject. There are hundreds of microbooks that describe in detail the education process and the final success of the legislation. It is probable that without the joining together of Mexico, Central and South America, Canada and the United States to form the United Western Hemisphere such population-limiting legislation could never have been passed. Slowly, unification was ratified. Then, by requiring an examination and a license for every potential parent, and with sterilization as a penalty for breaking this law, the population at last became stable. It would never have been possible without the intense hemisphere-wide sex education program and the comprehensive dissemination of both long- and short-term, male and female fertility control pills, in addition to the more recent injections and nasal sprays. It was a matter of developing the essential legislative mechanism and making it acceptable. An important factor was the adoption of the birth-to-maturity insurance program. This made it possible for any competent adult willing to give the necessary time to the rearing of a child the economic opportunity to do so. Government child support, under which all of you have benefited, did not become law in the United Continents until the year 2005. Although it must seem to you cruel and barbaric, in the years before the turn of the century, children were unplanned, bred in enormous numbers and had to be supported by their producers. Because this was impossible large numbers of these children became antisocial as a result of deprivation and, in some of the southern areas of our continent, many starved to death.

"Now let us turn to the history of sex activity for pleasure. Because of children's lack of freedom to explore and enjoy sex many males and females were affected with algolagnia and agonorgasmos; others with alphamegamia. There was little sex a cappella."

John 2BX1 pressed his circuit breaker and requested acknowledgement. Upon getting it, he said: "This is my first year in sex history and I'm not entirely sure I understand the meaning of the terms you used. Would you mind elucidating?"

"Algolagnia can be defined as the infliction of pain upon another person for sexual gratification. It was a prevalent problem in the seventies and eighties, and many males and females imprisoned one another in leather and metal harnesses and used whips to produce painful and sexually gratifying reactions.

"Agonorgasmos is the inability to achieve orgasm or ejaculation without prolonged and painful effort. This, too, was a widespread malady.

"Alphamegamia does not come under the heading of disease but is rather a natural tendency, unless it becomes the only sex outlet for an individual. It can be defined as the desire by older men for sex with young girls.

"A cappella simply means sex without embellishment — no rubber condom, no rubber diaphragm, no foams or jellies. It was rare because of fear of pregnancy and fear of venereal diseases, which were a major cause for concern until the immunological vaccines were developed. I would recommend that all of you check your medical history text regarding the seventies and eighties. We have only touched on the aberrations under "A" thus far. To understand how many of the sexual aberrations arose, it is important that you learn now that until approximately 1990 children had no sexual rights. In theory they were not supposed to know anything about the pleasures of the orgasm and were not expected to encounter each other sexually until they were married, or at least until they were able to support any progeny that resulted from their sexual connections."

Mary 2AXC1st received clearance for her next question. "Do you mean that teen-agers and pre-teens couldn't enjoy sex in the olden days?"

"Exactly," was the reply. "We know now that, no matter what steps parents took in those days to hinder or divert their children from sexual pleasures, the latter invariably found some outlet. With our current knowledge that sexual experience is imprinted on the child in much the same way that language is imprinted — that is, that it occurs in a very early period of the child's life — it becomes understandable that, with repression and punishment and a warped imprint, aberrations were inevitable. Masturbation, as a favorite, though hidden, pleasure, possibly led to limited antisocial behavior and alienation from parents for it, like all sexual experimentation, was viewed by society as sinful and harmful. It was not until the eighties that masturbation — including mutual masturbation between males and females, males and males, females and females — was recognized, if not entirely approved of, as a normal sexual outlet.

"A story that was considered daring in the seventies concerned a liberal Catholic priest who gave enlightening sex education lectures to a group of young boys at

Sunday school. On the subject of masturbation, he explained that it was not a harmful habit, that there was nothing shameful about it, and asked how many of his twelve-year-old students masturbated. All except the youngest and smallest boy raised their hands.

"'What about you, Billy,' he asked.

"'Oh, Father,' Billy replied, 'I'm already fucking.'"

Mary 2AXC1st pushed her buzzer. "What does that word 'fucking' mean that you just used in telling the story?"

"It was a socially acceptable word, used on every level by English-speaking people in the fifteenth and until the end of the sixteenth century, to describe sexual connection. After that date it became a taboo word, perhaps because the church proscribed sex — it was considered dirty. During the 1980s and '90s the word came back into common usage for a short time but was soon replaced by the words we now use.

"But, to get back to sex education for children. Young children, even infants, get pleasurable sensations by touching their genitals or having them touched by others. Most young children today may not need the sex education that is available from the age of two, for they now learn about sex from adult males and females and indulge in many kinds of sex play. Only fifty years ago such sex play was punished. With the sex act no longer hidden from view, children may freely give pleasure to each other without punishment. Adolescents began to demand the right to sexual pleasure during the latter part of the twentieth century. With the passage of the fertility control laws and all the fertility control methods available they succeeded in their quest for sexual freedom."

"Check," said Mary 2AXC1st. "We know all about that. But what about old people?"

"They were," said the leader, "treated like children until the beginning of this century. Society generally thought it unseemly for grandmothers and grandfathers to enjoy sex. By the early 1980s society was beginning to get a bit more tolerant of the older segment of the population. It became known that males and females in their sixties, seventies, eighties and even nineties enjoyed sex just as much as younger people. Health was the important factor."

"May I make a comment?" asked Mary 1XYJr. "I mated last week with a man old enough to be my grandfather — it was just great. He knew everything — much more than the younger men I've tried mating with — and he lasted longer too."

The discussion leader continued. "The older people had one advantage over the youngsters, as they still have. When they reached a certain age they were no longer expected to engage in as many work hours; however, their incomes from social security and pensions were also reduced. Elderly couples first banded together, sometimes in small communes, sometimes only in male and female couples, to maximize their economic benefits. Two small incomes were better than one. Economic liaisons led to sexual liaisons. So the older people found themselves benefiting both ways. Now, as you know, we have three groups of older people — the gays, the bis and the straights — some living in communes, some keeping house in pairs. Another great advantage to the world of the seniors has been the development of transplant techniques and the increased number of spare parts available.

"During the period between 1960 and the year 2000 there was so much emphasis on the importance of sex as a part of living that everyone though that unless they were happily engaged in sexual mating a considerable part of the time there was something biologically or psychologically wrong with them. Millions of psychiatrists made a living advising people, some of whom may not have needed sex at all, how to increase their sexual outlets or improve their performance. Now we know that the sex drive is a variable and that it is not essential that certain humans have any sex life at all so long as they have rewarding companionship. Yet sexual stimulation has become a government function, partly because the great majority of the people seem to need regular sexual contacts to keep their contractual marriages stable. Swinging clubs have helped, to a degree, even though it has been found that participants are likely to swap partners only for a short time. Changing sexual partners may be just as boring as continuing with the same one.

"A woman writer almost a hundred years ago expressed this same thought when she said: 'When I have sex with a different man every night, it is always the same. When I have sex with the same man every night, it is always different.'

"Now, let us leave the specific examples for the general historical vista. Most of you learned in primary school that in the United States, before we became the United Continents, blacks, Asians and whites did not tend to mix sexually. There was, in fact, a distinct prejudice against miscegenation. Historically, this was the result of nationalism, which dates back to the earliest civilizations. Each of the groups of Amerindians considered itself to be the only truly civilized society. All others were cultural strangers. This pattern was, in fact, true throughout the world. The Chinese, the French, the Russians, the Koreans, the Japanese, the Chileans — each country believed its civilization to be the first and the superior one. The result was, as you know, thousands of years of revolutions and wars. Finally, in the year 2000, the rapidly shrinking white population of the New World realized it must integrate to survive. This could not be token integration; it was a necessity, just as fertility control and child insurance had been. It was a long, slow political process. In some areas, integration was only accomplished by force. But the new gene pool of blacks, Indians, Asians and whites combined to make the United Continents of North and South America a great country."

John 2BX1 posed a question. "I need some specific information on sex education in the sixties and seventies for a report — what was happening?"

"There was still resistance to sex education in the schools in that period, but many males and females, young and old, began to receive limited sex education from two-dimensional, four-color porn, or, as they were referred to, X-rated films. This rating, imposed by censors, kept the films from being seen by those under eighteen. But even so the films made a deep impression on the sexual mores of their time. They were little more than demonstrations by naked males and females of the standard sexual procedures, heterosexual and homosexual matings and fondling and oral contact with breasts, penises and vaginas. Because the general population had little knowledge of such practices, or of the variety of sexual positions, these films, though never aesthetically tasteful, stimulated and educated many individuals. Such sex films vanished from the cultural scene, preserved only in archives, by the year 2000. As you know, now when a dramatic narrative calls for mating or using, such scenes are a natural part of television plays and, of course, are available to every age.

"In passing, I would like to mention how fortunate we are to have two-way, three-dimensional television, not only for classroom education and general entertainment but also because the use of audio-video telephone allows safe contact and the opportunity to be selective regarding one's casual companions. When these phones first came into use twenty-five years ago, there was still some prudery regarding nudity, especially in the south. Obsolete types were annoyed to pick up a telephone and find a flasher exposing penis, vagina or anus. This type of "obscene" call did not last long because no one took it seriously. It was somewhat tiresome because everyone knew what human genitals looked like anyway. Most people laughed and were not offended."

"What," asked Mary 2AXC1st, "do you consider our greatest sexual problem today?"

"There is the problem of sexual boredom," answered the leader. "Some political leaders are concerned because there have been no new stimuli — no way to interest the younger generation in rewarding sexual contact. Perhaps it will make no serious difference to future generations as artificial insemination and computerized incubator donors become available. But, at this time, if humans are not to meet extinction, sexual contact must be stimulated."

John 2BX1, who had popped a pill into his mouth and swallowed, asked: "What about drugs — don't they help to solve the problem of monotonous mating?"

"Indeed they do," answered the professor quickly, "and there are many types fully endorsed by the Food and Drug Administration that are harmless when taken in moderation. *Alco*, the pill that gives the individual something similar to an alcoholic high by affecting the cerebellum and the cortex, is recommended. The well-known *MJ*, which sexually stimulates males and females in much the same way as marijuana did fifty years ago, and the *SloGo*, which increases sexual pleasure but delays orgasm, are available. And, of course, there are the always useful controlled sleep-time pills that allow the body to regather sexual energies. These, of course, are but a sampling of our arsenal of sex-oriented drugs. A list of them includes. . . ."

But the leader had become fascinated by his theme and the sound of his own voice. There were no questions as he droned on and on. The students were all now unzipped — and they did not seem to be bored.

Picture Credits

Special Permission Notices
Lawson, John, A NEW VOYAGE TO CAROLINA, edited by Hugh
Talmage Lefler, Copyright 1967 The University of North Carolina
Press
From CAPTAIN JOHN SMITH by Bradford Smith. Copyright 1953
by Bradford Smith. Reprinted by permission of J.B. Lippincott
Company.
"Benjamin Franklin, His Wit, Wisdom, and Women. Copyright © '75
by Seymour S. Block, permission by HASTINGS HOUSE,
PUBLISHERS."
Billy King's Tombstone, by C.L. Sonnichsen, Tucson, Arizona (University
of Arizona Press), copyright 1972.
The Gentle Tamers: Women of the Old Wild West, by Dee Brown, G.P.
Putnam's Sons, New York, 1958. Reprinted by permission Harold
Matson Company.
VOODOO IN NEW ORLEANS by Robert Tallant (Copyright 1946
by Robert Tallant, renewed 1974 by Minnie Magruder Gibbs)
The Manuscript Journals of Alexander Henry and of David Thompson, by
Elliott Coues, 1965 (Mpls: Ross & Haines)
Eros Denied; Sex in Western Society, © by Wayland Young, 1964
From *Howl and Other Poems* by Allen Ginsberg copyright © 1956,
1959 by Allen Ginsberg. Reprinted by permission of CITY LIGHTS
BOOKS.
Herbert Asbury. *The Barbary Coast* © 1933 Alfred A. Knopf.
Herbert Asbury. *The French Quarter* Copyright 1936 by Alfred A.
Knopf, Inc. Renewal copyright 1964 by Edith Evans Asbury.
Herbert Asbury. The Gangs of New York © 1927, 1928 by Alfred
A. Knopf.
"Selections from the Princess with the Golden Hair" from *Memoirs of
Hecate County* by Edmund Wilson, Copyright © 1942, 1943, 1946
1959 by Edmund Wilson copyright renewed © 1973 by Elena
Wilson. Reprinted with the permission of Farrar, Straus & Giroux
Inc.

Bibliography

Much of the research in this book was done by consulting the files of the following newspapers: *New York Times, New York Mirror, New York Daily News, New York Graphic, San Francisco Chronicle, Alta Californian, New Orleans Item* and *New Orleans Picayune;* and numerous small pamphlets and journals.

Permission has been granted to quote from copyrighted material indicated by an asterisk (*).

Chapter 1

Benedict, Ruth. "Sex in Primitive Society." *American Journal of Orthopsychiatry* 9:570-73.

Bischof, Norbert. "The Biological Foundations of the Incest Taboo." Translated by Phyllis Rechten. Paper given at the twenty-seventh conference of Deutsche Gesellschaft für Psychologie, Kiel, West Germany, 1970.

Carey, Mathew, ed. *The American Museum, or, Universal Magazine,* vols. 1-12 (January 1787-December 1792). Philadelphia: Printed by Mathew Carey, 1787-92.

The Columbian Magazine, Or Monthly Miscellany, vols. 1-6 (September 1786-February 1790). Philadelphia: 1786-90.

The Columbian Museum, Or, Universal Asylum, part 1, (January-June 1793). Philadelphia: From the press of J. Parker, 1793.

The Dessert to the True American, vols. 1-2 (July 14, 1798-August 19, 1799). Philadelphia: S. Bradford, 1798-99.

Devereux, George. "Institutionalized Homosexuality of the Mohave Indians." *Human Biology* 9:498-529.

Dozier, Edward P. *The Pueblo Indians of North America.* New York: Holt, Rinehart and Winston, 1970.

Dragoo, Don W. "Transvestites in North American Tribes." Typescript. Indiana: Department of Anthropology, University of Indiana, 1950.

Farb, Peter. *Man's Rise to Civilization.* New York: E. P. Dutton & Co., 1968.

Forde, C. Daryll. "Ethnography of the Yuma Indians." *University of California Publications in American Archaeology and Ethnology* 28:83-278.

Friedl, Ernestine. *Women and Men.* New York: Holt, Rinehart and Winston, 1975.

The General Magazine, vol. 1 (June-July 1798). Baltimore: Printed by A. Hanna and H. Greene, 1798.

The Gentleman and Lady's Town and Country Magazine, vol. 1, nos. 1-8 (May-December 1784). Boston: Printed by Weeden and Barrett, 1784.

Hewitt, John N. B. *The American Anthropologist,* vol. 2 (October 1889).

The Journal of American Folk-Lore, vol. 12 (January-March 1899). Cambridge: The Riverside Press, 1899.

The Key, vol. 1, nos. 1-27 (January 13-July 14, 1798). Maryland: Printed by J. D. Cary, 1798.

Kirk, Thomas, ed. *The American Moral & Sentimental Magazine,* vols. 1-2 (July 3, 1797-May 21, 1798). New York: Printed by Thomas Kirk, 1797-98.

Lawson, John. *A New Voyage to Carolina.* Edited by Hugh T. Lefler. North Carolina: University of North Carolina Press, 1967.

Lorant, Stefan, ed. *The New World—The First Pictures of America.* New York: Duell, Sloan & Pearce, 1946.

The Massachusetts Magazine, vols. 1-8 (January 1789-December 1796). Boston: Printed by I. Thomas and E. T. Andrews, 1789-96.

The Medical Repository, vols. 1-3 (1797-1800). New York: Printed by T. & J. Swords, 1798-1800.

The New-Jersey Magazine, December 1786-February 1787. New Brunswick, N.J.: Printed by F. Quequelle and J. Prange, 1786-87.

The New Star, nos. 1-26 (April 11-October 3, 1797). Concord, Mass.: Russel & Davis, 1797.

The New-York Magazine, vols. 1-6 (January 1790-December 1795), vols. 1-2 (January 1796-December 1797). New York: Printed by T. & J. Swords, 1790-97.

The New-York Weekly Magazine, vols. 1-3, nos. 1-122 (July 1, 1795-August 23, 1797). New York: J. Bull, 1796-97.

Paine, Thomas, ed. *The Pennsylvania Magazine,* vols. 1-2 (January 1775-July 1776). Philadelphia: Printed by R. Aitken, 1775-76.

The Rural Casket, vol. 1, nos. 1-15 (June 5-September 11, 1798). Poughkeepsie, N.Y.: Printed by Power & Southwick, 1798.

The Rural Magazine, vol. 1, nos. 1-52 (February 17, 1798-February 9, 1799). Newark, N.J.: Printed by J. H. Williams, 1798-99.

Smith, William, ed. *The American Magazine and Monthly Chronicle for the British Colonies,* vol. 1. Philadelphia: Printed by W. Bradford, 1757-58.

South Carolina Weekly Museum, January 1-July 1797. Charleston: Printed by W. P. Harrison & Co., 1797.

Stewart, Omer C. "Homosexuality among the American Indians and other Native Peoples of the World." *Mattachine Review* 6(1):9-15, 6(2):13-19.

Stiller, Richard. "Homosexuality and the American Indian." *Sexology* 29(11):770-72.

Thomas, Isaiah, and Greenleaf, Joseph, eds. *The Royal American Magazine,* vols. 1-2 (January 1774-March 1775). Boston: Printed by I. Thomas, 1774-75.

United States Magazine, vol. 1, nos. 1-5 (April-August 1794). Newark: Printed by J. Woods, 1794.

The Vigil, nos. 1-6 (February 27-April 3, 1798). Charleston: Printed by W. P. Young, 1798.

Vogel, Virgil J. *American Indian Medicine.* Norman, Okla.: University of Oklahoma Press, 1970.

Webster, Noah, ed. *The American Magazine*, December 1787-November 1788. New York: Printed by S. Loudon, 1787-88.

Weslager, Clinton A. *The Delaware Indians*. New Brunswick, N.J.: Rutgers University Press, 1972.

Chapter 2

Bishop, Morris. *The Odyssey of Cabeza de Vaca*. New York: The Century Co., 1933.

Cabeza de Vaca, Alvar Nuñez. *La Relación que Dio Alvar Nuñez Cabeça de Vaca de lo Acaescido en las Indias en la Armada Dónde Iva por Governador Panphilo de Narváez*. Zamora: 1542.

Díaz, Bernal. *The Conquest of New Spain*. Edited by Genaro García. Hakluyt Society, 1908.

Herrera, Antonio de. *Historia General de los Hechos de los Castellanos*. Madrid: 1601.

Hodge, Frederick W. *Handbook of American Indians North of Mexico*. Washington: 1907-10.

Hodge, Frederick W., and Lewis, Theodore H., eds. *Spanish Explorers in the Southern United States, 1528-1543* of the Original Narratives Series. New York: 1907.

Horgan, Paul. *Conquistadors in North American History*. New York: Farrar, Straus & Co., 1963.

Las Casa, Bartolomé de. *Historia de Las Indias*. Edited by Gonzalo de Reparaz. Madrid: 1927.

Lawson, Edward W. *The First Landing Place of Juan Ponce de León ...in the year 1513*. Privately printed.

Lowery, Woodbury. *The Spanish Settlements within the Present Limits of the United States*, vol. 1, 1513-1561. New York: Russell & Russell, 1901.

Martyr, Peter. *De Orbe Novo*. Translated by Leonardo Olschki.

O'Crouley, Pedro Alonso. *The Kingdom of New Spain*. Translated and edited by Séan Galvin. John Howell Books, 1922.

Tío, Aurelio. *Nuevas Fuentes para la Historia de Puerto Rico*. Puerto Rico: 1961.

Weise, Arthur J. *The Discoveries of America to 1525*. New York: G. P. Putnam's Sons, 1884.

Winsor, Justin. *Narrative and Critical History of America*, vol. 2. Boston: Houghton, Mifflin & Co., 1886.

Chapter 3

Arber, Edward, ed. *Travels and Works of Captain John Smith*. New York: Burt Franklin.

Barth, John. *The Sot-Weed Factor*. New York: Doubleday & Co., 1960.

Dow, George F. *Every Day Life in the Massachusetts Bay Colony*. New York: Benjamin Blom, 1967.

Fowler, Samuel P. *Salem Witchcraft*. Salem, Mass.: 1823.

Garnett, David. *Pocahontas or the Nonpareil of Virginia*. New York: Doubleday & Co., 1958.

Hallowell, Richard P. *The Quaker Invasion of Massachusetts*. Boston: Houghton, Mifflin & Co., 1883.

Mapp, Alf J., Jr. *The Virginia Experiment, The Old Dominion's Role in the Making of America (1607-1781)*. Virginia: The Dietz Press, 1957.

Smith, Bradford. *Captain John Smith—His Life & Legend*. Philadelphia: J. B. Lippincott Co., 1953.

Wallechinsky, David, and Wallace, Irving. *The People's Almanac*. New York: Doubleday & Co., 1975.

Weeden, William B. *Economic and Social History of New England 1620-1789*, vols. 1-2. New York: Hillary House Publishers, 1963.

Chapter 4

Amacher, Richard E. *Franklin's Wit & Folly*. New Jersey: The Bagatelles, 1953.

Bigelow, John, ed. *The Complete Works of Benjamin Franklin*. New York: G. P. Putnam's Sons, 1887-1888.

*Block, Seymour Stanton. *Benjamin Franklin, His Wit, Wisdom, and Women*. New York: Hastings House, Publishers, 1975.

Brodie, Fawn M. *Thomas Jefferson, An Intimate History*. New York: W. W. Norton & Co., 1974.

Fleming, Thomas. *The Man Who Dared the Lightning*. New York: William Morrow & Co., 1971.

*Franklin, Benjamin. *The Complete Poor Richard Almanacks*. Massachusetts: The Imprint Society, Crown Publishers, 1970.

Franklin, W. T. *Memoirs of the Life and Writings of Benjamin Franklin*. Philadelphia: 1818.

Hatch, Alden. *The Byrds of Virginia*. New York: Holt, Rinehart and Winston, 1969.

Labaree, Leonard W., ed. *The Autobiography of Benjamin Franklin*. New Haven: Yale University Press, 1964.

Labaree, Leonard W., and Wilcox, William B., eds. *The Papers of Benjamin Franklin*. New Haven: Yale University Press, 1959-74.

Lopez, Claude-Anne, and Herbert, Eugenia W. *The Private Franklin, The Man and His Family*. New York: W. W. Norton & Co., 1975.

Moore, Charles, ed. *George Washington's Rules of Civility and Decent Behavior*. Boston: Houghton Mifflin Co., 1926.

Roberts, Kenneth, and Anna M., eds. *Moreau de St. Méry's American Journey (1793-1798)*. New York: Doubleday & Co., 1947.

*Roelker, William Greene, ed. *Benjamin Franklin and Catherine Ray Greene: Their Correspondence 1755-1790*. Philadelphia: American Philosophical Society, 1949.

Rosenbach, A. S. W. *The All-Embracing Dr. Franklin*. Philadelphia: Free Library of Philadelphia, 1932.

Seitz, Don Carlos. *Famous American Duels*. New York: Books for Libraries Press, 1929.

Smyth, Albert Henry, ed. *The Writings of Benjamin Franklin*. New York: 1905-07.

Stifler, James M., ed. *"My Dear Girl": The Correspondence of Benjamin Franklin with Polly Stevenson, Georgiana and Catherine Shipley*. New York: 1927.

Chapter 5

Cairncross, John. *After Polygamy Was Made a Sin.* London: Routledge & Kegan Paul, 1974.

Dixon, William H. *Spiritual Wives,* vol. 2. London: Hurst and Blackett, 1868.

Hinds, William A. *American Communities and Co-operative Colonies.* Chicago: Charles H. Kerr & Co., 1908.

Johnston, Johanna. *Mrs. Satan.* New York: G. P. Putnam's Sons, 1967.

Kisner, Arlene, ed. *Woodhull & Claflin's Weekly.* New Jersey: Times Change Press, 1972.

Lockwood, George B. *The New Harmony Movement.* New York: D. Appleton & Co., 1905.

Nordhoff, Charles. *The Communistic Societies of the United States.* New York: Schocken Books, 1966.

Noyes, Pierrepont B. *A Goodly Heritage.* New York: Rinehart & Co., 1958.

Shaplen, Robert. *Free Love and Heavenly Sinners.* New York: Alfred A. Knopf, 1954.

Veysey, Laurence. *The Perfectionists, Radical Social Thought in the North, 1815-1860.* New York: John Wiley & Sons, 1973.

Woodward, Helen B. *The Bold Women.* New York: Farrar, Straus and Young, 1953.

Chapters 6 and 7

Bancroft, Hubert H. *A History of California.* San Francisco: The History Company, 1886-90.

Gregory, Joseph W. *Gregory's Guide for California Travellers.* New York: Nefis & Cornish, 1850.

Russailh, Albert Bernard de. *Last Adventure.* San Francisco: The Westgate Press.

Wierzbicki, F. P. *California as It Is and as It May Be.* San Francisco: The Grabhorn Press, 1933.

Chapter 6

Asbury, Herbert. *Sucker's Progress.* New Jersey: Patterson Smith, 1969.

Basso, Etolia S., ed. *The World from Jackson Square.* New York: Farrar, Straus & Co., 1948.

*Benjamin, Harry, and Masters, R. E. L. *Prostitution and Morality.* New York: The Julian Press, Crown Publishers, 1964.

Brown, Dee. *The Gentle Tamers: Women of the Old Wild West.* New York: G. P. Putnam's Sons, 1958.

Chestnut, Mary Boykin. *Diary from Dixie.*

*Coues, Elliott, ed. *The Manuscript Journals of Alexander Henry and of David Thompson,* vols. 1-2. Minnesota: Ross & Haines, 1965.

Cox, Ross. *The Columbia River.* Oklahoma: University of Oklahoma Press, 1957.

Day, Caroline Bond. *A Study of Some Negro-White Families in the United States.* Massachusetts: Peabody Museum of Harvard University, 1932.

Drago, Harry Sinclair. *Notorious Ladies of the Frontier.* New York: Dodd, Mead & Co., 1969.

Drake, Philip. *Revelations of a Slave Smuggler.* Illinois: Metro Books, 1972.

Fisher, Vardis, and Holmes, Opal Laurel. *Gold Rushes and Mining Camps of the Early American West.* Idaho: The Caxton Printers, 1968.

Fryer, Peter. *The Birth Controllers.* London: Secker & Warburg, 1965.

Green, Shirley. *The Curious History of Contraception.* London: Ebury Press, 1971.

Henriques, Fernando. *Children of Conflict.* New York: E. P. Dutton & Co., 1975.

Johnston, James Hugo. *Race Relations in Virginia & Miscegenation in the South 1776-1860.* Massachusetts: University of Massachusetts Press, 1970.

Larsson, Clotye M., ed. *Marriage Across the Color Line.* Chicago: Johnson Publishing Co., 1965.

Marks, Edward B. *They All Had Glamour.* New York: Julian Messner, 1944.

Martin, Cy. *Whiskey and Wild Women.* New York: Hart Publishing Co., 1974.

Martinez, Raymond J., and Holmes, Jack D. L. *New Orleans: Facts and Legends.* Louisiana: Hope Publications.

Ransford, Oliver. *The Slave Trade.* London: John Murray, 1971.

Reuter, Edward Byron. *The Mulatto in the United States.* New York: Negro Universities Press, 1969.

Rogers, J. A. *Sex and Race,* vols. 2-3. New York: Helga M. Rogers, 1944.

Sonnichsen, C. L. *Billy King's Tombstone.* Arizona: University of Arizona Press, 1972.

Stern, Philip Van Doren. *The Annotated Uncle Tom's Cabin.* New York: Eriksson, 1964.

Tallant, Robert. *Voodoo in New Orleans.* New York: Macmillan Publishing Co., 1946.

Woodward, C. Vann. *American Counterpoint.* Boston: Little, Brown & Co., 1964.

Woolston, Howard B. *Prostitution in the United States.* New Jersey: Patterson Smith, 1969.

Chapter 7

Anderson, Sherwood. *Dark Laughter.* New York: Pocket Books, 1925.

*Asbury, Herbert. *The Barbary Coast.* New York: Alfred A. Knopf, 1933.

*———. *The French Quarter.* New York: Ballantine Books, 1973.

*———. *The Gangs of New York.* New York: Alfred A. Knopf, 1927.

Bailey, Thomas A. *The American Pageant.* Boston: D. C. Heath & Co., 1956.

Beebe, Lucius. *The Big Spenders.* New York: Doubleday & Co., 1966.

Carlson, Oliver, and Bates, Ernest S. *Hearst, Lord of San Simeon.* New York: The Viking Press, 1936.

Comfort, Alex. *The Anxiety Makers.* London: Panther Modern Society, 1967.

Deslandes, L. *Manhood; the Causes of Its Premature Decline.* Boston: Otis, Broaders and Co., 1843.

Dubois, Jean. *The Secret Habits of the Female Sex.* New York: 1848.

Fitch, Robert E. *The Decline and Fall of Sex.* New York: Harcourt, Brace and Co., 1957.

Kaplan, Justin. *Mr. Clemens and Mark Twain.* New York: Simon & Schuster, 1966.

Kipling, Rudyard. *From Sea to Sea,* vol. 2. London: Macmillan & Co., 1922.

Lewis, Arthur H. *La Belle Otero.* New York: Trident Press, 1967.

Lewis, Oscar. *This Was San Francisco.* New York: David McKay Co., 1962.

Mooney, Michael M. *Evelyn Nesbit and Stanford White.* New York: William Morrow and Co., 1976.

Murtagh, John M., and Harris, Sara. *Cast the First Stone.* New York: McGraw-Hill Book Co., 1957.

Muscatine, Doris. *Old San Francisco.* New York: G. P. Putnam's Sons, 1975.

Sanger, William W. *The History of Prostitution.* New York: Eugenics Publishing Co., 1939.

Saxon, Lyle. *Fabulous New Orleans.* New Orleans: Robert L. Crager & Co.

Sobel, Bernard. *A Pictorial History of Burlesque.* New York: G. P. Putnam's Sons, 1956.

Swanberg, W. A. *Citizen Hearst.* New York: Charles Scribner's Sons, 1961.

Tallant, Robert. *Voodoo in New Orleans.* New York: Macmillan Publishing Co., 1974.

Taper, Bernard, ed. *Mark Twain's San Francisco.* New York: McGraw-Hill, 1963.

*Thaw, Harry K. *The Traitor.* Philadelphia: Dorrance & Co., 1926.

Time-Life Books. *This Fabulous Century,* vol. 2. New York: Time-Life Books, 1969.

Untermeyer, Louis. *Makers of the Modern World.* New York: Simon & Schuster, 1955.

Woods, S. D. *Lights and Shadows of Life on the Pacific Coast.* New York: Funk & Wagnalls Co., 1910.

Writers' Program of the Work Projects Administration. *Louisiana: A Guide to the State.* New York: Hastings House, Publishers, 1941.

*Young, Wayland. *Eros Denied.* New York: Grove Press, 1964.

Chapter 8

American War Songs. Michigan: Gryphon Books, 1971.

Amory, Cleveland, and Bradlee, Frederic, eds. *Vanity Fair.* New York: The Viking Press, 1960.

Anderson, Sherwood. *Dark Laughter.* New York: Pocket Books, 1925.

Aristophanes. *Lysistrata.* Greece: 411 B.C.

Barnett, Walter. *Sexual Freedom and The Constitution.* Albuquerque: University of New Mexico Press, 1973.

Basso, Etolia S., ed. *The World from Jackson Square: A New Orleans Reader.* New York: Farrar, Straus & Co., 1948.

Bedroom Companion, The. New York; Farrar & Rinehart, 1935

Chaplin, Lita Grey. *My Life with Chaplin.* Vermont: Bernard Geis Assoc., distributed by Grove Press, 1966.

Cheney, Anne. *Millay in Greenwich Village.* Alabama: University of Alabama Press, 1975.

Churchill, Allen. *The Improper Bohemians.* New York: E. P. Dutton & Co., 1959.

Disch, Thomas M. "The Dumbbell Murder Case." In *Murder, My Love: The Great Crimes of Passion,* edited by Eric Corder. Chicago: Playboy Press, 1973.

*Goldman, Emma. *Living My Life.* New York: Alfred A. Knopf, 1931.

*———. *The Traffic in Women.* New York: Times Change Press, 1970.

Groddeck, Georg. *The Book of the It.* New York: Vantage Books, 1949.

Grove Press, ed. *Fille de Joie.* New York: Grove Press, 1967.

Hays, Arthur Garfield. *Trial by Prejudice.* Connecticut: Negro Universities Press, 1970.

*Herndon, Booton. *Mary Pickford and Douglas Fairbanks.* New York: W. W. Norton & Co., 1977.

Keating, Walter S. *Sex Studies from Freud to Kinsey.* New York: Plaza Book Co., 1954.

Naylor, Charles. "The Two-sided Triangle." In *Murder, My Love: The Great Crimes of Passion,* edited by Eric Corder. Chicago: Playboy Press, 1973.

Ramsey, Frederic, Jr., and Smith, Charles Edward, eds. *Jazzmen.* New York: Harcourt, Brace & Co., 1939.

Sobel, Bernard. *A Pictorial History of Burlesque.* New York: G. P. Putnam's Sons, 1956.

Stedman, Raymond William. *The Serials.* Oklahoma: University of Oklahoma Press, 1977.

Swanwick, Helena M. *The War in Its Effect upon Women and Women and War.* New York: Garland Publishing, 1971.

Untermeyer, Louis. *Makers of the Modern World.* New York: Simon & Schuster, 1955.

Wilk, Max. *They're Playing Our Song.* New York: Atheneum, 1973.

Chapter 9

Exner, Judith. *My Story.* New York: Grove Press, 1977.

Fang, Irving E. *Those Radio Commentators!* Ames, Iowa: Iowa State University Press, 1977.

Faulkner, William. *Sanctuary.* New York: Signet Books, 1931.

*Ginsberg, Allen. *Howl.* San Francisco: City Lights Books, 1956.

Gottlieb, David I. *The Gay Tapes.* New York: Stein & Day, Publishers, 1977.

Hite, Shere. *The Hite Report*. New York: Dell, 1976.

"J." *The way to become The Sensuous Woman*. New York: Lyle Stuart, 1969.

Lawrence, D. H. *Lady Chatterley's Lover*. New York: Grove Press, 1957.

*Miller, Henry. *My Life and Times*. New York: Playboy Press, 1972.

*———. *Quiet Days in Clichy*. New York: Grove Press, 1956.

*———. *Tropic of Cancer*. New York: Grove Press, 1961.

*———. *Tropic of Capricorn*. New York: Grove Press, 1961.

*Moran, Jim. *How I Became an Authority on Sex*. New York: Stein & Day, Publishers, 1973.

Nabokov, Vladimir. *Lolita*. Connecticut: Fawcett Publications, 1955.

Reuben, David R. *Everything you always wanted to know about sex but were afraid to ask*. New York: David McKay Co., 1969.

Roosevelt, Elliott, and Brough, James. *Mother R: Eleanor Roosevelt's Untold Story*. New York: G. P. Putnam's Sons, 1977.

———. *An Untold Story: The Roosevelts of Hyde Park*. New York: G. P. Putnam's Sons, 1973.

Rugoff, Milton. *Prudery and Passion*. New York: G.P. Putnam's Sons, 1971.

*Southern, Terry, and Hoffenberg, Mason. *Candy*. Paris: Olympia Press, 1958.

Whitman, Walt. *Leaves of Grass*. New York: The Book League of America, 1942.

*Wilson, Edmund. *Memoirs of Hecate County*. New York: The New American Library, 1942.

*Young, Wayland. *Eros Denied: Sex in Western Society*. New York: Grove Press, 1964.

Index